Party Politics and Economic Reform in Africa's Democracies

In *Party Politics and Economic Reform in Africa's Democracies*, M. Anne Pitcher offers an engaging new theory to explain the different trajectories of private sector development across contemporary Africa. Pitcher argues that the outcomes of economic reforms depend not only on the kinds of institutional arrangements adopted by states in order to create or expand their private sectors but also on the nature of party system competition and the quality of democracy in particular countries. To illustrate her claim, Pitcher draws on several original datasets covering twenty-seven countries in Africa and detailed case studies of the privatization process in Zambia, Mozambique, and South Africa. This study underscores the importance of formal institutions and political context to the design and outcome of economic policies in developing countries.

M. Anne Pitcher is professor of political science and African studies at the University of Michigan. She is the author of *Transforming Mozambique: The Politics of Privatization* (Cambridge 2002) and *Politics in the Portuguese Empire: The State, Industry, and Cotton, 1926–1974* (1993). She co-edited *African Postsocialisms* with Kelly Askew (2006), and her articles have appeared in *Comparative Politics*, the *Journal of Modern African Studies*, *African Studies Review*, and *Politique Africaine*, among other publications. In 2003–2004, she was a Fellow at the Woodrow Wilson International Center for Scholars in Washington, D.C. To explore patterns of political and economic reform across Africa, she has conducted extensive research in Mozambique, South Africa, Zambia, Angola, and Uganda.

AFRICAN STUDIES

The African Studies series, founded in 1968, is a prestigious series of monographs, general surveys, and textbooks on Africa covering history, political science, anthropology, economics, and ecological and environmental issues. The series seeks to publish work by senior scholars as well as the best new research.

EDITORIAL BOARD

A list of books in this series will be found at the end of this volume.

Party Politics and Economic Reform in Africa's Democracies

M. ANNE PITCHER

University of Michigan

CAMBRIDGE
UNIVERSITY PRESS

CAMBRIDGE UNIVERSITY PRESS
Cambridge, New York, Melbourne, Madrid, Cape Town,
Singapore, São Paulo, Delhi, Mexico City

Cambridge University Press
32 Avenue of the Americas, New York, NY 10013-2473, USA

www.cambridge.org
Information on this title: www.cambridge.org/9780521738262

© M. Anne Pitcher 2012

First published 2012

Printed in the United States of America

A catalog record for this publication is available from the British Library.

Library of Congress Cataloging in Publication data
Pitcher, M. Anne.
    Party politics and economic reform in Africa's democracies / M. Anne Pitcher.
        p. cm. – (African studies ; 119)
    Includes bibliographical references and index.
    ISBN 978-0-521-44962-5 (hardback) – ISBN 978-0-521-73826-2 (pbk.)
    1. Africa – Economic policy.   2. Political parties – Africa.   3. Democratization – Africa.
    I. Title.
    HC800.P58   2012
    338.96 – dc23   2011049204

ISBN 978-0-521-44962-5 Hardback
ISBN 978-0-521-73826-2 Paperback

Contents

Tables, Figures, and Maps

Tables

Figures

Maps

Acknowledgments

This study originated with my interest in comparing whether economic reforms adopted by African countries in the 1990s had become institutionalized over time. Having documented Mozambique's transition to a market economy in a previous work, I wanted to explore how other governments in Africa had coped with the multiple challenges of political and economic transformation. Did the formal institutions chosen by African governments to promote private sector development follow the prescriptions of the World Bank or did they reflect more domestic and more political considerations? Did parchment institutions implemented in the early 1990s look anything like the institutional arrangements that were operating by the mid-2000s or were they simply a veneer behind which African governments were practicing "business as usual" as the literature on Africa so commonly argues? And since many governments were also undergoing processes of democratization, how did the advent of multiparty politics affect economic reforms?

Similar to research on other regions where significant transitions have occurred over the last two decades, scholarly studies of political and economic reform in Africa are numerous. But I was surprised to discover that the literatures on multiparty politics and on market reforms hardly talk to each other in the context of Africa. To be sure, a number of scholars have attributed state collapse or political instability to the impact of neoliberal reforms. A few, especially in South Africa, have also suggested that party politics played a role in how privatization occurred or who benefited from it. But there has been little systematic, comparative examination of how party dynamics might have interacted with economic institutional choices to shape private sector development across Africa. This book is at once an effort to apply these two strands of research to an understanding of political and economic change in Africa and a plea for greater cross-fertilization between them.

Like most endeavors that are worthwhile, the crafting of this book has taken a long time. Extensive fieldwork in several African countries over the last decade greatly informed my understanding of political and economic reforms. Some of the places where I did research such as South Africa, Mozambique, and Zambia serve as case studies in the book. Others such as Uganda and Angola did not become cases; nonetheless, my experiences in those countries greatly informed my thinking about reform. I would like to thank especially those representatives of trade unions, business associations, governments, international financial institutions, nongovernmental organizations, and civil society groups who took time out of their busy schedules to share their knowledge and experiences of economic reform with me. I cannot begin to express my gratitude for their insights.

As anyone who has conducted fieldwork knows, a successful research experience often depends on the kindness of strangers and the generosity of friends. I want to express my deep appreciation for the research assistance I received from Benedito Machava in Mozambique and Lilian Muchimba in Zambia. Benedito's intellectual curiosity and his powers of observation demonstrate that he will make a fine scholar. I would also like to thank many colleagues in Zambia, Mozambique, and South Africa who welcomed me into their homes, gave me dinner or a place to sleep, and commented on my research. In Zambia, James Matale, Kathy Sikombe, Neo Simutanyi, and Andrew Sardanis shared insights about party politics and economic development that greatly helped me to conceptualize the project at an early stage in the research. In South Africa, Sakhela Buhlungu, Sean Jacobs, Cecil Madell, Tembakazi Mnyaka, and Trevor Ngwane were very generous with their time and their suggestions regarding some of the main arguments in the book. My dear friend, Doug Tilton, lifted my spirits and looked after me every time I was in Johannesburg. In Mozambique, the diverse points of view on private sector development expressed by Sid Bliss, Carlos Castel-Branco, Alexandre Munguambe, Boaventura Mondlane, Raul Sango, and Graeme White greatly informed my understanding of economic change there. Without their help and that of many others whom I met and interviewed during my research, the project would not have been as rewarding as it was.

It takes time and patience to digest fieldwork, to explore ideas fully, and to commit thoughts and theories to paper. I owe an enormous debt to the Woodrow Wilson International Center for Scholars in Washington, D.C., for granting me a fellowship in 2003–2004 just at the beginning of the research for this book. At WWICS, I was surrounded by a supportive scholarly community and engaging colleagues. I continue to cherish every moment of my time there and I am grateful for the help of my diligent and conscientious research assistant, Patrick Johnson. As the book progressed, Colgate University and the University of Michigan provided financial support and sabbatical leaves. In both places, students gave valuable help compiling references and checking data. In particular, I want to recognize the contributions of Courtney Dunlaevy,

George Henry, Dahlia Risk, John Mizzi, and Roberto Icaza. Additionally, Todd Austin gave technical support and advice that was much appreciated. Statistical guidance provided by the Center for Statistical Consultation and Research and especially Giselle Kolenic was invaluable.

I am grateful to seminar participants at Oxford University, the University of Michigan, Indiana University–Indianapolis, Queen's University in Belfast, the Graduate Institute of International Studies in Geneva, Georgetown University, Universidade Eduardo Mondlane, and the Danish Institute for International Studies and to conference attendees at the annual meetings of the African Studies Association, the Midwest Political Science Association, and the American Political Science Association for their helpful remarks. Kenneth Shepsle gave me useful feedback at a critical stage in the project's development. Many colleagues and friends at Colgate University and the University of Michigan also contributed to the stimulating intellectual exchanges and the personal happiness that I have enjoyed at both places.

Leslie Anderson, Nancy Bermeo, Cathy Boone, Lars Buur, Larry Dodd, Michael Johnston, Miles Larmer, Carrie Manning, Mary Moran, Eric Morier-Genoud, Martin Murray, Rachel Stringfellow, Manny Teodoro, Lindsay Whitfield, and Elke Zuern commented on earlier versions of the manuscript or exchanged ideas with me about parties and private sector development in, as well as beyond, Africa. I am greatly indebted to them not only for their observations and criticisms but also for their encouragement. I especially want to thank Larry Dodd for advising me to be patient with my ideas and Gavin Williams for giving me his copy of V. O. Key's classic work, *Politics, Parties and Pressure Groups*. Reading Key's description of party behavior in the United States reminded me again that politics in Africa is not exceptional.

Two anonymous reviewers at Cambridge provided beneficial comments that greatly improved the manuscript. The enthusiastic endorsement of the project by my editor at Cambridge, Eric Crahan, gave me the confidence to complete it. Finally, I want to thank my family and my cats for reminding me that work does not love you back. I hope that I have given them as much love as they have given me.

Abbreviations

AG	Auditor General
AHI	Afrikaanse Handleinstituut
AIM	Mozambique Information Agency
ANC	African National Congress
APF	Anti-Privatization Forum
ASGISA	Accelerated and Shared Growth Initiative for South Africa
BAZ	Bankers Association of Zambia
B-BBEE	Broad-Based Black Economic Empowerment
BCP	Botswana Congress Party
BEE	Black Economic Empowerment
BID	Business Improvement District
BMF	Black Management Forum
BUSA	Business Unity South Africa
CC	Central Committee
CCT	Consultative Labor Council
CDC	Commonwealth Development Corporation
CFM	Mozambique Ports and Railways Company
CID	City Improvement District
CONSILMO	National Confederation of Free and Independent Unions of Mozambique
COPE	Congress of the People
COSATU	Congress of South African Trade Unions
CPI	Center for Investment Promotion
CTA	Confederation of Economic Association
DA	Democratic Alliance
DPE	Department of Public Enterprises
EPWP	Expanded Public Works Program
EU	European Union

FDD	Forum for Democracy and Development
FDI	Foreign Direct Investment
FPTP	First Past the Post
Frelimo	Front for the Liberation of Mozambique
GDP	Gross Domestic Project
GEAR	Growth, Employment, and Redistribution
IFI	International Financial Institution
IFP	Inkatha Freedom Party
IGEPE	Institute for the Management of State Shareholdings
IMF	International Monetary Fund
INE	National Institute of Statistics
IRAI	International Development Association Resource Allocation Index
JSE	Johannesburg Stock Exchange
KZN	Kwazulu-Natal
MBO	Management Buyout
MCEL	Mozambique Cellular
MDM	Mozambique Democratic Movement
MIC	Mineworkers Investment Company
MMD	Movement for Multiparty Democracy
MPD	Movement for Democracy
NDC	National Democratic Congress
NEC	National Executive Committee
Nedlac	National Economic Development and Labour Council
NGO	Nongovernmental Organization
NPP	National Patriotic Party
OPE	Office of Public Enterprises
OTM	Organization of Mozambican Workers
PAICV	African Party for the Independence of Cape Verde
PBC	Produce Buying Company
PF	Patriotic Front
PHI	Presidential Housing Initiative
PIC	Public Investment Corporation
PNT	Privatization Negotiation Team
PPP	Public–Private Partnership
PSDRP	Private Sector Development Review Program
RDP	Reconstruction and Development Program
Renamo	Mozambique National Resistance
RID	Residential Improvement District
SABC	South African Broadcasting Corporation
SACCAWU	South African Commercial, Catering and Allied Workers Union
SACP	South African Communist Party
SAHRWU	South African Railways and Harbor Workers Union

SAMWU	South African Municipal Workers Union
SANCO	South African National Civic Organization
SATAWU	South African Transport and Allied Workers Union
SIH	Sanco Investment Holdings
SNP	Seychelles National Party
SOE	State-Owned Enterprise
SPPF	Seychelles People's Progressive Front
Tazama	Tanzania Zambia Mafuta Pipeline
Tazara	Tanzania Zambia Railways
TCLC	Tripartite Consultative Labour Council
TDM	Mozambique Telecommunications
UDA	United Democratic Alliance
UDF	United Democratic Front
UNDP	United Nations Development Programme
UNIP	United National Independence Party
UPND	United Party for National Development
USAID	U.S. Agency for International Development
UTRE	Technical Unit for Enterprise Restructuring
WTO	World Trade Organization
ZACCI	Zambia Association of Chambers of Commerce and Industry
ZAM	Zambia Association of Manufacturers
Zamtel	Zambia Telecommunications
Zanaco	Zambia National Commercial Bank
ZBF	Zambia Business Forum
ZCCM	Zambia Consolidated Copper Mines
ZCCM-IH	Zambia Consolidated Copper Mines–Investment Holdings
ZCSMBA	Zambia Chamber of Small and Medium Business Associations
ZCTU	Zambia Congress of Trade Unions
ZDAA	Zambia Development Agency Act
ZESCO	Zambia Electricity Supply Corporation
ZFE	Zambia Federation of Employers
ZIBA	Zambia Indigenous Business Association
ZIBAC	Zambia International Business Advisory Council
ZLA	Zambia Land Alliance
ZNFU	Zambia National Farmers Union
ZNTC	Zambia National Tourism Council
ZPA	Zambia Privatisation Agency
ZSIC	Zambia State Insurance Corporation

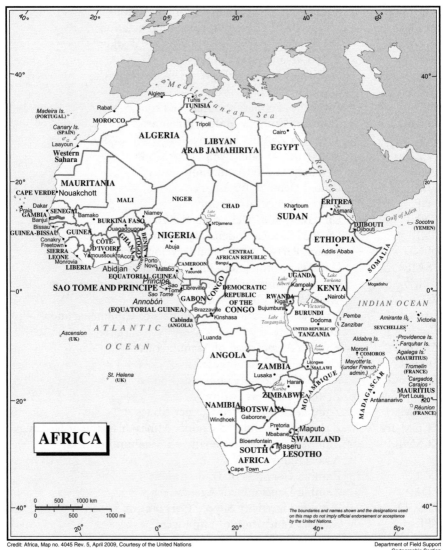

MAP 1. Sub-Saharan Africa.

1

Understanding Institutional Development in Africa

An Introduction

For many countries in East and Central Europe, Latin America, and Asia, the implementation of political and economic reforms over the last quarter century has constituted a sharp break from the past. Words such as "transition," "transformation," "schism," and "shock therapy" suggest ruptures of momentous proportions. Many countries have become democratic and adopted market economies. Prices have increased; imports have risen. Workers, consumers, and citizens now rely on blogs or newspapers, the ballot box, or street demonstrations to demand secure jobs, free elections, or fair trade.

In Africa, no less than in the former Soviet Union or Latin America, political and economic changes have been just as transformative. Many African governments now practice some form of democratic electoral politics and many citizens enjoy basic political rights and civil liberties that were denied to them just twenty years ago. To varying degrees, countries have also liberalized trade, set up investment centers, established stock markets, and passed privatization laws. Governments in Mali and Uganda have sold their parastatals to foreign and domestic investors. Malls, fast food restaurants, and cafes selling flavored coffees have sprouted up from Kampala to Cape Town. A dizzying array of consumer goods are hawked on the streets of Lagos or displayed in upscale shops in the northern suburbs of Johannesburg.

As in Europe or Latin America, transition in Africa has come with costs. Fraud and violence have marred elections in Kenya, Madagascar, and Zimbabwe; citizens in Senegal and Mozambique are less enthusiastic about democracy today than they were just a few years ago.[1] Political parties are poorly

[1] Afrobarometer Survey Findings, "Summary of Results, Round 3 Afrobarometer Survey in Senegal, 2005" and "Summary of Results, Round 3 Afrobarometer Survey in Mozambique, 2005," question 47; "2008 Round 4 Afrobarometer Survey in Senegal" and "2008 Round 4 Afrobarometer Survey in Mozambique," question 43, compiled by Michigan State University, accessed 9/7/2010, http://www.afrobarometer.org.

organized in many countries, and many of them prefer to rely on patronage or threats instead of programmatic manifestos to gain votes. Furthermore, the shift to market economies has produced rising inequality, a decline in formal sector employment, and increased casualization of the workforce. In Mali, Madagascar, Mozambique, Niger, and Zambia, more than half the population lives below the poverty line: formal sector employment now constitutes a mere fraction of total employment in these countries. Even in South Africa, which is routinely cited as the most developed country south of the Sahara, nearly half of the economically active population is un- or underemployed. Like their counterparts elsewhere, citizens across Africa have thus demanded better representation and greater equity. Facing rising prices for basic amenities such as food, water, and electricity coupled with bleak prospects for a stable and sustainable income, they have used the available political space to articulate and advance their interests.

Although countries in Africa have experienced changes as profound as those in Latin America or East Central Europe, the scholarly literature on political and economic transition has treated the changes in Africa unevenly. As the book will discuss, African countries are well represented in studies that explore why transitions to democracy have occurred; whether democracy is likely to become institutionalized; how varied patterns of democracy have been; and what types of political parties exist. However, theoretical and comparative work on the development of economic institutions or the relationship between political and economic reforms in Africa has been limited. Whereas in Latin America and East Central Europe, scholars have asked how formal and informal institutional arrangements shape the economic preferences of individual and collective players, what credible commitments look like and how they are made, and why some governments stick to the rules while others abuse their discretionary authority, most of these questions remain unanswered and undertheorized in the literature on Africa.

This book contributes to comparative scholarship on transitions by examining how new formal institutions and fluctuating political dynamics have interacted to shape the process of economic reform in African countries over the last two decades. Focusing specifically on privatization – one of the most controversial and far-reaching of the economic reforms adopted by transitional, developing countries – I discuss the institutional arrangements enacted by African governments in order to create or expand their private sectors. Tracking their development over time, I assess the effectiveness of new institutions alongside continued uses of discretionary power by the state. Further, I explore the distributional conflicts triggered by the implementation of privatization and how democratic governments have resolved them. I demonstrate that differences in the quality of democracy and the nature of the party system combined to influence divergent trajectories of institutional development in Africa.

Briefly, my argument is the following. Much of the conventional wisdom on the role of formal institutions in Africa claims that governments consistently devalue or ignore them, often because they are imposed by outside actors such as Western donors or the World Bank. By contrast, I find that although the World Bank was often the exogenous proponent of institutional reform, many African governments modified the institutional prescriptions they received from the Bank in order to fit local circumstances prior to adoption. For example, laws on private property rights might contain special provisions acknowledging and protecting communal, rather than individual, property rights in the rural areas as they did in Mozambique, or investment laws might require foreigners to partner with indigenous investors or the state in order to purchase strategic assets as in Mauritius.[2] As a consequence, I find that formal arrangements enacted by African governments demonstrate greater variation than scholars have previously recognized.

Furthermore, I claim that the kinds of institutional arrangements created by African governments in order to build a private sector are strongly associated with the degree to which these institutions operate effectively at a later moment in time. To illustrate this point, I rely on a theoretical distinction between two types of credible commitment made by Kenneth Shepsle and develop a pair of indices that assesses these two types of commitment at different points in time for twenty-seven countries in Africa. The approach captures empirically and temporally the degree to which the enactment of formal institutions ultimately becomes embedded in the ordinary practices and everyday norms of individual and collective actors. Moreover, it highlights those instances in which governments employ their discretionary authority to bend or break the rules.

As many institutionalists acknowledge, institutional development is enormously complex. Even when the rules are clear and consistent, the dynamics accompanying transformative political and economic change can produce unintended consequences. Some change agents may see in new rules an opportunity to advance their interests, and in doing so, they help to institutionalize the rules; while those who are disadvantaged by new rules may endeavor to subvert them.[3] The privatization process especially has generated multiple forms of resistance by parastatal administrators, bureaucrats, organized labor, consumers, and the unemployed over the loss of jobs, benefits, or status; over rising prices or declining services; over unfair or unwelcome competition.

I assume that authoritarian governments can simply turn a blind eye to these outbursts or resort to coercion if they wish to proceed. Alternatively, they can cancel the whole project if they are politically threatened. As Olson points out, "any autocracy must sooner or later have a short time horizon," and short time

---

[2] Mozambique, Assembleia da República, Lei no. 19/97, October 1, 1997; Percy Mistry, "Commentary: Mauritius-Quo Vadis?," *African Affairs*, 98 (1999): 551–569.

[3] Although they are examining incremental change rather than institutional development following a transition, James Mahoney and Kathleen Thelen identify four analytically distinct roles played by change agents, see "A Theory of Gradual Institutional Change" in James Mahoney and Kathleen Thelen, eds., *Explaining Institutional Change: Ambiguity, Agency and Power* (New York: Cambridge University Press, 2010), 22–28.

horizons eventually encourage autocrats to become roving bandits, to subvert the rules that they themselves have created.[4] As other scholars have shown, these settings are not particularly conducive to the maintenance of credible commitments.[5]

Democratic governments face a different but no less problematic set of trade-offs between rules and discretion. In theory, democratic governments must navigate between maintaining regime credibility by adhering to their commitments or responding to constituents by using their discretion to bend or break rules if those rules cause harm to a favored group. To offer a stylized example from the privatization process, this may mean choosing between the sale of a highly indebted public utility, with expected job losses and higher prices for consumers if a private investor purchases it, or continuing to run it at a loss in order to protect workers' jobs, to subsidize rates for consumers, and to favor insiders. In the former case, the government follows the rules and gains credibility with those who favor privatization. In the latter case, the government uses its discretionary authority to ignore the institutional arrangements it just adopted. By continuing to retain a loss making parastatal, it illustrates that it is accountable to several sets of constituents, but it may lose credibility with those who favored privatization if it bends the rules too often. The political and economic trade-offs inherent in such decisions have long-term consequences. If the government decides to sell a parastatal, unemployment may rise, and the government may lose office at the next election as a result; if it reneges on agreements to privatize, growth may be jeopardized; reform may be curtailed; and the government may be punished at the polls for not sticking to its commitment.

How do Africa's new democracies resolve these dilemmas and what are the consequences for emerging markets? My theoretical argument is that under conditions where governments have already adopted formal institutional arrangements consistent with creating or expanding their private sectors, the trade-off between rules and discretion that governments negotiate depends on the quality of democracy and the logic of party politics. Democratic quality and party system logics interact with each other. They can vary over time and across cases. Where democratic quality is high and the party system is stable, governments exercise their discretion to manage conflicts arising from privatization, but they do so within the limits of the law and without reneging on the policy choice. As such, the privatization process will reflect the compromises that governments make in order to sustain the policy. Where democratic quality

---

[4] Mancur Olson, "The New Institutional Economics: The Collective Choice Approach to Economic Development" in Christopher Clague, ed., *Institutions and Economic Development: Growth and Governance in Less-Developed and Post-Socialist Countries* (Baltimore: Johns Hopkins University Press, 1997), 47.

[5] See also Timothy Frye's comment on this point, *Building States and Markets After Communism: The Perils of Polarized Democracy* (New York: Cambridge University Press, 2010), 33–34 and ch. 1, fn. 25.

is low and the party system is fragmented, uses of government discretion are more arbitrary and the consequences for privatization are more unpredictable. In these cases, the process may lose focus and become ad hoc.

The theory will be more fully elaborated later, but two examples will suffice to illustrate the claim. Just two years after coming to office, the democratic government of South Africa announced plans to privatize three hundred parastatals, including several large state-owned enterprises in sectors such as transport and electricity. As privatization proceeded, resistance to job losses and higher prices for services intensified, aided by the many outlets for expressing grievances afforded by South Africa's liberal (or high-quality) democracy. At the same time, the kind of democracy that existed in South Africa increased the likelihood that the government would respond to protesters *and* maintain its commitments.

The high quality of the democratic setting in which these struggles were played out also interacted with the nature of party politics in South Africa. For an emerging democracy, party politics in South Africa has been relatively stable. Parties are well organized and have identifiable constituencies. Party loyalty tends to endure over time. This means that the governing party can depend on a devoted base to sustain it through a tough transition, but it cannot take that base for granted.[6] If policy outcomes are likely to harm the base of the party, the leadership may have to bend the rules. In South Africa, the combination of a democratic setting that encouraged contestation and participation and a stable party system, where supporters of the ruling party were able to hold it accountable, promoted compromises around the privatization policy. Over time, these compromises affected the trajectory of economic reform in South Africa. Instead of outright privatization, the government commercialized and corporatized parastatals so that they operated according to market principles. While the government continued to embrace a private sector economy, it also financed public works projects in order to provide formal sector employment to likely supporters.[7]

By contrast, consider the political dynamics surrounding privatization in Zambia. After a nearly twenty-year hiatus, the Zambian government returned to multiparty politics in 1991. Democratic elections brought a new party to power, the Movement for Multiparty Democracy or MMD, under the leadership of its charismatic president, Frederick Chiluba. Consistent with its election manifesto, the new government adopted a privatization law, created an agency to value and sell parastatals, and changed the land law to favor private property rights. But when the outcome of initial sales failed to meet the expectations of a broad spectrum of Zambian civil society, anger and disappointment ensued. Unlike South Africa, outlets for the expression of grievances were more restricted in Zambia and the Zambian government reacted more harshly to

---

[6] The recent formation of Congress of the People in South Africa illustrates this point.

[7] Chapter 6 will discuss (and reference) more fully the process of privatization in South Africa.

popular contestation than its South African counterpart. Rather than using its discretionary authority to forge compromises as the South African government did, the Zambian government subverted new economic and political institutions for its own ends.

Alongside the low quality of Zambia's democracy, party fragmentation also explains state responses and the subsequent outcome of privatization. Parties were poorly organized; party loyalty was weak; and volatility was high. Although the MMD remained the ruling party throughout the 1990s, the base of the party was unstable as were those of many opposition parties in Zambia. Uncertain about the electoral impact of privatization policies on a shifting base, Zambian governments adopted inconsistent approaches to sales of parastatals; to relations with the business sector; and to land, labor, and financial reforms. President Chiluba disbursed companies to allies in a failed effort to use privatization to build partisan support for his presidency during the 1990s. After 2001, President Mwanawasa stalled privatization in favor of populist appeals to the electorate. The result was that although economic institutions appeared to be reasonably effective nearly a decade after they were adopted, the ensuing political dynamics produced partial, ad hoc reforms characterized by extensive uses of patronage.

To explore the dynamics of the privatization process and its consequences for the character of capitalism in Africa, I employ a multidisciplinary and multimethod approach. I rely on two databases assessing the institutional development of privatization over time in twenty-seven countries, descriptive statistics, interviews with key stakeholders, comparative analysis of other regions, and process tracing to examine the nature of commitment to reforms. I explore the distributional conflicts that arose from reform implementation and how states responded to them; I also investigate how different state responses contributed to the diverse reform trajectories witnessed across the continent. As I develop the theoretical argument, I also vary the sample size to illustrate patterns and trajectories more effectively. First, I broadly evaluate the privatization experiences of twenty-seven democratic and authoritarian countries in Africa; second, I examine more specifically the political dynamics of the process in nine African democracies with different party systems. Finally, I offer detailed case studies of three countries in Southern Africa. To more fully delineate patterns of economic and political development in one of the poorest regions of the world, I discuss below the substance of debates regarding institutional change in Africa, the comparative literature that informs them, and the theoretical approach taken by this book.

Debates About Economic Reform in Africa

Over the last two decades, many African countries have designed economic reforms for the purpose of selling state assets, attracting investors, expanding their private sectors, and creating market economies. Governments from

Benin to Zambia changed their constitutions and land tenure laws to favor private property and to reduce arbitrary appropriations by public officials. In thirty-eight out of forty-eight Sub-Saharan African countries, governments established agencies to value state assets, to choose the appropriate method of sale, to find buyers, and legally to transfer state-owned enterprises to private sector ownership.[8] They created investment centers to advertise potentially profitable sectors, to lure foreign firms, to advise domestic investors, or to promote public private partnerships. Finally, they altered domestic regulations and signed regional and world trade agreements in order to create environments conducive to private sector–driven economic growth.

These measures produced tangible results. By 2005, approximately 3,000 privatization transactions had taken place across the continent. They included not only the sale of state-owned enterprises through competitive tender or the exercise of preemptive rights to them, but also the creation of joint ventures, the signing of management contracts, or the offering of public shares in key sectors such as telecommunications, electricity, water, and sanitation. The revenue from sales reached US$8.8 billion. In addition, after sluggish growth in the 1990s, foreign direct investment (FDI) into Sub-Saharan Africa totaled about $70 billion by 2007. Countries such as Senegal, the Seychelles, Madagascar, Botswana, and Mozambique saw yearly FDI inflows increase dramatically from 1990 to 2007. Whereas total annual FDI inflows for these five countries averaged around US$44 million between 1991 and 1995, they had skyrocketed to an average of nearly US$1 billion between 2000 and 2007.[9]

Scholars and policymakers have responded to these changes with praise, skepticism, and outrage. For some, the adoption of institutional arrangements that protect private property, the creation of agencies to sell state-owned enterprises, and sales of parastatals suggest that African countries finally *committed* to market reforms.[10] By the early 1990s, several scholars and policymakers had begun to argue that commitment, rather than conditionality imposed by the World Bank and the International Monetary Fund (IMF), would lead to the successful implementation of reforms by governments in developing countries. The justification that advocates gave for emphasizing commitment to reforms was that if a government voluntarily enacted reforms rather than acting under

---

[8] Jean-Claude Berthélemy, Céline Kauffmann, Marie-Anne Valfort, and Lucia Wegner, eds., *Privatisation in Sub-Saharan Africa: Where Do We Stand?* (Paris: OECD, 2004), 23.

[9] World Bank, *World Development Indicators (WDI) and Global Development Finance (GDF)*, *World dataBank*, accessed 11/22/2011, http://databank.worldbank.org.

[10] Oliver Campbell White and Anita Bhatia, *Privatization in Africa* (Washington, D.C.: The World Bank, 1998); Jose Campos and Hadi Esfahani, "Credible Commitment and Success with Public Enterprise Reform," *World Development*, 28, 2 (2000): 221–244; World Bank, "The Role and Effectiveness of Development Assistance: Lessons from World Bank Experience," Research Paper, Development Economics Vice Presidency 2002, 42–46, accessed 2/10/2007, http://econ. worldbank.org.. Ownership and commitment tend to be used interchangeably in the literature. I shall discuss this further in Chapter 2.

pressure from outside agencies, it was more likely to sustain them through the challenges of the implementation process. Convinced that the government's commitment was credible, investment would increase and the outcome would be successful.[11] Although donor pressures on African countries were considerable in the 1990s, the breadth of reform efforts by governments indicated that they had begun to "own" or commit to neo-liberal economic policy approaches.[12]

Yet not everyone agrees that these commitments were *credible*. Many scholars find that the positive aggregate data mask significant cross-national differences in both the implementation and the outcome of these reforms. Scholars adopt at least two positions regarding these findings. On the one hand, from Madagascar to Zambia, they document erratic approaches to implementation, continued state intervention in the largest and most profitable firms, the sales of firms to cronies of the government, and widespread rent seeking by insiders.[13] Extrapolating from these results, they conclude that African governments were afflicted with the "partial reform syndrome," where reforms generated some structural economic changes but rent-seeking opportunities and clientelistic practices by "neo-patrimonial" elites persisted, notably through continued state regulation of prices, manipulation of supply chains, the formation of quasi-private organizations, and the maintenance of parastatals in key economic sectors.[14]

[11] Miles Kahler, "External Influence, Conditionality, and the Politics of Adjustment" in Stephan Haggard and Robert R. Kaufman, eds., *The Politics of Economic Adjustment: International Constraints, Distributive Conflicts, and the State* (Princeton: Princeton University Press, 1992), 114. World Bank, *Bureaucrats in Business: The Economics and Politics of Government Ownership* (Oxford: Oxford University Press, 1995), ch. 4; Henry Bienen and Jeffrey Herbst, "The Relationship between Political and Economic Reforms in Africa," *Comparative Politics*, 29, 1 (1996): 31.

[12] Steve Kayizzi-Mugerwa, "Privatization in Sub-Saharan Africa: On Factors Affecting Implementation" in Steve Kayizzi-Mugerwa, ed., *Reforming Africa's Institutions: Ownership, Incentives, and Capabilities* (New York: United Nations University Press, 2003), 250.

[13] Roger Tangri, *The Politics of Patronage in Africa: Parastatals, Privatization and Private Enterprise* (Trenton, N.J.: Africa World Press, 1999); John Nellis, "Privatization in Africa: What Has Happened? What Is to Be Done?" in Gérard Roland, ed., *Privatization: Successes and Failures* (New York: Columbia University Press, 2008), 109–135; Berthélemy et al., *Privatisation in Sub-Saharan Africa*, 102–107, fn. 1; Peter Lewis, "Economic Reform and the Discourse of Democracy in Africa: Resolving the Contradictions" in Mark R. Beissinger and Crawford Young, eds., *Beyond State Crisis? Postcolonial Africa and Post-Soviet Eurasia in Comparative Perspective* (Washington, D.C.: Woodrow Wilson Centre Press, 2002), 290–320.

[14] The term derives from Kevin Murphy, Andrei Shleifer, and Robert Vishny, "The Transition to a Market Economy: Pitfalls of Partial Reform," *The Quarterly Journal of Economics*, 107, 3 (1992): 889–906 and was popularized by Joel Hellman in his work on Eurasia, see "Winners Take All: The Politics of Partial Reform in Postcommunist Transitions," *World Politics* 50, 2 (1998): 203–204. For its application to Africa, see Nicolas van de Walle, *African Economies and the Politics of Permanent Crisis, 1979–1999* (New York: Cambridge University Press, 2001) and "Economic Reform: Patterns and Constraints" in E. Gyimah-Boadi, ed., *Democratic Reform in Africa: The Quality of Progress* (Boulder: Lynne Rienner, 2004), 54–56; Tony Addison, "Do

On the other hand, several scholars highlight the disastrous consequences of structural adjustment.[15] In some countries, the combination of reduced state intervention, increased capital flows, and more open trade weakened national states and channeled revenue to natural resource extraction or private city building projects in isolated, securitized enclaves. Where states withdrew, "horizontal contemporaries" such as international financial institutions, transnational nongovernmental organizations, and private investors stepped into the breach, assuming functions that most states routinely exercised twenty years ago.[16] In the worst cases, global liberalization allowed rulers to create privatized and personalistic alliances with shadow networks of drug cartels and other illicit enterprises, resulting in the "criminalization" of states such as Chad, Angola, or Nigeria.[17] Some states such as Congo, Sierra Leone, or Somalia collapsed all together partially due to the impact of reforms.[18]

Each of these interpretations captures part of the experience of private sector creation and expansion across the continent, but also each embodies conceptual and theoretical inconsistencies. First, those approaches that stress the importance of commitment rather than conditionality differ with regard to what factors or combination of factors (institutions, partisan control, reputation, signaling, external agencies of restraint, etc.) made a commitment credible

Donors Matter for Institutional Reform in Africa" in Steve Kayizzi-Mugerwa, ed., *Reforming Africa's Institutions: Ownership, Incentives, and Capabilities* (New York: United Nations University Press, 2003), 59–61; Lise Rakner, *Political and Economic Liberalisation in Zambia 1991–2001* (Stockholm: Nordiska Afrikainstitutet, 2003); M. Bratton, Robert B. Mattes, and E. Gyimah-Boadi, *Public Opinion, Democracy, and Market Reform in Africa* (Cambridge: Cambridge University Press, 2005), 20–23; Antoinette Handley, *Business and the State in Africa: Economic Policy-Making in the Neo-Liberal Era* (New York: Cambridge University Press, 2008).

[15] Thomas Callaghy, "Vision and Politics in the Transformation of the Global Political Economy: Lessons from the Second and Third Worlds" in Robert Slater, Barry Schutz, and Steven Dorr, eds., *Global Transformation and the Third World* (Boulder: Lynne Rienner, 1993), 161–257; Peter Gibbon, "Structural Adjustment and Structural Change in Sub-Saharan Africa: Some Provisional Conclusions" in Peter Gibbon and Adebayo Olukoshi, *Structural Adjustment and Socio-Economic Change in Sub-Saharan Africa: Some Conceptual, Methodological and Research Issues*, Research Report 102 (Stockholm: Nordiska Afrikainstitutet, 1996), 9–47; Béatrice Hibou, "The Political Economy of the World Bank's Discourse: From Economic Catechism to Missionary Deeds (and Misdeeds)," *Les Etudes du Centre d'études et de recherches internationales*, 39 (March 1998), English translation (January 2000).

[16] James Ferguson, *Global Shadows: Africa in the Neoliberal World Order* (Durham, N.C.: Duke University Press, 2006), 103.

[17] Jean-François Bayart, Stephen Ellis, and Béatrice Hibou, *The Criminalization of the State in Africa* (Oxford: International African Institute in Association with James Currey, 1999); Will Reno, "The Privatisation of Sovereignty and the Survival of Weak States" in Béatrice Hibou, ed., *Privatizing the State* (New York: Columbia University Press, 2004), 95–119.

[18] Anastase Nzeza Bilakila, "The Kinshasa Bargain" in Thedore Trefon, ed., *Reinventing Order in the Congo: How People in Kinshasa Respond to State Failure* (New York: Zed Books, 2004), 31; David Keen, "Liberalization and Conflict," *International Political Science Review*, 25, 1 (2005): 73–89.

or how governments created it.[19] In the policy-making literature especially, the use of commitment to explain the success or failure of neo-liberal reforms often relies on circular reasoning: If a particular reform succeeded, then the government was committed to it; if it failed, then the government was not committed to it.[20]

Second, those who argue that African governments failed to commit credibly or only partially committed to institutional reforms often minimize the ways in which a major reform such as privatization produced legitimate distributional conflicts that governments had to confront. In emerging democracies, the political expression of these conflicts through the party system, at the ballot box, or via formal or informal channels of influence, and the range of institutional and extra-institutional responses to them undertaken by state officials may have reshaped reforms during implementation. Rather than being manipulated by venal government officials, reforms may have changed because governments were trying to be accountable to particularistic interests, to their base, or to the electorate. Lastly, those approaches that stress the unsuitability or negative impact of reforms such as privatization underspecify the extent to which governments actually enacted formal institutional changes consistent with privatizing their economies and the degree to which they implemented them.

This book addresses these inconsistencies in the literature by examining the ways in which formal economic institutions and political dynamics interacted in African countries undergoing privatization. Despite frequent claims by scholars that formal institutions are merely a veneer behind which African governments engage in more ubiquitous and unseemly informal practices, I claim that the formal adoption of institutions consistent with the creation or expansion of a market economy constitutes a necessary building block in the development of such an economy over time. As I will demonstrate, because their adoption can

---

[19] For the debate over commitment and what mechanisms might best be used to make it credible, see Dani Rodrik, "Promises, Promises: Credible Policy Reform via Signalling," *The Economic Journal*, 99, 397 (1989): 756–772; Silvio Borner, Aymo Brunetti, and Beatrice Weder, *Political Credibility and Economic Development* (New York: St. Martin's Press, 1995); Pablo Spiller, "Institutions and Commitment," *Industrial and Corporate Change*, 5, 2 (1996): 421–452; Paul Collier, "Learning from Failure: The International Financial Institutions as Agencies of Restraint in Africa" in Andreas Schedler, Larry Diamond, and Marc F. Plattner, eds., *The Self-Restraining State: Power and Accountability in New Democracies* (Boulder: Lynne Rienner, 1999), 313–330; David Stasavage, *Public Debt and the Birth of the Democratic State* (New York: Cambridge University Press, 2003); S. H. Haber, A. Razo, and N. Maurer, *The Politics of Property Rights: Political Instability, Credible Commitments, and Economic Growth in Mexico, 1876–1929* (Cambridge: Cambridge University Press, 2003); Timothy Frye, "Credible Commitment and Property Rights: Evidence from Russia," *American Political Science Review*, 98, 3 (2004): 453–466. I take up this issue again in Chapter 2.

[20] On the dangers of circularity, see Graham Bird, "The Effectiveness of Conditionality and the Political Economy of Economic Policy Reform: Is It Simply a Matter of Political Will?," *The Journal of Policy Reform*, 2, 1 (1998): 89–113.

act as powerful signals of government intentions or encourage economic actors to change their preferences, the study of formal economic institutions in Africa merits more serious analysis than it has received.

As much of the institutional literature argues, however, the process of institutional change is lengthy and complex; reversals are common and resistance may be great. This book argues that differences in the quality of democracy and in the nature of party politics condition economic institutional development because they influence the types of conflicts that will emerge and how the state will respond to them. Whether a state will adhere to the rules it has adopted or whether it will resort to discretionary authority to assuage its critics is a function not only of the constraints imposed by new economic institutions but also of the political environment. The political and economic choices that states ultimately make will shape the character of capitalism in transitional countries.

Institutions and Credible Commitments

The theoretical literature underpinning my argument is derived from studies of credible commitment, democratization, and party politics. The concept of commitment has been central to the literature on institutional reform for several decades. As is the case with any reform that is not the outcome of incremental change, the implementation of privatization requires transitional governments actively to commit to it.[21] But for governments with authoritarian histories and large state sectors, this act embodies a paradox, which is that governments themselves must elect to restrict their discretionary authority over the economy in order for private sector actors to prevail. To quote a widely cited observation by Barry Weingast, "Any government that is strong enough to provide the minimal institutional requirements of markets...is also strong enough to extract the wealth of its citizens."[22]

Scholars have offered a number of theoretical and policy solutions to resolve the paradox but for reasons that Chapter 2 will discuss more fully, most of these are inadequate in the context of developing countries that are undergoing transition. I resolve the dilemma by relying on Kenneth Shepsle's distinction between "motivationally credible" commitments and commitments that are "credible in the imperative sense."[23] Like other institutionalists, Shepsle uses

---

[21] Most African governments adopted privatization when they were at a "critical juncture." Nevertheless, the reforms have undergone change during the implementation process in ways that parallel the claims regarding incremental change made by Mahoney and Thelen, eds. and contributors to *Explaining Institutional Change*.

[22] Barry Weingast, "The Political Commitment to Markets and Marketization" in David Weimer, ed., *The Political Economy of Property Rights: Institutional Change and Credibility in the Reform of Centrally Planned Economies* (Cambridge: Cambridge University Press, 1997), 43.

[23] Kenneth Shepsle, "Discretion, Institutions, and the Problem of Government Commitment" in Pierre Bourdieu and James S. Coleman, eds., *Social Theory for a Changing Society* (Boulder: Westview Press and New York: Russell Sage Foundation, 1991), 245–263.

the adoption of rules and regulations as the litmus test for gauging whether a commitment to reform has been made. Yet, he distinguishes analytically and temporally between two types of credible commitment that attach to such changes. According to Shepsle, "motivationally credible" commitments are those that a government adopts because such a change is compatible with the government's current set of incentives. By contrast, commitments are "credible in the imperative sense" if the discretionary authority of the government to adopt some other course of action is disabled by the practice of existing institutional arrangements.[24] Thus, at time t, a commitment is motivationally credible if a government has adopted a series of institutional reforms that indicate a change in policy direction. Such a commitment becomes credible in the imperative sense if at time $t + n$, those arrangements prevent the government from engaging in any other course of action.

As an example, suppose that in exchange for a sizable loan to an ailing government, the World Bank requires that an African government adopt a package of policies that includes the privatization of the country's large stable of state-owned enterprises (SOEs). To receive the loan, the government adopts a private property law, sets up an agency to handle the privatization of SOEs, and passes a privatization law detailing the SOEs that will be sold and how the process will take place. The commitment to institutional reform is motivationally credible because although regulations have been passed and organizations have been created to implement them, at this stage the reform depends on the government's willingness to honor it. If the government wants to renege on this commitment in the short-term, it is certainly possible to do so, although it will risk losing aid from the Bank. As the literature on aid indicates, there were many instances in which African governments disregarded parchment institutions especially after they received their tranche of loans.[25]

Yet imagine that a government makes a motivational commitment and decides to follow through with the reforms, in spite of the fact that the content of the reforms is exogenously determined by the preferences of the World Bank and Western donors. This government passes laws *and* sells parastatals; it welcomes foreign investors and enforces private property rights; it finances domestic investors and provides incentives for the creation of infant industries. Over time, the existence of these institutions may structure the preferences of multiple economic actors; these actors develop interests in sustaining the new rules, and those interests act to constrain the state from reneging on its earlier decision. At this point, commitments are "credible in the imperative sense,"

---

[24] Ibid., 245–263. Henceforth I drop the quotation marks when using these phrases.

[25] Miles Kahler, "International Financial Institutions and the Politics of Adjustment" in Joan Nelson, and Contributors, *Fragile Coalitions: The Politics of Economic Adjustment* (Washington, D.C.: Overseas Development Council, 1989), 139–159; Kahler "External Influence"; Paul Mosley, Jane Harrigan, and John Toye, *Aid and Power: The World Bank and Policy-Based Lending* (London: Routledge, 1991, 2nd ed., 1995), 187–301.

meaning that institutional constraints are effective at disabling discretionary attempts by the government to overturn them.

In this book, I operationalize Shepsle's distinction between motivationally credible commitments and commitments that are credible in the imperative sense with regard to the creation or expansion of private sector–driven market economies in Africa. To assess the former, I systematically compare the institutional arrangements associated with privatization and private sector expansion that African countries adopted or inherited in the 1990s. Through careful analysis and comparison of countries' constitutions, land and privatization laws, and agencies charged with selling state assets, I devise an index that gauges the motivationally credible commitments of twenty-seven democratic and nondemocratic countries in Africa between 1988 and 2000. The index developed in Chapter 2 looks at whether and how African governments altered their constitutions to acknowledge and promote private property rights in the 1990s. It examines whether land laws embodied rights to buy and sell property freely or, alternatively, whether they contained restrictions on the rights to purchase land by groups such as foreigners and provisions for indigenous communities to enjoy communal land rights. It specifies whether privatization and investment laws existed and how favorable they were to investors. The index also determines whether governments established agencies to implement privatization and if they gave these agencies sufficient autonomy to carry out their responsibilities. Finally, the index gauges whether governments and/or agencies made clear which companies would be sold and the methods by which sales would occur.

To ascertain whether motivational commitments to a private sector–driven economy became commitments that were credible in the imperative sense, I then establish criteria for judging what such imperative commitments would look like. To most analysts, sales of state assets would appear to be obvious indicators of a commitment that has imperative credibility because they suggest that private sector interests are emerging with a stake in maintaining the new rules. I find a positive and statistically significant, but moderate correlation between the existence of privatization rules and sales of SOEs. The relationship between rules and sales is more attenuated because countries with established private sectors such as Mauritius or South Africa opted to restructure, rather than to sell, many of their SOEs. On the other hand, some countries such as Kenya or Guinea divested parastatals even though the extent to which they adopted formal institutional arrangements consistent with privatization was low.

To account for the possibility that some countries might not engage in sales even though private sector rules were in place and others might divest in the absence of rules, I incorporate sales into a broader index that gauges the effectiveness of institutions that are typically associated with a private sector–driven economy. On the supposition that if these institutions were performing properly, they would act to disable the state's discretion, institutional effectiveness became a proxy for commitments that were credible in the imperative sense.

What made these commitments imperative rather than motivational was that rules and regulations became institutionalized and self-enforcing over time. In the area of property rights and corporate governance, they acted effectively to restrict the state's discretionary authority.[26]

The index evaluates the extent to which the government engaged in sound macroeconomic management; whether regulatory, trade, and finance policies were consistent with the building of a market economy; and if major infrastructural assets such as water, electricity, and telecommunications were sold or restructured. The assessment also examines whether state-business relationships either facilitated or hindered the expansion of the private sector. This last category is an equally important indicator of commitments with imperative credibility because the capacities of institutions to constrain the use of government discretion largely depend on the strength and organization of those preferences they represent.

The criteria and the assessments of individual countries in the index partly derive from indicators used by the International Development Association Resource Allocation Index (IRAI), which a number of scholars have relied on to assess economic reforms.[27] The IRAI (formerly the Country Policy and Institutional Assessment) analyzes the effectiveness of the institutional and policy framework implemented by a range of countries. Country teams associated with the World Bank rate a range of countries according to sixteen criteria organized into four components: Economic Management, Structural Policies, Policies for Social Inclusion and Equity, and Public Sector Management and Institutions. Not only do I select from the IRAI those indicators that are relevant to this study's objectives but also I rely on the IRAI criteria to assess countries such as Botswana, Mauritius, Namibia, South Africa, and the Seychelles that the IRAI index does not cover. In addition, I devise three indicators on privatization and restructuring, infrastructure reform, and relationships with the private sector to capture more explicitly the performance of institutional reforms designed to create or expand the private sector.[28] For these three measures, I rely on privatization databases of the World Bank and the Organization for Economic Cooperation and Development (OECD); government and company reports; interviews with key stakeholders in government, the private sector, and civil society; and secondary sources on

---

[26] Kenneth Shepsle, "Discretion, Institutions" and personal communication, January 18, 2008.

[27] World Bank, International Development Association, "2005 International Development Association Resource Allocation Index (IRAI)," 2005, accessed 5/11/2009, http://www.worldbank. org /IDA/. On other uses of the index, see Benno Ndulu, Stephen O'Connell, Robert Bates, and Paul Soludo, eds., *The Political Economy of Economic Growth in Africa, 1960–2000*, Vol. 1 (New York: Cambridge University Press, 2008) especially Paul Collier and Stephen O'Connell, "Opportunities and Choices," 76–136 and Robert Bates, "Political Reform," 348–390.

[28] Several of these were adapted from European Bank for Reconstruction and Development, "Transition Indicators Methodology," accessed 1/9/2008, http://www.ebrd.com/country/sector/ econo/stats/timeth.htm.

privatization outcomes to assess each country in the dataset. Allowing for a five-year lag between the final year included in the index on motivational commitment and the beginning of the imperative commitment index, I determine the extent to which countries approximated imperative, credible commitments by 2005.

A comparison of the two indices suggests that there is a relationship between the formal changes that African governments adopted or did not adopt with respect to privatization and the extent to which those institutions were effective at a later point in time. If African countries made formal institutional changes to the Constitution and land laws to protect private property rights, passed privatization laws, and created privatization agencies, the institutional and policy framework was more conducive to private sector growth and expansion ten to fifteen years later. Where African countries did not make initial motivational commitments, the measure of their imperative credibility was also correspondingly low. This finding suggests that formal adoption of the institutional architecture designed to create or expand a market economy constitutes a necessary building block in the development of such an economy over time. It reinforces the claims of many historical as well as rational choice institutionalists that the implementation of institutions structures bargaining, shapes preferences, and affects the calculations of politicians.[29]

The findings also highlight the varied institutions that African governments chose and, correspondingly, the divergence in the extent to which they realized commitments that were credible in the imperative sense. The motivational commitment scores show that many countries demonstrated greater variation in the degree and kinds of formal institutions they adopted than critics of the World Bank's "one size fits all" approach would have us believe. The variation suggests that individual governments were imposing their preferences on the reform process and trying to shape it in anticipation of future gains and losses. Moreover, the extent to which countries approximated commitments that were credible in the imperative sense also showed considerable divergence.[30] The scores of many countries fell short of what might constitute an ideal type of imperative credibility.

---

[29] See the contributions to Sven Steinmo, Kathleen Thelen, and Frank Longstreth, eds., *Structuring Politics: Historical Institutionalism in Comparative Analysis* (New York: Cambridge University Press, 1992, reprinted 1998); Jack Knight and Itai Sened, eds., *Explaining Social Institutions* (Ann Arbor: University of Michigan Press, 1995) and Clague, ed., *Institutions and Economic Development*. These two approaches are not as far apart as some of their adherents suggest, see John Campbell and Ove Pedersen, "The Rise of Neoliberalism and Institutional Analysis," 1–23 and Jack Knight, "Explaining the Rise of Neoliberalism: The Mechanisms of Institutional Change," 27–50 in John Campbell and Ove Pedersen, eds., *The Rise of Neoliberalism and Institutional Analysis* (Princeton, N.J.: Princeton University Press, 2001).

[30] For a similar claim regarding the divergence of banking sector reform across Africa, see Cathy Boone's work of careful scholarship, "State, Capital, and the Politics of Banking Reform in Sub-Saharan Africa," *Comparative Politics*, 37, 4 (2005): 401–420.

These results remind us that transformative institutional change is time-consuming, multifaceted, and contextual. Many of these countries were responding to crisis; many were democratizing at the same time that they were adopting market principles. New social groups with different levels of organizational strength and power were exerting contradictory pressures on governments, forcing them to face new and challenging trade-offs. To understand more fully the ways in which institutions interacted with these changing dynamics, and the broader implications for the kind of capitalism that was emerging, we have to examine the politics of the process.

The Politics of Institutional Development

Common to the privatization experience in many Sub-Saharan African countries is that even if formal institutions reflected the historical and political context in which they were situated, they were adopted by governments only after pushing and prodding from international financial institutions. Liberal institutions in Africa did not emerge from the strategic interaction of various interests, in contrast to the descriptions of their emergence in eighteenth-century England or France depicted by scholarly accounts.[31] Because of the intentionality behind their design, therefore, liberal institutions in Africa became sites of political struggles between distributional interests and the state *after* they were adopted. These ex post moments of strategic interaction intertwined with other changes such as democratization to determine the extent, pace, and sequencing of reforms and to influence who would benefit and who would lose from them. The bargains that were struck and the compromises that were made affected the material ends and normative goals to which institutions were directed. Those who engaged in bargaining and negotiation had different preferences, information, and power; therefore, trajectories of private sector development have varied across countries. [32]

Privatization, in particular, has often provoked distributional conflicts between large commercial enterprises and indigenous communities over the private allocation of land; between investors and trade unions over the possible retrenchment of labor; and between private utility operators and consumers over the payment of fees for services such as water or electricity. Threatened by

---

[31] See, for example, Douglass C. North and Barry R. Weingast. "Constitutions and Commitment: The Evolution of Institutions Governing Public Choice in Seventeenth-Century England," *The Journal of Economic History*, 49, 4 (1989): 803–832 and Stasavage, *Public Debt*.

[32] The explanation I offer draws on the work of Daniel Diermeier, Joel Ericson, Timothy Frye, and Steven Lewis, "Credible Commitment and Property Rights: The Role of Strategic Interaction between Political and Economic Actors" in David Weimer, ed., *The Political Economy of Property Rights: Institutional Change and Credibility in the Reform of Centrally Planned Economies* (Cambridge: Cambridge University Press, 1997), 20–42; Jack Knight, *Institutions and Social Conflict* (Cambridge: Cambridge University Press, 1992), especially ch. 5 and 6; and Knight, "Explaining the Rise of Neoliberalism."

privatization, bureaucrats may cling to clientelistic and rent-seeking practices; alternatively they may engage in *sub rosa* resistance against policies with which they ideologically, technically, or morally disagree.[33]

Unlike eighteenth-century England or contemporary China, where the struggle over property rights largely occurred in the absence of mass enfranchisement, many of these conflicts over job losses, private property, and the withdrawal of benefits transpired in contexts where norms and rules of democratic representation, contestation, and accountability have recently emerged. These newly democratic arenas provided opportunities as well as drawbacks for stakeholders to influence the reform process and to demand accountability from the state for its actions. In Africa, as in parts of Latin America and Eurasia, interests had varied financial resources, levels of expertise, and national visibility; some were well connected to international networks or largely local affairs; and the appropriate mechanisms for aggregating these interests in individual states may have been weak or strong.[34] In recently democratic countries, new means for aggregating interests such as political parties and business associations also existed. Finally, periodic elections, legislatures, and intraparty caucuses in some countries checked and diffused executive authority.

The book examines economic institutional development in such democratic settings. From the initial set of twenty-seven countries discussed in Chapter 2, I identify nine democracies in Chapter 3 that made high or very high motivational commitments to economic reform. Keeping the initial commitment constant allows us to examine the trajectory of reform over time: what conflicts arose, which interests were involved, how government acted on their demands, and what the impact was on the process of privatization. I claim that under conditions where motivational commitments were high or very high, two factors critically shaped private sector development over time and across cases: first, differences in the quality of democracy and second, variations in the logic of party system competition. Although they remain underspecified in

---

[33] On principled challenges by bureaucrats to land reform, as opposed to rent-seeking practices cited in much of the literature, see Jessica Allina-Pisano, "Sub Rosa Resistance and the Politics of Economic Reform: Land Redistribution in Post-Soviet Ukraine," *World Politics,* 56, 4 (2004), 554–581; on Botswana, see Amy Poteete, "Ideas, Interests, and Institutions: Challenging the Property Rights Paradigm in Botswana," *Governance,* 16, 4 (2003): 527–557.

[34] The literature on coalitions and distributional conflicts is vast. On Latin America, see H. E. Schamis, *Re-forming the State: The Politics of Privatization in Latin America and Europe* (Ann Arbor: University of Michigan Press, 2002); Dag MacLeod, *Downsizing the State: Privatization and the Limits of Neoliberal Reform in Mexico* (University Park: Pennsylvania State University Press, 2004); Ben Ross Schneider, *Business Politics and the State in Twentieth-Century Latin America*; on Africa, see Robert Bates and Anne Krueger, *Political and Economic Interactions in Economic Policy Reform: Evidence from Eight Countries* (Oxford: Blackwell Publishers, 1993); Deborah Bräutigam, Lise Rakner, and Scott Taylor, "Business Associations and Growth Coalitions in Sub-Saharan Africa," *Journal of Modern African Studies,* 40, 4 (2002): 519–547; Peter Lewis, *Growing Apart: Oil, Politics, and Economic Change in Indonesia and Nigeria* (Ann Arbor: University of Michigan Press, 2007).

the literature on privatization, differences in the quality of democracy and the character of the party system in privatizing countries affected the organization and expression of partisan pressures in response to the implementation of new institutions as well as the ways in which the government used its discretionary authority to cope with those pressures. The outcomes of these interactions, in turn, molded the trajectory of private sector development.

Democratic Demands and Constraints on Reform

As moments of transition recede into history, theoretical scholarship has begun to assess more critically the quality of democracy in those countries that have become democratic in the last few decades. Building on the work of Robert Dahl, scholars have evaluated not only procedural aspects of democracy such as the holding of regular, competitive, and fair elections or the existence of the rule of law but also its substantive dimensions such as citizens' rights to participate, to express themselves, and to organize free from harassment or repression. Together, the different dimensions have allowed analysts to assess more comprehensively the quality of democracy across a range of countries.[35]

In this study, I use Freedom House indicators to proxy for these dimensions of democratic quality in the countries that are the subject of analysis. Countries in the sample are classified as liberal or limited democracies according to the extent of political rights and civil liberties that they have. I argue that whether a country exhibits only a few (which I call "limited democracy") or, alternatively, most of the characteristics that Dahl identified as important attributes of democracy (which I designate "liberal democracy") impacts the ability of partisan pressures to articulate their interests, to give voice to their demands, and ultimately to influence the policy process. If those who stand to lose their jobs from labor retrenchments or casualization have few effective avenues for voicing their concerns to government or for holding government accountable, likely the kind of market economy that takes shape in a given country will not reflect the interests of labor. By contrast, where diverse interests are able to rely on extensive formal mechanisms to gain access to government officials, we can expect that the outcome of privatization will reflect their influence.

Moreover, differences in the quality of democracy condition the government's response to the claims and conflicts that emerge from the privatization process. Even the most democratic governments may choose to ignore the demands of selected constituencies if they are determined to proceed with

---

[35] See Robert Alan Dahl, *Polyarchy: Participation and Opposition* (New Haven: Yale University Press, 1971); Larry Diamond, "Thinking about Hybrid Regimes," *Journal of Democracy*, 13, 2 (2002); Bratton, Mattes, and Gyimah-Boadi, *Public Opinion*, ch. 1; Larry Diamond and Leonardo Morlino, eds., *Assessing the Quality of Democracy* (Baltimore: Johns Hopkins University Press, 2005); Daniel Levine and José Molina, eds., *The Quality of Democracy in Latin America* (Boulder: Lynne Rienner, 2011).

policy change and have the votes, but governments that actively repress or manipulate interests in their efforts to privatize realize different outcomes than those who do not. Over time, I argue that such interactions influenced the trajectory of private sector development. They shaped the extent to which crony capitalism occurred; whether some compromises with labor took place; and whether the public viewed the process as legitimate.[36]

Invariably, to discuss differences in democratic quality means revisiting previous debates about the importance of regime-type to the outcome of economic reform.[37] To date, most of the findings regarding whether democratic or authoritarian regimes are "better" at privatization are contradictory. In his study of Mexico, MacLeod found that an authoritarian regime was instrumental in the process of organizing potential winners to capture the benefits of privatization. Not only did it consciously and selectively direct benefits toward particular elites and businesses in Mexico to advance privatization – a process we see also in a number of African cases such as Uganda – but also it worked actively to reduce opposition from losers by "penetrating, co-opting, disorganizing, and where necessary, repressing these groups."[38]

In the case of Mexico, regime-type did seem to shape the outcome. Here an authoritarian regime had greater liberty than a democratic one to manipulate and stifle those who were disaffected with the process. It had more discretion to cultivate selectively and consciously the beneficiaries of the process. Initially at least, it did not have to answer for its actions to voters at the polls. Similarly,

---

[36] In emerging democracies, there is a potential endogeneity problem when examining the influence of democratic quality on the process of economic reform, because the way that a government deals with distributional conflicts may contribute to its democratic quality scores. Some endogenous cycling is probably unavoidable, but I try to address the problem in two ways. First, Freedom House scores assess a broad array of political rights and civil liberties thus reducing the likelihood that the score reflects simply the expression and resolution of economic conflicts over any given period. Second, I rely on process tracing to tease out causal sequences.

[37] Most of the debate has focused on broader issues than the one I address here but their insights have informed my own thinking on the relationship between privatization and regime type. For a theoretical discussion of regime types and economic reform, see Stephan Haggard and Robert R. Kaufman, *The Political Economy of Democratic Transitions* (Princeton, N.J.: Princeton University Press, 1995) and Stephen Haggard, "Democratic Institutions, Economic Policy, and Development" in Christopher Clague, ed., *Institutions and Economic Development: Growth and Governance in Less-Developed and Post Socialist Countries* (Baltimore: Johns Hopkins University Press, 1977), 121–149. A comprehensive quantitative study of the relationship between regime type and per capita income, which addresses a longstanding question on whether more democratic countries also have a higher per capita income and why this is the case, is David Epstein, Robert Bates, Jack Goldstone, Ida Kristenson, and Sharyn O'Halloran, "Democratic Transitions," *American Journal of Political Science*, 50, 3 (2006): 551–569. In addition, for an interesting study on a related issue regarding the political determinants of policy choice and economic growth, see Macartan Humphreys and Robert Bates, "Political Institutions and Economic Policies: Lessons from Africa," *British Journal of Political Science*, 35 (2005): 403–428.

[38] MacLeod, *Downsizing the State*, 105.

those seeking to influence the state did not have at hand multiple institutional means of access to express their positions. As MacLeod's findings show, these conditions made collective action difficult.[39]

Joel Hellman's study of transitions in formerly communist countries reinforces the claim that regime-type matters. Hellman concluded that in less democratic countries, "early winners" such as insiders and local state officials who benefited from initial effects of privatization then used their clout to block further reform so that they could gain substantial rents from a partial reform equilibrium. By contrast, Hellman found that this scenario was less likely in more democratic countries because the increased participation and voice of potential losers would act to reduce the power of early winners and force governments to disperse the gains from reforms more broadly.[40] Diermeier et al. deepen and extend Hellman's claims by demonstrating that the kind of bargaining around significant reforms that takes place in democratic countries helps to institutionalize the process. As they state, "Other things equal, governments with dispersed political power are better able to make a credible commitment to property rights than are governments with more concentrated powers."[41]

However, comparative work by Hector Schamis across different regime-types raises doubts about the importance of democratic regimes to the privatization process. He found that even under democratic regimes, whether in Argentina or Britain, economic crises and the state response that followed often ushered in a period of "extraordinary policy making" that centralized power in the state, conferring an "autocratic quality" on the process.[42] Moreover, both Schamis and MacLeod effectively challenged Hellman's argument that nondemocracies were more likely to achieve a partial reform equilibrium by showing that regardless of regime-type, collusion between the state and beneficiaries allowed rents to be acquired even after full liberalization.[43] Peter Lewis's comparison of Nigeria and Indonesia, though not explicitly focused on privatization, also challenges the importance of regime-type to outcomes by tracing the divergent reform results of two countries with similar regime-types.[44]

The case studies I examine initially appear to support the claims by Schamis, MacLeod, and Lewis. I highlight the coercive features of the reform process, the efforts to silence critics, and the lack of transparency in the two limited democracies of Zambia and Mozambique. Moreover, even in the more liberal democracy of South Africa, the legacy of apartheid left a highly centralized state. Under the African National Congress (ANC), which has been in power since 1994, centralizing tendencies have continued in the postapartheid period. Some of the effects of privatization replicate patterns found in

---

[39] Ibid.
[40] Hellman, "Winners Take All," 203–234.
[41] Diermeier et al., "Credible Commitment and Property Rights," 36.
[42] Schamis, *Re-Forming the State*, 137.
[43] Schamis, *Re-Forming the State* and MacLeod, *Downsizing the State*.
[44] Lewis, *Growing Apart*.

limited democracies or in authoritarian regimes such as that controlled by the Institutional Revolutionary Party in Mexico; political elites have used the process to cement alliances that enhance power at the apex of the political system. As the Mexican government did, the South African government has actively tried to cultivate some constituencies and to marginalize others.

But, there are historical and contextual differences among African countries that underline the importance of regime-type as well as differences within regime-type to the privatization process. These have to do with the means by which some countries in Africa became, or continue to be, democratic, in contrast to those in Latin America such as Mexico, Chile, and Argentina studied by Schamis. In the case of South Africa, the democratic transition brought to power not only a national liberation movement that adheres to the tenets of representative democracy but also one whose main pillar of support is organized labor. In Mauritius, too, another liberal democracy, support from labor is often critical to the survival of coalitions. These countries demonstrate marked variation from those where democratization was installed following a peace accord as in the case of Mozambique or occurred following only a brief popular uprising as in the case of Zambia. The roles played by various social movements in the political history of individual countries and the way that democratization took place in Africa offer theoretical insights for comparativists studying institutional change in new democracies. They suggest that regime-type and *variation within a regime-type* such as democracy may exercise greater influence on the trajectory of privatization than the current literature acknowledges.[45] The study of democratic variation within Africa and its impact on institutional development therefore pushes comparative scholarship in new directions.

Party Politics and Economic Reform

Whereas a number of scholars working on Latin America and East, Central, and Southern Europe have debated the impact of democracy on the process of economic reform, few have analyzed the effects of political parties on an institutional change as far-reaching as privatization.[46] Scholarship on this topic

---

[45] In their work on the relationship between regime type and per capita income, Epstein et al., "Democratic Transitions," also suggest that scholars have failed to pay attention to variation within regime types, which may have skewed their results. They identify "partial democracies" as worthy of greater study. Although my category, "limited democracy," is narrower than theirs and relies on Freedom House rather than Polity scores, I agree that further study of the differences among democratic countries is warranted.

[46] Frye's recent book is an exception to the trend, see *Building States and Markets*. For insightful work on the role of party politics and state building in transitional countries, though not privatization per se, see Haggard and Kaufman, *Political Economy of Democratic Transitions*, 163–182; Haggard, "Democratic Institutions"; Conor O'Dwyer, *Runaway State-Building: Patronage Politics and Democratic Development* (Baltimore: The Johns Hopkins University

in Africa is nearly nonexistent with the exception of the literature on South Africa. By examining party system differences along with the quality of democracy, this book offers a more robust theoretical analysis of institutional development than existing comparative work. I claim that the dynamics of party politics influence the engagement of governments with those distributional pressures arising from privatization. Parties are the building blocks of democracies. They act as mechanisms for identifying, aggregating, and mobilizing interests in support of elites and their policies. They serve as conduits for the expression of popular discontent or, alternatively, adoration and loyalty by particular constituencies. Differences in political party formation, organization, and support influence how a ruling party will deal with the consequences of privatization, whether it will ignore or incorporate the demands of those affected by it. Further, party system dynamics shape how the opposition will respond and what mechanisms the opposition will use to express its policy objections.

Because the activities of party politics under democratic conditions in Africa are relatively recent, most observers highlight the fragility of African parties. Many parties suffer from a chronic lack of finances and lack internal democratic procedures. They are uncertain of their membership and weakened by factional in-fighting and ethno-regional cleavages. Many fail to campaign on substantive issues and serve as personalistic vehicles for Africa's "big men." In places such as Zambia or Mali, small, weak opposition parties generally come and go with every election while incumbent parties monopolize resources, control appointments, dispense patronage, and even commit fraud, in order to maintain their grip on political power.[47]

These generalizations about the weakness of party politics have reinforced the theme of African exceptionalism that pervades the comparative literature.[48]

Press, 2006). A useful examination of party politics and structural adjustment in the context of Spain's democratization is Nancy Bermeo, "Sacrifice, Sequence, and Strength in Successful Dual Transitions: Lessons from Spain," *The Journal of Politics*, 56, 3 (1994): 601–627.

[47] Nicolas van de Walle and Kimberly Smiddy Butler, "Political Parties and Party Systems in Africa's Illiberal Democracies," *Cambridge Review of International Affairs*, 13, 1 (1999): 14–28; Vicky Randall and Lars Svåsand, "Political Parties and Democratic Consolidation in Africa," *Democratization*, 9, 3 (2002): 30–46; Nicolas van de Walle, "Presidentialism and Clientelism in Africa's Emerging Party Systems," *Journal of Modern African Studies*, 41, 2 (2003): 297–321; Carrie Manning, "Assessing African Party Systems after the Third Wave," *Party Politics*, 11, 6 (2005): 707–727.

[48] A recent contribution to the archive of African exceptionalism was the counterintuitive claim by Mozaffar, Scarritt, and Galaich that high ethno-political fragmentation does NOT increase the number of parties, see Shaheen Mozaffar, James Scarritt, and Glen Galaich, "Electoral Institutions, Ethnopolitical Cleavages and Party Systems in Africa's Emerging Democracies," *American Political Science Review*, 97 (2003): 379–390. This claim was convincingly challenged by Thomas Brambor, William Roberts Clark, and Matt Golder, "Are African Party Systems Different?," *Electoral Studies*, 26, 2 (2007): 315–323. On areas where more systematic research is needed, see Giovanni Carbone, "Political Parties and Party Systems in Africa: Themes and Research Perspectives," *World Political Science Review*, 3, 3 (2007): 1–29.

Moreover, a lack of cross-national research on substantive aspects of party systems in Africa has occluded a key distinction between party systems on the continent – the distinction between a fragmented and a stable party system.[49] Stable party systems show greater continuity in parliament and more consistent voter support over time. Fragmented or fluid systems show greater variation in the support that parties receive from voters and less continuity from election to election.[50] I argue that whether a party system is stable (or solid), fragmented (or fluid), affects a government's calculations regarding whether it will react to partisan pressures and how it will use its discretion to solve conflicts.

As forthcoming chapters will discuss, transient parties populate fluid systems. In these systems, parties rise and decline; supporters are fickle; and voter loyalty is low. Even in cases where one party repeatedly wins elections, on closer inspection, the "dominant" party may lack a stable membership and loyal supporters. Even though fluid party systems such as those in Malawi or Mali may produce more competitive elections and offer more choices to voters, they produce policy dilemmas for governments. A ruling party such as the Movement for Multiparty Democracy (MMD) in Zambia, for example, regularly confronted party switching and defections within its own party as well as threats from new parties, and it relied on its discretionary authority to stall or distort policies to satisfy or woo constituents. At the same time, fluid parties

[49] Use of the word "system" here does not mean to imply that patterns of party interaction are already institutionalized between 1990 and 2005, the time period of my study. I use the word "system" to call attention to emerging patterns or logics of party politics in particular countries, while recognizing that these are nascent democracies. The same caution should be exercised with use of the word "dominant" or "predominant." During the period between 1990 and 2005, some parties may have been trending dominant, but they were not yet dominant or predominant according to Sartori's definition.

[50] The categorization of fluid (or floating) and stable (or solid) party systems draws on Lawrence Dodd, *Coalitions in Parliamentary Government* (Princeton: Princeton University Press, 1976), 88–94; Scott Mainwaring and Timothy R. Scully, eds., *Building Democratic Institutions: Party Systems in Latin America* (Stanford, Calif.: Stanford University Press, 1995); Michael Coppedge, "Political Darwinism in Latin America's Lost Decade" in Larry Diamond and Richard Gunther, eds., *Political Parties and Democracy* (Baltimore: Johns Hopkins University Press, 2001), 173–205. For Africa, see Michelle Kuenzi and Gina Lambright, "Party System Institutionalization in 30 African Countries," *Party Politics*, 7, 4 (2001): 437–468 and "Party Systems and Democratic Consolidation in Africa's Electoral Regimes," *Party Politics*, 11, 4 (2005): 423–446; Shaheen Mozaffar and James Scarritt, "The Puzzle of African Party Systems," *Party Politics*, 11, 4 (2005): 399–421 and the critique of the latter work by Matthijs Bogaards, "Dominant Party Systems and Electoral Volatility in Africa: A Comment on Mozaffar and Scarritt," *Party Politics*, 14, 1 (2008): 113–130. For recent efforts to construct typologies of party systems in Africa, see Bogaards, "Dominant Party Systems"; Staffan Lindberg, "Institutionalization of Party Systems? Stability and Fluidity among Legislative Parties in Africa's Democracies," *Government and Opposition*, 42, 2 (2007) and Matthias Basedau, "Do Party Systems Matter for Democracy? A Comparative Study of 28 Sub-Saharan Countries?" in Matthias Basedau, Gero Erdmann, and Andreas Mehler, eds., *Votes, Money and Violence: Political Parties and Elections in Sub-Saharan Africa* (Uppsala: Nordiska Afrikainstitutet and Scottsville: University of Kwazulu-Natal, 2007), 105–137.

frustrate organized interests. Their uncertain membership undermines efforts by interests to develop linkages with particular parties or to lobby around policy initiatives.

On the other hand, parties in more stable systems such as those in Ghana and Mozambique show higher survival rates from election to election, higher levels of party loyalty from members, and more consistent bases of support. They tend to have more resources, lower supporter turnover, and greater organizational cohesion. They cultivate and attract organized interests in support of mutually beneficial opportunities. In these systems, policy tends to be better coordinated and more coherent.[51] But governments in stable party systems usually design policies to benefit their supporters, fearing distributional squabbles if they do not. They may use their discretion to pursue economic strategies intended to strengthen the party's hold on power rather than to benefit the country as a whole. Such trade-offs risk unintended political consequences in democratic settings, however, as opposition parties may seize on inequitable policy outcomes to gain seats or power.[52]

Since party systems are not static and the time span of African democracies is so recent, observers should expect that systems may move from stable to fluid or vice versa over time and should choose indicators that reflect such changes. By capturing changes in support for winning and losing parties from election to election, Pedersen's index of volatility not only registers the rate of party system change but also makes it possible to detect patterns in party stability or volatility over time, even in cases where a trend toward one party dominance is beginning to prevail.[53] Together with public opinion data on party loyalty, evidence on party switching by members, and other quantitative and qualitative assessments, these indicators allow us to categorize for heuristic purposes

---

[51] Recent findings by Sebastian Elischer that parties in Africa are more ideological than conventional views acknowledge provide additional support for my claim. However, Elischer only examines parties in three countries, and he does not draw a link between party stability and more programmatic approaches. See Sebastian Elischer, "Measuring and Comparing Party Ideology in Nonindustrialized Societies: Taking Party Manifesto Research to Africa," GIGA German Institute of Global and Area Studies Working Paper, 139 (June 2010).

[52] Here I draw on Haggard and Kaufman, *The Political Economy of Democratic Transitions*, 163–182.

[53] Mogens Pedersen, "On Measuring Party System Change: A Methodological Critique and a Suggestion," *Comparative Political Studies*, 12, 4 (January 1980): 387–403. Because it captures the rise and decline of support for parties over time, Pedersen's index is appropriate for our purposes along with the more commonly used Laakso-Taagapera index. The latter calls attention to the effective number of parties in the legislature – an important measure – but it cannot indicate if those parties are the same as or different from the parties in the previous legislature. Therefore, I rely on both measures. For a critique, see Matthijs Bogaards, "Counting Parties and Identifying Dominant Party Systems in Africa," *European Journal of Political Research*, 43, 2 (2004): 173–197. The emphasis here is on the pattern of interaction within and between parties in individual countries not simply whether there is a dominant party or not. See Chapter 3 for further discussion.

the particular attributes of each system in order to trace their effects on policy making and implementation.

It might be asked why I do not examine party polarization instead of party system volatility as a guide to how these conflicts might be resolved and how they will affect the privatization process, particularly since privatization has been so controversial. Basedau has rightfully observed that scholars of Africa have mostly overlooked party polarization in Africa. Moreover, in his study of private sector creation in East Central Europe and Russia, Timothy Frye argues that political polarization was a significant factor affecting the outcome of economic and institutional reforms.[54] It is reasonable to assume that the same might be true for Africa.

My reasons not to focus on this dimension of party politics are conceptual as well as empirical. In Frye's work, polarization is understood as the "policy distance on economic issues between the executive and the largest opposition faction in parliament."[55] This is a very different use of polarization than that employed by Basedau who has been one of the few scholars systematically to study polarization among African parties. According to Basedau, polarization is the degree to which parties adhere to the democratic rules of the game or alternatively reject them. Basedau finds that there is a strong correlation between low democratic performance (or quality) as measured by Freedom House scores and high party polarization (selected measures on election boycotts, violence, acceptance of the outcome by losers).

Basedau's understanding of polarization is restricted to acts of conflict during electoral periods or the rejection of electoral outcomes, which is not particularly helpful for a study that assesses the process of economic reform. Moreover, Basedau's model of polarization suffers from an endogeneity problem, since Freedom House assessments of democratic performance include some of the same measures as Basedau's model of polarization (the presence or absence of boycotts and violence, for example).[56] My approach avoids that by keeping party system characteristics separate from the quality of democracy.

Adopting Frye's definition of polarization also presents empirical difficulties. First, the survey data that would allow a precise measurement of party polarization on economic issues is poor with respect to African countries. Second, in many African countries, the implementation of privatization has sparked protests and influenced vote choice at elections in many countries. It has generated episodes or moments of polarization in which voters or supporters express strong preferences for one candidate over another, one party over another, or one policy over another.[57] But in most places, privatization has not provoked

[54] Frye, *Building States and Markets*.
[55] Ibid., 3.
[56] Basedau, "Do Party Systems Matter," 105–137.
[57] My view is informed by Leslie Anderson and Lawrence Dodd, *Learning Democracy: Citizen Engagement and Electoral Choice in Nicaragua, 1990–2001* (Chicago: University of Chicago Press, 2005), 122–127.

the adoption of substantive, opposing, and lasting ideological positions by parties that Frye finds in East and Central Europe, nor generated the kind of party polarization that Basedau describes. This finding accords with those of Nicholas van de Walle and Gero Erdmann, who claim that ideological differences among African parties are not substantial.[58]

Of greater significance in these transitional countries are the degree of party system cohesion and the quality of democracy in different political settings. They provide the context within which distributional conflicts unfold. More importantly, the party system and the quality of democracy influence how the state uses its discretion to resolve such conflicts. As the case studies illustrate, three patterns are possible under conditions where the degree of motivational commitment was high or very high. In the first pattern, the privatization process occurred in political settings where democracy was limited and the party system was volatile. In these cases, which characterize countries such as Malawi, Mali, and Zambia, governments opportunistically used their discretionary authority to resolve contention arising from privatization and to staunch fragmentation within the ruling party. They relied on sales of state firms to dispense benefits to potential supporters, to curb defections from the party, and to disrupt the formation of opposition parties. Over time, manipulation of the process for political gain produced an ad hoc privatization. The pace was marked by delays and deferrals, while the outcome was misaligned with the original policy intent. To empirically illustrate opportunistic uses of state discretion and ad hoc private sector development, Chapter 4 examines the privatization process in Zambia.

Like the cases that characterize the first pattern, countries that conform to the second pattern resort to illiberal practices to pursue their interests during the period of privatization. But unlike the fragmented party systems that populate the first scenario, the presence of stable party systems explains the purposeful management of privatization by states in the second category. In cases such as Ghana, Mozambique, and the Seychelles, ruling parties used their discretion deliberately to anticipate, avoid, and react to distributional conflicts arising from privatization and they did so in ways that protected their bases of support. In these systems, organized opposition parties offered some check on the uses of deliberate discretion, but these were counterbalanced by the authoritarian impulses of the ruling party. In such settings, privatization nearly always served the partisan interests of the ruling party. Moreover, as the case study of Mozambique in Chapter 5 illustrates, the outcome may have surprising consequences. In this case, a cohesive, disciplined ruling party in a nearly failed state used privatization to reconfigure the party and to consolidate the state.

A final scenario depicts liberal democracies with stable party systems such as South Africa, Cape Verde, and Mauritius. These are cases that most

---

[58] See van de Walle, "Presidentialism and Clientelism"; Gero Erdmann, "Party Research: The Western European Bias and the 'African Labyrinth'," *Democratization*, 11, 3 (2004): 63–87.

closely approximate commitments that are credible in the imperative sense. In situations where countries have a stable party system, but where reforms encounter highly mobilized, well-organized interests, governments in liberal democracies are likely to respond to distributional conflicts arising from privatization by resorting to "contingent" uses of authority in order to build consensus. The idea derives from Robert Barro's observation that the policy effects of a commitment or changes to the context in which a commitment is made, sometimes require a government to modify the rules, to engage in a "contingent reaction."[59] Such uses of discretionary authority do not constitute a repudiation of the policy commitment; rather their purpose is to secure strategic compromises that will maintain policy and regime stability. The privatization process in South Africa illustrates such a pattern, and it is one that the book will discuss in Chapter 6.

To investigate these three different trajectories, I use process tracing to examine the interaction of formal as well as informal institutional arrangements and partisan pressures in Zambia, Mozambique, and South Africa.[60] All three countries became democratic in the 1990s, and all made high motivational commitments to privatization by adopting institutional arrangements consistent with the privatization of existing state enterprises and the creation or expansion of private sector investment. Nevertheless, the logic of their party systems and the qualities of their democracies produced the observed variance in their reform paths. After analyzing the institutional arrangements that they designed to restructure their economies or expand their private sectors and comparing them with other African democracies, I examine how party politics and democratic quality contributed to their varied reform trajectories. To do so, I rely on datasets that I have compiled, which depict those state assets that were privatized; to whom they were sold; the procedure by which the sales took place; and the characteristics of the buyers. I also discuss new investment projects in these countries.

Further, I complement and enrich the findings of the data through semistructured interviews with key stakeholders in the privatization process including government officials from selected ministries; members of business associations; private foreign and domestic investors; trade unionists; members of nongovernmental organizations; and representatives of privatization agencies, major donor governments, and international financial institutions. Although the patterns of privatization found in these countries do not exhaust the range of outcomes across Africa, they are largely representative of those African

[59] Robert J. Barro "Recent Developments in the Theory of Rules Versus Discretion," *The Economic Journal*, 96, Supplement: Conference Papers (1986): 28.

[60] South Africa is often treated as an exception in comparative studies of economic reform. Yet, in spite of its size, it shares many features with other countries in Africa, including SOEs in strategic sectors. Moreover, although many institutions of a market economy existed in South Africa prior to democratization, the apartheid government used them selectively to favor the white minority as did many colonial governments throughout Africa.

countries that were, or became, democratic in the early 1990s. What is not covered are those cases where nondemocratic states formally or informally adopted reforms and collapsed (Congo) or used the reforms to continue or increase their discretionary use of power (Angola) or sustained the reforms (Uganda).

The implications of my argument for comparative scholarship on private sector development are the following. The empirical application of Shepsle's distinction between two understandings of commitment allows us to explore much more systematically how institutions develop over time. Greater specification of differences in democratic quality and party systems sharpen our understanding of how institutional arrangements interact with the political dynamics of a country. It allows us to better explain the substantial variation in patterns of private sector development across cases. Lastly, detailed examination of institutions and interests in the African context should provide extensive data for larger cross-national studies on economic policy choices and their outcomes.

Organization of the Book

This chapter has presented the theoretical framework and identified the key variables that are the subject of study. The following chapters will illustrate how these variables have produced the divergent reform trajectories that characterize patterns of private sector development across Africa. Chapters 2 and 3 develop systematically the theoretical justification for focusing on institutions and partisan coalitions in the case of privatization reform. Chapter 2 delineates the paradox of institutional adoption in the case of privatization and explains why Shepsle's distinction between motivational commitment and commitment in the imperative sense offers a solution to the puzzle. Relying on data from the privatization experiences of twenty-seven countries across Africa, Chapter 2 offers an empirical illustration of the relationship between motivational commitments and commitments that are credible in the imperative sense.

Chapter 2 establishes that the adoption of formal institutions is a necessary condition for the institutional development of a market economy to occur, but formal institutions do not sufficiently explain the varied trajectories of reform across the continent. After describing the qualitative differences among the trajectories of even the most committed reformers, Chapter 3 argues that differences in the logic of party politics and the quality of democracy are responsible for variation in outcomes. It illustrates the argument by examining patterns of privatization for nine cases that were nominally democratic and initially made high or very high commitments to reform. Holding motivational commitment constant reveals the effects of party politics and the quality of democracy on distributional conflicts, state responses, and privatization outcomes. Chapters 4, 5, and 6 then explore more fully the patterns that produced divergent outcomes in Zambia, Mozambique, and South Africa. The book concludes by extending the argument to other cases in Africa and by exploring the theoretical implications of the findings for the study of credible commitments, the political trade-off between rules and discretion in emerging democracies, and patterns of private sector development.

2

From Motivational to Imperative Commitment

Variation and Convergence of Private Sector Institutions across Africa

Introduction

Since the 1980s, many governments in Eastern Europe, Latin America, Asia, and Africa have designed new formal institutions to foster democracy, to reduce the role of the state, to build market economies, and to develop their private sectors. In many countries, the arrangements were not the product of incremental institutional evolution. Rather, they reflected deliberate choices made by governments to address economic crisis, control spending, court investors, or assuage popular protest. In some cases, conditions attached to loans by international financial institutions and donors forced countries to adopt new rules; other governments enacted new laws owing to pressures from social actors or the global diffusion of neo-liberal ideas.

The adoption of new formal institutions has raised interesting questions with respect to their contribution to the complex and contentious process of economic and political transition. Regardless of whether they are rational choice theorists or historical institutionalists, scholars of institutionalism have been especially concerned with the kinds of institutions governments have adopted; how governments have demonstrated their commitment to these institutions; and whether such commitments can be credible in the context of a country undergoing a multifaceted transition. Furthermore, scholars have sought to explain the dynamics and consequences of institutional development as well as whose interests are, or are not, served by particular institutional choices.[1]

---

[1] See especially the contributions to David Weimer, ed., *The Political Economy of Private Property Rights: Institutional Change and Credibility in the Reform of Centrally Planned Economies* (Cambridge: Cambridge University Press), and Campbell and Pedersen, eds., *The Rise of Neoliberalism*.

These questions gain particular significance in the context of Africa because much of the scholarly literature argues that African governments lack the capacity fully to implement formal institutional changes conducive to producing a robust democracy or a vibrant, free market economy. Simultaneously, scholars have documented numerous instances where African politicians have manipulated, ignored, or sabotaged formal institutions such as private property rights or electoral laws in order to pursue their own interests. These abuses tend to occur particularly when governments have adopted formal institutions in response to pressure from international financial agencies or donors. In these circumstances, is it really possible for an African government credibly to commit to a reform as sweeping as privatization? If so, what would such a commitment look like? Moreover, even if a government does demonstrate "ownership" of a reform that requires the state to divest assets to private sector actors, what is the likelihood that such a reform will survive the political dynamics of implementation – the challenges by parastatal management, public sector employees, or even ordinary citizens?

I offer answers to these questions by applying insights from the theoretical literature on credible commitment to an empirical assessment of the institutions adopted by African governments to create or extend their private sectors. I examine the puzzle that neo-liberal institutional change poses for governments that have been heavily involved in their economies. I also look at how scholars and policymakers have tried to resolve this puzzle in order to determine the likelihood of commitment to new policies. I contend that Kenneth Shepsle's conceptual distinction between motivational commitment and commitments that are credible in the imperative sense offers a useful solution for the problem.

After exploring the differences between Shepsle's two types of commitment, I operationalize them by categorizing and rating the institutions and agencies created (or not created) by twenty-seven African governments to reform their economies in the 1990s. I then analyze the outcomes and outputs of efforts to foster private sector development using data on sales of parastatals and indicators on the effectiveness of institutions in these countries. On the basis of the cross-national findings, I argue that despite claims by scholars that African governments adopted a "one size fits all" formula of arrangements devised by the World Bank, most African governments have exercised more autonomy and demonstrated more variation in the choice of formal institutions than some scholars have acknowledged.

Second, the variation in the extent to which African governments initially committed to privatization policies is associated with the degree to which they sold state firms and developed more effective market institutions at a later moment in time. The more that states adopted formal institutional arrangements at the outset, the more likely they were to have sold public enterprises. In addition, these states were more likely to have "effective" institutions later, that is, to have institutions that constrained the state's use of discretionary authority.

These institutions were shaping preferences and structuring bargaining by new private sector actors in emerging markets. How the process occurred, whose preferences were shaped, and what the implications were for the kind of capitalism that emerged depended on the interaction of those institutions with the political dynamics specific to each country, but formal institutions were a critical building block in effecting economic transformation.

From Conditionality to Commitment

Like their counterparts in Latin America, African governments increasingly turned to international financial institutions (IFIs) for aid during the 1980s owing to economic crisis. Requests for aid coincided with heightened activism on the part of IFIs to attach conditions to aid disbursements. To receive funds, grants, or loans, governments had to agree to a package of reforms, recommended and overseen by the IFIs and bilateral donors. The rationale (now well known) behind the recommendation of measures designed to effect broad institutional change was that state economic intervention was part of the reason for the extent and depth of the crisis that afflicted developing economies. In their diagnosis of economic breakdown in Africa, IFIs and their most powerful members, the industrialized countries, agreed that bloated, overextended states had produced economic inefficiencies through the operation of exchange controls, state monopolies, the imposition of protectionist tariffs, and the overemployment of labor. Poor management and corruption also undermined the efficiency of parastatals. The solution (coined by John Williamson as the "Washington consensus") rested heavily on the transformation of economic institutions. The objective was to reduce state intervention in the economy by liberalizing the exchange rate, streamlining the tax system, eliminating subsidies, promoting foreign investment, privatizing state assets, and embracing an export-led development strategy.[2]

As the implementation of neo-liberalism accelerated globally in the 1990s, the IFIs recommended a series of "second-generation" reforms. These extended the scope of the previous initiatives by including additional administrative and political reforms. These required that governments adopt secure private property rights, grant judiciaries greater independence to enforce the rule of law, implement measures to alleviate poverty, practice "good governance," and professionalize the civil service.[3] The IFIs claimed they would enhance the effectiveness of the first-stage reforms or reduce the severity of their impact on

---

[2] John Williamson, "What Washington Means by Policy Reform" in John Williamson, ed., *Latin American Adjustment: How Much Has Happened?* (Washington, D.C.: Institute for International Economics, 1990), 5–38.

[3] Manuel Pastor and Carol Wise, "The Politics of Second-Generation Reform," *Journal of Democracy*, 10, 3 (1999): 34–48; A. Geske Dijkstra, "The Effectiveness of Policy Conditionality: Eight Country Experiences," *Development and Change*, 33, 2 (2002): 309.

vulnerable populations. With regard to privatization, several of the reforms intended to make privatization measures more transparent and to offer greater security to private investors. Additional recommendations included an expansion of privatization to incorporate those SOEs that previously had remained off the list of firms to be privatized, novel methods for restructuring management in so-called strategic sectors such as water or electricity, and the adoption of tax incentives to attract investment.[4]

Even as the number of conditions attached to funding climbed, scholars and analysts began to criticize sharply the effectiveness of conditionality.[5] Not only did conditions threaten state sovereignty, critics argued, but also they had failed to bring about the expected reforms. For example, Dollar and Svensson demonstrated that policy-based lending or lending with conditions attached did not increase the likelihood of reform. They noted that loans to Zambia from the World Bank totaled US$212 million in the 1980s, and the Bank itself had concluded that all were failures.[6] Similarly, Przeworski and Vreeland showed that growth rates for those countries that had adopted IMF programs were actually lower than growth rates for those countries that had not adopted them.[7]

Regardless of the merits of the reforms or the severity of the conditions attached to them, most African governments inconsistently adopted privatization programs in the 1980s. Unlike Latin America, where second-stage reforms were expected to follow first-stage reforms that had already been implemented, many African governments had not yet completed the first stage of the reform process when the IFIs began attaching second-generation reforms as conditions on loans and grants. In the 1980s, many African governments were still focused on stabilization and liberalization measures; most were attempting to reform their public enterprise sectors, not privatize them. Figures suggest that only four countries (Uganda, Guinea, Côte d'Ivoire, and Togo) divested over twenty companies each prior to 1988. Many of these were liquidations of poorly performing SOEs. Where equity sales occurred, most of the parastatals bought by private sector investors were small.[8]

---

[4] Pastor and Wise, "The Politics of Second-Generation Reform."

[5] Kahler, "International Financial Institutions," 139–159; "External Influence"; Paul Mosley, Jane Harrigan, and J. F. J. Toye, *Aid and Power: The World Bank and Policy-Based Lending* (London: Routledge, 1995), 187–301; Tony Killick, "Principals and Agents and the Failings of Conditionality," *Journal of International Development*, 9, 4 (1997): 483–495. For a summary of the findings and the debate about conditionality, see Ajay Chhibber, R. Kyle Peters, and Barbara Yale, eds., *Reform and Growth: Evaluating the World Bank Experience* (Piscataway, NJ: Transaction Publishers, 2006).

[6] David Dollar and Jakob Svensson, "What Explains the Success or Failure of Structural Adjustment Programs?" Policy Research Working Paper 1938, Macroeconomics and Growth, Development Research Group, World Bank (June 1998).

[7] Adam Przeworski and James Vreeland, "The Effect of IMF Programs on Economic Growth," *Journal of Development Economics*, 62 (2000): 385–421.

[8] Ademola Ariyo and Afeikhena Jerome, "Privatization in Africa: An Appraisal," *World Development*, 27, 1 (1999), 202. See Paul Bennell, "Privatization in Sub-Saharan Africa: Progress

Dijkstra's study of stabilization, structural adjustment, and conditionality lends support to these findings. In his comprehensive examination of conditions applied by the IMF and the World Bank to eight less-developed countries in Asia, Africa, and Central America, Dijkstra found that compliance with conditions was limited. In some cases, the aid that accompanied conditionality actually yielded effects that were the opposite of what was intended: The availability of aid allowed governments to delay the imposition of reforms altogether. Regarding certain second-order, political conditions such as demands for good governance, accountability, and democratic decision making, Dijkstra observed that most countries ignored them unless they were of a very specific nature and relatively unimportant. He argued that compliance tended to occur when governments already agreed with the IMF and the World Bank about the need for reform and when domestic opposition was low.[9] Based on the evidence, Dijkstra concluded that "domestic factors were most important in explaining policy reforms."[10] Rather than conditions, the economic policy choices of governments were more consistent with their ideological orientation, their assessment of the gravity of the crisis, or the political pressures that acted on them within their countries.[11] These findings echoed those of Dollar and Svensson, who stated that "there are institutional and political factors that affect the probability of success of a reform program. Given those factors, *none* (emphasis added) of the variables under the World Bank's control affects success or failure of adjustment programs."[12]

The importance accorded to domestic institutional and political factors by Dollar and Svensson and Dijkstra were representative of a consensus within policy circles and academia that conditionality was inappropriate and should be abandoned in favor of policy "ownership" or "commitment" on the part of governments engaging in reform.[13] The consensus around commitment began to emerge in the early 1990s and rested on the rationale that if governments "owned" or were "committed" to reforms, they would be more likely to marshall them through the challenges of the implementation process and policies would be successful. For example, without dismissing the use of conditions altogether, Miles Kahler, an early advocate of commitment, found that in the case of adjustment programs "prior commitment and policy action (taken before external support is offered) is a good predictor of successful implementation."[14] Following the conclusions of numerous studies, the

and Prospects during the 1990s," *World Development*, 25, 11 (1997): 1788–1789 and Jacques Dinavo, *Privatization in Developing Countries: Its Impact on Economic Development and Democracy* (Westport: Praeger, 1995), 60–63.

[9] Dijkstra, "The Effectiveness" 307–334.

[10] Ibid., 330.

[11] Ibid., 307–334.

[12] Dollar and Svensson, "What Explains the Success," 18.

[13] For references, see Chapter 1, footnote 11.

[14] Kahler, "External Influence," 114.

Bank adjusted its approach to aid-based lending. Although it did not drop completely its reliance on conditions, the Bank changed the content and timing of conditions; the packaging and disbursement of aid.[15] Over the course of the 1990s, the Bank highlighted the importance of governmental ownership or commitment to a range of reforms targeting growth and poverty reduction in developing countries.[16]

The emphasis on commitment as the preferred approach for aid-based lending represented a major policy shift. However, the meaning of the term, what it looked like, and how it was to be achieved or measured were ambiguous. One of the central objectives of this book is to develop a conceptual understanding of commitment and to assess empirically what constitutes a credible commitment to privatization and restructuring.

Theoretical and Conceptual Dilemmas of Commitment

Although many scholars and policymakers agree on the merits of government commitment to policy agendas, they continue to debate the question of when a credible commitment has been made. In a now classic articulation of the dilemmas of establishing credible commitments, North and Weingast argue that a government can create commitment by one of two means: first, "by setting a precedent of responsible behavior, appearing to be committed to a set of rules that he or she will consistently enforce" (*Means 1*) and second, "by being constrained to obey a set of rules that do not permit leeway for violating commitments" (*Means 2*).[17] *Means 1* is similar to the understanding of commitment employed in much of the policy-making literature and often used interchangeably with the term "ownership" or "political will." For example, the IMF characterizes ownership as

A willing assumption of responsibility for an agreed program of policies, by officials in a borrowing country who have the responsibility to formulate and carry out those policies, based on an understanding that the program is achievable and is in the country's own interest.[18]

Yet, North and Weingast reject such approaches because the scope for the use of discretionary authority is high. They anticipate that if the criterion for commitment is a "precedent of responsible behavior" (or similarly "a willing assumption of responsibility"), governments will easily renege on it. With regard to privatization for example, although the aim of the policy is to get the state out of the

[15] This began in the early 1990s, see Mosley et al.; *Aid and Power*, 39–45.
[16] World Bank, "The Role and Effectiveness."
[17] North and Weingast, "Constitutions and Commitment: The Evolution of Institutions Governing Public Choice in Seventeenth-Century England," *The Journal of Economic History*, 49, 4 (1989): 804. Means 1 and 2 are my clarifications.
[18] International Monetary Fund. "Strengthening Country Ownership of Fund-Supported Programs" Policy Development and Review Department (December 5, 2001: 6).

economy, ironically it is the state that must "commit" to selling state enterprises. Many states in Africa have poor reputations for acting responsibly: Prior behavior does not provide a useful guide to whether they will concede discretion over the running of parastatals nor does a voluntary assumption of responsibility mean that they will sustain it. If *Means 1* is the benchmark by which commitment is judged, then it leaves the state ample room to repudiate agreements.

Some scholars have tried to correct the defects of *Means 1* by developing criteria to evaluate whether a commitment is credible. They have asked business elites if they believe the government will follow through on a stated policy or what they think about a government's bureaucratic practices.[19] However, even though investment decisions are critical to the commitment process and I shall return to that point later, using investor beliefs to determine the credibility of a commitment is problematic in the context of many transitional countries for two reasons. First, there is a time-consistency problem that may lead to inaccurate judgments about the degree of state commitment. As Collier has noted, investors may fear that if they respond to a policy reform too quickly, governments will choose to change it at some later date.[20] Yet, if a government is taking a direction that signals a marked shift from the way it behaved in the past, investors may choose to wait to see how the reforms turn out. For example, investors might buy a firm but not make needed improvements until other reforms are enacted. Alternatively, a country may be assessed as riskier than it really is, which may lead investors to delay investments or not to invest at all. African countries in particular suffer from such overestimations of risk.[21] The time lag by investors may cause the state to lose faith in the reforms, which, in turn, may produce precisely what investors feared – a policy reversal.

Second, investors may simply differ regarding the credibility of a government's commitment. In a survey of investors' beliefs regarding the security of property rights in Russia, Frye found that around 39 percent of respondents believed that state courts could defend their interests against local or regional governments, whereas a nearly equal percentage (41 percent) believed that state courts could not defend their interests. Among those who were skeptical, "managers said that local and regional governments were much less likely to abide by judicial decisions than were private businesses."[22] The nearly equal split among business managers in Russia regarding the scope of the state's discretionary power makes it difficult to draw conclusions about the government's commitment to secure property rights and whether the government was likely to sustain the commitment over time.

[19] Borner, Brunetti, and Weder, *Political Credibility*; Frye, "Credible Commitment."
[20] Paul Collier, "Learning from Failure," 316.
[21] Nadeem Ul Haque, Nelson Mark, and Donald J. Mathieson, "Rating Africa: The Economic and Political Content of Risk Indicators" in Paul Collier and Catherine Pattillo, eds., *Investment and Risk in Africa* (New York: St. Martin's Press, 2000).
[22] Frye, "Credible Commitment," 458.

If a reliance on reputation or investors' beliefs is insufficient to resolve the dilemma posed by *Means 1*, what about *Means 2*? North and Weingast argue that government can create it "being constrained to obey a set of rules that do not permit leeway for violating commitments." Based on their study of the Glorious Revolution of 1688 in England, they claim that the constraints that compelled governments to commit to play by the rules included institutions such as legislatures, constitutions, and private property rights.[23] In countries undergoing comprehensive restructuring, however, it is unlikely that institutional constraints could act initially in the manner suggested by *Means 2*, since that is what the reforms intended to create. When African countries began economic reforms in the 1990s, many were also undergoing a transition to democracy. Constitutional provisions that protected against arbitrary expropriation of goods and property were recent, legislatures were less than five or ten years old in some countries, and judiciaries were weak. As in many post-Soviet countries, multiple institutional rearrangements were occurring in the economy and in politics.

I argue that a more elastic, and temporal, notion of credible commitment is required to capture that transformative moment when previous formal institutions have not yet disappeared, informal institutions still have salience, and new formal arrangements have not yet consolidated. Because it incorporates elements of both Means 1 and 2 and is grounded in the creation and development of institutions, Kenneth Shepsle's distinction between a commitment that is "motivationally credible" and a commitment that is "credible in the imperative sense" is useful here. As Shepsle asserts, a government may initially elect to make a costly institutional change with the intention of limiting its discretionary power because such a decision is compatible with its current incentives (which he terms "motivationally credible"). Yet the maintenance of that commitment *over time* may solidify structures and procedures that restrict the ability of the government to exercise discretionary authority, making the commitment "credible in the imperative sense."[24] This conceptualization builds on the distinction by North and Weingast, but it allows for the possibility of institutional consolidation.

Shepsle's distinction offers a number of advantages for the analysis of privatization in Africa. First, it rejects the common tendency in the policy literature to equate commitment with political will – a nebulous concept, too rooted in intentionality to be analytically useful. Instead, it isolates costly institutional changes as key criteria for establishing commitments. Second, the distinction recognizes the dynamic, processual, and temporal nature of developing new institutional frameworks for complex changes such as privatization or private sector expansion. Third, it acknowledges that institutional rearrangements

[23] North and Weingast, "Constitutions and Commitment," 806–808, 817–819.
[24] Shepsle, "Discretion, Institutions," 247.

may generate partisan pressures and distributional conflicts that will enhance or diminish commitment – an issue to which later chapters will return.[25]

An Index of Motivationally Credible Commitments

Did African countries adopt the institutions and agencies necessary for privatizing state assets and building a market economy more generally? What did these institutions look like, how were they designed? Is there a relationship between the institutions that were adopted at time *t* and the institutions that exist at time *t + n*? Is there a relationship between institutional arrangements and sales of parastatals later? The following sections rely on a pair of indices that evaluate institutional changes and a dataset on parastatal sales to answer these questions. The indices seek to operationalize Shepsle's concepts of motivationally credible commitments and commitments that are credible in the imperative sense. The first index, which details motivationally credible commitments, records and evaluates those institutions and agencies formally enacted by African countries to create or expand their private sectors over a twelve-year period between 1988 and 2000. The findings of this index are then correlated with sales of parastatals by African countries to demonstrate the relationship between formal institutional change and the outcome of privatization. Next, the index of motivationally credible commitments is compared to one that gauges commitments that are "credible in the imperative sense." This latter index evaluates the effectiveness of institutions at a later moment in time. It allows for at least a five-year lag between the formal adoption of a rule or regulation by 2000 and judges the extent to which that institution has become effective by 2005.

The first index of motivationally credible commitments assesses those economic institutions and agencies considered critical to privatization and private sector expansion. Rather than constituting a comprehensive guide to every rule or procedure associated with private sector development, I adopt some simplifying restrictions to establish a baseline for judging whether and how governments in Sub-Saharan Africa created or did not create motivationally credible commitments to the most important components of privatization. The index includes twenty-seven Sub-Saharan countries for which there was available data from 1988 until 2000 – the endpoint for this index. The twenty-seven countries are geographically representative and include countries from West, East, Southern, and Central Africa. They vary in population, resources, and per capita income. Countries also varied according to the type of regime from authoritarian regimes to democracies. Average Freedom House scores for political rights and civil liberties in these countries ranged between 1 and 7 over the time period.

[25] Adam Przeworski and Fernando Limongi criticize Shepsle for ignoring the "political process by which such commitments are established"; see "Political Regimes and Economic Growth," *Journal of Economic Perspectives*, 7, 3 (1993): 66. Yet, Shepsle, "Discretion, Institutions," 256, appears to recognize a possible trade-off between representation and governance. The political process is central to the model I present here.

Since I examine democracies in more detail in subsequent chapters, I explain the criteria for categorizing the different regimes. Countries classified by Bratton and van de Walle as already democratic or as having undergone flawed or democratic transitions at least by 1994 *and* that remained democratic through 2005 (the endpoint for the second index) are considered democratic. Moreover, I classify countries as democratic if Freedom House scores for the two categories of political rights and civil liberties averaged 4 or less in each category over the time period, whereas I classify as authoritarian those that received Freedom House scores greater than 4.[26] By this criteria, the sample contains fifteen democratic and twelve authoritarian cases. Some countries such as Djibouti, Angola, and Sierra Leone were excluded because data were unavailable or unreliable. Moreover, countries such as Sierra Leone, Liberia, or Congo that experienced major conflicts during the time period of the study were excluded on the assumption that they either did not attempt seriously to create or expand their formal private sectors during the time period or their efforts were interrupted. Since the purpose is to determine whether there is any association between the adoption of rules and the development of those rules over time, it did not seem fair to include countries that were engaged in sustained conflicts during the period under study. Obviously, these countries cannot normally be expected to adopt rules and/or sell state enterprises if they are at war (though of course some have done both).

The index assesses the creation of motivationally credible commitments by these twenty-seven countries between 1988 and 2000. I chose this twelve-year period for four reasons. First, by the late 1980s, privatization was clearly on the agenda of donors and developing countries. After several abortive efforts to restructure rather than privatize public enterprises, countries from Ghana to Côte d'Ivoire began to move beyond weak policy pronouncements on privatization to the adoption of more detailed institutional arrangements. They changed their Constitutions and passed land laws to promote more secure private property rights by the early 1990s. Others such as Zambia and Uganda could no longer ignore pervasive economic crises in their countries and had turned to more comprehensive reforms. For countries in either of these two situations, divestiture of state-owned enterprises and private sector creation became standard elements of the reform lexicon across the continent.[27]

---

[26] By this criteria, the fifteen democracies are Benin, Botswana, Cape Verde, Ghana, Madagascar, Malawi, Mali, Mauritius, Mozambique, Namibia, São Tomé and Principe, Senegal, Seychelles, South Africa and Zambia. The rest are authoritarian. See Michael Bratton and Nicholas van de Walle, *Democratic Experiments in Africa: Regime Transitions in Comparative Perspective* (Cambridge: Cambridge University Press, 1997), 116–120; Larry Diamond, "Thinking about Hybrid Regimes," *Journal of Democracy*, 13, 2 (2002): Table 2, 30–31; Freedom House, "Comparative and Historical Data," accessed 3/12/2009, http://www.freedomhouse.org. Unfortunately, Polity IV does not include data on Cape Verde, São Tomé and Principe, and the Seychelles, which are included in my study.

[27] Ariyo and Jerome, "Privatization in Africa," 201–213.

Second, although conditionality continued to influence negotiations between international financial institutions and African governments, IFIs had recognized the failure of conditionality to bind governments to their commitments and began to stress the importance of ownership by governments (as noted earlier). This does not mean that countries resolved to "own" reforms by passing comprehensive reform packages, but simply that the rhetoric and the approach changed. It therefore marks a useful time period to judge whether countries altered their approaches and what the effects were. Third, many African countries from Mozambique to Mali became democratic during the 1990s, a development which both complemented and conflicted with efforts to expand the private sector. The interaction of these two processes is an issue I have alluded to already and I shall return to it in more detail later. It is sufficient to note here that transformative political events were occurring alongside economic transition as they were in East Central Europe, for example.

Last, no institutional or agency changes made after 2000 are recorded in the index of motivationally credible commitments. Setting the parameters for institutional change between 1988 and 2000 recognizes that there may be a time lag in which distributional, electoral, or investment responses may emerge either to accelerate or to stall the process. Since these responses may affect sales of SOEs or the degree to which commitments became credible in the imperative sense, it seemed prudent to set parameters for the adoption of policy changes in order to avoid the possible overestimation of institutional change in the first index and the subsequent underestimation of institutional effectiveness or sales at a later point in time. Furthermore, it is also noteworthy that eighteen countries enacted privatization laws between 1991 and 1997; two other countries revised and strengthened existing privatization policies during this time period. Three countries that already had substantial private sectors adopted policies that intended to encourage private sector investment. Therefore, establishing the parameters between 1988 and 2000 for assessing motivational commitment and then allowing a five-year lag before examining sales and institutional effectiveness does not unduly advantage or disadvantage any country with respect to scoring.

There are two categories in the index – legislation and agencies (within which are several subcategories) – which provide a benchmark for empirically evaluating what governments adopted (see Appendix 1). Using ideal types that resemble policies recommended by the World Bank as the basis for evaluation, the first category assesses the extent of Constitutional protection from arbitrary alterations of property rights; the extent to which land tenure laws made provisions for individual property rights; and the content of laws or decrees to privatize state assets and encourage investment by the private sector. Unlike the vague, ill-defined policy pronouncements made by some African countries in the 1980s, these are institutional reforms. They are more costly to adopt; the likelihood of reneging on them should theoretically decline.

Second, the index examines whether agencies were created and how they were organized. Many scholars and policymakers have acknowledged the importance of agencies with clear mandates to value companies, carry out sales, and attract investment to the sustainability of privatization. As North observes, agencies are "initiators of institutional change."[28] Following the insights of John Waterbury on the importance of agency independence from political interference,[29] the index posits as an ideal type an agency that has sole responsibility to make decisions regarding sales of state assets and can act with relative autonomy from politicians. Further, the index looks at whether companies were listed for sale and how the methods for purchase were defined. In the context of laws and regulations that transform property rights, a detailed list of those SOEs that the government intends to sell and a clear statement regarding the method by which they will be sold act as signaling devices for investors. They indicate the seriousness of a government's commitment, particularly in those cases where a government cannot rely on its reputation to establish credibility.[30] Here the category assesses the extent to which SOEs were listed for sale, whether the methods for purchase were clearly and consistently defined, with the ideal type defined as one in which those conditions were fully met.

Based on the coding scheme shown in Appendix 1, I assign numerical values to represent different institutional or organizational arrangements by each government within each of the subcategories.[31] The numerical value assigned to each component is weighted according to my evaluation of its importance to privatization and private sector creation with the top score (a 4 or 3 depending on the category) approximating ideal-type arrangements envisioned in many World Bank recommendations on privatization and a score of zero indicating that either the arrangement was not adopted or deviated substantially from the ideal type. I model the values and the weights of my rating system on the format used by the International Country Risk Guide. Like their assessments of qualitative data, mine are necessarily subjective, and small differences between

[28] Douglass C. North, "Institutions and Credible Commitment," *Journal of Institutional and Theoretical Economics*, 149, 1 (1993): 12–13.

[29] John Waterbury, "The Heart of the Matter? Public Enterprise and the Adjustment Process" in Stephan Haggard and Robert Kaufman, eds., *The Politics of Economic Adjustment: International Constraints, Distributive Conflicts, and the State* (Princeton: Princeton University Press, 1992), 191 and see also John Williamson, on the value of technocrats who staff these agencies, "In Search of a Manuel for Technopols" in John Williamson, ed., *The Political Economy of Policy Reform* (Washington, D.C.: Institute for International Economics, 1993), 9–28.

[30] For the reasons cited earlier regarding the poor reputation of African governments, signaling alone likely would not work. But as part of a more comprehensive package of reforms, it serves a useful function. On the importance of signaling in other contexts, see Rodrik, "Promises, Promises" and J. D. Fearon, "Signaling Foreign Policy Interests: Tying Hands Versus Sinking Costs," *The Journal of Conflict Resolution*, 41, 1 (1997): 68–90.

[31] See Barbara Geddes, *Paradigms and Sand Castles: Theory Building and Research Design in Comparative Politics* (Ann Arbor: University of Michigan Press, 2003): 142–148 on nonquantitative operationalization and measurement.

TABLE 2.1. *Motivational Commitments to Privatization and Private Sector Creation, 1988–2000*

Category	Legislation				Agencies			Grand Total
Country	Constitutional Constraints on Arbitrary Alterations of Property Rights (0–4)	Property Rights/ Land Law/Land Allocations (0–4)	Privatization Law and Investment Codes Favorable or Not? (0–4)	Total (0–12)	Existence of an Agency Mandated to Undertake Privatization (0–3)	Process of Sale (0–3)	Total (0–6)	
Benin	2	2	2	6	1	2	3	9
Botswana	4	3	2	9	0	0	0	9
Burkina Faso	2	1	2	5	1	1	2	7
Cameroon	1	1	2	4	2	2	4	8
Cape Verde	4	3	3	10	2	3	5	15
Côte d'Ivoire	1	2	4	7	2	2	4	11
Ghana	3	2	3	8	2	2	4	12
Guinea	2	2	2	6	1	0	1	7
Kenya	2	2	1	5	1	1	2	7
Lesotho	2	1	3	6	2	3	5	11
Madagascar	2	2	2	6	2	1	3	9
Malawi	3	3	3	9	2	2	4	13
Mali	3	3	4	10	1	1	2	12
Mauritius	4	3	3	10	0	1	1	11
Mozambique	3	2	4	9	2	2	4	13
Namibia	3	2	2	7	0	0	0	7
Niger	1	2	3	6	2	1	3	9
Nigeria	3	1	2	6	1	1	2	8
São Tomé &Principe	2	1	2	5	1	1	2	7
Senegal	3	1	3	7	1	2	3	10
Seychelles	4	3	3	10	0	1	1	11
South Africa	4	3	3	10	1	2	3	13
Tanzania	2	2	3	7	2	2	4	11
Togo	2	1	2	5	1	2	3	8
Uganda	3	3	4	10	2	3	5	15
Zambia	2	2	4	8	3	3	6	14
Zimbabwe	2	2	2	6	1	0	1	7

Note: See Appendix 1 for coding scheme.

Authors' calculations based on primary and secondary sources on constitutions, land laws, privatization laws, privatization agency creation, lists of

TABLE 2.2. *Motivational Commitments: Composite Categories and Scores*

Highest Possible Score is 18
Very High Motivational Commitment (15–18)
Cape Verde, Uganda
High Motivational Commitment (11–14)
Côte d'Ivoire, Ghana, Lesotho, Malawi, Mali, Mauritius, Mozambique,
Seychelles, South Africa, Tanzania, Zambia
Moderate Motivational Commitment (8–10)
Benin, Botswana, Cameroon, Madagascar, Niger, Nigeria, Senegal, Togo
Low Motivational Commitment (7 and below)
Burkina Faso, Guinea, Kenya, Namibia, São Tomé and Principe (STP), Zimbabwe

total scores do not signify much. Ideally, it would be useful to have an independent panel of experts rate motivationally credible commitment. I compensated for this weakness by comparing my evaluations with those of several research assistants who conducted assessments. I consulted primary and secondary sources on all the countries extensively in order to evaluate each country in each subcategory.[32] I also conducted fieldwork and interviews with government officials, donors, business elites, and organized labor regarding private sector development in five countries; three of the countries, Zambia, Mozambique, and South Africa comprise the case studies discussed in subsequent chapters.

Following the assignment of values, I summed these numerical assessments to obtain a reasonable approximation of the level of motivationally credible commitment to sales of state assets and private sector creation by category. The index then combines the individual categories to produce a composite commitment rating for each country. The higher the score, the greater the country's motivational commitment to privatization and private sector development.

The categories selected and the substantive issues included in the model are based on what policymakers considered ideal institutional arrangements at the time. Moreover, any classification scheme has to be general enough to accommodate diverse approaches to privatization by particular countries, but also rigorous enough to determine the character of commitment to reform. Even though the ability of the state to act unilaterally cannot be entirely overcome by new institutions and organizations, the justification for including the categories was that the existence of private property rights, agencies to attract private buyers, and legislation on privatization potentially offer "lock-in mechanisms" to bind governments to their commitments over time, which many institutionalists have argued is an important part of commitment (Tables 2.1 and 2.2).[33]

---

[32] I would like to thank Patrick Johnson, Dahlia Risk, and especially Courtney Dunlaevy for their assistance with this effort.

[33] On lock-in mechanisms, see Collier, "Learning from Failure."

Motivationally Credible Commitments: Institutional Variation and Convergence

Nearly all of the countries changed legislation to create more favorable environments for private investors as Tables 2.1 and 2.2 illustrate. The clustering of new laws, "one stop shops for investment" or privatization agencies during the 1991–1997 period suggest not only the diffusion of ideas and structures articulated by donors and international financial institutions but also the continued application of conditions to loans and grants. Thus, prescriptions by the World Bank and the global economic environment established the parameters of institutional change.

Although some countries approximated the ideal-type reformer, no country received a perfect score of eighteen. Thirteen countries in the sample made very high or high motivational commitments to privatize their state-owned sectors with scores between 11 and 15. Some countries in the sample such as South Africa, Mauritius, or Botswana already had institutions that delineated and protected private property rights and welcomed private investors, but even these countries revised their rules in the 1990s. Mauritius announced its intention to privatize and restructure some of its state assets in a White Paper on Privatization in 1997. That same year, the Mauritian government stated its intention to sell part of its shares in the parastatal, Mauritius Telecom, and to liberalize the telecommunications sector.[34]

In South Africa, the National Framework Agreement on the Restructuring of State Assets and the Growth, Employment, and Redistribution (GEAR) strategy adopted in 1996 expressed the government's intention to sell parastatals in the tourism and forestry sectors, to find strategic equity partners for existing SOEs in sectors such as telecommunications, and to combine management contracts and cost recovery approaches in the service delivery sector.[35] Botswana, too, enacted laws to privatize grazing lands that formerly were in the state's domain.[36] In cases such as Ghana, Cape Verde, Mali, Zambia, and Mozambique, which had substantial state sectors until the 1990s, the adoption of institutions and organizations associated with privatization or private sector creation indicated a significant institutional shift. Their constitutions acknowledged private property rights, they established agencies to handle the

[34] Republic of Mauritius, Ministry of Telecommunications and Information Technology, "White Paper on the Telecommunications Sector: Fostering the Info-Communications Society," December 1997.

[35] South Africa, "National Framework Agreement on the Restructuring of State Assets," approved 2/7/1996, accessed 4/15/2004, http://www.gov.za/reports/1996/nfa.htm; South Africa, Department of Finance, "Growth, Employment and Redistribution: A Macroeconomic Strategy," 1996.

[36] Amy Poteete, "When Professionalism Clashes with Local Particularities: Ecology, Elections, and Procedural Arrangements in Botswana," *Journal of Southern African Studies*, 29, 2 (2003): 461–485.

evaluation and sale of their SOEs; they passed privatization and investment laws that were welcoming to private capital.

The index also reveals considerable divergence in the degree and substance of institutional choice, which most other studies of privatization in Africa have overlooked.[37] Similar to governments in Latin America, most governments in Africa adopted institutions and designed agencies in accordance with their own history, strategic calculations, ideological beliefs, and the influence of partisan constituencies.[38] As Knight's theory on the emergence of social institutions expects, governmental efforts to tailor new legislation to existing social concerns reflected evolving and dynamic political processes.[39] Yet the intentional design of much privatization legislation and the contradictions embodied in the new arrangements equally laid the groundwork for struggles after implementation. As subsequent chapters in the book will demonstrate, these ex post conflicts and the ways in which they were resolved shaped the contours of capitalist development.

Motivational commitments range from a low score of 7 to a high score of 15. In cases such as Uganda and Ghana, governments enacted far-reaching economic reforms. In other cases, countries did very little or proceeded very slowly, either because they wanted to maintain the status quo (Botswana) or because the political and economic environment was already unstable (Zimbabwe). To explore the variation in more detail, I examine three elements of the privatization process addressed by the index: land and privatization laws, agency design, and the logistics of the sale process.

First, the institutional design of land and investment laws by governments in South Africa, Namibia, and Mozambique, for example, reflected concerns about historically disadvantaged groups in their countries. In South Africa and Namibia, revised land laws and credit policies included explicit provisions for empowering black smallholders and black capital. In Mozambique, laws and decree laws on investment aimed to privilege national capital by offering generous terms of credit, more favorable tax and duty regimes, a lower threshold than foreigners for the purchase of equity capital, and a longer period of time to conclude the purchase process. Moreover, as in several other countries, the land law in Mozambique not only asserted that all land belonged to the state,

---

[37] White and Bhatia and Kayizzi-Mugerwa also examine institutions of privatization in Africa, but have a restricted number of cases, see White and Bhatia, *Privatization in Africa* and Kayizzi-Mugerwa, "Privatization in Sub-Saharan Africa," 227–253.

[38] For the influence of coalitions on institutional choice associated with privatization in Latin America, see Victoria Murillo, "Political Bias in Policy Convergence," *World Politics*, 54 (July 2002): 470 and Schamis, *Re-forming the State*. On the causes of variation in state building in Africa, Catherine Boone offers a sophisticated theoretical study of the ways in which bargaining between national and subnational political elites conditioned institutional choice, see *Political Topographies of the African State: Territorial Authority and Institutional Choice* (Cambridge: Cambridge University Press, 2003).

[39] Knight, *Institutions and Social Conflict*, 21–47.

but also it made provisions for long leases by private actors *and* recognized the rights of communities. These features of the law referenced simultaneously a colonial past that gave preference to leasehold arrangements, continuing government beliefs in the efficacy of statist approaches, a strategic governmental response to a civil conflict partly fueled by smallholder resentment at *dirigiste* land policies, and a new predilection for private sector creation.[40]

Second, the index exposes variation in the design of the agencies mandated to carry out privatization. Fifteen countries receive a score of 0 or 1 for the creation of a privatization agency, indicating that they did not create an agency to privatize their state-owned sectors prior to 2000 or that the existing agency was highly circumscribed by other government bodies, and had other responsibilities besides privatization. For example, in spite of a constitution that protected private property rights, legislation that encouraged private sector development, and a 1991 policy that expanded the amount of communal range available for privatization, Botswana did not establish a Public Enterprises Evaluation and Privatisation Agency until early 2001, hence its score of 0 for a privatization agency. Likewise, Mauritius and Namibia had private sectors, and their governments recognized private property rights. In the case of Namibia, these rights had been extended to the black population following independence.[41] Yet, neither country created privatization agencies prior to 2000. In the case of Namibia, the ruling party opted to retain parastatals in order to provide employment to those who had shown loyalty to the movement during the liberation struggle. Moreover, it restricted foreign ownership of commercial land in order to reduce the country's dependence on foreign capital and to benefit historically disadvantaged domestic groups.[42]

Similarly, South Africa did not create a separate agency to handle the privatization of its most important SOEs such as electricity supply and generation, defense manufacture, telecommunications, and transport services. Instead, it located responsibility within government in the Department of Public Enterprises (DPE). Since DPE's mandate included the management of these same companies, a potential conflict of interest existed within the organization between retaining and relinquishing SOEs.

There are several plausible explanations for the decision by governments in Mauritius, Botswana, and South Africa not to create stand-alone agencies. First, whereas all three of them had sizeable state sectors, they also had substantial private sectors. These countries did not experience economic crisis in the same way and to the same degree as countries with larger state sectors. Second, they did not depend on donor financing nor were they subjected to donor pressures

[40] Mozambique, Assembly of the Republic, Lei 19/97 (October 1997) and Decreto-lei 69/98 (December 1998) and see Chapter 5.
[41] Republic of Namibia, The Constitution of the Republic of Namibia, article 16.
[42] Willem Odendaal, "The SADC Land and Agrarian Reform Initiative: The Case of Namibia," NEPRU Working Paper No. 111 (December 2006), 9, 20–47.

to the same extent as smaller, weaker economies like Zambia or Mozambique. These arguments help to explain why the substance of neo-liberal reforms in these countries varied from those countries with larger state sectors, but they do not sufficiently explain why governments did not entrust the execution of privatization reforms to independent agencies staffed by technocrats.

As I will demonstrate in Chapter 6 on South Africa, the democratic context largely explains both the hesitation and the difficulty of governments to create independent agencies. These are the most democratic countries in Africa. Governments are more accountable to their citizens and more exposed to conflicting pressures than those in less democratic countries. Adopting a new institution, particularly one whose purpose is to privatize parastatals, is more challenging because organized interests rely on multiple institutional channels to shape governmental policies on privatization, which often leads to incremental change and compromise.

Countries such as Kenya, Burkina Faso, and Zimbabwe demonstrate low motivational commitments to privatization, but the reasons are different from those of the most capitalist and most democratic countries. Both Kenya and Burkina Faso issued privatization policy papers or passed privatization laws in the early 1990s indicating that they were prepared to divest some of their parastatals. As early as 1991, the Kenyan government indicated that it was prepared to sell equity in 207 parastatals. Consistent with their stated policy goals, both countries created agencies to undertake divestiture. Yet agencies were not granted independent statutory authority in either case nor were their mandates solely focused on privatization of parastatals. Instead, high level government officials from the president to sector level ministers directed or controlled agencies. In Kenya, the agency assumed additional responsibilities besides privatization such as the management of existing government investments and assets, parastatal reform and restructuring. In addition, these countries advertised companies inconsistently and methods of sale were often nontransparent and noncompetitive. Nigeria's privatization program was only slightly better than these two cases, whereas Zimbabwe's was arguably worse for most of the 1990s. It did not establish a semiautonomous privatization agency until 1999.[43]

By contrast, many countries, including those with previously large state sectors such as Zambia, Tanzania, and Ghana, created agencies whose main

---

[43] White and Bhatia, *Privatization in Africa*; World Bank, "Privatization Database, 1988–1999" and "Privatization Database, 2000–2008," accessed 11/4/2009, http://rru.worldbank.org/privatization/; Gurushri Swamy, "Kenya: Patchy, Intermittent Commitment" in Ishrat Husain and Rashid Faruqee, eds. *Adjustment in Africa: Lessons from Country Case Studies* (Washington, D.C.: The World Bank, 1994), 193–237; Rashid Faruqee, "Nigeria: Ownership Abandoned" in Ishrat Husain and Rashid Faruqee, eds., *Adjustment in Africa: Lessons from Country Case Studies* (Washington, D.C.: The World Bank, 1994), 238–285; Burkina Faso, "Le programme de privatisations au Burkina Faso," accessed 4/20/2011, http://www.fdi.net/documents/WorldBank/databases/plink/burkina/burki.htm.

objective was to privatize and whose responsibilities were formally delineated in legislation on privatization. Only in Zambia, however, did the
government statutorily grant the agency full autonomy to make decisions
regarding the privatization of assets. After submitting a list to cabinet, the
Zambia Privatisation Agency (ZPA) had broad powers to identify, value, and
sell SOEs. Moreover, the legislation stipulated that the board was accountable to Parliament not to the president. Last, only three members of ZPA's
twelve-person board were government officials. The majority of the board
represented trade unions, parastatal management, the private sector, and civil
society organizations.[44]

In most of the other cases, formal opportunities for political interference in
the composition of the agency board or in the decision-making process were
greater than those in Zambia. Where privatization agencies were given a score
of 2, they were formally subject to the authority of the president, the prime
minister, the council of ministers, or an individual ministry. In Malawi, the
president appointed the board of the Privatization Commission; the board followed the guidelines of the cabinet on privatization and answered to the cabinet.[45] In Ghana, the minister of finance chaired the Divestiture Implementation
Committee, and the office of the presidency had the authority to approve those
companies subject to privatization.[46] Similarly in Cameroon and Lesotho, privatization commissions were located within the ministry of finance and overseen by the minister.[47] Mozambique had a complex arrangement characterized
by multiple levels of authority depending on the size and sector of the parastatal under consideration. The government created a restructuring unit specifically to handle the privatization of larger firms, but the unit worked closely
with the council of ministers and the prime minister throughout the process
from the identification of firms to the final approval of sales. No decision
regarding the privatization of a parastatal worth more than US$10 million was
taken without the approval of the Council of Ministers.[48]

Third, in ten out of twelve cases, the more autonomous agencies were and
the more clearly defined their mandates, the more likely they were to issue
detailed lists of companies to be sold, to delineate the methods of sale, and to

---

[44] Zambia, Privatisation Act (1992), sections 5–9.
[45] Malawi, The Privatisation Commission, Public Enterprises (Privatisation) Act, no. 7 of 1996
(April 17, 1996), accessed 5/26/2008, http://www.privatisationmalawi.org.
[46] Ghana, Divestiture Implementation Committee, "The Divestiture Program," accessed 1/21/2010,
http://www.dic.com.gh/info/faq.html. Kojo Appiah-Kubi, "State-Owned Enterprises and
Privatization in Ghana," *Journal of Modern African Studies*, 39 2 (2001): 206.
[47] Cameroon, Ministere de L'Economie et des Finances, Commission Technique de Privatisation
et de Liquidations, accessed 4/10/2006, http://www.ctpl.cm and Lesotho, Lesotho Privatisation
Unit, "The Lesotho Privatisation Program," Privatization Link: Project Opportunities in
Emerging Markets, February 3, 2000, accessed 1/21/2010, http://www.fdi.net/documents/
WorldBank/databases/plink/lesotho/pprogram.htm.
[48] M. Anne Pitcher, *Transforming Mozambique: The Politics of Privatization, 1975–2000*
(Cambridge: Cambridge University Press, 2002), 131–138.

advertise broadly. Agencies in countries such as Cape Verde, Ghana, Lesotho, Malawi, Mozambique, Tanzania, Uganda, and Zambia that received a 2 or above for agency autonomy and responsibilities also tended to list which companies would be sold and the method of sale. Alternatively, in seven out of eleven cases where a country received a score of 1, the country also scored poorly with regard to specifying which companies would be privatized, advertising them, and explaining the method of sale. This evidence lends support to claims by scholars that greater agency autonomy generally produces greater reform transparency and faster sales. Moreover, the evidence suggests that when agencies are more independent, signals about the intention to reform are stronger.[49] Agencies whose primary purpose is to privatize, then, appear to be important elements of motivational commitment.

To summarize, a comparison of countries in the sample shows variation in the extent to which governments made motivational commitments to privatization in the period between 1988 and 2000. Governments with very high or high motivational commitments such as Cape Verde, Uganda, Mali, or Ghana adopted constitutional constraints on arbitrary appropriations of private property rights, and land laws that recognized the rights of individuals to own, buy, sell, and title land. Many, such as Uganda, Malawi, and Zambia had privatization agencies whose primary responsibility was to undertake the sale of existing parastatals. Governments with very high or high motivational commitments circulated lists of companies to be privatized, advertised those companies that were for sale, and indicated the methods by which companies could be purchased.

Governments that demonstrated moderate or low motivational commitment varied considerably from each other and from those with very high or high motivational commitment. I have already pointed out that several of them such as Botswana and Namibia were largely market economies, and they were not experiencing economic crises to the same degree that other countries were. Although they made changes to their economic policies in the 1990s, they did not fully embrace privatization strategies nor make major alterations to their institutional arrangements. These cases are distinct from the remaining cases of moderate or low motivational commitment such as São Tomé, Niger, Nigeria, Kenya, or Madagascar. In many of these latter cases, constitutional constraints on arbitrary alterations of property rights were vague. Existing land laws did not clearly guarantee individual rights. Privatization and investment laws largely maintained the status quo. These countries had agencies that were dependent on the government and lacked detailed mandates for their organization and operation. Their privatization strategies were unclear and uneven.

[49] White and Bhatia, *Privatization in Africa*, 54–58 and see Anne Pitcher and Manuel Teodoro, "The Impact of 'Technocratic Change Teams' on the Outcome of Political and Economic Reforms: Some Findings from Africa," Paper prepared for the Annual Meeting of the Midwest Political Science Association, Chicago (April 22–25, 2010).

Substantively, institutional choices made by these countries did not appear to provide potential "lock-in mechanisms" to bind governments to their commitments over time.[50]

From Motivationally Credible Commitments to Commitments that are Credible in the Imperative Sense

I have analyzed the variation in the degree and the substance of motivational commitment by the twenty-seven countries in the sample. I now want to determine whether there is a relationship between the institutional choices that governments made and the results they achieved (if any) at a later point in time. Are very high or high motivational commitments to privatization associated with the privatization of parastatals? Did those countries with high motivational commitments also reach the point where, as Shepsle advises, constraints existed to disable the discretionary power of governments? Is low motivational commitment associated with low asset sales? Do states with low motivational commitments continue to rely heavily on their discretionary authority at a later point in time? Does an association exist between motivational commitments and commitments that are credible in the imperative sense?

To answer these questions, I examine, first, the relationship between motivational commitment and sales of parastatals and, second, the relationship between motivational commitment and the effectiveness of economic institutions, which I use as proxies for commitments that are credible in the imperative sense. Examining both of these associations yields different but important insights into the commitment dilemma with respect to private sector creation and expansion.

Relationship between Motivational Commitment and Sales of SOEs
Since divesting parastatals is the intention behind the adoption of a privatization law, the formation of a privatization agency, and the advertising of companies, then, all things being equal, we should expect to find that sales have occurred if governments have made motivational commitments. Moreover, if the adoption of formal institutions plays a role in the process of transitioning to a private sector–driven economy then we should expect to see a relationship between the degree to which states made motivational commitments to privatization and the extent of sales some five to ten years later.

Because the size and value of state sectors across the twenty-seven countries varies tremendously, I calculate the percentage of SOEs out of the total number of existing SOEs divested by each country by 2005 (the last year for which reliable data are available for all countries) in order to compare whether privatization occurred or not across cases. My dataset on sales combines primary

---

[50] See Collier, "Learning from Failure."

TABLE 2.3. *Africa: State-Owned Enterprises Divested, 1988–2005*

Country	Total SOEs c.1980s	SOEs Privatized	%
Benin	60	37	62
Botswana	35	0	0
Burkina Faso	77	28	36
Cameroon	180	98	54
Cape Verde	53	50	94
Côte d'Ivoire	147	82	56
Ghana	350	335	96
Guinea	181	122	67
Kenya	240	108	45
Lesotho	50	10	20
Madagascar	184	116	63
Malawi	110	65	59
Mali	84	62	74
Mauritius	15	2	15
Mozambique	1,248	1,200	96
Namibia	52	0	0
Niger	54	34	63
Nigeria	485	116	24
STP	22	6	27
Senegal	87	50	57
Seychelles	20	3	15
South Africa	300	26	9
Tanzania	425	304	72
Togo	86	51	59
Uganda	159	120	75
Zambia	282	260	92
Zimbabwe	90	20	22

Sources: Author's compilation from John Nellis, "Public Enterprises in Sub-Saharan Africa," World Bank Discussion Paper no. 1, Washington, D.C. (1986); Berthélemy et al., *Privatisation in Sub-Saharan Africa*; White and Bhatia, *Privatization in Africa*; World Bank, "Privatization Database, 1988–1999," and "Privatization Database, 2000–2008," accessed 11/4/2009, http://rru.worldbank. org/privatization/. Each database has missing information. Where possible, the author has attempted to find primary sources, especially government data, from selected countries.

data reported by national privatization agencies and government ministries in selected countries with that available in existing databases on privatization in Africa, notably those by John Nellis, the World Bank, and the OECD.[51] This dataset addresses gaps and errors in previous databases (see Table 2.3). By calculating the percentage of the state sector that was privatized. it avoids

[51] See sources for Table 2.3.

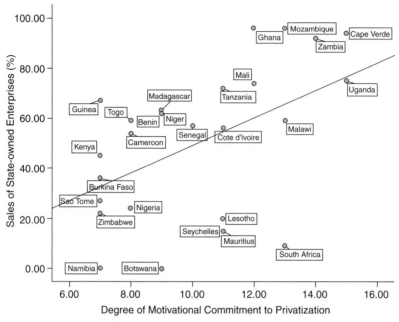

FIGURE 2.1. Relationship between motivational commitments and sales of state-owned enterprises.

overestimation or underestimation of the extent of privatization that may result from a reliance on the absolute number or value of firms sold by each country. These calculations complement absolute sales figures and values in other datasets by allowing researchers to evaluate what countries have done in relation to the existing size of their state sector and to compare these meaningfully across cases.

The dataset makes possible a comparison of the motivational commitments that governments made (or did not make) from 1988 to 2000 and the percentage of the SOE sector that was sold by 2005. This relationship is represented by the scatterplot in Figure 2.1 and Pearson's correlation coefficient in Table 2.4 indicating the association between a country's level of motivational commitment and the percentage of its state sector that was privatized.

As Table 2.4 shows, the coefficient of .484 is positive and statistically significant at the .05 level, and the association is moderate. With the exclusion of South Africa, which shows considerable deviation from the line of best fit, the association is stronger at .581 and statistically significant at the .01 level. Some justification can be made for running the correlation without South Africa since it is evident that it is a clear outlier.[52] With such a small number of

---

[52] Chapter 6 will explain why the South African government adopted a privatization policy and then changed course.

TABLE 2.4. *Correlation between Motivational Commitments and Sales of SOEs*

		Sales of SOEs
Degree of Motivational Commitment	Pearson Correlation Coefficient	0.484*
	Sig. (2-tailed)	0.011
	N	27

* Correlation is significant at the .05 level.

cases, the inclusion or removal of a few outliers can noticeably affect the trend of the data. But a scatterplot can also take advantage of the small number to illustrate more usefully what the patterns are. As Figure 2.1 demonstrates, a moderate and positive relationship exists between the degree of motivational commitment and the percentage of SOEs divested. For example, Burkina Faso, São Tomé and Principe, and Zimbabwe exhibit low motivational commitment to privatization and the percentage of the state sector that they sold is also correspondingly low. By contrast, countries such as Cape Verde, Cote D'Ivoire, Mali, Uganda, and Zambia, which demonstrated high or very high commitments to privatization, also divested a majority of their state sectors. This is what we would expect to find if there is an association between the adoption of formal institutions and sales of state assets.

Close examination of the scatterplot also helps to explain which countries deviated from the general trend. Two different kinds of cases occupy two different places on the plot, pulling at the line of best fit in two different directions. First, there is a group of countries such as Botswana, Seychelles, Mauritius, and South Africa that had many of the institutions characteristic of a private sector–driven economy and already had a private sector. During the 1990s, they undertook a few initiatives to privatize their state-owned enterprises. Because of the existing institutional arrangements as well as the reforms, their motivational commitment scores are consequently high or moderate. Although these countries have higher scores, they privatized little by 2005. Botswana, Mauritius, Seychelles, and South Africa divested 15 percent or less of their state sectors by 2005.

Second, a number of countries score low with regard to their motivational commitment, yet they appear to have sold a sizable percentage of their parastatal sector. In the case of Kenya, formal institutional arrangements conducive to the expansion of their private sector were circumscribed and its privatization law during the 1990s was unfavorable to investors, yet Kenya sold approximately 108 firms out of a total of 240 SOEs or 45 percent of its SOEs by 2005. Interestingly, while the number of sales was relatively high, the character of the sales was consistent with what might be expected of a low motivational commitment. Many of these firms were small and in poor shape at the time of sale; most were returned to private sector shareholders via preemptive rights or sold to foreigners by nontransparent means.[53] Similarly, Guinea demonstrated a very low score with regard to its motivational commitment to privatization yet is listed as having privatized 67 percent of its SOE sector. Although Guinea began its privatization process in 1985, which was earlier than many other countries, the legislation governing private property rights and the privatization process was weak. The government did not give an agency a clear mandate for privatizing companies and it interfered in the privatization process. With respect to sales during the late 1980s and 1990s, the World Bank reported that "Some of the divestitures were no more than accounting transactions: they accomplished only a change in legal status without any real change in ownership, management structure, or business ethos."[54] These findings indicate that although countries like Kenya and Guinea sold firms, they did so without having adopted an institutional environment conducive to the growth of the private sector.

The positive, statistically significant, and moderate-to-strong association between motivational commitment and divestitures of SOEs in Africa indicate that we can be reasonably confident that governments will privatize their SOEs in a manner consistent with their level of commitment. If their commitment is low, then sales will be correspondingly low whereas higher levels of commitment will yield higher sales. Yet, some caution should be used when relying on divestitures alone to evaluate the extent of commitment to privatization. Figures on sales reveal little about the quality of the privatization process undertaken by the government or the degree to which the government is maintaining an institutional environment conducive to private sector growth. Divestitures do not tell us about the sale of large versus small firms, and they do not tell us if the firm was liquidated, returned to its original owner, sold to cronies, or publicly bid for in an open and transparent bidding process. Sales alone do not tell us about the characteristics of investors or what kind of relationship they may have had with the state officials who sold the SOE. Finally, they do not direct us to possible distributional conflicts and challenges that governments encounter in their efforts to expand the private sector. These issues require a different dataset and "thicker" approaches.

Relationship between Motivational Commitments and Commitments That are Credible in the Imperative Sense

Forthcoming chapters will rely on qualitative case studies to address the many challenges associated with the divestiture process. Here, I want to incorporate divestitures into a broader dataset that examines not only *outcomes* such as the extent of divestitures or restructuring but also institutional *outputs*, that is, the extent to which economic institutions, organizations, and relationships are

[53] White and Bhatia, *Privatization in Africa*, 26.
[54] World Bank, Operations Evaluations Department, Country Evaluation and Regional Relations, "Project Performance Assessment Report: Guinea," Report no. 27166 (October 31, 2003), 11. After 2000, Guinea established a new Privatization Unit and passed a new privatization law, which were intended to address the weaknesses of the earlier arrangements.

acting effectively to promote and sustain a market economy. Because many of the indicators in this dataset evaluate the extent to which rules exist and are being followed, they capture well Shepsle's understanding of commitments that are "credible in the imperative sense." In the ideal-type case of imperative credibility, rules act effectively to constrain the state's use of discretionary authority, and they do so because norms and preferences consistent with the rules have emerged among players affected by them. I am interested in the extent to which African countries in the sample approximate these commitments and whether there is an association between the degree of motivational commitment and commitments with imperative credibility.

The following index evaluates institutional effectiveness in 2005, which gives a sufficient lag time to evaluate any development of institutions adopted between 1988 and 2000. It combines criteria from the World Bank's International Development Association Resource Allocation Index (IRAI), which examines institutional performance, and criteria that I adapt from the transition indicators of the European Bank for Reconstruction and Development (EBRD).[55] The EBRD developed a set of indicators in the 1990s to evaluate the extent and impact of privatization outputs in East and Central Europe.[56] The coding scheme in Appendix 2 explains the assignment of values and the sources used for the imperative commitment index.

The index includes assessments of trade and financial sector policy as well as the quality of the regulatory environment for business, since these are necessary for the private sector to function. Equally, it judges how predictable property rights laws are, and whether states are able or willing to uphold and enforce them. Sales of state enterprises are folded into a broader question about the percentage of the state sector that has been privatized *or* restructured, which allows us to assess those private sector–driven economies such as Namibia and South Africa that may have commercialized their state sectors without engaging in full divestiture. Further the dataset evaluates the extent to which large sectors such as electricity and telecommunications have been reformed, and the kinds of institutional relationships that governments have developed with their private sectors. This latter indicator, which I added, reflects scholarly work

[55] World Bank, International Development Association, "2005 IRAI." These indicators were formerly known as the Country Policy and Institutional Assessment (CPIA). For a justification of their use as well as the limitations of the data, see Paul Collier, V. L. Elliott, Håvard Hegre, Anke Hoeffler, Marta Reynal-Querol, and Nicholas Sambanis, *Breaking the Conflict Trap: Civil War and Development Policy* (Washington, D.C.: World Bank, 2003) and Humphreys and Bates, "Political Institutions," 43, fn. 42. The 2005 data addresses some of these earlier concerns. However, the data remain categorical and unweighted and researchers should bear that in mind. I have compensated for this by using only those indicators that are most relevant to private sector development, incorporating additional indicators, and not exaggerating small differences in scores in my analysis.
[56] European Bank for Reconstruction and Development, "Transition Indicators Methodology," accessed 1/9/2008, http://www.ebrd.com/country/sector/econo/stats/timeth.htm. The indicators are widely used and respected, but African countries were not included.

56 *Party Politics and Economic Reform*

on Africa and Latin America that examines the circumstances under which business associations influence government decisions and the impact of their influence on economic policy choices. The evidence suggests that where business forms associations and/or establishes regular contact with government through meetings or symposia, it is more likely to exercise influence on government policy. Findings indicate that regular consultation between government and business tends to foster more coherent, pro-business policy formulation and greater policy consistency.[57]

For this category, I build on the work of Dirk Willem te Velde and Kunal Sen, which examines the relationship between state–business relations and economic growth in Africa.[58] To capture state-business relations, te Velde devised an indicator that measured several aspects of state–business relations over time in fifteen African countries. These include the organization of the public sector, the organization of the private sector, and the ways in which states and businesses interact. I adjust his scores in order to incorporate them into the larger imperative commitment dataset for twenty-seven countries.[59]

Like the IRAI, the dataset uses a six-point scale. Where it overlaps with the IRAI, it also adopts the IRAI's coding scheme. The different categories are rated from 1 to 6 with 1 equivalent to an environment that is utterly hostile to private sector creation and development and 6 equivalent to an ideal-type environment that is very highly conducive to private sector growth and sustainability.

The IRAI ratings evaluate twenty-two of the twenty-seven countries that are in my study. Since the IRAI does not include several middle-income countries such as Botswana, Mauritius, South Africa, Seychelles, and Namibia, I rate these countries using existing countries in the IRAI dataset as benchmarks for assigning scores in each category. I rely on national government reports and the secondary literature on economic policy to determine their scores. With regard to the last three categories in the dataset, privatization and restructuring, infrastructural reform, and institutional relationships with the private sector (which I either adapt from the EBRD transition indicators or devise myself), I assign individual scores for these categories according to the coding scheme in Appendix 2. To do so, I draw on government sources, World Bank reports, and secondary material to assign values for each category (see Table 2.5).

---

[57] Ben Ross Schneider, *Business, Politics, and the State in Twentieth-Century Latin America* (Cambridge: Cambridge University Press, 2004); Bräutigam et al., "Business Associations and Growth Coalitions," 519–547.

[58] Dirk Willem te Velde, "Measuring State-Business Relations in Sub-Saharan Africa", Discussion Paper Series no. 4, Research Programme Consortium for Improving Institutions for Pro-Poor Growth, University of Manchester (November 2006), accessed 1/25/2010, http://www.ippg.org.uk; Kunal Sen and Dirk Willem te Velde, "State-Business Relations and Economic Growth in Sub-Saharan Africa," *Journal of Development Studies*, 45, 8 (2009): 1267–1283.

[59] In several African countries, te Velde's figures for 2005 were based on outdated and incomplete information. I therefore adjusted them accordingly. They have also been scaled to fit with my scoring system for imperative commitment. See te Velde, "Measuring State-Business Relations."

TABLE 2.5. *Imperative Commitments to Private Sector Development, 2005*

Country	Trade	Financial Sector	Privatization and Restructuring	Infrastructure Reform	Business Regulatory Environ.	Property Right & Rule based Govern.	Institutional Relationship-Gov/ Private sector	Total Score
Benin	4.5	3.5	4	3	3.5	3	3	24.5
Botswana	5.5	5.5	4	4	5	5.5	4.5	34
Burkina Faso	4	3	3	3	3	3.5	4.5	23.5
Cameroon	3.5	3	4	3	3	2.5	2.5	21.5
Cape Verde	4	4	5	4	3.5	4	3.5	28
Côte d'Ivoire	3.5	3	4	3	3	2	2.5	21
Ghana	4	3.5	5	4	4	3.5	4	28
Guinea	4.5	3	4	1.5	3	2	3	21
Kenya	4	3.5	3	1	4	3	4	22.5
Lesotho	3.5	3.5	2	4	3	3.5	3	23.5
Madagascar	4	3.5	4	2.5	4	3.5	2	23.5
Malawi	4	3	4	3	3.5	3.5	4	25
Mali	4	3	5	3.5	3.5	3.5	3.5	26
Mauritius	4.5	5	4	4	5	5.5	5	33
Mozambique	4.5	3	5	4	3	3	3.5	26
Namibia	5	4.5	5	4	4	3	4	29.5
Niger	4	3	4	2.5	3	3	2	21.5
Nigeria	3	3	2	1	3	2.5	2.5	17
STP	4	2.5	3	3	3	2.5	2	20
Senegal	4	3.5	4	3	3.5	3.5	4.5	26
Seychelles	5	4	3	3	3.5	3.5	3.5	25.5
South Africa	5	4.5	5	4.5	4	4.5	5	32.5
Tanzania	4	3.5	4.5	2.5	3.5	3.5	4	25.5
Togo	4	2.5	4	1.5	3	2.5	2.5	20
Uganda	4	3.5	5	4.5	4	3.5	3.5	28
Zambia	4	3	5	3	3	3	3.5	24.5
Zimbabwe	2	2.5	2	1	2	1	2.5	13

Note: See Appendix 2 for coding scheme.

Sources: Author's calculations. See Appendix 2 for sources consulted for each category.

Did African countries approximate commitments that were credible in the imperative sense? Is there an association between motivational and imperatively credible commitments? The highest possible score, which represents an ideal-type commitment, is 42. To receive this score, countries in the sample have to demonstrate that private property rights are fully protected and enforced and that the state sector is fully privatized or restructured so that it operates according to market principles. With respect to the reform of infrastructure such as water, roads, railways, and telecommunications, an ideal type has a coherent institutional framework governing tariffs, licensing, and concession fees, effectively administered by an independent entity. Strong relationships between the government and the business are also characteristic of ideal types. In these cases, business is actively and regularly consulted on major policy decisions, and there are regular opportunities for interaction between government and business.

The findings in Table 2.5 show that most countries fell short of the ideal type – an issue that qualitative analysis in subsequent chapters will discuss. Scores ranged from a high of 34 for Botswana to a low of 13 for Zimbabwe. Like Botswana, many of those countries that achieved high scores already had well-developed private sectors such as Mauritius (33 points) and South Africa (32.5). Although neither Mauritius nor Botswana actively promoted privatization, existing practice and/or reforms in other sectors of their economies produced high scores with respect to institutional effectiveness. In these countries, formal institutional arrangements acted to constrain and limit the state's discretion to intervene arbitrarily in the economy.

Besides Namibia (29.5) and the previously mentioned countries that already had an established private sector, eight other countries including Uganda, Ghana, Cape Verde, Mali, Mozambique, Tanzania, and the Seychelles underwent substantial reforms and achieved scores that were 25.5 points or more. Limits on state discretion were emerging with respect to trade flows, financial transactions, the exercise of private property rights, and ordinary business operations. Countries such as Uganda, Ghana, Cape Verde, and Mozambique sold over 75 percent of their SOEs – an indication that their states were ceding authority to the private sector.

Many of these countries also went beyond the divestiture of parastatals to demonstrate a greater commitment to privatization and restructuring. They commercialized and regulated electricity production and distribution, railways, roads, telecommunications, water, and sanitation. In contrast to what had existed before the reforms, governments improved the legal framework for business, reduced licensing requirements for business activities, and adopted more flexible employment laws in accordance with the prevailing neo-liberal principles of the time. Most governments, with the exception of Cape Verde, only partially enforced private property rights and inadequately protected their citizens against crime and violence, yet their judiciaries became more professional and made greater efforts to enforce the rule of law. Lastly, governments in this group sought to establish formal relationships with the private sector in order to solicit their views. The score for the seventh criterion, institutional relationships, captured this dynamic.

The median score was 24.5–25 obtained by Malawi, Zambia, and Benin. All together, eleven countries including Benin, Madagascar, Burkina Faso, Kenya, Lesotho, Malawi, Cote D'Ivoire, Niger, Guinea, Cameroon, and Zambia had scores that ranged from 21 to 25. Countries within this range of scores had limits on the use of state discretion and formal institutions that were starting to work as intended. Generally, they reduced tariffs less that 16 percent, their banking sectors were vulnerable to shocks but expanding, and they had payment and clearance systems that were moderately functional. They privatized more than 50 percent of their state sector and made modest to substantial progress on commercialization of their infrastructure. Most of them had de jure property rights but enforcement of these rights was still weak and inconsistent. Last, even though business associations in many of these countries were active, institutional relationships between business and government were still in their infancy. Some governments were beginning to have regular meetings with business but there was also evidence of collusion between government and selected businesses.

Those countries such as São Tomé and Principe, Togo, Nigeria, and Zimbabwe with low scores relative to other countries demonstrated very inconsistent patterns of reform. They made some effort to liberalize trade and published their laws and regulations, but duty collection was slow, and there were frequent allegations of corruption. Their banking sectors were vulnerable to shocks; capital markets were generally weak, and payment and clearance systems were underdeveloped. They made half-hearted efforts to privatize their state sectors or restructure their infrastructure. Licensing requirements were complex and burdensome; laws and regulations on property rights rarely enforced and largely informal. Relationships with the private sector were intermittent and unreliable and no competition law existed. Countries with low credible commitments allowed ample room for the exercise of discretionary authority by the state.

I then compare the findings in this dataset with the index of motivational commitments to produce the scatterplots in Figures 2.2 and 2.3. Pearson's correlation coefficients are presented in Tables 2.6 and 2.7.

As Table 2.6 and Figure 2.2 suggest, there is a moderate, positive, and statistically significant association between motivational commitments and imperative commitments. The association is statistically significant at the .01 level in a two-tailed test. As seen in Table 2.7 and Figure 2.3, this association becomes strong (.732), positive, and statistically significant at the .01 level with the removal of three outliers (Botswana, Namibia, and Mauritius). The reason for excluding these cases is conceptual, not statistical. Namibia, Botswana, and Mauritius achieve high credible commitments even though none of them had very high motivational commitments to privatization. These cases are different

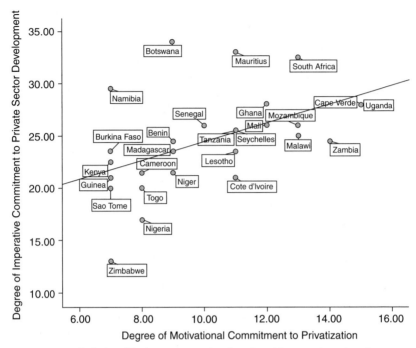

FIGURE 2.2. Relationship between motivational and imperative commitments.

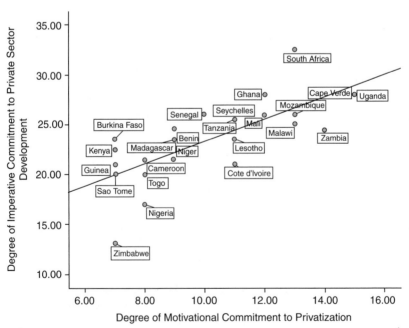

FIGURE 2.3. Relationship between motivational and imperative commitments (excluding Botswana, Mauritius, and Namibia).

TABLE 2.6. *Correlation between Motivational and Imperative Commitments*

		Degree of Imperative Commitment
Degree of Motivational Commitment	Pearson Correlation Coefficient	.497**
	Sig. (2-tailed)	0.008
	N	27

** Correlation is significant at the .01 level.

TABLE 2.7. *Correlation between Motivational and Imperative Commitments (Excluding Botswana, Mauritius, and Namibia)*

		Degree of Imperative Commitment
Degree of Motivational Commitment	Pearson Correlation Coefficient	.732**
	Sig. (2-tailed)	<.001
	N	24

** Correlation is significant at the .01 level.

from other countries in the sample with the exception of South Africa. They already had in place many of the institutional arrangements typically associated with private sector–driven economies. Although in the 1990s they made policy adjustments that were consistent with the global neo-liberal agenda, they were very cautious about the sale of state assets to the private sector as one of their policy tools. Instead, they favored restructuring and commercializing to make their state sectors more efficient. They also had formal relationships with their business sectors, and relatively strong banking sectors. These strengths produced high scores for commitments that were credible in the imperative sense.

The different historical trajectories of these cases conceptually justify running the correlations without including them, but I shall return to some of these countries in subsequent chapters. The purpose here is to explore whether the pattern demonstrated by the remaining cases supports the claim that there is a relationship between the degree of motivational commitment and the extent to which commitments are credible in the imperative sense (Figure 2.3 and Table 2.7).

As the figures and tables indicate, the more that states adopted institutional arrangements consistent with the creation or expansion of their private sectors, the more likely that the quality of those arrangements improved over time. The relationship is even stronger when Namibia, Botswana, and Mauritius are excluded. Although it is important to note that countries fall short of ideal-type commitments, those governments that demonstrate high or very high commitments to privatization and private sector expansion during the 1990s, for the most part, also achieve higher credible commitment scores by 2005. Those that score low on motivational commitment to private sector creation or expansion of the private sector also tend to attain low scores for imperatively credible commitment ten to fifteen years later.

For example, Uganda and Cape Verde made very high motivational commitments to privatization; subsequently, they extended and sustained an environment conducive to private sector growth. These are impressive developments considering their starting points. Uganda ended a lengthy civil war in 1986 with the coming to power of Yoweri Museveni and privatization was part of the postwar strategy of economic rehabilitation. In Cape Verde, the government embraced market principles and private property rights after achieving only modest growth following the adoption of socialism at independence in 1975. In the 1990s, both governments revised land laws and acknowledged private property rights. They passed privatization laws and established privatization agencies to sell SOEs. Nearly a decade later, both governments had privatized most of their state sectors and engaged in substantial infrastructural reform. They promoted trade polices that reduced average tariffs and decreased the number of tariff bands to four or fewer. They also reformed their customs administrations in order to increase efficiency and limit corruption. They reduced the vulnerability of their banking sector to shocks; and their financial and capital markets, while still weak, were growing.

Conversely, lower scores for motivational commitments tend to correlate with lower scores for imperative commitments. The figures indicate that countries such as São Tomé and Principe, Togo, and Guinea with lower motivational commitments also receive lower credible commitment scores (20, 20, and 21, respectively). Guinea, which sold over 50 percent of its state sector, obtains a lower imperative commitment score relative to other countries because of its poor performance in other categories. In several cases, countries with low imperative commitments sold SOEs and reformed their trade regimes just as those that made greater credible commitments did, but they did not accompany these efforts with substantial changes to their financial sectors or major reforms in key strategic areas of their infrastructure. Enforcement of property rights was unpredictable and licensing requirements for investors were burdensome. Last, many governments engaged in only superficial efforts to establish meaningful working relationships with the private sector. These findings suggest that, in the case of some countries, continuing economic difficulties after the turn of the century may not have been because they adopted reforms, but rather, because they *failed* to adopt them.

The associations suggest that the extent to which African governments adopted formal institutions provided a good barometer as to whether they would follow through on that commitment at a later date. Where governments made high or very high motivational commitments, they were more likely to engage in sales of SOEs following the adoption of institutions to protect private property and welcome investors. At a later point in time, they were more likely to have reformed their infrastructure and utilities; favored free trade and promoted an effective banking sector. They were also more likely to have established a relationship with the private sector. Conversely, as should be evident from the data, a number of countries including São Tomé and Principe, Guinea, and Cameroon combined a weak motivational commitment to privatization with poor institutional effectiveness at a later date. These findings demonstrate that what African countries formally did, or did not adopt, was related to their later institutional development.

Conclusion

To a greater extent than other policies of liberalization such as the adoption of exchange rate flotation or tariff reductions, the implementation of privatization requires a series of complex, interdependent, institutional, ideological, and organizational changes. Moreover, private sector development is a lengthy process that occurs unevenly over time. Because of these characteristics, knowing when a government has made a credible commitment to privatization presents conceptual and empirical dilemmas. I have argued that understanding when and how states commit to it requires a more elastic approach to the concept of credible commitment. Ken Shepsle's distinction between a commitment that a government makes because it is motivated to do so at that particular moment (motivational commitment) and a commitment that a government adheres to because it is prevented from engaging in any other action without costly consequences (a commitment that is credible in the imperative sense) provides a useful conceptual solution to the problem. It recognizes that institutional development takes time, and it allows for a differentiation between the moment of adoption and a later moment when institutions may become more firmly entrenched.

Through the use of indices that measured motivational and imperatively credible commitments and data on divestitures, the chapter also attempted to rate the commitment experiences of African countries. I found that despite the continuing presence of conditions in many countries, African governments did not adhere to a single, standard, package of reforms. Rather, the substance of their reforms diverged considerably, and they adapted policy reforms to suit local conditions and preferences. Moreover, the chapter demonstrated that there was a positive relationship between motivational commitments and sales of assets as well as commitments that were credible in the imperative sense. High or very high motivational commitments were associated with higher imperatively credible commitment scores whereas lower motivational commitments were related to lower credible commitments by 2005. These findings suggest that even in Africa where informal institutions abound, the enactment of formal institutional changes increases the likelihood that commitments will become more credible over time.

Finally, the additive ratings for commitments that were credible in the imperative sense not only demonstrated considerable variation amongst the twenty-seven countries but also illustrated that many countries fell short of ideal-type credible commitments. Countries such as Cape Verde, Mali, Mozambique, Tanzania, and Uganda, for example, achieved scores for institutional effectiveness by 2005 that were quite impressive considering their starting points. Yet, the ratings indicated that states in these countries still exercised considerable discretionary authority over the functioning of those arrangements. Institutions still did not act sufficiently to constrain state behavior.

These findings serve as a reminder that there is a long, long road between the adoption of institutions and their eventual institutionalization. They raise important questions about how institutions function once they are adopted, how they interact with interests, whose preferences they are shaping, and which bargains they are structuring. Did African governments confront distributional conflicts that derailed or diverted privatization as countries in Latin America or East and Central Europe did? As the process unfolded, what trade-offs did states have to make between adhering to the rules or exercising discretion? What were the implications for the kind of capitalism that emerged, or for the degree of state stability? These questions highlight the importance of the often-contentious political dynamics that accompany major policy reforms such as privatization, and it is to those dynamics that I now turn.

3

The Impact of Party Politics and Democratic Quality on Economic Reform

The previous chapter established theoretically that commitments to private sector development have imperative credibility when constraints exist on the state's ability arbitrarily to renege on market reforms. Empirically, it documented a considerable range in the extent to which most African governments approximated ideal type, imperatively credible commitments. With respect to cases such as Botswana, Mauritius, and South Africa, which already had private sectors that had been operational for some time, institutions largely acted to constrain the state's discretionary behavior. On the other end of the spectrum, cases such as Zimbabwe or Guinea illustrated that governments continued to intervene arbitrarily in strategic sectors or to encourage corrupt practices by customs officials. Although they did not approximate the ideal type, countries such as Mozambique, Cape Verde, Ghana, or Mali, with histories of significant state intervention, sold state assets, liberalized trade, and built formal relationships with an emerging private sector. Finally, the scores of countries such as Madagascar, Niger, and Cameroon indicated that state discretion competed with institutional constraints across a range of economic arenas.

This chapter explains these divergent trajectories of institutional development by investigating the ways in which the political dynamics of particular countries propel or constrain the privatization process. Not only do existing political coalitions mold institutions over time, but state responses to their actions also produce unanticipated outcomes. Moreover, reforms generate new constituencies that have a vested interest in maintaining new institutional arrangements. For example, growing numbers of foreign and domestic investors brought their preferences to bear on states in Malawi or Ghana. Investors helped to make commitments more credible because, in selected instances, the pursuit of their interests acted to curtail state discretion. Alternatively, institutional changes may catalyze interests that seek to undermine existing arrangements in order to maintain a status quo more coincident with their preferences. Zimbabwe and Nigeria have demonstrated such patterns.

In addition, as private property expands, workers lose jobs, companies are liquidated, or competition increases, distributional conflicts generated by former state managers, workers, bureaucrats, consumers, and even previously protected private sector actors act as countervailing pressures, either hijacking the process or restraining the state in a manner unanticipated at the time of policy enactment. These actions find parallels in transitional countries in Eurasia where, in some instances, groups who stood to lose from reforms organized to block their implementation or individuals who experienced short-term gains distorted the original intent of reforms.[1] Finally, external actors such as the IMF and the World Bank, major donors, and transnational nongovernmental organizations also exert their interests at crucial points in the process.[2]

To resolve these distributional conflicts, states rely on their discretionary authority. Different states use their discretion in a variety of ways when confronted with the struggles induced by policy change. Whether to enforce, bend, or break the rules in order to resolve struggles over power and resources poses few dilemmas for those autocrats who do not have to defend their actions at the polls, but it creates challenging paradoxes for transitional countries that are also emerging democracies. In these instances, if a government adheres to the institutional arrangements it has adopted, it indicates that it respects the rule of law, and that it can be trusted not to renege on policy decisions. Such a stance builds credibility among supporters of the rules, but, at the same time, it suggests to opponents that the state is inflexible and unresponsive. On the other hand, if a government bends or breaks the rules in favor of some aggrieved group, it demonstrates that it is accountable to the group's concerns. But in doing so, it risks forfeiting its credibility with those interests that favor the new institutional arrangements.

The responses of newly democratic governments to these dilemmas have economic and political consequences. Different uses of discretionary authority affect the trajectory of the privatization process as well as electoral results. Governments that abide by the institutions or rules they have adopted often succeed in creating or expanding their private sectors – as the policy intended. By contrast, those governments that break the rules to favor rent-seeking insiders or to engage in clientelism inflict further damage on an already weakened economy. Politically, those groups who lose out in distributional conflicts may punish ruling parties by voting them out at the next election or by expressing their discontent in more destructive ways.

To illustrate the myriad pathways that countries travel on to build market economies, I focus especially on a subset of nine democratic countries from the

[1] J. Hellman, "Winners Take All."

[2] Joseph Stiglitz, "The World Bank at the Millennium," *The Economic Journal*, 109, 459, Features (1999): F583.

larger sample that made high or very high motivationally credible commitments to privatization and private sector expansion. The previous chapter established that the extent to which states made motivational commitments is associated with the degree of imperative credibility at a later moment in time, but how does the process work? Do countries with similar motivational commitments demonstrate similar privatization trajectories, or do they vary according to the ways in which institutions interact with the political dynamics in selected countries?

I identify three types of imperatively credible commitments achieved by the countries in our smaller sample and show how each type combined institutional arrangements that constrained arbitrary government actions with continued uses of state discretion. To account for the variation in imperative credibility among these cases, I argue that differences in the quality of democracy and in party system dynamics explain why some governments resort to discretion, whereas others are more likely to follow the rules. Whether a country is a limited or liberal democracy affects how and if partisan pressures organize effectively to influence policy. Differences in democratic quality also determine whether, and how, a government deploys its discretionary authority in response to distributional conflicts.[3]

Equally, the logic of party competition shapes policy implementation and policy outcomes. Surprisingly, the literature on reform in Africa has largely ignored the impact of the party system on economic policy choice.[4] In emerging democracies, the characteristics of the party system condition government decision making and determine who benefits from reforms. Whether parties rise and decline from election to election or are relatively stable over time affects the interaction of the government with different constituencies. The degree of stability in the party system influences the kinds of constituencies that mobilize in response to economic change, how governments react to them, and, consequently, what trajectory the reform process will take.

Ruling parties in fragmented systems tend to manipulate the reform process over time because they are uncertain of their base and are afraid that the consequences of privatization will result in a loss of political power. Party factionalization may stall the privatization process as breakaway parties or caucuses within parties seek modifications or benefits from existing policies. In more stable party systems, ruling parties seek to design and implement policies in a manner consistent with the interests of their base of support.[5] Greater

---

[3] For sources underpinning my categories and arguments, see Chapter 1.

[4] My usage of the term draws on O'Dwyer, *Runaway State-Building*, 23–29. In his work, O'Dwyer constructs a fourfold typology of party systems to examine different patterns of state building in East and Central Europe. With respect to party politics and privatization, I explain my own approach later.

[5] On the categorization of fluid (or floating) and stable (or solid) party systems, see sources in Chapter 1, footnote 50. For two recent and important studies of party aggregation, see Allen Hicken, *Building Party Systems in Developing Democracies* (Cambridge: Cambridge University

party cohesion facilitates the concentration of power and allows ruling parties to act more decisively with regard to economic reform. Collectively, differences in the quality of democracy and party system dynamics help to explain why African governments engage in trade-offs between rules and discretion during the privatization process. In some cases, these trade-offs compromise or derail economic reforms. Moreover, their consequences can undermine or enhance the stability of the state.[6]

After discussing the challenges to policy reform faced by authoritarian versus democratic countries, the chapter explains the method of case selection for the nine democratic countries that are the object of focus. It describes and classifies the balance of rules versus discretion that comprise their imperative credibility. It then details the theoretical argument regarding differences in the quality of democracy and party system competition and gives the criteria used to distinguish those differences for each variable. To conclude, the chapter will illustrate empirically the implications of the trade-off between rules and discretion for trajectories of privatization in the nine cases.

Imperative Credibility in Emerging Democracies

To investigate the variation in imperative credibility, the analysis focuses on the democratic countries in the sample. The decision to focus on democratic countries is two fold. First, the embrace of democratization by so many developing countries has prompted extensive comparative analysis of interests, institutions, and identities within newly democratic regimes. With its particular focus on the institutional development of a private sector in countries undergoing democratization, this work sheds light on an area of study that has received less attention in the scholarly literature. Second, I assume that the explanation for the continued exercise of discretionary behavior in nondemocratic countries is that authoritarian leaders reserve the right to cancel or modify their commitments if they feel like it. This does not mean that they do not make or even maintain commitments (Museveni showed consistent support for economic reform in Uganda throughout the 1990s for example), but rather, as Olson suggests, such commitments eventually become vulnerable to succession crises and the short-term thinking of insecure leaders.[7] The credibility of commitments is thus harder to establish under such circumstances.[8]

Press, 2009), 2, fn. 2, and Pradeep Chhibber and Ken Kollman, *The Formation of National Party Systems* (Princeton, N.J.: Princeton University Press, 2004). Hicken (p. 2, fn. 2) defines aggregation as "the extent to which competitors from different districts join together to form regional or national political parties."

[6] See Haggard and Kaufman, *The Political Economy of Democratic Transitions*, 151–182.

[7] Mancur Olson, "Dictatorship, Democracy and Development," *American Political Science Review*, 87, 3 (1993): 572.

[8] See also Frye, Building States and Markets, 33–34.

Theoretically, the likelihood of policy reversals under democratic as opposed to authoritarian conditions should decrease *once a policy is in place*. As the literature on veto players demonstrates, democracies offer partisan interests numerous institutional avenues (such as legislatures or the courts) to thwart policy change.[9] The efficacy of these veto points is enhanced by the enforcement of regulations governing the relationship between the executive and the legislative branches, or by the number of votes required by the legislature to override a presidential veto, or by the procedures in which judges acquire their positions.

For democratic governments that attempt to privatize parastatals, the challenge may arise in getting such a policy change enacted. The more institutional access points a political system has, the greater the likelihood that veto players will use them to block a reform if they disagree with it. Moreover, since multiple policy initiatives such as constitutional changes to property rights, the creation of privatization agencies, procedures for the sale of assets, and regulations on investment characterize the privatization process, they offer numerous opportunities for players to exercise veto power. These constraints on government risk creating political instability if groups in favor of the reforms resort to extra legal means of forcing them through.

By the same rationale, once privatization is adopted it should be difficult to reverse in a democracy. Not only does privatization disperse the power of the state into new institutional arrangements for private property, investment, land ownership, and commercial operations, but also the increased number of veto points provided by democratic arrangements acts to restrict the government's discretion to reverse policy.[10]

Examination of the democratic countries in the sample allows us to evaluate how newly emerging democracies in Africa balanced the challenges of economic reform. The criteria used to select the cases are the following. Only those countries that became and/or remained democratic during most of the time period under study were included. To merit inclusion in the sample, countries had to have undergone at least a "flawed" or "democratic" transition by 1994 and remained democratic up to 2005 – the endpoint of the study.[11] This allows a sufficiently lengthy time period to examine the trade-off between rules and discretion in countries that have privatized as well as democratized.

---

[9] George Tsebelis, *Veto Players: How Political Institutions Work* (New York and Princeton, N.J.: Russell Sage Foundation and Princeton University Press, 2002), 67–115.

[10] Ibid., 209–221.

[11] On the criteria for determining a flawed or democratic transition, see Bratton and de Walle, *Democratic Experiments in Africa*, 116–120. By these criteria, Lesotho ought to have been included in the sample as it averaged less than 4 for political rights and civil liberties. Yet, it was excluded on additional criteria including a near monopoly of seats held by the ruling party in the legislature, political instability, and military intervention in the 1990s. In addition to Freedom House scores, these criteria suggest that democracy in that country was questionable at least until 2002.

		Party System	
		Stable	Fluid
Democratic Quality	Liberal	Contingent Uses of Authority	Null
		Strategic Compromise (Mauritius, Cape Verde, South Africa)	
	Limited	Purposeful Discretion	Opportunistic Discretion
		Partisan Private Sector Development (Ghana, Mozambique, Seychelles)	Ad Hoc Private Sector Development (Zambia, Mali, Malawi)

FIGURE 3.1. Party system type, quality of democracy, state responses, and privatization outcomes in cases of high or very high motivational commitment.

Note: Above the dotted line captures state actions. Below dotted line describes the outcome of such actions.

Recall from Chapter 2 that the broad criteria relied on to identify those countries that were democratic over the time period were average Freedom House scores between 1 and 4 for political rights and civil liberties at least by 1994 up to 2005.[12] In addition, I target here those democratic countries (nine cases) where governments demonstrated high or very high motivational commitments during the period from 1988 to 2000. Holding the initial institutional arrangements more or less constant permits the identification of substantive differences among the nine cases regarding the balance of rules versus discretion, the key factors contributing to the balance, and the implications for outcomes of privatization (see Figure 3.1). These findings are based on the descriptive statistics from the larger dataset on imperative credibility by 2005 and careful tracing of the reform process by these nine countries. In subsequent chapters, three case studies on Zambia, Mozambique, and South Africa draw on extensive fieldwork, interviews with key stakeholders, and analytic narratives to substantiate further this chapter's theoretical claims. These cases are fully explored in Chapters 4, 5, and 6.

Figure 3.1 indicates that even where motivational commitments were similar, states relied on their discretionary authority to serve different objectives such that the composition and extent of their imperative credibility diverged over time. For heuristic purposes, these are classified into three types (one quadrant is empty). First, over the course of the privatization process, governments such as Zambia, Mali, and Malawi relied on opportunistic uses of discretion in response to distributional conflicts that arose from the process of selling SOEs.

[12] See Freedom House, "Comparative and Historical Data." For a defense of the use of Freedom House indicators of democracy over other indices, see Bogaards, "Counting Parties," 175.

This type of capricious behavior was unsystematic and arbitrary. Government officials bent and broke the rules in order to realize short-term gains and to deliver benefits to individuals or selected groups in exchange for electoral and legislative support. Over time, the central characteristic of private sector development was that it was "ad hoc." It followed no consistent pattern and was marked by government interference and delays.

Second, other governments such as Mozambique, Ghana, and the Seychelles employed their discretionary authority more deliberately and systematically to preserve or enhance the power of the ruling party. The initial design of private sector institutions and the process of implementation reflected biases in favor of ruling party supporters. In response to opportunities or threats, ruling parties manipulated or interpreted the rules to privilege party loyalists. Because the beneficiaries of the process were often tied to the party in power, I label this "partisan private sector development."

Last, governments in Mauritius, Cape Verde, and South Africa primarily adhered to the rules they adopted. Their uses of discretion were neither arbitrary nor systematic; rather, they were "contingent" on the particular circumstances or interests that the process generated. Governments sometimes bent the rules, but they did so in order to sustain policy continuity.[13] Economic restructuring in these cases was chiefly characterized by strategic compromises that maintained the reform and assuaged the demands of disaffected groups. I discuss these patterns after examining the determinants of different combinations of rules and discretion.

Explaining Divergent Combinations of Rules Versus Discretion

My argument regarding the varied patterns exhibited by these governments is that differences in the quality of democracy and in the logic of party competition largely explain the divergent expressions of opportunistic behavior by democracies in Africa and their subsequent impact on privatization trajectories. I assume that in these as in other democracies, ruling parties and their opponents have a strategic incentive to build coalitions in exchange for electoral support. To acquire party members and votes, party leaders in more democratic countries typically make programmatic appeals to the general welfare or to particular districts, sectors, or interest groups. Alternatively, in less democratic countries, they often engage in clientelistic practices by distributing private goods to individuals or club goods to selected groups to gain votes.[14]

---

[13] This notion of contingent uses of discretion builds on Barro, "Recent Developments," 28–29.

[14] Herbert Kitschelt and Steven Wilkinson, "Citizen-Politician Linkages: An Introduction" in Herbert Kitschelt and Steven Wilkinson, eds., *Patrons, Clients, and Policies: Patterns of Democratic Accountability and Political Competition* (New York: Cambridge University Press, 2007), 11. Like Kitschelt and Wilkinson, I recognize that club goods such as those sought by trade unions or business occupy the "murky middle ground" between a programmatic position or a clientelistic relationship between a party and a constituency. The quality of democracy

After it gets into power, a ruling party may interfere in the implementation of policy to direct benefits to specified constituencies as a reward for their support or to encourage them to join the governing coalition.[15] In addition, governments may have ideological or political motives for favoring particular groups that go beyond a simple electoral calculus.

Since privatization tends to generate multilayered conflicts during implementation, democratic governments confront several challenges: mediating the conflict, retaining electoral support, and maintaining the policy. In a newly democratic country, differences in the quality of democracy and the nature of the party system affect greatly what the challenges are and how ruling parties employ their discretionary authority to address them. Whether a government honors or restricts the rights of individuals to express their views, to join parties or organizations, or to hold their government accountable influences the privatization process. Whether a government abides by or evades the rule of law impacts how privatization takes place. Finally, whether private sector development occurs in a system where parties are weak, fragmented, and inchoate or, alternatively, stable and cohesive shapes its outcome.

Variation in Democratic Quality

As the era of one-party states, military dictatorships, and authoritarian regimes recedes and democracy persists across many of the world's regions, scholars have turned their attention to the quality of those democracies that have been established. They have been interested to isolate procedural as well as substantive dimensions of democracy in order to rank and evaluate democratic quality.[16] A recent edited volume by Daniel Levine and José Molina brings greater clarity to the concept of democratic quality and it theoretically informs my claim.[17] According to Levine and Molina, democratic quality is

the extent to which citizens can participate in an informed manner in processes of free, fair, and frequent elections; influence the making of political decisions; and hold those who govern accountable. Determination of the level of quality of a democracy also involves *the extent* to which those who govern are those who really make decisions and do so in a way that is responsive to popular will.[18]

in a country provides a useful indication of the extent to which parties engage in one versus the other.

[15] On these practices across cases see Kitschelt and Wilkinson, "Citizen-Politician Linkage," 1–49 and selected chapters in *Patrons, Clients*.

[16] See, for example, Diamond and Morlino, eds., *Assessing the Quality*; Guillermo O'Donnell, Jorge Cullell, and Osvaldo Iazzetta, *The Quality of Democracy: Theory and Applications* (Notre Dame, Ind.: University of Notre Dame Press, 2004); Larry Diamond, Jonathan Hartlyn, Juan Linz, and Seymour Martin Lipset, eds., *Democracy in Latin America*, 2nd ed. (Boulder, Colo.: Lynne Rienner, 1999).

[17] Levine and Molina, eds., *The Quality of Democracy*.

[18] Daniel Levine and José Molina, "Evaluating the Quality of Democracy in Latin America" in Levine and Molina, eds., *The Quality of Democracy*, 8.

Levine and Molina devise an index of democratic quality that consists of five dimensions: Electoral Decision, Participation, Accountability, Responsiveness, and Sovereignty. They analyze the conduct of elections, the degree to which governments are accountable to those who elect them, and the extent to which governments are sovereign. To evaluate each one of these dimensions for Latin American countries in the year 2005, they rely on Freedom House indicators of political rights and press freedom; answers to public opinion surveys on the extent to which respondents participate in their communities, and whether they agree that their vote makes a difference; and an assessment of the degree to which civilians have control over the military.[19] Moreover, they stress that their evaluations are not based on normative judgments about "good" or "bad" policies but rather on the degree to which citizens choose and hold to account those who enact such policies.[20] Their analysis provides a foundation for understanding how qualitative differences in democracy might affect the privatization process in our cases.

In addition, the implications of their approach closely parallel those of Lawrence Broz regarding the potential political costs democratic governments have to bear if they renege on their promises.[21] The basic claim here is that the more democratic a country is, the more constrained it is to engage in opportunistic behavior. Because democratic countries have more institutions through which interests can express their preferences, these interests have greater means to hold governments accountable. As Broz observes, "In a transparent polity, civil liberties are afforded to a heterogeneous population, political parties compete openly for votes in regular and free elections, and the media is free to monitor the government."[22]

To capture the differences in democratic quality for my sample of cases, I rely on Freedom House indicators of political rights and civil liberties as proxies for democratic quality rather than the Levine/Molina index for three reasons. First, for some of my cases, there is a lack of data comparable to that which they used for Latin America.[23] Second, the construction of Levine and Molina's index makes it possible to evaluate only one year, whereas my study of institutional development over time requires that I rely on an average of democratic quality for the time period in question. Third, there is a very high correlation between the results of their study and Freedom House indicators.[24] I therefore felt confident using Freedom House indicators as proxies for democratic quality in Africa.

---

[19] Daniel Levine and José Molina, "Measuring the Quality of Democracy" in Levine and Molina, eds., *The Quality of Democracy,* 21–37.
[20] Levine and Molina, "Evaluating the Quality," 4–5.
[21] J. Lawrence Broz, "Political System Transparency and Monetary Commitment Regimes," *International Organization,* 56, 4 (2002): 861–887.
[22] Ibid., 868.
[23] I also could not use Polity IV data since it includes neither the Seychelles nor Cape Verde.
[24] Levine and Molina, "Measuring the Quality," 31.

TABLE 3.1. *Average Democratic Quality of Selected African Countries*[a]

Country	Political Rights	Civil Liberties
Cape Verde[b]	1.07	1.87
Ghana	3.0	3.21
Malawi	2.92	3.33
Mali	2.21	2.79
Mauritius	1.13	1.88
Mozambique	3.0	4.08
Seychelles	3.0	3.15
South Africa	1.08	2.08
Zambia	3.9	3.87

[a] Average calculated from year of first election, or, if already democratic prior to 1990, from 1992 to 2005.
[b] Countries in bold are liberal democracies.
Source: Freedom House, "Comparative and Historical Data," accessed 3/12/2009, http://www.freedomhouse. org.

The countries in the sample were divided into two categories, liberal or limited democracies according to the following criteria.[25] I defined liberal democracies as those countries that averaged a Freedom House score between 1 and 2 for either political rights or civil liberties (or both) from the date of their first election (or, from 1992, if they were already democratic like Mauritius) to 2005. By contrast, limited democracies received average scores of more than 2 and less than or equal to 4 for political rights and civil liberties.[26]

Whether a government is a liberal or limited democracy influences the nature of those pressures that arise from the implementation of privatization and how governments will respond to them. Governments in liberal democracies such as Mauritius or South Africa are more likely to abide by the rule of law, to listen to stakeholders with an interest in the policy, and to respect their rights during implementation. In liberal democracies, fewer restrictions on the media mean that opposition parties and members of the public have access to more information with which to hold governments accountable for their actions. Functioning judiciaries that uphold established rules make it more difficult for a state to behave opportunistically. At the same time, political parties, trade unions, and civil society organizations also rely on institutional channels

[25] The categories of liberal and limited broadly correspond to Diamond's liberal and electoral types. See Larry Diamond, "Thinking about Hybrid Regimes," 30–31, table 2.
[26] See Freedom House, "Comparative and Historical Data," and "Freedom in the World Survey, 2005," accessed 3/15/2009, http://www.freedomhouse.org.

to influence policy in liberal democracies. Depending on their resources and degree of mobilization, they can organize into associations, launch demonstrations, arrange meetings with officials, or use the media. Multiple channels of access by such pressures increase the chances of effective oversight and likely reduce egregious deployment of discretionary authority. This may explain why countries such as South Africa and Mauritius have been slow to privatize. Not only do opponents take advantage of extensive political rights and civil liberties to challenge policy change, but also governments are listening to multiple stakeholders advance a multitude of interests.

As scholars have observed, however, African democracies vary considerably in the degree to which political rights are exercised and civil liberties are respected. Legacies of colonialism and authoritarianism following independence continue to shape the rules as well as the behavior of Africa's current leaders.[27] Citizens of countries such as South Africa and Mauritius enjoy many of the rights and freedoms enjoyed by citizens living in developed Western democracies, whereas most residents of countries such as Malawi and Mozambique do not. These countries are limited democracies: Their governments are less constrained by the checks and balances exerted by an active legislature, a competent judiciary, or a robust media. Their governments are more likely to encroach on individual liberties if they are threatened by the distributional conflicts that arise from privatization or if they wish to advance their interests.[28] As a result, the implementation and consequences of privatization are likely to be more unpredictable because governments in these democracies exercise greater discretionary authority than those in liberal democracies. Thus, commitments to privatization that are credible in the imperative sense are not likely to be fully realized.

Moreover, as the case of Zambia illustrates, we can expect that the privatization process in a limited democracy will be more prone to corruption owing to the lack of transparency. On the one hand, because democratization in Zambia increased the number of opportunities for veto players to block policy change, the Zambian government did not renege completely on its commitment to privatization when conflict and slow growth accompanied the process. On the other hand, although the policy remained in place, government officials took advantage of extensive formal and informal executive authority to raid the privatization process. Over time, politicians manipulated privatization to build or maintain loyalty for the highly factionalized ruling party.[29]

---

[27] Diamond, "Thinking about Hybrid Regimes"; Bratton et al., *Public Opinion*, 13–26; Nicolas van de Walle, "Meet the New Boss, Same as the Old Boss? The Evolution of Political Clientelism in Africa," in Kitschelt and Wilkinson, eds., *Patrons, Clients*, 58–59; John Harbeson, "Promising Democratization Trajectories in Africa's Weak States," in John Harbeson and Donald Rothchild, eds., *Africa in World Politics: Reforming Political Order* (Boulder: Westview, 2009), 109–139.
[28] See Diamond, "Thinking About Hybrid Regimes."
[29] Chapter 4 will document the Zambian case.

Even though differences in the quality of democracy determine the contours and character of the privatization process, variation in the dynamics of party politics equally shape its trajectory. Owing to their central role in democratic governance, the way that parties are organized and how they attract support can influence greatly institutional development, especially in regions such as Latin America and Africa where control over state power is both highly contested and so valuable.[30] Scholars of Africa have suggested that party fragmentation or stability might affect policy making, but few studies have focused in any detail on the interaction of parties and the policy process.[31] To explain how parties might shape the implementation of privatization requires, first, an understanding of the general characteristics of parties across Africa and, second, how scholars have categorized particular cases.

Party Characteristics and Party System Typologies in Africa

Many political parties in Africa have shallow foundations because they function in poor countries that have only recently democratized. Many of them are internally undemocratic, lack adequate finances, and have poor linkages with civil society.[32] Together with the dominance of the executive branch in most African political systems, these features generally give incumbents a decided advantage over opposition parties. Their proximity to state resources allows them to create clientelistic networks consisting of key political brokers, who mobilize regional, ethnic, religious, or other identities to attract votes. Incumbents may also take advantage of their positions to offer food, t-shirts, and other items to potential supporters at campaign rallies in the hope that such gifts will translate into votes at election time.[33]

By contrast, opposition parties often are hobbled by an inability to attract voters at a national level owing to inadequate resources, poor leadership, a lack of experience, or their own regional or local orientation. Consequently, they tend to weaken and split leading to a proliferation of smaller parties without clear bases of support or established identities. Although opposition parties in some African countries have grown stronger recently, they still face formidable challenges owing to the prominence of presidentialism, electoral districting systems that favor ruling parties, and doubts about their legitimacy by voters. Given the advantages of incumbency, alternations in power between ruling and opposition parties following democratization have been infrequent.[34]

---

[30] On this point, see Scott Mainwaring and Timothy R. Scully, "Introduction: Party Systems in Latin America" in Mainwaring and Scully, eds., *Building Democratic Institutions*, 3.

[31] See for example Kuenzi and Lambright, "Party Systems and Democratic Consolidation" and Matthijs Bogaards, "Crafting Competitive Party Systems: Electoral Laws and the Opposition in Africa," *Democratization*, 7, 4 (2000): 163–190.

[32] Randall and Svåsand, "Political Parties and Democratic Consolidation."

[33] Van de Walle, "Meet the New Boss," 59–66.

[34] Randall and Svåsand, "Political Parties and Democratic Consolidation"; Manning, "Assessing African Party Systems;" Lise Rakner and Nicolas van de Walle, "Democratization by Elections? Opposition Weakness in Africa," *Journal of Democracy*, 20, 3 (2009): 108–121.

Owing to the slow turnover rate of ruling parties in a number of countries, scholars have referred to these as "dominant party systems" or "dominant one-party systems" in typologies of African party politics. The term "party system" refers to patterned interaction between or among parties. The qualifier "dominant" or "dominant one party" indicates that the same party has controlled the legislature and the presidency over a long period of time.[35] Most applications of the term "dominant party system" are problematic, however, owing to uses of multiple criteria to determine dominant party status. Scholars use different thresholds to calculate the share of the vote that parties must capture in order to be considered dominant (from a simple plurality to a supermajority of seats) and different electoral or time periods to label the prevailing logic a "dominant party system" (from three to four electoral periods, twenty years or more), and these differences reduce the usefulness of the category.[36] Moreover, as Carbone has observed, dominant parties in countries with very different levels of political competition tend to be grouped under the same umbrella.[37] A further complication arises when scholars try to explain particular patterns of behavior by noting that a country has a dominant party system. This is essentially a retrospective evaluation. It is very difficult to rely on party dominance as an explanatory variable when it cannot be verified until the third or fourth election. On a related point, some scholars code dominant party systems as undemocratic if there is no alternation of the party in power over the course of three elections and/or twenty years. Bogaards has criticized this position for its overreliance on outcome at the expense of the procedure by which it was obtained, a concern I share, and which my focus on democratic quality takes into account.[38]

A recent typology of African party systems by Erdmann and Basedau tries to address some of these criticisms but it raises new concerns.[39] Drawing on Sartori's 1976 typology of party systems, the Erdmann-Basedau model introduces a two-level typology of party systems in Africa with four party system classifications per level. The two levels refer to the extent to which a party system has been institutionalized. All party systems receive a classification in the first level of fluid/inchoate if they have had one or two elections. After three consecutive elections, the longer the age of the party and the lower the volatility (less than 40 according to Pedersen's index) then the greater the chances that Erdmann and Basedau will code it as institutionalized.[40]

Within each level, the party system is then categorized according to regime type. Among party systems that have been institutionalized, Erdmann and

[35] Bogaards, "Counting parties," 175.
[36] Ibid., 176.
[37] Carbone, "Political Parties," 15.
[38] Matthijs Bogaards, "Elections, Election Outcomes, and Democracy in Southern Africa," *Democratization*, 14, 1 (2007): 73–91.
[39] Gero Erdmann and Matthias Basedau, "Party Systems in Africa: Problems of Categorizing and Explaining Party Systems," *Journal of Contemporary African Studies*, 26, 3 (2008): 241–258.
[40] Ibid., 246.

Basedau classify as "predominant" party systems those cases where ruling parties have gained absolute majorities in at least three elections, have exhibited low seat volatility, and have Freedom House scores of less than 3.5.[41] If conditions under which parties became institutionalized were noncompetitive then the party is classified as "hegemonic." If procedures were more competitive and there is a change of the party in power, cases are coded as "moderate pluralism" or "two-party."[42]

Erdmann and Basedau's typology is more systematic and comprehensive than previous ones, but it is not very parsimonious. The distinction between fluid/inchoate and institutionalized party systems is a temporal not a categorical one. The temporal distinction suggests that countries evolve to a stage where parties persist over time and volatility declines. Further, the sorting of fluid/inchoate versus institutionalized party systems precludes comparison between the two systems even though parties in Benin, Mali, and Zambia have been fragmented for as long as parties in Namibia and Cape Verde have been stable.[43]

The focus on the degree of institutionalization also comes at the expense of a focus on the democratic context in which the party is operating. The institutionalized level excludes by definition parties in countries such as Senegal, Zambia, and Malawi where the party age is low or volatility is high despite the fact that these countries have been democratic for fifteen years or more and have average Freedom House scores of less than 4 since the 1990s. Moreover, the inchoate/fluid category groups parties in these countries with parties from countries such as Guinea-Bissau and Zimbabwe, even though these latter countries have experienced violent unrest or a regime change and have very high Freedom House scores.[44]

Additionally, the creation of such a low threshold for qualification as a democracy (3.5 or less according to Freedom House scores) in the institutionalized category leads to the inclusion of regimes as different as Seychelles and Mozambique alongside regimes such as South Africa and Mauritius.[45] The designation of Seychelles and Mozambique as "predominant party systems" seems to disregard a critical observation that Sartori made regarding "predominant party systems," which is that to merit the designation "predominant," the continuation in office of the ruling party for three or more elections is largely the result of "fair competition." As Sartori states

The monopolistic permanence in office of the same party, election after election, cannot reasonably be imputed to conspicuous unfair play or ballot stuffing. In other words, we can close an eye to electoral irregularities as long as it can be reasonably assumed that

[41] Ibid., 245 and 254, fn. 4.
[42] Ibid., 245–246.
[43] Ibid.
[44] Ibid.
[45] Ibid.

in a situation of fair competition the predominant party would still attain the absolute majority of seats.[46]

By these criteria, it is questionable whether the Seychelles and Mozambique qualify as "predominant" rather than "dominant" party systems since electoral irregularities have been a conspicuous feature of elections in both cases.

Thus, even though the substitution by Erdmann and Basedau of "dominant party system" by "predominant party system" represents an improvement over earlier typologies, it does not fully address Carbone's criticism regarding the grouping of different democratic regimes under the same umbrella or the analytical awkwardness of retrospective assessments. Although the number of cases I investigate is necessarily limited, I adopt a more parsimonious approach to understanding party systems by decoupling differences in democratic quality from the logic of party competition.

Fragmented versus Stable Party Systems

Since differences in the quality of democracy already account for how a party might use its power, I depart from the conventional practice in the literature of treating dominant or predominant parties as special types of party systems. The distinction I draw is that between a stable (or solid) and a fragmented (or fluid) party system, terms that are commonly used in the literature on European, Latin American, and African party systems.[47] Parties in stable systems interact with other parties in more or less predictable ways. These parties have identities that extend beyond their leadership; their party labels provide recognizable points of reference for voters as in many established democracies. By contrast, fluid, fragmented, or "floating" party systems may be more

---

[46] Giovanni Sartori, *Parties and Party Systems: A Framework for Analysis* (Cambridge: Cambridge University Press, 1976, republished Colchester: European Consortium for Political Research, 2005): 173.

[47] The literature uses a variety of terms to describe similar phenomena. Dodd, in his pioneering work, *Coalitions in Parliamentary Government*, refers to stable and unstable parties, see pp. 88–94. For Europe, Stefano Bartolini and Peter Mair, *Identity, Competition and Electoral Availability: The Stabilisation of European Electorates 1885–1985* (Cambridge: Cambridge University Press, 1990) refer to stabilization versus fragmentation of party systems; in Africa, Staffan Lindberg distinguishes between stable and fluid systems in "Institutionalization of Party Systems? Stability and Fluidity among Legislative Parties in Africa's Democracies," *Government and Opposition*, 42, 2 (2007): 215–241; Stephen White, "Russia's Client Party System" in Paul Webb and Stephen White, eds., *Party Politics in New Democracies* (Oxford: Oxford University Press, 2007) refers to stable versus floating party systems in Russia; Mainwaring and Scully, "Introduction" refer to solid versus inchoate party systems in Latin America. It should be stressed that most party systems demonstrate stable as well as fluid properties from time to time regardless of their classification. For novel explanations of *why* African parties in various countries demonstrate these and other properties, see Rachel Riedl, "Institutions in New Democracies: Variations in African Political Party Systems," Ph.D. diss., Princeton University (November 2008) and Adrienne LeBas, *From Protest to Parties: Party-Building and Democratization in Africa* (Oxford: Oxford University Press, 2011).

"competitive" owing to an increased number of parties, but parties in these systems frequently rise and decline, merge and divide.[48] In these systems, seat volatility or the percentage of seats that change parties in the legislature may exceed 20 percent from election to election.[49] In addition, voters split their party loyalties among many parties and switch parties often. What fragmented parties stand for also changes frequently since their base is so fluid. Owing to a lack of cohesion, their leaders may resort unabashedly to patronage to gain or retain support.[50]

To distinguish stable from fragmented systems, I use three indicators derived from electoral data and survey research on Africa: first, average seat volatility in the legislature; second, the degree to which voters feel close to a party; and third, the effective number of parties in the legislature.[51] Stable party systems in Africa demonstrate lower seat volatility, a higher degree of party loyalty (or closeness), and a lower number of effective parties in the legislature.[52] With regard to the first criterion, I rely on Pedersen's index of volatility to assess seat volatility in the legislature as most comparative work on party systems does.[53] Ideally, it would have been useful to gauge voter volatility also since rules on the allocation of seats often exaggerate the seat shares of major parties (and

---

[48] See Stephen White, "Russia's Client Party System" in Paul Webb and Stephen White, eds., *Party Politics in New Democracies* (Oxford: Oxford University Press, 2007), 23.

[49] Seat volatility of 20 percent would be considered high in a European democracy, but because we are examining emerging democracies, we allow some room for preferences to change as these democracies institutionalize. Erdmann and Basedau adopt an extremely high volatility threshold of 40 percent for their study.

[50] See White, "Russia's Client Party System" and examples.

[51] This approach not only builds on but also updates several earlier typologies of African party systems. In addition to Erdmann and Basedau, see Lindberg, "Institutionalization of Party Systems;" Matthias Basedau, "Do Party Systems Matter," and Bogaards, "Dominant Party Systems." As I do, Lindberg disentangles regime quality from the type of party system after establishing a minimum threshold for a democracy. Lindberg's typology uses eight indicators to distinguish between stable and fluid party systems in Africa. The indicators support his claim that stable party systems demonstrate lower seat volatility in the legislature, not only with regard to the total number of parties that enter and depart, but also with regard to the shift in the share of seats controlled by the largest and runner-up parties. By contrast, fluid party systems show greater volatility with regard to the entry and exit of parties at each election; the percentage of seats won by these new parties and the total number of parties that receive votes, and, the percentage of seats that change hands from one election to another. Using more parsimonious criteria and a longer time frame, my findings reinforce his claims except where noted below.

[52] Seat volatility and ENPP are standard in the literature on party systems; voter closeness to parties is a less common measure. There are additional criteria regarding party organization and length of time in parliament that may also prove to be useful indicators, but data are complete for only a few cases in the sample. I shall examine some of these indicators in the more detailed case studies.

[53] It may be argued that since my index of credible commitment ends in 2005, I should not include elections that occurred after 2005. However, since election outcomes often reflect changes that have been several years in the making, I opted to include a recent election if 2005 fell between election periods.

therefore underestimate voter volatility), but the data on actual votes were incomplete.[54]

Measuring volatility requires some decisions about how to treat parties. Following the criteria adopted by Bartolini and Mair in their study of European party systems, Bogaards opted not to treat mergers, splits, and name changes as new parties in Africa, arguing that this approach enables comparison across cases.[55] Bartolini and Mair were concerned to identify the degree to which the decline in party identities in Europe reflected changes in long-standing cleavages within established democracies. In a European country, a party split may not indicate a cleavage of significance; hence, Bartolini and Mair do not count party splits as new parties. Rather, they sum the percentage of votes won by the two new parties and subtract it from the percentage received from the original party before the split.[56]

I depart from Bartolini and Mair's approach. In a transitional country, a party split may signify a new era of more competitive politics or it may call attention to the prevalence of personalism, two features of a party system worth noting because in this context they may affect processes of economic reform. In a number of emerging democracies in Africa, party splits have provoked a crisis of profound proportions. Witness the split in the African National Congress (ANC) in South Africa prior to the 2009 elections. Most observers agree that despite the fact that the new party, Congress of the People (COPE), only received 7 percent of the vote, the split provoked a serious crisis within the ANC and challenged its hegemony in South African politics. Although it is too early to tell, the formation of COPE may ultimately produce more competitive politics in South Africa in the future.[57] Accordingly, I count splits and mergers (but not coalitions where parties retain their identities) as new parties. Regarding name changes and the formation or dissolution of coalitions, I follow the criteria of Bartolini and Mair. I do not count a change of name if it is essentially the same party. For coalitions, the percentage won by the coalition is subtracted from the percentage gained by the sum of the parties that are participating in the coalition. Similarly, if a coalition splits, then the percentages gained by parties that participated in the previous coalition are summed and subtracted from the percentage gained by the coalition in the previous election.[58]

Since Pedersen's index cannot discern whether voter or seat volatility is occurring among parties that endure over time or is owed to new parties

---

[54] Bogaards makes a good case for examining voter as well as seat volatility. Unfortunately extensive searches did not produce election results for Mali, which is one of my cases and which Bogaards left out of his study, see Bogaards, "Dominant Party Systems," 11.

[55] Bogaards, "Dominant Party Systems," 117.

[56] Bartolini and Mair, *Identity, Competition,* 311–313.

[57] Adam Habib and Collette Schulz Herzenberg, "Democratisation and Parliamentary Opposition in Contemporary South Africa: The 2009 National and Provincial Elections in Perspective," unpublished manuscript (February 2010).

[58] Bartolini and Mair, *Identity, Competition,* 311–313.

arising at each election, the second indicator supplemented this measure with available public opinion data from the Afrobarometer surveys on partisan political loyalty. The percentage was derived from answers to two questions about whether respondents felt close to parties and if so, to which parties they felt close.[59] I assumed that in cases where parties were more fluid, the percentage of respondents who felt close to particular parties would be lower than in those cases where parties endured from election to election, or that loyalties by voters in fragmented systems would be spread among several parties. Conversely, in more stable party systems, I expected that the percentage of respondents who felt close to particular parties would be higher than in fragmented systems. This expectation is consistent with the existing literature on partisanship and parties. Where parties tend to endure over time, citizens are likely to have, and to express, partisan attachments.[60]

The first two indicators examine the electoral environment and the views of voters regarding parties in their respective countries. The third indicator, the effective number of parties in parliament or the legislature (ENPP), reflects the consequences of weak or strong voter identity with parties. Moreover, it allows us to assess whether the formal political context in which governments make and implement policy is populated by many parties or by a few. For this indicator, calculations are based on the Laakso-Taagapera index and are computed using the instructions and excel spreadsheet supplied by Michael Gallagher.[61] I also update the figures on Cape Verde, South Africa, and Zambia in the Gallagher dataset.

Used in conjunction with the other indicators, ENPP casts light on the extent to which party stability exists in the legislature and what the implications are for governments. In cases where there are many parties in the legislature or where the number of parties varies from one term to the next, governments may have to revise their policy-making strategies in order to deal with new political players. It is not that presidents lack the formal power to make policy if they wish. Rather, because they cannot count on consistent support in fragmented party systems, they may spend valuable political capital, rely on personalism,

[59] Partisan loyalty percentages are calculated from Afrobarometer Survey Findings, Round 3, 2005. The 2005 data is used because it corresponds to the endpoint of the imperative commitment index. Data of 2008 are referred to where appropriate. Unfortunately Afrobarometer Surveys were not conducted in Mauritius and Seychelles.

[60] Mainwaring and Scully, "Introduction," 21–28, but see the debate regarding partisan dealignment in the older, industrialized democracies in Russell J. Dalton, Ian McAllister, and Martin P. Wattenberg, "The Consequences of Partisan Dealignment" in Russell J. Dalton and Martin P. Wattenberg, eds., *Parties without Partisans: Political Change in Advanced Industrial Democracies* (Oxford: Oxford University Press, 2000), 37–63.

[61] See Michael Gallagher "Election Indices," ElectionsIndices.pdf, accessed 5/25/2011, http://www.tcd.ie/Political_Science/staff/michael_gallagher/ElSystems and Indices.xls, accessed 5/25/2011, http://www.tcd.ie/Political_Science/staff/michael_gallagher/ElSystems/Docts/IndicesCalc.pdf. For more information on calculating ENPP, see Michael Gallagher and Paul Mitchell, eds., *The Politics of Electoral Systems* (Oxford and New York: Oxford University Press, 2005).

break the rules, or resort to short-term populist measures to appease factions and retain support.[62]

By contrast, in systems where the effective number of parties remains more or less constant over time and volatility is lower, ruling parties are more likely to have established a means for managing contestation, a protocol for communicating with the party in parliament, and an agenda for enacting policy. Voters are more consistent in their support for particular parties and less likely to change their vote to another party in response to offers of token gifts by candidates.[63] Policy beneficiaries are more likely to be associated with the ruling party in these systems. At the same time, opposition parties tend to be more experienced and more organized than in systems where the ENPP is larger or varies from one period to the next. They are thus in a stronger position than opposition parties in fluid party systems to offer critical appraisals of policy making and outcomes by the ruling party. The results for the indicators are in Table 3.2 and Appendix 3.

As Table 3.2 suggests, stable party systems show much lower seat volatility from one election to the next. Seat volatility in Ghana, Mozambique, Seychelles, Cape Verde, and South Africa has been less than 15 percent since these countries became democratic. Mozambique exhibits the lowest total net shift of seats at 10 percent while Seychelles's shift is the highest at 14 percent (excluding Ghana's first election which was boycotted by four parties). At nearly 48 percent, Mauritius shows a higher degree of volatility than we would expect for this established democracy. Because coalitions have been such a common feature of Mauritian politics since 1976, Mauritius is a special case.

In addition, stable party systems also demonstrate greater party loyalty by the electorate to fewer parties as Ghana, South Africa, Cape Verde, and Mozambique demonstrate. According to Afrobarometer surveys, a majority of respondents from *all* countries in the sample claimed that they felt close to a party. But in Ghana, Mozambique, South Africa, and Cape Verde, a majority felt close or very close to just one or two parties. In Mozambique, for example, 82 percent of respondents to an Afrobarometer survey claimed they felt close to a political party. When asked to name the particular party they felt close to, 73 percent of those asked responded by naming the ruling party, the Front for the Liberation of Mozambique (Frelimo).[64] Sixty-six percent of

[62] Mainwaring and Scully, "Introduction," 22–27; Ronald Archer and Matthew Shugart, "The Unrealized Potential of Presidential Dominance in Colombia" in Scott Mainwaring and Matthew Shugart, eds., *Presidentialism and Democracy in Latin America* (Cambridge: Cambridge University Press, 1997), 110–159.

[63] On this point, see Staffan Lindberg and Minion Morrison, "Are African Voters Really Ethnic or Clientelistic? Survey Evidence from Ghana," *Political Science Quarterly*, 123, 1 (2008): 95–122 and chapters 5 and 6.

[64] Afrobarometer Survey Findings, "Summary of Results: Round Three, Afrobarometer Survey in Mozambique, 2005," Compiled by João Pereira, Domingos de Rosário, Sandra Manuel, Carlos Shenga, and Eliana Namburete, Afrobarometer Survey, Round 3, 2005, accessed 3/6/2008,

TABLE 3.2. *Average Seat Volatility, the Effective Number of Parliamentary Parties and Partisan Loyalty*

Country	Seat Volatility (%)	ENPP	Partisan Loyalty (top two parties in 2005, %)
Cape Verde[a]	11	1.90	50
Ghana	13 (18)	2.07 (1.88)	64
Malawi[e]	41	2.90	43
Mali[c]	43	1.97	32
Mauritius[d]	48	1.49	—[b]
Mozambique	10	1.90	81
Seychelles[e]	14	1.57	—[b]
South Africa	13	2.11	55
Zambia	34	2.14	38

[a] Stable party systems are in bold. In the case of Ghana, initial figures do not include the first elections, which four opposition parties boycotted. Figures in parentheses include the first election.
[b] Missing data.
[c] In 2006 the president of Mali did not belong to a party in Parliament.
[d] Because of the prevalence of coalitions, Mauritius has demonstrated a stable pattern of volatility for several decades now. It is therefore a special case, and I have included it with the stable, liberal democracies in the two by two table.
[e] These results differ from those of Lindberg and Bogaards in the cases of Malawi and Seychelles because I include all elections that occurred on or before 2009 on the assumption that the antecedents of any current trends began in an earlier period. In Malawi, which was already trending fluid by 2004, a new party formed and won a majority of the vote in 2009 producing a seat volatility over three elections of 41 percent. As a result, I classified Malawi as fluid. Seychelles looked like a fluid system in 2002 because a new opposition party gained seats. However, seat share has been stable through 2007 producing a relatively low score of 14 percent. These characterizations are consistent with Lindberg's observation that stability and fluidity represent a continuum; they are not dichotomous.
Source: Author's compilation of volatility scores based on Pedersen', "On Measuring Party System Change," the African Elections Database, accessed 2/9/2010, http://africanelections.tripod.com/; and election results from selected African countries. ENPP was calculated based on the Laakso-Taagapera Index using the spreadsheet supplied by Michael Gallagher, Indices.xls, accessed 5/25/2011, http://www.tcd.ie/Political_Science/staff/michael_gallagher/ElSystems/Docts/IndicesCalc.pdf. Party loyalty compiled from Afrobarometer Barometer Survey Findings, Round 3 Surveys for selected countries. See Appendix 3 for election dates.

respondents in Ghana answered that they felt close to a political party, and nearly the same number said they were close to either the National Democratic Congress (NDC) or the New Patriotic Party (NPP).[65] In Cape Verde, only

http://www.afrobarometer.org. The explanation for the disproportionately high number of respondents who favored Frelimo may have been because they thought that surveyors were from the government. Bob Mattes, personal communication, September 2008.
[65] Afrobarometer Survey Findings, "Summary of Results: Round Three, Afrobarometer Survey in Ghana, 2005," Compiled by Edem Selormey, Joseph Asunka, and Daniel Armah-Attoh, Afrobarometer Survey, Round 3, 2005, accessed 11/29/2007, http://www.afrobarometer.org.

52 percent of respondents identified with a political party, but the loyalties of most of them clustered heavily around two parties, the Movement for Democracy (MPD) and the African Party for the Independence of Cape Verde (PAICV).[66] The pattern suggests that although parties are relatively stable in Cape Verde, party identity is weaker than in other African democracies with stable party systems.

Combined with the observations on seat volatility and partisan loyalty, stable party systems also have fewer effective numbers of parties in the legislature than fragmented systems. Most stable party systems have nearly two effective parties in the legislature though they rarely average above two, with the exception of South Africa. Of the six cases considered here, Seychelles and Mauritius have the lowest ENPP at 1.57 and 1.49, respectively. In the case of the Seychelles, the ruling Seychelles People's Progressive Front (SPPF) dominated politics until the 2002 election when a new opposition party, the Seychelles National Party (SNP), began to make inroads into the ruling party's majority, capturing a third of the seats in both the 2002 and 2007 elections. Interestingly, in the Mauritian case, even though the presence of coalitions contributes to high seat volatility since each party's share of the vote is counted separately, it is also responsible for an extremely low average number of effective parties at 1.49.[67] Such a low score indicates that parties are forming maximum, rather than minimum, winning coalitions in order to gain power – a puzzle that goes beyond the scope of this work but that is nevertheless interesting.

By contrast, seat volatility and the ENPP tend to be higher in fluid party systems, whereas voter closeness to the top two parties is lower. The average net shift in seats in Mali, Zambia, and Malawi was 43, 34, and 41 percent even though they became democratic nearly twenty years ago. In Zambia and Malawi, the ENPP was higher than 2, whereas in Mali the ENPP was higher than 2 in two out of four elections.[68] As Appendix 3 indicates, the ENPP also shows volatility over time, which is another contrast with stable party systems.

---

[66] Afrobarometer Survey Findings, "The Quality of Democracy and Governance in Cape Verde," 2005, Accessed 11/29/07, http://www.afrobarometer.org and Afrobarometer Survey Findings, "Summary of Results: Round Four, Afrobarometer Survey in Cape Verde, 2008," Compiled by Afro-Sondagem and Michigan State University, Round 4, 2008, accessed 7/21/2010. The original figure for Cape Verde of 97% for party closeness suggests that they calculated the percentage of voters who were loyal to particular parties from those who answered yes. This is supported by the findings in Round 4 where 63 percent of respondents in Cape Verde said they felt close to a party and 55 percent of respondents said they were close to either the PAICV or the MPD. I recalculated the figure for consistency with the other cases.

[67] Coalitions in the legislature are counted as one party for calculation of the ENPP.

[68] The design of institutional arrangements for party participation and the allocation of seats in many African countries reduces ENPP as compared with Europe, see Matthijs Bogaards, "Electoral Systems, Party Systems, and Ethnicity in Africa" in Matthias Basedau, Gero Erdmann and Andreas Mehler, eds., *Votes, Money and Violence: Political Parties and Elections in Sub-Saharan Africa* (Uppsala: Nordiska Afrikainstitutet and Scottsville: University of Kwazulu-Natal, 2007), 168–193.

In Mali, the ENPP more than doubled between the 1997 election and the 2002 election as new coalitions formed, existing parties gained seats, and new parties won seats in parliament. In the 2007 elections in Mali, the ENPP was reduced owing to the formation of new, larger coalitions that contested those elections, but volatility and party fragmentation continued to characterize the party system. The ENPP scores for Malawi and Zambia also reflect their higher seat volatility. Because voters distribute their votes among multiple parties, the ENPP remains greater than 2.

Feeling close to a party also varies in fragmented party systems. As the data on party closeness indicate, either the percentage of respondents who felt close to parties was low (as in Zambia) or respondents felt close to many parties as in the case of Mali. Respondents in Zambia split nearly evenly on the question of party closeness in 2005. A little less than half of those surveyed did not feel close to any particular party. For respondents in urban areas, the percentage increased to 56 percent who did not feel close to any party. Moreover, only 38 percent of respondents in Zambia felt close to one of the top two parties.[69] These findings indicate that voters did not have strong attachments to political parties in Zambia.

A majority of respondents in Mali and Malawi stated that they felt close to a political party just as those voters in stable party systems did. In Mali, 61 percent of respondents in 2005 and 69 percent in 2008 felt close to a party suggesting that voters were beginning to have more fixed party identities. However, party identities clustered around five or six parties in 2005 and 2008. When respondents in Mali were asked what parties they felt close to in 2005, the top two parties only received 32 percent of responses, whereas six parties reflected the summed opinions of a majority of respondents. This pattern was more or less replicated in 2008. Although the percentage of respondents who were close to parties had climbed to 69 percent, a majority expressed closeness to as many as five parties.[70]

In Malawi, around 61 percent of respondents to the 2005 Afrobarometer survey felt close to a political party, a figure that at first glance seems respectable. It is better than that of Cape Verde at 52 percent, comparable to Mali, and slightly lower than South Africa at 64 percent. Yet, a majority of respondents were close to three parties: notably, 21 percent of respondents felt close to a party that had just formed prior to the survey.[71] By 2008, a majority felt close

---

[69] Afrobarometer Survey Findings, "Summary of Results: Round Three Afrobarometer Survey in Zambia, 2005," Compiled by Peter Lolojih, Afrobarometer Survey, Round 3, 2005, questions 85 and 86, accessed 7/21/2010, http://www.afrobarometer.org.

[70] Afrobarometer Survey Findings, "Summary of Results: Round Three, Afrobarometer Survey in Mali, 2005," Compiled by Michigan State University, Round 3, 2005, accessed 11/29/2007, http://www.afrobarometer.org and Afrobarometer Survey Findings, "Summary of Results: Round Three, Afrobarometer Survey in Mali, 2008," Compiled by Michigan State University, Afrobarometer Survey, Round 3, 2008, accessed 7/21/2010, http://www.afrobarometer.org.

[71] Afrobarometer Survey Findings, "Summary of Results: Round Three, Afrobarometer Survey in Malawi, 2005," Compiled by Stanley Khaila and Catherine Mthinda, Round 3, 2005, accessed

to two parties, the Democratic Progressive Party (DPP), which formed in 2004 (48 percent felt close) and the United Democratic Front (UDF) (9 percent felt close).[72] Feeling close translated into a victory for the DPP, which captured a majority of parliamentary seats in the 2009 elections. The UDF was less fortunate: It captured only 17 out of 192 seats, less than the Malawi Congress Party and a group of Independents.

As the indicators suggest, loyalties to multiple parties and shifting party identities tend to translate into greater volatility at election time and a higher ENPP in fragmented than in stable party systems. Because there are so many parties, voters have difficulty distinguishing among them and holding them accountable. Instead of acting as vehicles for organizing voters around a set of core, substantive issues, parties in fragmented systems are the means by which elites mobilize voters in order to contest elections. So-called big men in these countries employ patronage to stitch together coalitions of support based on particularistic interests. Typically, these coalitions collapse when the leader departs or when there are no more favors to dispense.[73] As a Kenyan politician quipped, "Parties are like matatus...when one matatu leaves you, you simply jump into another."[74]

Parties and Economic Transformation

Most of these countries have been democratic for less than twenty years. Their party systems continue to fluctuate. Nevertheless, it is still possible to trace how differences in the logic of party competition might influence uses of discretion or conformity with the rules by newly democratic governments that are undergoing economic reform.[75] Although fragmentation may signal competitiveness, it usually results in divided, weak governments.[76] In these systems, policy making and implementation reflect the uncertainty and the ceaseless bargaining that characterizes party politics. These governments are often unable to resist the pressures of the World Bank for reform, but they also

7/21/2010, http://www.afrobarometer.org and Afrobarometer Survey Findings, "Summary of Results: Round Three, Afrobarometer Survey in South Africa, 2006," compiled by Citizen Surveys and Institute for Democracy in South Africa, Afrobarometer Survey, Round 3, 2006, accessed 7/21/2010, http://www.afrobarometer.org.

[72] Afrobarometer Survey Findings, "Summary of Results: Malawi, Round Four, Afrobarometer Survey, 2008," Maxton Tsoka and Blessings Chinsinga, Afrobarometer survey, Round 4, 2008, questions 85 and 86, accessed 7/21/2010, http://www.afrobarometer.org.

[73] Randall and Svåsand, "Political Parties and Democratic Consolidation," 37–46; Carrie Manning, "Assessing African Party Systems," 721–724.

[74] George Ogola, "Kenya: 'Matatu' Hopping Culture of Politics," *Business Daily* (Nairobi) 9/20/2007. allAfrica.com, accessed on 9/30/2010, http://allafrica.com/stories/200709201140.html.

[75] Coppedge, "Political Darwinism," 173–205, discusses general characteristics of fluid and solid party systems in Latin America, and I draw on his analysis here.

[76] Christopher Fomunyoh, "Francophone Africa in Flux: Democratization in Fits and Starts," *Journal of Democracy*, 12, 3 (2001): 37–50.

fail to sustain policies consistently. "Unfettered by party platforms, they make policy choices that tend to be short-term and erratic,"[77] note Mainwaring and Scully with reference to such parties in Latin America. The observation also applies to fragmented systems in Africa, where policies often lack coherence and those that are implemented may be subject to policy drift.[78] For example, in Zambia, critics have referred to the "ambiguity" of government policy with respect to the sale of the Zambia National Commercial Bank after 2001.[79] In Malawi, host to another fragmented party system, analysts observed that the government quit referring to privatization in public after the 2004 election produced divided government.[80]

Distracted by party switching and internal feuds, governments in fragmented systems often neglect or delay needed reforms. Because avenues of institutional access get jammed up with requests from interested stakeholders, the status quo may prevail, even though there may be broad agreement that reforms are necessary. In Mali, for example, factionalization, unrest, and an election boycott by opposition parties were responsible for the slow progress of privatization in the mid 1990s.[81] Despite enormous pressure from the World Bank, privatization of the cotton sector in Mali was also postponed until after the 2007 reelection of President Touré, an election in which he ran under no single party banner.[82]

In Malawi, the formation of the Privatisation Commission in 1996 included representatives from three political parties as ex officio members.[83] The incorporation of opposition party members into the organization responsible for economic transformation in Malawi mirrored the three way split amongst the parties in Congress and clearly reflected the balance of power in Malawi, but also it contributed to numerous delays in the privatization process. As party fragmentation increased after 1999, privatization was suspended on several occasions.[84] Under such circumstances, uses of discretion during the privatization process assume an erratic character because ruling parties are uncertain

---

[77] Mainwaring and Scully, "Introduction," 25.
[78] Isaline Bergamaschi, "Mali: Patterns and Limits of Donor-Driven Ownership" in Lindsay Whitfield, ed., *The Politics of Aid: African Strategies for Dealing with Donors* (Oxford: Oxford University Press, 2009), 217–245 and on Zambia, see Chapter 4.
[79] Alistair Fraser, "Zambia: Back to the Future?" in Lindsay Whitfield, ed., *The Politics of Aid: African Strategies for Dealing with Donors* (Oxford: Oxford University Press, 2009), 313.
[80] Bertelsmann Transformation Index (BTI), "Malawi Country Report." BTI 2006: 9, accessed 7/9/2010, http://bti2006.bertelsmann-transformation-index.de/fileadmin/pdf/en/2006/Eastern AndSouthernAfrica/Malawi.pdf.
[81] Shantayanan Devarajan, "Mali" in Shantayanan Devarajan, David Dollar, Torgny Holmgren, eds., *Aid and Reform in Africa* (Washington, D.C.: World Bank, 2001), 227–286.
[82] Bergamaschi, "Mali," 221.
[83] Malawi, Privatisation Commission, "Commissioners, 1996–2001." Accessed 11/11/2006. http://www.privatisationmalawi.org.
[84] BTI, "Malawi," 9.

how the opposition will respond to policies or what the consequences of a conflict with opposition parties and their supporters will be.

Drawing on an analysis of personnel spending by provincial governments in Argentina, Karen Remmer has argued that governments are more likely to increase patronage spending when their base is weak.[85] The claim captures well the uses to which ruling parties have directed the privatization process in Africa's fragmented party systems. Governments have depended on parastatal sales to cultivate allies or placate enemies, which has affected the outcome. For example, frequent interventions by President Chiluba in Zambia's privatization process in order to allocate patronage to potential supporters not only undercut the credibility of privatization in Zambia but also contributed to the sales of valuable assets at prices that were much lower than the government might have gotten had the process been more transparent.[86]

Equally, vulnerable presidents may rely on sales of SOEs or other sources of patronage as useful tools to build alliances with key power brokers. In exchange for a flour mill or tourist complex, power brokers promise loyalty to the party or the voters of their districts. Electoral support may be purchased from rural or urban constituencies through promises of land or housing or fiscal transfers to key political players as was the case in Malawi prior to the 2004 election. However, the use of patronage to retain members may be ineffective. In a fragmented system, if those powerbrokers who benefitted from government patronage perceive that the ruling party or the president is vulnerable (as they did when Chiluba and Muluzi tried and failed to gain third terms in Zambia and Malawi, respectively), they may look for better arrangements from other parties. Voters may follow suit.[87]

The frequent appearance and disappearance of vanity parties built around popular leaders also means that the opposition tends to be weaker, less experienced, and more disorganized in fluid systems.[88] Under these conditions, opposition parties are less able to exercise systematic oversight of government policy or to provide a viable and consistent policy alternative to the government of the day. Indeed, the opposition itself is susceptible to poaching by the government if the offers are attractive enough. Mali's "consensus" government after 2002 exemplifies the difficulties with trying to create a unified and legitimate opposition in the face of a government that relies on patronage to create a viable base.[89] In Malawi, too, one commentator noted that

[85] Karen Remmer, "The Political Economy of Patronage: Expenditure Patterns in the Argentine Provinces, 1983–2003," *The Journal of Politics*, 69, 2 (2007): 363–377.

[86] For more details, see Chapter 4.

[87] BTI, "Malawi," 4–6 and see Chapter 4 on Zambia.

[88] Rakner and van de Walle, "Democratization by Elections?" Although they do not use the terminology, most of the examples they use to support their claims about opposition parties are drawn from cases that I code as fragmented party systems.

[89] Bergamaschi, "Mali."

The new government has to struggle for a new power base recruited from the members of parliament from the opposition parties who will expect to be rewarded for their support. To obtain a new power base usually becomes costly due to the expected patronage and/or the opportunity for enrichment.[90]

Yet not all party systems follow this logic. Mozambique, South Africa, Cape Verde, Ghana, Seychelles, and Mauritius have more stable party systems. Parties in several of these countries originated in national liberation movements, and they have retained a solid base of supporters in the postliberation period. In Mauritius, the party system and the shifting pattern of coalitional politics associated with it since independence over forty years ago have become institutionalized.[91] To be sure, just as in fragmented systems, there are ephemeral parties that rise and decline at each election. Politicians in stable systems also "cross the carpet": They resign from one party to join another that they think will exercise more influence.[92] In contrast to fragmented systems, however, parties in stable systems have a greater tendency to survive over time. Ruling as well as opposition parties are more skilled at maintaining discipline and aggregating interests within their parties. Within ruling parties, there is better coordination among branches of government and between the party and the state. The policy process is more certain.

In cases where parties have won an absolute majority in at least three, consecutive, multiparty legislative and presidential elections (which other scholars classify as dominant or predominant parties), the political system tends to be characterized by an increase in centralization and a decline in tolerance. Former liberation movements such as the ANC and Frelimo tend to treat opposition parties as enemies much as they treated their opponents during the period of struggle. These historical experiences help to explain their current behavior toward opposition parties.[93] Moreover, parties such as the Seychelles Progressive People's Front, the PAICV in Cape Verde, and Frelimo in Mozambique were ruling parties during the era of the interventionist, one-party state and that history influences their leadership style.[94]

The democratic context in which parties operate can constrain or facilitate the expression of authoritarian tendencies by ruling parties. In liberal as

[90] BTI, "Malawi," 12.

[91] Raymond Suttner, "Transformation of Political Parties in Africa Today," *Transformation: Critical Perspectives on Southern Africa*, 55 (2004): 1–27; Randall and Svåsand, "Political Parties and Democratic Consolidation," 36–37; Sara Dorman, "Post-Liberation Politics in Africa: Examining the Political Legacy of Struggle," *Third World Quarterly*, 27, 6 (2006): 1085–1101. The necessity of forming coalitions to win elections in Mauritius mitigates some of these characteristics of stable parties.

[92] Stevens Ahiawordor, "Issues and Dilemmas in Ghana's 2000 Elections" in Joseph Ayee, ed., *Deepening Democracy in Ghana: Politics of the 2000 Elections*, Vol. 1 (Accra: Freedom Publications, 2001), 116.

[93] Dorman, "Post-Liberation Politics," 1092.

[94] Heritage Foundation, "Seychelles," *2010 Index of Economic Freedom* (2010), accessed 8/1/2010, http://www.heritage.org/index/pdf/2010/countries/seychelles.pdf.

well as limited democracies, ruling parties seek to retain power through the provision of club goods to loyalists, ideological and interest-based appeals, the strategic deployment of organizational capabilities, and the generous allocation of financial resources. Alternatively, ruling parties in limited democracies such as Ghana, the Seychelles, and Mozambique have resorted to intimidation, outright coercion, or electoral fraud in order to stay in office.[95] They have been adept at manipulating rules and electoral agendas in their favor, running sophisticated campaigns, and delivering well-timed public goods. For example, just before the 2004 elections, the Guebuza government abolished primary school fees in Mozambique.[96] Guebuza won handily.

The opposition in stable party systems tends to have a more programmatic agenda, to be more experienced, and to engage in more sustained criticism of ruling party policy than in fragmented systems. These features are further enhanced if the opposition has been in power as has been the case in Ghana and Cape Verde.[97] As with ruling parties in stable systems, opposition parties generally have an identifiable base, and they more consistently articulate the interests of that base than do opposition parties in fragmented systems. Ethnoregional identities partially explain loyalty to different parties as they do in fragmented systems, but other factors also contribute to observable divisions. Divergent "founding mythologies" may distinguish one party from another as is the case of the NDC and the NPP in Ghana, or differences may be ideological as they are with respect to the Democratic Alliance (DA), the Inkatha Freedom Party (IFP), and the ANC in South Africa.[98] Alternatively, they may stem from lengthy and violent power struggles as is the case between Renamo (Mozambique National Resistance) and Frelimo in Mozambique. Although it is important not to exaggerate the power of opposition parties, these characteristics strengthen their ability to challenge the negative effects of privatization or to lobby for economic policies that will benefit their supporters.

Where ruling parties in these countries made very high or high commitments to privatize, they tried to design and implement institutions that benefitted key constituencies or that mitigated the worst effects of privatization for elements of their base. Sometimes parties anticipated how their base would be affected

[95] Heritage Foundation, "Seychelles," 372, and see Chapters 5 and 6.
[96] World Bank, "Moçambique Análise de Pobreza e Impacto Social Admissão e Retenção no Ensino Primário – o Impacto das Propinas Escolares," Relatório N° 29423-MZ (January 31, 2005), xv.
[97] Lindsay Whitfield, "Ghana since 1993. A Successful Democratic Experiment?" in Abdul Raufu Mustapha and Lindsay Whitfield, eds., *Turning Points in African Democracy* (Rochester: James Currey, 2009), 64 and for Cape Verde, see Inter-Parliamentary Union, "Cape Verde: Assembleia Nacional," Parline database, accessed 8/1/2010, http://www.ipu.org/parline/reports/2057_E.htm.
[98] Lindsay Whitfield, "Change for a Better Ghana: Party Competition, Institutionalization and Alternation in Ghana's 2008 Elections," *African Affairs*, 108, 433 (2009): 630; for South Africa, see Chapter 6. Even in these cases, ideological divisions around economic policies are not great.

and built protections into the design of the arrangements as in the case of Frelimo. In the case of the ANC, a sustained challenge from the base of the party drove the leadership to compromise on key aspects of the policy. How ruling and opposition parties in stable systems respond to a conflict arising from privatization or how they cater to a group that has a stake in the privatization process also varies from those in fragmented systems. Because the base of support in stable systems is more constant, policy agendas are more consistent over time, and the reaction of parties to the distributional impact of privatization is more predictable.[99] Ruling parties tend to ignore pressures from constituencies that do not support them and to reward individuals or party networks for their loyalty. Their greater organizational skills and more stable base also enable them better to withstand pressures from the World Bank and the IMF. This latter issue will be further illustrated in Chapter 5 on Mozambique.

During the process of privatization, ruling parties in stable systems can be expected to deliver club goods to particular voting blocs, not simply because they want their vote, but also because they share the principles of that group and are sympathetic to their appeals. Those individuals who benefit from privatization almost certainly do so because they have served the party well over the course of many years. This kind of clientelism is more positional than it is personalistic. Those individuals who benefit from it are not simply friends and relatives of high government officials; rather, they have demonstrated their loyalty to the party in numerous instances. A reliance on clientelism to manage the effects of privatization in stable systems is likely to blur the line between state and party over time, however. Where other institutions of the democratic process are weak, privatization programs in these countries may be manipulated to serve the partisan interests of the ruling party.[100]

Empirical Illustration of the Argument

Having traced how differences in party politics and democratic quality independently affect policy formation and outcomes, we are now in a position to present the argument in its entirety. Here I explore briefly the ways in which the two variables interact with institutional arrangements to determine privatization trajectories before turning to case studies of Zambia, Mozambique, and South Africa in later chapters. The quality of democracy affects how coalitions will mobilize and how the state will respond to their actions. It influences how privatization is formulated and implemented, in short, who will be able to exercise "veto power" and how many constituents will be able to exercise agency. Equally, political party formation sheds light on how the ruling party

---

[99] The general theory here is informed by Coppedge, "Political Darwinism," 173–205 and supported by empirical findings on the cases mentioned.

[100] This pattern will be demonstrated in Chapters 5 and 6.

will deal with the consequences of privatization, for example, whether it will ignore or incorporate the demands of those interests harmed by privatization. Further, it affects how the opposition will respond and what mechanisms the opposition will use to express its policy objections.

For heuristic purposes, I identified in the preceding matrix four possible uses of discretionary authority by the state resulting from the interaction of differences in the quality of democracy and in the character of the party system. These uses hold under conditions where governments adopted those rules consistent with the creation of a private sector economy. Since no country in the group of nine occupies the category where there is a liberal regime and a fluid party system, I shall exclude that one and focus on the other three quadrants. The patterns indicate the predominant type of discretion used; they are not meant to suggest that states do not resort to each of the three types throughout the privatization process.

Examining the category of a limited democracy and a fluid party system, the sample includes three cases of this type – Zambia, Malawi, and Mali. In a limited democracy, policy implementation occurs under conditions where transparency is reduced and accountability of the state is low. Manipulation of the policy arena by elites is common as is the tendency to censor the release of information that is unfavorable to the regime. Governing elites also restrict opportunities for open contestation by those who are affected by policy and resort instead to violence and intimidation to buy off or silence opponents.

Along with limited democracy, a fluid party system exists in this first quadrant. Parties lack institutional roots; and voter loyalty is divided among multiple, smaller parties. Parties do not have substantive ideological and policy positions with which voters or interests can identify. In such systems, splits and mergers among and within parties are common, and defections are frequent. Unstable support for the ruling party serves to delegitimize policy positions; intraparty factionalization and departures also produce divided government. In Zambia until 2011 and Malawi until 2004, for example, the party controlling the presidency did not change for twenty years and ten years, respectively, thereby suggesting a stable party system. Yet in both cases, the party of the president gradually lost its majority in parliament. Presidents presided over governments where their own parties did not have absolute majorities in the legislature and new parties captured a share of the vote.[101] In Malawi, the sitting president in 2005 decided to address the problem by founding his own party, the DPP. That new party was able to capture a majority of the seats in parliament in the 2009 elections, and President Mutharika was reelected for a second

---

[101] On Malawi's party configurations, see Peter VonDoepp, "Institutions, Resources, and Elite Strategies: Making Sense of Malawi's Democratic Trajectory" in L. Villalón and P. VonDoepp, eds. *The Fate of Africa's Democratic Experiments: Elites and Institutions* (Bloomington: Indiana University Press, 2005), 175–198 and Lise Rakner, Lars Svåsand, and Nixon Khembo, "Fissions and Fusions, Foes and Friends: Party System Restructuring in Malawi in the 2004 General Elections," *Comparative Political Studies*, 40, 9 (2007): 1112–1137.

term.[102] The question now is whether the DPP will survive as a party when Mutharika reaches the end of his constitutionally mandated two terms as head of government.

Since power is formally concentrated in the office of the presidency in many African countries, presidents in fragmented systems may use the power of office to build an independent base of support. Yet, because party loyalties are so ephemeral, presidents may be subject to the particularistic demands of rivals within their own and other parties, including members of parliament as well as appointed civil servants. A few comparative examples from Latin America serve as a template for similar patterns in Africa. Archer and Shugart highlight the extensive powers of the Colombian president during the 1980s to make most high-level appointments, to issue decrees, to control the fiscus, to veto legislation, and to declare states of emergency. These are powers that many African presidents also formally have been granted. But Archer and Shugart note that even though there was a legislatively mandated, two-party system in Colombia, the process of candidate selection was so decentralized and intra-party competition was so high that it produced members of parliament that were more loyal to the personalistic networks that put them in office than to the president.[103]

Mali, Malawi, and Zambia offer parallel examples. Because presidents in the 1990s and 2000s were uncertain about their base, they used their institutional and political leverage to bargain with individuals from their own parties and opposition parties in the legislature who threatened their power. In the case of Mali, the president refused to be in any party, and instead used his powers of appointment to fill positions in twenty-eight ministries with representatives from at least six parties.[104] Similar examples of what O'Dwyer calls "runaway statebuilding" were evident in Malawi and Zambia where the number of ministries was twenty-eight and twenty-one, respectively, in 2006. The size of ministries was high in comparison with the size of the population. By comparison, the government in South Africa had only twenty-seven ministries although the population there is much higher than those of Malawi and Zambia.[105]

With respect to those who are appointed to positions, party fragmentation in the context of a limited democracy may encourage a "lone ranger" approach

---

[102] For seats allocated by party in Malawi's National Assembly, see Web site, accessed 1/11/2010, http://www.parliament.gov.mw and Rakner et al., "Fissions and Fusions." On the elections, see South African Press Association, Associated Press, "Malawi vote gives president control of Parliament," *Mail and Guardian Online*, May 25, 2009, accessed 1/11/2010 http://www.mg.co.za/article/2009–05–25-malawi-vote-gives-president-control-of-parliament.

[103] Archer and Shugart, "The Unrealized Potential of Presidential Dominance."

[104] BTI, "Mali," 10.

[105] See O'Dwyer, *Runaway State Building*; figures are from BTI, "Malawi," "Zambia," http://bti2006.bertelsmann-transformation index.de/fileadmin/pdf/en/2006/EasternAndSouthernAfrica/Zambia.pdf and "South Africa," BTI 2006, accessed 7/18/2010, http://bti2006.bertelsmann-transformation-index.de/fileadmin/pdf/en/2006/EasternAndSouthernAfrica/SouthAfrica.pdf.

by civil servants, appointed ministers, and insiders in the remaining parastatals who use their positions to pursue short-term interests. Lacking a sense of loyalty to a particular party and not subject to oversight provided by the checks and balances of a more democratic country, "lone rangers" rent seek for their own personal benefit.[106]

Moreover, privatization becomes a useful weapon in the bargaining that occurs between presidents and their supporters or detractors. As presidents or a ruling party struggle vainly to curb defections or buy off opponents, they may offer state assets as patronage or bribes or stall the process altogether, hence the label ad hoc private sector development. For example, after adopting rules consistent with the creation of a private sector–driven economy, presidents in Zambia used their discretion to change or stall privatization to satisfy potential defectors from their own party who were critical of the policy's impact. In Zambia, both Presidents Chiluba and Mwanawasa, raided the privatization process, and used offers of land and private companies to poach opposition members, silence internal critics, or favor loyal insiders. They relied on extra-institutional means to interfere in the process in order to build new constituencies of support. In the face of widespread criticism, both presidents intervened to delay the privatization of the copper mines (President Chiluba) and to halt privatization of the electricity parastatal, ZESCO (President Mwanawasa) fearing a loss of electoral support. Although such responses may indicate that voters are holding the ruling party accountable, the handling of the sale of the copper mines in Zambia indicates that the results rarely worked to the benefit of voters nor were Zambian voters fooled by such tactics. The MMD's vote on the Copperbelt declined dramatically between 1991 and 2001.

Alternatively, governments may intervene to sever linkages between the private sector and an opposition party. In Malawi, legislation passed by the new government in the 1990s deprived the opposition Malawi Congress Party (MCP) of access to a major holding company created during the Banda era.[107] Since opposition party members are just as fragmented and self-interested as the ruling party in fluid party systems, they are susceptible to patronage and undermined by the more repressive tactics of governments. As such, they do not present a sustained critique of existing policy nor offer a meaningful alternative to voters.[108] As voters shop around for better representation or more favors at each election, volatility continues.

---

[106] This behavior is encouraged by high government turnover, see Chapter 4 on Zambia.

[107] VonDoepp, " Institutions, Resources," 181.

[108] This is a claim about general patterns and is not meant to suggest that there are no cases where parties are becoming more programmatic or more institutionalized. For example, the party system in Zambia has demonstrated greater stability in the last few years, an encouraging trend. See Nic Cheeseman and Marja Hinfelaar, "Parties, Platforms, and Political Mobilization: The Zambian Presidential Election of 2008," *African Affairs*, 109, 434 (2009): 75–76.

Finally, half-hearted populist appeals and policy drift on key aspects of reform are common in countries with fragmented party systems.[109] As the reintroduction of fertilizer subsidies in both Malawi and Zambia suggest, governments with weak bases and low party loyalty often resort to populism in the hope of gaining voter support at election time. Although both of these projects have brought benefits to small farmers, they have also been marked by delays, mismanagement, and corruption.[110]

In our lower left quadrant are countries that are also limited democracies but that have more stable party systems such as Mozambique, Ghana, and the Seychelles.[111] Like the cases in the first quadrant, the democratic quality of countries in this quadrant is poor. With few checks on their power, partisan supporters of ruling parties largely control institutional channels. As with the preceding cases, ruling parties in these three countries try to rely on the advantages of incumbency to monopolize resources such as access to the media, the use of state vehicles for campaigning, and their proximity to foreign and domestic businesspersons in order to influence voters at election time, while opposition parties fight over the remaining spoils. They also set the agenda, of which the privatization process was a significant component in the 1990s, and ignore or even repress those interests who do not constitute actual or potential bases of support.

In contrast to the fluidity and instability displayed by the previous cases, party identities are stronger and parties exhibit greater continuity from one election to the next. Parties have more identifiable bases of support, more independent sources of financing, and greater internal discipline. They have party headquarters in major cities and towns, and tend to adopt more substantive policy positions.

Over time, opposition parties in stable systems develop strategies to hold ruling parties accountable, such as serving on particular legislative committees, or attempting to offer a meaningful alternative to voters at election time by calling attention to the flaws of the ruling party.[112] In Mozambique and Ghana, the stability produced a more predictable pattern of negotiation among the parties and enabled the opposition to more consistently expose the weaknesses

---

[109] Mainwaring and Scully, "Introduction," 22–27.

[110] Ziggy Magombo, "Malawi's subsidised fertilizer smuggled and embezzled," *The Chronicle*, 7 February 2006 and Steen Jorgenson and Zlatina Loudjeva, "A Poverty and Social Impact Analysis of Three Reforms in Zambia: Land, Fertilizer, and Infrastructure," The World Bank, Social Analysis, Social Development Papers, no. 49 (January 2005).

[111] Although the opposition party that gained power in Ghana in 2000 appeared to have been formed only in 1996, I considered this a name change as the roots of this party are considerably older. Hence Ghana was classified as a stable party system. See Lindberg, "Institutionalization of Party Systems" and Minion Morrison, "Political Parties in Ghana through Four Republics: A Path to Democratic Consolidation," *Comparative Politics*, 36, 4 (2004): 421–442.

[112] See Chapter 5 on Mozambique for more information and Whitfield, "Change for a Better Ghana," 621–641.

and errors of the ruling party. In Ghana, a sustained effort by the opposition, the NPP, to challenge the ruling party eventually resulted in victory in 2000, which it was able to maintain in a subsequent election in 2004. With the return to power of the NDC in the 2008 elections where it captured the presidency and a slim majority in parliament, Ghana now appears to have institutionalized a two-party system and the alternation of those two parties in power.[113]

The change of the party in power in Ghana after 2000 initiated a trend toward a more liberal democracy in that country. Although a change of the party in power is not a priori sufficient to improve both Freedom House scores as Ghana's scores indicate; nevertheless, the improvement of its score for Political Rights after 2000 and for Civil Liberties after 2004 suggest that it was becoming a liberal democracy. Patterns of bargaining and negotiation between government and interested stakeholders by 2005 should therefore share similarities with those found in liberal democracies such as South Africa or Cape Verde.

Like Ghana, Mozambique has a stable party system. The two parties (who were previously combatants on the battlefield) and voters have become habituated to the rules of the game over the last decade and a half, and they largely conduct politics within those rules.[114] Unlike Ghana, however, where the stability of the party system also resulted in the development of a responsible opposition and alternation of the party in power, the same party has been reelected to the presidency and the legislature four times in Mozambique. Frelimo, the ruling party, controls both the executive and legislative branches of government. The opposition in Mozambique has so far been unable to constitute a viable alternative to Frelimo. Internal weaknesses partially explain its inability to attract voters but also the continuation of a more restricted democratic environment in Mozambique as opposed to Ghana helps to explain the challenges any opposition faces in exposing Frelimo practices or unseating them at the polls. When threatened, the government has resorted to ballot rigging, intimidation, secrecy, and abuse of funds to retain power, which helps to explain its classification as a limited democracy. This pattern is also found in the Seychelles, where the same party has retained control of the executive and legislative branches since the return to multiparty politics in 1993.

The combination of a limited democracy and a stable party system help to explain the course of privatization and state responses to the distributional conflicts that accompanied the process for countries in this quadrant. Owing to limited information on the Seychelles, I shall focus primarily on Ghana and Mozambique here. By the 1980s, economic crisis and, in the case

---

[113] Whitfield, "Change for a Better Ghana," 623.

[114] On elite habituation in Mozambique, see Carrie Manning, "Elite Habituation to Democracy in Mozambique: The View from Parliament, 1994–2000," *Journal of Commonwealth and Comparative Politics*, 40, 1 (2002): 61–80. On changing political risks in transitional countries, see Nancy Bermeo, "Sacrifice, Sequence, and Strength in Successful Dual Transitions: Lessons from Spain," *The Journal of Politics*, 56, 3 (1994): 619–621.

of Mozambique, a violent civil conflict had significantly eroded state power such that governments in Ghana and Mozambique approached international financial institutions for assistance. Although they implemented the prescriptions advocated by the IMF and the World Bank, ruling parties tried to fashion policies in ways that preserved and rebuilt their bases of power. In all three cases (including the Seychelles, which did not receive Fund support), the ruling parties who were in charge of economic reforms were the heirs of those parties or movements that had intervened into the economy in the 1970s and the 1980s. Consistent with their statist legacies, privatization was controlled from the top.

In Ghana and Mozambique, ruling parties consciously employed their discretionary authority either to avoid or to resolve distributional conflicts arising from privatization in a manner that would ensure party survival and protect loyalists, hence I term the outcome of the process partisan private sector development. Frelimo in Mozambique not only designed and implemented privatization in ways that preserved its traditional base of support from urban workers, worker/peasants in the south, and rural smallholders based in the north where the liberation movement began, but also it used the policy shift to transform itself into the party of capital after espousing socialism for nearly two decades. Policy continuity has marked the period since the country underwent the transition to a private sector–driven economy and to democracy, but it does not exist because institutional access has increased and constant bargaining among multiple veto players maintains the status quo as might occur in liberal democracies. Rather, the risks associated with a policy change as far reaching as privatization have declined because the base of support for the ruling party in this limited democracy has developed economic and political interests arising from the policy changes undertaken in the early 1990s.[115]

Beyond their longevity in power, high-ranking party loyalists in the party occupy key positions in finance, services, tourism, and commerce. Throughout the process, state officials repeatedly put together joint ventures that included either state participation or domestic investors who were party loyalists. In association with foreign capital, these groups have now branched out into new investments such as the Maputo Corridor, aluminum smelting, and shopping malls in Maputo. Each step of the way the state facilitated and sustained these new business ventures with accompanying legislation, loans, and advice. Furthermore, formal sector workers who historically have constituted the base of the party were spared some of the more deleterious consequences of privatization. Even though they lost many of the benefits they enjoyed during the socialist period, they continue to enjoy social protections and access to key state officials long ago dropped by other countries.[116] Where concessions to sustain

---

[115] See Chapter 5.

[116] M. Anne Pitcher, *Transforming Mozambique*, chapter 4 and Mozambique, *Boletim da Republica*, Serie III, selected years.

policy continuity and the flow of benefits to party supporters have not been possible, the ruling party has also sought to disable its critics as we indicated earlier. Low turnout in the 2004 and 2009 elections and recent protests over the rising cost of consumer goods have clearly unsettled the regime recently, but its near monopolization of political and economic power is undiminished.

In Ghana, the NDC faced a different but equally difficult task, which was to build a broad coalition based in the rural areas and to incorporate cross-cutting ethnic and class support into a party that previously had harassed and ridiculed business.[117] In that endeavor, privatization played a role in helping to create a new core of business people who were both loyal to, and dependent on, the NDC. As in Mozambique, NDC party loyalists served on the board of the Divestiture Implementation Committee (DIC), which was under the authority of the minister of finances. Although technocrats handled the day-to-day operations of DIC, political interference by the ruling party directed sales of state assets to loyal party members, while supporters of the opposition were systematically denied opportunities to participate in privatization. Moreover, when cocoa marketing was liberalized in the early 1990s, regime allies used their connections to NDC elites to receive the few licenses made available by the government to market cocoa beans. In turn, the company that they formed allegedly financed the party.[118]

Restructuring of other parastatals further illustrates that the NDC protected party loyalists during the process of privatization. Gyimah-Boadi notes that because the existing private sector had lukewarm relations with the NDC, the NDC tried to build a new domestic capitalist class that would be loyal to the ruling party. Beyond favoring NDC loyalists during the privatization process, the NDC either formed joint ventures between parastatals and the private sector or held onto key sectors staffed by NDC loyalists such as the media, the Ghana National Petroleum Corporation, and the Ghana National Procurement Agency so that it could control the privatization process for political and financial benefit. As Gyimah-Boadi observes, "The officials who manage these bodies know that their tenure depends on the NDC; they line up alongside the ruling party with varying degrees of openness, and some have served as top political advisors to the regime."[119] This fusion of the state, the party, and the market was not only a legacy of the previous period of state interventionism but also an effort to ensure political survival by safeguarding

---

[117] Eboe Hutchful, "The Fall and Rise of the State in Ghana" in Abdi Samatar and Ahmed Samatar, eds., *The African State: Reconsiderations* (Portsmouth: Heinemann, 2002), 120; Darko Opoku, "Political Dilemmas of Indigenous Capitalist Development in Ghana under the Provisional National Defence Council," *Africa Today*, 55, 2 (2008): 35–36.

[118] Darko Opoku, *The Politics of Government-Business Relations in Ghana, 1982–2008* (New York: Palgrave Macmillan, 2010), 147–148, 152–157; Lindsay Whitfield, "The Politics of Production: Challenges to Economic Transformation in Ghana," unpublished manuscript, May 2011.

[119] E. Gyimah-Boadi, "The Challenges Ahead," *Journal of Democracy*, 8, 2 (1997): 85–86.

access to resources. By relying on loyalists to straddle the public and private sectors, the NDC hoped successfully to navigate the transition to a private sector economy.

Just because their base is more identifiable, however, ruling parties in stable systems that are limited democracies are not immune to the negative effects of policy change. Economic choices can backfire politically, contributing to protests or even electoral loss. Because parties in stable party systems cultivate loyalty from particular ethno-regional or socioeconomic groups, they may lack the flexibility to adjust to the impact of distributional conflicts, even when those conflicts are not marked by sharp differences. In the Ghanaian case, for example, highly polarized differences regarding the implementation of privatization did not define the positions of the two major parties nor was it the cause of the NDC's loss in 2000. Rather, the perception by the public that the NDC had mismanaged the process of economic reform was a contributing factor in the defeat of the NDC.[120] In spite of economic growth during its tenure, ironically the NPP faced nearly identical charges regarding its mismanagement of the economy in the election campaign of 2008, which led to its defeat by the NDC.[121] The chief conclusion to be drawn from the process of privatization in these cases is that ruling parties in stable party systems that are limited democracies deliberately and consciously try to pursue strategies that will benefit their base of support in the hope that they will remain in power. The central characteristic of private sector development in such contexts is that it is highly partisan in nature.

Our last configuration consists of those countries in the quadrant categorized as liberal democracies with stable party systems. These countries are more likely to adhere to the rules they adopt. Like the previous set of countries, party identities and loyalties in these countries are more fixed. Parties have an administrative structure and access to resources, which helps them to sustain and build party membership and support. Opposition parties tend to survive in-between elections. Parties in power do change, as they did in Mauritius and Cape Verde, but they do so within a context of party system continuity.

In liberal democracies, moreover, there are institutional checks and balances that circumscribe the government's power, provide access to those who both disagree with and support policy changes, and allow interests to hold governments accountable for their actions.[122] With respect to privatization,

[120] Joseph Ayee, "The 2000 General Elections and Presidential Run-Off in Ghana" in Ayee, *Deepening Democracy in Ghana: Politics of the 2000 Election*, Vol. 1 (Accra: Freedom Publications, 2001), 42 and 52. These findings additionally support my decision not to focus on polarization as indicated in Chapter 1.

[121] Newsafrica, "Complacency and Corruption Cost the NPP," February 9, 2009, accessed 9/28/2010, http://www.modernghana.com/news/201881/1/complacency-and-corruption-cost-the-npp.html.

[122] BTI, "Mauritius," accessed 8/1/2010, http://bti2006.bertelsmann-transformation-index.de/fileadmin/pdf/en/2006/EasternAndSouthernAfrica/Mauritius.pdf.

the utilization of such channels by organized groups to challenge aspects with which they disagree or to encourage the government to continue the policy has resulted in compromise around particular aspects of the privatization process. Even in South Africa, where there has been no change of the party in power since the founding election, the government resorted to compromises because it faced pressure from partisan coalitions inside and outside of the party who used their institutional access to struggle over the policy. In Mauritius and Cape Verde, opposition parties together with other sources of pressure have forced compromises or adjusted policy when they got into power. This is particularly evident in Mauritius where successive governments sustained the welfare system and only haltingly engaged in privatization despite extensive integration of the Mauritian economy into the larger global economy.[123]

The compromises account for the slow pace of privatization in both Mauritius and South Africa and its particular characteristics in each country. In South Africa, the privatization process reflected the ANC's preference for commercialization, restructuring, and the use of black economic empowerment legislation over sales of parastatals to bolster the position of black South African investors and managers and to protect jobs in new and existing companies.[124] The explanation for the compromise stems from the polarized, but well-organized, factions that exist in South Africa's liberal democracy and their overlapping membership with the ruling party. Using multiple points of access to the government including personal contacts, the legislative and local branches of government, intraparty lobbying, popular mobilization, and the media, these interests sought to influence the government's policy choices. For example, efforts to privatize state companies or restructure local service delivery for water, electricity, and sanitation spawned intense distributional conflicts between supporters and opponents of privatization. In order to satisfy consumers and workers who form the base of the party, to promote black economic empowerment via managerial positions, and to concede to the power of the private sector, the government's preferred policy compromise was commercialization, that is, increasing efficiency or rationalizing production, rather than privatization. Governments in liberal democracies tend to rely on "contingent" uses of discretionary authority when confronted with the pushing and shoving of partisan players, in and outside of government. Although it deviates from the policy process, the discretion is "contingent" because it is situational and contextual. It does not signal that the government has abandoned the policy commitment in favor of the arbitrary use of discretionary powers.

---

[123] BTI, "Mauritius," 11–12.

[124] On the recently revised and strengthened legislation on affirmative action, see South Africa, Department of Trade and Industry, "The Broad-Based Black Economic Empowerment Act," 53 (2003), accessed 6/13/2007, http://www.dti.gov.za/bee/BEEAct-2003–2004.pdf and see Chapter 6.

Conclusion

Credible commitments to institutional arrangements designed to establish or extend fully private sector–driven economies in Africa have constrained uses of discretionary power by states, but they have not rendered inoperable the capacity of states to interfere in the economy. Uses of discretion in response to the contentious politics and distributive pressures that often accompany reform have typically assumed one of three types: opportunistic, partisan, or contingent uses of authority. The theory proposed in this chapter is that differences in the party system and in the quality of democracy explain why states employ different types of discretion and thus fall short of commitments that are fully credible in the imperative sense. These two factors not only influence the context in which distributional coalitions form and articulate their interests, but also they determine how the state will react to pressures to stall, modify, or distort the process.

Ultimately, the trade-off that the state makes between rules and discretion shapes the privatization process. Where motivational commitments have been high or very high, capricious uses of authority by governments that are limited democracies with weak party systems usually produce private sector development that is ad hoc in character. Here vulnerable presidents may rely on the transfer of parastatals to groups or individuals in exchange for political support or to prevent defection from the ruling party.

By contrast, governments in limited democracies with stable party systems are more partisan about the uses of their discretion. These governments practice patronage, and they display authoritarian impulses like governments in the first category, but they are also more deliberate in the pursuit of their goals. In these cases, they bring the organizational resources of the party and the instruments of the state to bear on the process in a systematic and conscious way in order to secure benefits for the base of the party through public–private partnerships, the provision of credit, and procurement contracts. In some cases, the political space provided by democracy brings opportunities for the opposition in stable party systems to challenge policies of the ruling party, but the likelihood is high that once in power, opposition parties will also seek to use the power of the state to benefit party loyalists. Over time, repeated intervention to protect and serve the ruling party produces a private sector characterized by the selective club or individual benefits it bestows on the party faithful.

Lastly, governments in liberal democracies with stable party systems may employ their discretion to change the rules, but such uses are typically contingent on the particular circumstances. The purpose is not to renege on the policy but to maintain stability and credibility in the eyes of an engaged and critical public. In these cases, multiple channels of access afforded by liberal democracy provide opportunities for diverse, organized interests to constrain the power of government but also to establish formal relationships with government to express their views. In general, contingent uses of authority produce strategic compromises without derailing reforms. In the following chapters, I illustrate these patterns by exploring the cases of Zambia, Mozambique, and South Africa in greater depth.

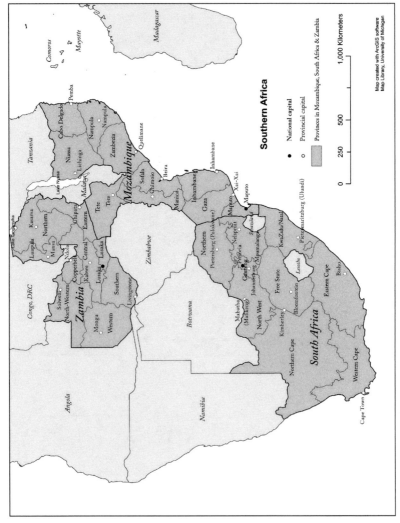

Note: The map reflects place names as of 2007. Since that date, several names of cities, particularly in South Africa, have been changed.

Credit: Karl Longstreth, University of Michigan Library

MAP 2. Southern Africa.

4

Party Fragmentation and Ad Hoc Private Sector Development in a Limited Democracy

Zambia

Introduction

By the early 1990s, conditions in Zambia appeared highly favorable to the implementation of economic reforms. Previous efforts by the one-party state to address structural imbalances in the economy had failed.[1] Copper production, Zambia's greatest asset, had stagnated; by the late 1980s, even that sector's powerful trade union was calling for private sector investment to revitalize the mining industry.[2] Declining formal sector employment amidst rising prices for basic staples such as mealie-meal, left a majority of households struggling to meet their daily needs. Furthermore, by 1991, voters of Zambia had channeled their discontent into support for a new party, the Movement for Multiparty Democracy. The MMD was elected by a landslide when the country returned to multiparty elections after a hiatus of two decades. Notably, the election manifesto of the party pledged to adopt privatization once it assumed office. Donors responded to the new government's plans to transform the economy by increasing aid.[3]

Nearly fifteen years later, however, the implementation of institutional arrangements designed to foster a private sector–driven economy had brought mixed results. On the one hand, the Zambian government made a high motivational commitment to expand its private sector and the extent of this commitment was associated with the extent to which Zambia approximated a commitment that was credible in the imperative sense by 2005. The government sold firms, liberalized trade, passed legislation favorable to business, and

---

[1] Robert Bates and Paul Collier, "The Politics and Economics of Policy Reform in Zambia" in Bates and Krueger, eds., *Political and Economic Interactions*, 387–443.
[2] Neo Simutanyi, "The Politics of Structural Adjustment in Zambia," *Third World Quarterly*, 17, 4 (1996): 835–836.
[3] World Bank, World Development Indicators and Global Development Finance, World databank.

reformed the banking sector. On the other hand, owing to opportunistic actions by the ruling party, that commitment failed to be fully credible. Zambia's imperative commitment score of 24.5 is the median score of those countries analyzed in Chapter 2. Such results do not reflect well on a program that observers once labeled "one of the most successful in sub-Saharan Africa."[4]

To explain the abuse of discretionary authority, the chapter describes the government's implementation of privatization and the distributional conflicts that arose as a result of it. It details how and why these conflicts occurred, and the response to them by the Zambian government. It analyzes the ways in which a fragmented party system and the limited quality of democracy in Zambia encouraged opportunistic uses of discretionary authority by the ruling party, which in turn, affected the institutional development of the private sector. Its implementation was inconsistent, and its outcome was ad hoc. These dynamics influenced not only the results of economic change but also the course of state formation.

The Beneficiaries of Privatization in Zambia

Since coming to power in 1991, the ruling MMD government has overseen the transition of the Zambian economy from one dominated by parastatals to one driven by the private sector. Praised by international financial institutions for its commitment to private sector development, the government selected, valued, advertised, and sold a majority of its assets. Out of a portfolio of 282 companies, it divested around 260 companies by 2005.[5] Sales included businesses in almost every sector from manufacturing to tourism. The majority of firms (60 percent or around 156 companies) were sold to Zambians: Most of these were small companies. In addition, the government sold or gave away thousands of council houses and hundreds of small shops to local residents.

By contrast, purchases of state assets by foreigners accounted for the bulk of the revenue of nearly US$906 million received from sales. Joint ventures between foreigners and Zambians or foreigners and the state accounted for 83 percent of sales. Foreigners solely purchased 12 percent of the total value of assets sold, whereas Zambians accounted for the remaining 5 percent.[6] Of

---

[4] Bornwell Chikulo, "Corruption and Accumulation in Zambia" in Kempe Hope and Bornwell Chikulo, eds., *Corruption and Development in Africa: Lessons from Country-Case Studies* (New York: Palgrave, 2000), 168 and see also White and Bhatia, *Privatization in Africa*, 4.

[5] Stuart Cruickshank, Acting Chief Executive Officer, Zambia Privatisation Agency, Interview, 6/14/2005, Lusaka, Zambia and Zambia, Zambia Privatisation Agency, "Status Report as at 30th April, 2005," mimeo, 2005: 1. From 1998, this number excludes about fifty companies that were not under control of the ZPA. Most of the fifty companies were liquidations or companies returned to their former owners.

[6] World Bank, "Zambia Privatization Review: Facts, Assessment and Lessons." Report prepared at the request of the minister of finance and national planning, Zambia (December 5, 2002), 23 and see Robert Rolfe and Douglas Woodward, "Attracting Foreign Investment Through Privatization: The Zambian Experience," *Journal of African Business*, 5, 1 (2004): 12.

those foreigners who purchased existing parastatals (excluding the mining sector), the United Kingdom and South Africa topped the list, followed by India, China, the United States, and a few other African countries. Mostly via competitive tenders, South African investors purchased retail operations, tourist facilities, breweries, former dairy produce boards, and food and beverage companies. In addition, NLPI Limited, a holding company based in Mauritius, received the concession to run Zambia Railways. NLPI Limited included participation by Nedbank, Sanlam, and NLP of South Africa and it agreed to pay US$254 million in fixed concession fees over a twenty-year period.[7]

Companies from the United Kingdom and the Commonwealth Development Corporation (CDC), an investment company owned by the U.K. government under independent commercial management, invested in sugar, cement, mining, oil refining, soap making, and cotton ginning. Moreover, British companies and Zambians of Indian origin used preemptive rights and restitution to receive approximately twenty-eight firms in agriculture, milling, services, and fisheries.[8]

Amidst numerous administrative delays and charges of corruption, the government completed the privatization of the country's greatest asset, the copper mines in 2002. After breaking the parastatal into ten separate packages, the government sold a percentage of the mines at extremely low prices to foreign investors from Canada, South Africa, Great Britain, the United States, and Australia, among others. Development Agreements that were signed with each investor at a moment when world copper prices were low provided generous tax and royalty rates to companies.[9] Via a government-owned holding company, Zambia Consolidated Copper Mines-Investments Holdings (ZCCM-IH), the government retained shares from 10 to 20 percent in nine mining or mining-related companies. Proceeds from sales equalled about US$338.8 million in revenue, an amount that was insufficient to cover estimated liabilities of US$770 million.[10]

The government complemented the sales of parastatals by revising financial, land, and labor laws in order to create a regulatory environment more conducive to private sector growth. It undertook banking reforms to enable the sector to become more competitive and efficient. In 1994, it opened the Lusaka Stock Exchange. A decade later, many of the twenty-one companies it listed had been former parastatals and/or were largely foreign owned.[11] Furthermore,

[7] Zambia, "Status Report," and see http://www.nlpi.net (NLPI was originally in a consortium with Spoornet to manage the concession but Spoornet withdrew from the consortium in 2006).

[8] Zambia, "Status Report."

[9] Dan Haglund, "From Boom to Bust: Diversity and Regulation in Zambia's Privatized Copper Sector" in Alastair Fraser and Miles Larmer, eds., *Zambia, Mining, and Neoliberalism: Boom and Bust on the Globalized Copperbelt* (New York: Palgrave Macmillan, 2010), 93–95.

[10] See ZCCM Investments Holdings PLC, accessed 1/29/2009, http://www.zccm-ih.com.zm and World Bank, "Zambia Privatization Review," 17 and 21.

[11] Lusaka Stock Exchange, accessed 2/6/2009, http://www.luse.co.zm.

the government reduced import tariffs and export subsidies and established industrial free zones and export development zones so that investors and traders could benefit from trade and tariff incentives. It joined bilateral and multilateral trade organizations. The government also put mechanisms in place to encourage a formal dialogue between government and business.

The creation of the Zambia Investment Center facilitated foreign and domestic investment by providing information on projects, identifying sources of finance, locating suitable partners, and managing the process of purchase and sale on behalf of investors.[12] After averaging approximately US$140 million in foreign direct investment per year from 1990 to 2000, average FDI between 2004 and 2007 skyrocketed to around US$800 million per year owing to increased demand for copper from India and China. Consistent with the surge in demand for copper, most FDI occurred in the mining sector: Private investors opened new mines, introduced new technology, upgraded equipment or expanded operations. In addition, there were investments in cellular phone technology, tourism, gemstone mining, and retail outlets for consumer goods.[13]

The Distributional Consequences of Reform

Despite the high quantity of sales and the attraction of investors, privatization and associated reforms such as trade liberalization, the commercialization of utilities, and the introduction of cost recovery schemes negatively affected a broad swathe of the Zambian population. For nearly a decade, Zambia experienced stagflation, and most of the macroeconomic indicators did not meet expectations. Between 1991 and 2000, growth rates barely inched past 1 percent, whereas inflation rates averaged over 70 percent. In combination, these two factors undermined purchasing power, discouraged savings, and drove up interest rates. Owing to increases in demand followed by a rise in the price of copper, growth rates improved to an average of 5 percent per year between 2000 and 2006, and inflation rates dropped to around 21 percent per year.[14]

Privatization severely affected formal sector employment. By 1999, Zambia had about 4. 6 million people in the labor force of which only about half a million or about 10 percent were in the formal sector. This was a drop from 1992 where 17 percent of 3.3 million people in the labor force were in the formal sector.[15] By 2006, the official unemployment rate was 14 percent. Employment in the mining sector, declined from 56, 582 workers in 1991 to 22, 280 in 2000

---

[12] Jerome Mweetwa, Zambia Investment Centre, Interview, Lusaka, 6/13/2005.

[13] United Nations Conference on Trade and Development (UNCTAD), "Country Fact Sheet: Zambia," World Investment Report 2009, accessed 1/29/2010, http://www.unctad.org.

[14] World Bank, World Development Indicators and Global Development Finance, World databank.

[15] Austin Muneku, "Trade Union Membership and Profile in Zambia," ZCTU Economics and Research Department (December 2002), 10.

before climbing to 31,199 workers by 2006.[16] As a consequence of declines in formal sector employment, total trade union membership also dropped. At 60 percent, the unionization rate in Zambia was amongst the highest in Africa; nevertheless, the number of trade unionists decreased from about 380,000 members in the early 1980s to approximately 229,000 members by 2000 before rising to approximately 320,000 members in 2008.[17]

Poor economic results produced a broad political backlash against neo-liberal reforms by the mid-1990s. In the domestic business community, disappointment with the effects of reform extended from small Zambian manufacturers who could not compete with imports of Chinese textiles to indigenous investors who lacked low-interest financing at reasonable rates in order to expand or modernize their firms.[18] Disgruntled with the influx of foreign capital and foreign goods, negative protection, or high taxes, some Zambian businessmen abandoned the MMD: Either they joined other parties or formed their own. Opposition politicians assailed the lack of transparency, asset stripping, and plunder by the MMD government.[19] Trade union officials and workers criticized the loss of social services formerly provided by the state, increasing casualization of the labor force and rising unemployment. Consumers bemoaned rising prices for everyday staples. By the turn of the century, public opinion polls indicated that two out of three Zambians were against privatization and opposition party leaders were vigorously denouncing it.[20] Michael Sata, the leader of a new opposition party, campaigned explicitly on an antiprivatization (and anti-Chinese) platform and nearly unseated the ruling party in the 2006 elections. In addition to receiving votes from members of his own ethnic group, Sata's votes were drawn from the more urban areas of Lusaka and the Copperbelt, both of which were affected by job losses, casualization, and price increases.[21] Sata subsequently won the 2011 presidential election.

In a political context characterized by fragmented party politics and limited democracy, the government relied on opportunistic uses of discretionary authority to confront the distributional conflicts generated by privatization. By the eve

---

[16] Neo Simutanyi, "Copper Mining in Zambia: The Developmental Legacy of Privatization," South Africa Institute for Security Studies, Paper 165 (July 2008), 7.

[17] Muneku, "Trade Union Membership," 14; Steven Mumbi, Director of Organization and Trade Union Development, Zambia Congress of Trade Unions – Regional Office, Interview, Lusaka, 6/4/2008.

[18] David Simpson, "A Catalogue of Ills: Business People Outline their Problems to the World Bank," *Profit* (August 1995), 18–19; "Beating Business Constraints: Government comes up with the draft National Action Plan for Private Sector Support," *Profit* (July 1998), 26–27.

[19] David Simpson, "Do We Really Have a Democracy?" *Profit* (May 1995), 26–27.

[20] Bratton, Mattes, and Gyimah-Boadi, *Public Opinion,* 120 and Sheikh Chifuwe, "Privatization Will Be Over Zambians' Dead Bodies," *The Post (Lusaka)*, December 9, 2002.

[21] Zambia, Electoral Commission of Zambia, "General Elections 2006: Presidential-Constituency Result by Candidate," 2006, mimeo; and Nic Cheeseman and Marja Hinfelaar, "Parties, Platforms, and Political Mobilization: The Zambian Presidential Election of 2008," *African Affairs*, 109, 434 (2009): 71–75.

of the country's second elections in 1996, the ruling party had harnessed the objectives of privatization to the political exigencies of the ruling party. Officials bent and broke the rules in order to realize short-term gains and to deliver benefits to individuals or vested interests in exchange for electoral and legislative support. In some cases, sales of parastatals were withdrawn in response to public pressure or accelerated in accordance with donor demands. With regard to related reforms such as revision of land and labor laws, government behavior was erratic and contradictory. In one instance, the president used the considerable institutional power at his disposal to interfere personally in the sale of the copper mines during the late 1990s, capturing the reforms for his own benefit. By contrast, the government stubbornly maintained the status quo with respect to the 1995 land law in spite of broadly based criticism of the law's institutional ambiguity and its associated impact on land tenure security.

Just as opportunistic government interference affected the pace and substance of privatization, it also conditioned the character of the new private sector economy, hence the description of the outcome as ad hoc private sector development. In some instances, state firms were sold to party loyalists or potential political allies rather than to those who had expertise or capital. Where the government retained parastatals, they were used to finance the ruling party's political campaigns or plundered by corrupt managers and staff. In addition, efforts by business to cultivate a formal institutional relationship with the government were stymied by divisions and policy drift on issues of key importance to the business sector.

Explaining Reform Outcomes: Institutional Design, 1991–1996

Understanding how economic reforms interacted with party politics and the quality of democracy helps to explain why the shift to a private sector–driven economy in Zambia has been accompanied by repeated abuses of discretionary authority. Although the one-party state under Kenneth Kaunda made halting attempts to privatize SOEs during the 1980s, the Zambian government did not motivationally commit to privatization until 1991, when the MMD came to power after the country's return to multiparty elections. A heterogeneous coalition of labor, business, and academia, the MMD under the former trade union leader, Frederick Chiluba, incorporated privatization into its election manifesto, trumpeting it as a solution to the country's chronic economic malaise. Aided by the ambivalence of the trade union movement, pushed by donors, and motivated to purge UNIP supporters from parastatals, the ruling party decisively implemented the policy after victory.[22]

In its first five years, Zambia offered a textbook example of the World Bank's recommended procedures for the implementation of a successful

---

[22] Xinhua General Overseas News Service, "Top Executives of Zambian Parastatals Fired," 11/6/1991; and Zambia National Broadcasting Corporation, "Zambia Opposition Criticises Sacking of Parastatal Chiefs," 12/20/1991. Accessed 9/18/2006, http://www.LexisNexis.com

privatization policy. Both its institutional and organizational reforms illustrate why its motivational commitment score was high. It changed the constitution to allow for the protection of private property rights, passed a new land law that expanded leasehold tenure and provided for the granting of titles to individuals with the intent of creating a land market in Zambia (1995 Lands Act), and relaxed restrictions on foreign investment (Investment Act). By 1992, it had established the Zambian Privatisation Agency (ZPA), granting it statutory authority to undertake the privatization of SOEs. Notably among African countries, the Zambian government formally gave ZPA a great deal of independence to select, advertise, and process the sale of companies.[23]

The design of the ZPA on paper was consistent with the claims of a number of scholars in the early 1990s that to be effective, agencies needed to be insulated from political interference and staffed by technocrats. Even though the president had the power to appoint members of the agency, his appointments were subject to parliamentary oversight and approval. Moreover, the composition of the agency's board was broad based, and nongovernment representatives outnumbered government officials. In addition to three government officials, nine additional members of the board were from diverse sectors of civil society such as business, the trade unions, universities, and churches. Importantly, since voting members of the board only met once every two months, agency technical staff was subject to little oversight by politicians. Following the cabinet's authorization of those firms eligible for privatization, the ZPA was free to undertake privatization without further interference.[24] With regard to its activities and its actions, the ZPA submitted progress and annual reports to the minister of commerce, trade, and industry who was required to deposit the report with parliament within seven days of its next sitting.[25]

Despite a lack of experience, which delayed initial attempts to privatize the first tranche of between twelve and fourteen companies, ZPA moved systematically after its creation to dispose of parastatals. Unlike officials in other African countries, ZPA officials did not have to be convinced or threatened into privatizing parastatals. On the contrary, they were ideologically committed to the process and were not simply responding to World Bank conditionality, although, of course, Bank pressure was substantial. According to the former chief executive, James Matale,

We really thought privatization would deliver. We believed that with the injection of funds it would help create more employment. We had these objectives we wanted to meet. We thought that by the end, at least 60% would be doing better: investment and employment would increase because those had been the constraints under the previous system. So even though there was conditionality, we shared the views. We thought the goals were achievable.[26]

[23] Cruickshank, Interview; and Zambia, "Status Report," 1.
[24] Zambia, Privatisation Act, 1992 and Cruickshank, Interview.
[25] Ibid.
[26] James Matale, Former Chief Executive Officer, ZPA, Interview, Lusaka, 6/12/2008.

Matale observed that "By the third tranche of 12 to 14 companies, we started to catch on to how to privatize." According to Matale, the ZPA tried to conduct privatization "by the book." "We wanted to follow the rules and be professional."[27] With technical expertise and advice provided by the United Nations Development Program (UNDP), the World Bank, the U.S. Agency for International Development (USAID), Danida, and other donors, agency personnel valued assets, broadly advertised companies for sale, selected independent negotiating teams for each sale, and published quarterly status reports detailing particular transactions.[28] As its capacity for selling assets expanded, the pace of privatization increased.

Perhaps the most noteworthy feature of the period was not the quantity or pace of the sales, but the fact that the ZPA sold or attempted to sell a number of companies with sizable assets. With respect to these cases, disagreement between the ZPA and donors emerged over the timing of the sales. Whereas the ZPA preferred a more cautious approach owing to the high value of the assets, the Bank pushed for rapid sales. The Bank eventually triumphed.[29] Five large companies – Chilanga Cement, Zambia Breweries (broken into two companies), Zambia Sugar, and Metal Fabricators – with substantial assets and large workforces were the prizes in the sales or restitutions of assets that took place in this period. Aside from Metal Fabricators, whose sale was delayed on legal grounds, sales of the other four companies followed established guidelines and were done quickly. For the larger companies, ZPA recognized the exercise of preemptive rights by existing minority shareholders, and it also offered a percentage of company shares for purchase by the Zambian public on the newly created Lusaka stock exchange.[30]

Foreign companies took a controlling interest in many former parastatals. South African Breweries assumed control over both breweries in the country, creating a virtual monopoly in the Zambian beer industry, while the U.K.-based Tate and Lyle assumed a controlling interest in Zambia Sugar. Among other purchases, the CDC initially acquired 30 percent interest in Zambia Sugar through a debt equity swap. The CDC also underwrote the purchase of shares in Chilanga Cement, which was returned to a Zambia subsidiary of Anglo-American through the exercise of preemptive rights.[31]

As a result of these efforts, the ZPA soon gained a reputation among foreign investors, donors, and independent analysts for its methodical approach to

---

[27] ibid.
[28] Caleb Fundanga and Andrew Mwaba, "Privatization of Public Enterprises in Zambia: An Evaluation of the Policies, Procedures and Experiences," African Development Bank, Economic Research Papers no. 35 (1997), 8.
[29] Valentine Chitalu, "Quickly Now," *Profit* (April 1995): 22–24.
[30] Matale, interview.
[31] Zambia, ZPA, "Privatisation Transactions Summary Sheets 1992–2005," 2005, mimeo and see John Craig, "Privatization and Indigenous Ownership in Africa," *Annals of Public and Cooperative Economics*, 73, 4 (2002): 567.

TABLE 4.1. *Privatization of Parastatals in Zambia 1991–1995: Methods of Sale*

Competitive Sale of Shares Including Tenders	12
Competitive Sale of Assets	18
Direct Sale of Shares Including Private Placement and Negotiations	5
Public Flotation on Stock Exchange	1
Management Employee Buyout	16
Liquidation	14
Restitution/Return to Former Owner	11
Other	4
TOTAL	81

Source: Zambia, Zambia Privatisation Agency.

privatization. Zambia was singled out by an influential World Bank publication for its "appropriate legislation," "transparency," "adequate support by donors," "decisive action against constraints, and efforts to inform the public."[32] In concrete terms, the ZPA had sold, liquidated, or returned to their former owners about eighty-one SOEs out of a total of two hundred eighty-two firms between 1993 and 1995.[33] The total revenue expected from sales was over US$100 million, making Zambia one of only twelve countries in Africa whose sales revenue exceeded US$50 million.[34]

Yet textbook privatization also yielded serious economic and political consequences for the ruling party, which the 1996 landslide victory by the MMD initially obscured. Despite the ZPA's commitment to privatization, the kinds of firms that ZPA privatized in the first three years did not improve the economic situation for ordinary Zambians in the short term nor did they benefit Zambian business people. First, most of the companies that the ZPA sold were small and medium-sized companies. These companies were the easiest to dispose of, and they allowed the agency staff to gain experience with the privatization process. While such an approach was rational from a technical point of view, it did not produce immediate tangible benefits for ordinary Zambians or for the ruling party. As Table 4.1 indicates, just over half of the eighty-one companies that were sold were restitutions to former owners, management buyouts, or liquidations. Liquidations and restitutions brought in little revenue, whereas management buyouts were rarely paid for in full and performed poorly for the most part. These sales failed to contribute to economic growth, which was barely 1 percent in the 1990s, nor did Zambians see substantial increases in social spending as a result of the revenue generated from sales.

Second, 61,000 jobs were lost in the formal sector between 1991 and 2000; only after 2000 did a partial recovery of jobs occur. For example, the

---

[32] White and Bhatia, *Privatization in Africa*, 5.
[33] Zambia, "Status Report."
[34] White and Bhatia, *Privatization in Africa*, 71.

liquidation of United Bus Company and the Zambia Industrial and Mining Corporation (ZIMCO) resulted in a combined loss of 8,000 positions.[35] The continuing deterioration of the state sector in anticipation of privatization also contributed to unemployment and wages that were in arrears; a preference for casual labor by private sector firms further altered conditions of employment.[36] Moreover, the liquidation of Zambia Airways, which was a great source of national pride, reinforced the sentiment that economic policy changes were not benefiting Zambians.[37]

Third and related, job losses had a consequent negative impact on organized labor in Zambia, which had supported the MMD, especially in the economically important Copperbelt. Historically, Zambia has one of the highest rates of unionization among formal sector workers in Africa. However, as privatization proceeded during the 1990s, union membership declined owing to layoffs, increased casualization of the workforce, and the hostility of private owners to unionized workers. By 2000, union membership consisted of 250,000 members, a decrease of 130,000 members from the 1980s. The copper sector suffered a net loss of about 24,000 members over a ten-year period from 1991 to 2001.[38]

Fourth, although the sale of large companies to foreign investors brought high praise from the international financial institutions, the results of the textbook privatization approach reinforced cleavages within the business community in Zambia, which in turn, affected the MMD. Importantly, the early phases of the process did not produce a critical mass of Zambian capitalists who had benefited from privatization and who wholeheartedly endorsed the policy.[39] Sales of larger companies to foreigners fueled resentment. As several representatives of the business sector pointed out, Zambians had managerial expertise gained from running parastatals, but because they lacked capital and access to inexpensive credit, they were at a disadvantage in the privatization process.[40] Although there were approximately sixteen management buyouts

[35] Keith Somerville, "Limits of Patience?," *African Business*, no. 197 (March 1995), 20; World Bank, "Zambia Privatization Review," 18–19; and Kane Consult, University of Zambia Research Staff, Ness Associates and Participatory Assessment Group, "Post Privatization Impact Assessment Study," Zambia Privatisation Agency (ZPA) (May 31, 2005), ix, 48–50, 110.

[36] World Bank, "Zambia Privatization Review," 18–19.

[37] On the perceptions by civil society of privatization, see Kane Consult, "Post Privatization," 133–136.

[38] Zambia Congress of Trade Unions. *Zambia: Socio-Economic Issues and Unionization.* Global Policy Network: Zambia Congress of Trade Unions, 2001, accessed 1/3/2006, http://www.globalpolicynetwork.org.

[39] Craig, "Privatization and Indigenous Ownership in Africa," 568.

[40] Abel Mkandawire, previous chair of ZACCI quoted in Antoinette Handley, *Business and the State: Economic Policy-Making in the Neo-Liberal Era* (New York: Cambridge University Press, 2008), 226; Glenam Kasumpa, Management Information Officer, Zambia Business Forum, interview, Lusaka, 6/14/2005; Justin Chisulo, Chief Executive, Zambia Association of Chambers of Commerce and Industry (ZACCI), Interview, Lusaka, June 17, 2005.

(MBOs) by 1995, they were undercapitalized, and many did not survive long after privatization. Their use of the option to defer payments also meant that unlike those companies purchased by foreigners, MBOs did not generate substantial sales revenue for the government.[41]

All investors in Zambia in the mid-1990s faced challenges that are common in developing countries such as poor infrastructure, onerous taxes, antiquated legislation, and bureaucratic red tape. Indigenous investors confronted additional financial and administrative obstacles that hindered their ability to take advantage of privatization. The government established few financing mechanisms for them nor did it give them incentives to engage in joint ventures as governments did in Mozambique and South Africa. High interest rates (100 percent in 1994) and the reluctance by banks within the country to lend to local investors undercut their efforts to purchase existing firms or to establish new ones.[42] Furthermore, the government created a Privatisation Trust Fund to offer shares of companies listed on the Lusaka stock exchange to Zambian investors. But the fund established a minimum threshold for the quantity of shares to be purchased by each investor that was too high for most Zambians.[43]

Structural constraints on domestic investment coupled with the government's policy choices left foreigners in a better position to purchase larger, more viable firms. The resulting pattern of purchases and control then reinforced existing divisions by ethnicity, region, race, nationality, firm size, and sectoral interests within the business class, which in turn affected the composition of party politics in Zambia. The divisions within the business class were then mirrored in different demands the private sector began to place on the state. While indigenous Zambians argued for more favorable treatment and easier credit, foreigners lobbied for a more favorable tax regime and more attractive investment incentives. In the 1990s, businesses articulated these demands to government in diverse and uncoordinated ways – an issue I return to in subsequent sections. Some had one-on-one meetings with ministers, whereas others expressed their grievances within various sectoral organizations, each of which was individually weak.

These consequences arose in the other countries that are the subject of study. Nearly all countries in Africa were affected by the global spread of neo-liberal norms and practices by the 1990s. As they did in Zambia, donors in Mozambique exercised enormous influence on the design and process of economic policy making. And like Zambia, Mozambique saw rising unemployment in the formal sector and an increase in popular dissatisfaction resulting from sales of parastatals to the private sector. The South African government too experienced widespread consumer protests at the imposition

---

[41] Fundanga and Mwaba, "Privatization of Public Enterprises," 14.
[42] Cheryl Jones, "Did we liberalise too quickly?" *Profit* (November 1994), 15–16.
[43] Craig, "Privatisation and Indigenous Ownership in Africa," 566–568.

of tariffs on electricity and water following the creation of public private partnerships with private sector operators. Furthermore, in many countries, business was divided between small and large investors, locals and foreigners, trade and industry. Business interests were also split among a diverse array of organizations, each of which lacked the capacity and the clout to influence government.

What was different in the Zambian case was that the nature of the party system and the quality of its democracy interacted with the privatization process to produce opportunistic and undemocratic uses of discretion by the state. It was not simply that privatization produced *unintended* consequences that the government had to confront. Rather, the results of a privatization process that followed the recipe exacerbated growing factions and divisions in a party system where, unlike that of Mozambique or Ghana, for example, loyalties were fluid not fixed, and where changing parties became a common exit strategy for politicians and voters after 1991.

Furthermore, the president's response to the distributional conflicts arising from privatization reinforced the authoritarian pattern that the executive had already demonstrated with respect to other political and economic challenges faced by the regime. This preference for authoritarian solutions became glaringly apparent prior to the 1996 election when President Chiluba's main rival, Kenneth Kaunda, was disqualified from running on the grounds that he was not a Zambian citizen. In response, Kaunda's party, the United National Independence Party (UNIP), and five other parties boycotted the election and at least one donor-funded, democracy-building organization suspended its activities in protest. Under these conditions, President Chiluba easily won his bid for reelection, and the MMD retained its majority in the National Assembly (Zambia's national parliament).[44]

Explaining Reform Outcomes II: Party Politics and Limited Democracy

The response by the ruling party to the effects of privatization suggests that while privatization contributed to divisions within the MMD and the electorate, the causal arrow also pointed in the other direction. That is, party fragmentation and the quality of democracy in Zambia strongly influenced the implementation of privatization and associated neo-liberal reforms. A number of scholars have traced the ways in which democratic politics in Zambia affected the ability of actors such as business and labor to articulate their interests to government and when I discuss the quality of democracy, I shall return

[44] Lise Rakner and Lars Svåsand, "Stuck in Transition: Electoral Processes in Zambia, 1991–2001," *Democratization*, 12, 1 (2005): 86 and 93; National Democratic Institute, "Statement by NDI President Kenneth Womack on Suspension of Program Activities in Zambia," June 17, 1996, accessed 10/06/2010, http://www.accessdemocracy.org/files/869_zm_statement_061796.pdf; Zambia, Electoral Commission of Zambia, "Election Results Index."

TABLE 4.2. *Numbers of Parties and Independents Participating in Zambia's Parliamentary Elections, 1991–2006*

	Parties	Independents
1991	5	19
1996^a	11	93
2001	18	89
2006	15	158

^a UNIP and five other parties boycotted the 1996 elections.

Source: Zambia, Electoral Commission of Zambia, Election Results Index, Parliamentary Results, 1991–2006, accessed 1/11/2009, http://www.elections.org.zm

to the challenges faced by these stakeholders.[45] Yet, few scholars have examined extensively how the logic of party politics in Zambia shaped the government's responses to pressures arising from the transition to a market economy.

Party Politics

Following V.O. Key's classic framework, I explore three constituent elements of political parties that inform their nature and function: party organization, the party in the electorate, and the party as policymaker in government.[46] Taken together, the absolute number of parties and independents that participate in elections has grown steadily since Zambia's return to multiparty politics in 1991. As Table 4.2 shows, candidates from five parties and nineteen independents participated in the 1991 elections; by 2006, the total number of office seekers had grown to candidates representing fifteen parties and one hundred fifty-eight independents.

While the proliferation of parties and independents suggests that there was space within Zambia for political expression, it is difficult to see how the organization of these parties "facilitate[d] collective activity," in the sense that Key implies it.[47] Few of the parties had offices established throughout the country nearly a decade after the restoration of multiparty politics. Some did not conduct national campaigns nor have headquarters in the capital. Few had the

[45] David Bartlett, "Civil Society and Democracy: A Zambian Case Study," *Journal of Southern African Studies*, 26, 3 (2000): 429–446; Rakner, *Political and Economic Liberalisation*; Scott Taylor, *Business and the State in Southern Africa* (Boulder: Lynne Rienner, 2007); Antoinette Handley, *Business and the State*, 207–241.

[46] V.O. Key, *Politics, Parties and Pressure Groups*, 4th ed., New York: Thomas Crowell Company, 1958.

[47] Key, *Politics, Parties*, 345.

basic requirements of a functioning political party such as staff, equipment, and lists of current members. Many did not have an organizational presence at provincial, district, and local levels of state administration. In 2003, only four out of seventeen parties had an identifiable leader, at least 10 seats in parliament, and more than 125 parliamentary candidates and 750 candidates participating in local elections. Of these four, two were formed just prior to the 2001 national elections. Six parties had no identifiable leader and fielded no more than five parliamentary candidates in the 2001 elections.[48]

Apart from the ruling party, which relied on state resources to conduct campaigns and sustain party activities, many of the parties were organized around wealthy, charismatic leaders and depended on the financial largesse of their leaders to survive. For example, after its founding in 1998, the United Party for National Development (UPND) took advantage of generous financing from the two businessmen who served as leaders of the party, Anderson Mazoka and his successor, Hakainde Hachilema. As a result, the electorate identified this and parties like it with individuals, not with policy platforms or ideological orientation. The identification of parties with particular individuals reduced incentives to develop national party structures or to sustain party loyalty over time through the development of a programmatic agenda. Alternatively, "because the party leaders spend their personal money on party organization, they expect loyalty from lieutenants and subordinates," according to a study of parties in Zambia.[49] These practices reduced the likelihood that parties would gain national recognition, survive their leaders' departure, or outlast their defeat.

Another characteristic of party organization in Zambia was the lack of well-defined procedures for career advancement within the party or into political office. Even before the MMD got into office, local and provincial party leaders were manipulating appointments within that party to favor their own supporters and to build networks in order to advance their own interests in the party.[50] These maneuvers were not confined to the early formation of the MMD but were common to all parties in Zambia as late as 2003. The centralization of power by party leaders stifled the development of democratic processes for the selection of candidates for party and government offices. Instead, party leaders often hand-picked candidates for national and provincial level positions, on the basis of their personal connections or their professed loyalty to those above them.[51]

As such, party structures offered no real opportunity for providing the depth of political experience or inculcating the sense of loyalty offered by parties such

---

[48] National Democratic Institute (NDI) and the Foundation for Democratic Process (FODEP), "The State of Political Parties in Zambia – 2003: Final Report," Lusaka, Zambia (July 2003), 4, 14–16.

[49] Ibid., 14.

[50] Bartlett, "Civil Society and Democracy," 438–439.

[51] NDI and FODEP, "The State of Political Parties," 17.

as Frelimo and Renamo (until recently) in Mozambique, the NDC and the NPP in Ghana, or the ANC and the DA in South Africa. Instead, defections were common, and expulsions were frequent. Parties in Zambia were marked by a lack of discipline and an absence of loyalty stretching from the electorate to the party hierarchy. Appeals to ethnic loyalty played a part in splitting support among numerous parties,[52] but those instances where leaders have drawn on cross-regional and multiethnic support as Sata did in 2006 (and with success in 2011) suggest that causality also ran in the other direction. That is, in the presence of fragmented, chaotic parties, some voters fell back on ethnic cues to cast their votes. These cues, however, did not serve to link voters consistently to parties, and voters could not be counted on to sustain their parties either in or out of office.

Related to the centralization of leadership, poor organization, and the lack of loyalty, few attempts were made to cultivate a solid, consistent base of supporters through the development of distinct, coherent positions on key policy issues.[53] Notwithstanding the antiprivatization rhetoric espoused by several parties during the 2006 elections, party manifestos of nine political parties that attended a workshop on policy development in 2008 indicated that most parties including the ruling party, exhibited few policy differences on paper.[54] With the exception of UNIP, most party leaders preferred to rely on patronage rather than policy to attract supporters.[55] With few programmatic differences to distinguish them, most parties in Zambia had difficulty sustaining support.

As Zambia's ruling party from 1991 to 2011, the MMD enjoyed structural advantages that sustained it in power, but it was not immune to party fragmentation. The base of the party was heterogeneous when it first formed: intraparty factionalization has only multiplied over the past twenty years. Many intellectuals, businessmen, and trade unionists became estranged from the party during the 1990s. Despite the financial and logistical support that MMD received from small business in the 1991 campaign,[56] for example, the early effects of privatization and liberalization offered few benefits for local businesses as I have demonstrated. Economic policy making reflected little input from this group over the course of the 1990s, indicating that it had largely been marginalized from the policy process. Larmer and Fraser report that "moderate business-oriented

[52] For a detailed study of ethnic voting in Zambia, see Daniel Posner, *Institutions and Ethnic Politics in Africa* (New York: Cambridge University Press, 2005).
[53] Lise Rakner and Lars Svåsand, "From Dominant to Competitive Party System: The Zambian Experience 1991–2001," *Party Politics*, 10, 1 (2004); 49–68; Neo Simutanyi, "Political Parties and the Party System in Zambia," background paper prepared for Friedrich Ebert Stiftung, Lusaka, Zambia, October 5, 2005, mimeo.
[54] Center for Policy Dialogue/Friedrich Ebert Stiftung-Zambia, Political Parties Policy Development Seminar, Lusaka, Zambia, June 12, 2008.
[55] NDI and FODEP, "The State of Political Parties," 17.
[56] Adrienne LeBas, *From Protest to Parties: Party-Building and Democratization in Africa* (Oxford: Oxford University Press, 2011), 192.

figures" began leaving the party as early as 1993.[57] The recovery of copper prices after 2000 only worsened the marginalization of smaller commercial businesses and manufacturing since the national treasury derived much of its revenue from taxes and royalties on copper extraction and sales.[58]

After 1991, organized labor was initially ambivalent about privatization and refrained from criticizing the MMD's promarket policy choices, but job losses and casualization reduced their support for the MMD over the course of the decade. Not only did the decline in support cost the MMD votes by 2001, but also it damaged the party organizationally. According to Akwetey and Kraus, "Compared to other members of the [MMD] coalition, the organizational capabilities of the Zambia Congress of Trade Unions (ZCTU) were immense and could be mobilized quickly."[59] In the first and second elections, the MMD was able to rely on an established network of local unions and union organizers to mobilize support for the party, to transmit information to the grassroots, and to get out the vote.[60] As the linkages between the unions and the party deteriorated, the MMD lost its coherence.

Alongside the entry and exit by particular constituencies, senior members of the MMD who were critical of the policies and/or practices of the leadership either were expelled from the party or abandoned it. Many of those who were among the core supporters of MMD at its founding and served in the cabinet or parliament after the 1991 elections left the party before the second elections in order to form new parties.[61] President Chiluba's ultimately unsuccessful bid for a third term also generated strong dissent within the party. At least fifteen members of the MMD's National Executive Committee and nearly sixty members of parliament from the MMD joined efforts to prevent Chiluba from overturning the constitutionally mandated two-term limit.[62] Many resigned on principle; whereas others departed when they saw their own presidential aspirations blocked by Chiluba's attempt. Anderson Mazoka and Ben Mwila, wealthy businessmen who had helped finance the MMD, left to found their own political parties at this time.[63] As leader of UPND, Mazoka ran a close

[57] Miles Larmer and Alastair Fraser, "Of Cabbages and King Cobra: Populist Politics and Zambia's 2006 Election," *African Affairs*, 106, 425 (2007): 615.
[58] Miles Larmer, "Historical Perspectives on Zambia's Mining Booms and Busts" in Alastair Fraser and Miles Larmer, eds., *Zambia, Mining, and Neoliberalism: Boom and Bust on the Globalized Copperbelt* (New York: Palgrave Macmillan, 2010), 5.
[59] Emmanuel Akwetey and Jon Kraus, "Trade Unions, Development, and Democratization in Zambia: The Continuing Struggle" in Jon Kraus, ed., *Trade Unions and the Coming of Democracy in Africa* (New York: Palgrave Macmillan, 2007), 134.
[60] LeBas, *From Protest to Parties*, 193–194.
[61] Na. "Zambia's Newest Political Force: An Interview with the ZAP," *The Courier*, 176 (1999), 28–29 and see additional examples in Rakner, *Political and Economic Liberalisation*, 123.
[62] Daniel Posner and Daniel Young, "The Institutionalization of Political Power in Africa," *Journal of Democracy*, 18, 3 (2007), 133.
[63] Melinda Ham, "Zambia: A New Page," *Africa Report*, 37, 1 (1992), 20; Isaac Malambo, "BY's Party Plans for the Future," *The Times of Zambia*, 2005.

second to Mwanawasa in the 2001 presidential elections. In addition, Michael Sata, who held several ministerial positions in Chiluba's two administrations, resigned to form the Patriotic Front (PF) in 2001.

Further evidence of weak party composition comes from analyzing the average number of years served by members of parliament. Out of the one hundred thirty-six members of parliament in 2008 for which there was reliable data on their date of election and numbers of terms served, over half of them were elected in 2006. A short tenure in office is understandable with respect to a party such as the PF, which gained forty-three out of its forty-four seats in the National Assembly that year. Yet the life span in office of members of the MMD was also surprisingly short. Out of a total of seventy-two members of the MMD in the National Assembly, approximately forty-five were elected to office in 2006. In 2001 and 2006, previous members of parliament representing the MMD either left the party or were expelled by the new leadership and replaced by others deemed more loyal. Taken together, the entry and exit of parties and party members reinforced the pulverization of the party system.

Rather than discouraging multiple parties and numerous independents, Zambia's institutional arrangements encouraged their proliferation. The centralization of authority at the national level and the adoption of a single-member, first-past-the-post system should have favored the development of a two-party system, but they did not. Since a candidate could obtain a seat in parliament by winning only one district, competition for assembly seats at the local level was fierce. Often, three, or as many as ten, candidates competed for a parliamentary seat in each district. Although chiefs were barred from seeking political office, local notables or individuals with national name recognition could, and did, run as independents in order to capture a seat, hence the high number of independent candidates noted previously.

The number of parties or independent candidates that received a share of the vote and the number who were seated in parliament were also consistent with the pattern of a fragmented party system. Over four electoral periods from 1991 to 2006, the effective number of electoral parties averaged 3.38, whereas the effective number of parliamentary parties averaged 2.14. In the last two elections, the number of parties to capture a share of the vote averaged 4.7, and the number of parliamentary parties averaged 2.94. By 2001, eighteen parties competed in elections; the number of parties capturing seats rose to eight parties before "falling" to six parties that gained seats in 2006. However, one of the parties was an alliance of three parties meaning that nine parties held seats in 2006.[64]

Moreover, under Zambia's simple plurality system, presidents could be elected to office without winning an absolute majority of the votes. In 2001,

---

[64] Zambia, Electoral Commission of Zambia, "Election Results Index"; Gallagher, "Election Indices," and Indices.xls.

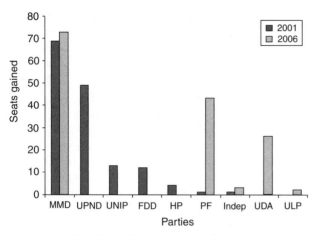

FIGURE 4.1 Zambia parliamentary election results, 2001–2006.

Source: Zambia, Electoral Commission of Zambia, Election Results Index, Parliamentary Results, 2001–2006, accessed 1/11/2009, http://www.elections.org.zm.

President Mwanawasa won elections with only 29 percent of the vote.[65] He improved his share of the vote to 43 percent in the 2006 election campaign, but he struggled to respond to the populist agenda of his main rival, Michael Sata. Beyond the standard appeals to ethno-regional loyalties, Sata also attracted support by criticizing privatization, corruption, and the neglect of urban housing and infrastructure.[66] In the special presidential election of October 2008, which followed the sudden death of President Mwanawasa, the MMD candidate, Rupiah Banda, narrowly achieved victory, winning by just under two points against Sata. Like his predecessor, Banda governed as a minority president with 40 percent of the vote (as will Sata having won 42 percent of the vote in 2011) and a relative majority of nine in the National Assembly. After 2001, the MMD maintained relative majorities in parliament because the president had the right to appoint directly eight members of parliament.[67]

Only the fragmentation of the opposition parties exceeded that of the MMD. As Figure 4.1 shows, party fragmentation between 2001 and 2006 increased. The PF, which had one seat in the 2001 elections, captured forty-four seats five years later. By contrast, three out of the top four parties to gain seats in the 2001 elections UNIP, UPND, and the Forum for Democracy and Development (FDD) did worse when they formed an alliance in 2006 (the United Democratic Alliance), than they did running separately in 2001. This resulted in an overall

[65] Mweelwa Muleya, "Heading Towards a Minority President," *The Post*, September 5, 2006, accessed 9/7/2006, http://allafrica.com/stories/200609051754.html.

[66] Larmer and Fraser, "Of Cabbages and King Cobra," 611–637.

[67] Zambia, Electoral Commission of Zambia, "2008 Presidential Election: National Results Totals for 150 Constituencies," November 2, 2008.

volatility between 2001 and 2006 of 33 percent. Some members of these parties shifted to new parties suggesting that there was stability of personnel; however, the reorganization of old parties and the rise of new parties complicated the process of building a stable base of support and constructing a sustained opposition to the ruling MMD.

Fragmented party loyalty paralleled the fluctuating voting patterns. As the results from an Afrobarometer survey conducted in 1999 show, 52 percent of people in Zambia declared they felt close to a party, but only 38 percent of respondents stated that they felt close to one of the top two vote getters in the 2001 election. Those two parties were the MMD and the UPND.[68] By 2006, the PF had become the second most important party, suggesting again that party loyalties were short-lived and limited. Discussions with party spokespersons, business executives, trade union officials, and scholars bore this out. According to Neo Simutanyi, director of the Center for Policy Dialogue in Zambia, the lack of clear policy differences expressed in party manifestos limited their attraction to voters.[69] Instead, the poverty of many voters made them susceptible to the appeals of those parties who could offer something tangible in return. As one-party official at a workshop for Zambia's political parties stated, "It's not just the manifesto that you have to sell in the countryside, you have to offer *chitenge* (cloth), a t-shirt, or food."[70] Consequently, "at election time," one trade union official observed, "the power base of politicians becomes the unemployed because they can be wooed with *chitenges* and beer."[71]

These offerings hardly create loyal clients. First, there are limits on the degree to which dyadic exchanges between candidates and their constituents can be employed to sustain loyalty. Available goods are insufficient to satisfy potential supporters.[72] Second, even if goods were available, public opinion data from Zambia and Kenya on voter expectations of members of parliament suggests that the ability of an MP to provide particularistic favors did not significantly influence vote choice. Rather respondents were more inclined to reelect MPs who visited their constituencies, presumably because the visits indicated an MP's concern with his or her district.[73] Anecdotal evidence introduces an interesting twist on these suggestive results. In those instances where voters are presented with particularistic goods, they may subvert the motivation behind a dyadic exchange by taking advantage of not just one but several candidates. As one Zambian party official observed, "Some people join four

[68] Afrobarometer Survey Findings, "Round Three Zambia, Questions 85 and 86."

[69] Neo Simutanyi, Presentation to the Political Parties Development Workshop, Lusaka, June 12, 2008.

[70] Political Party Representative, contribution to the Political Parties Development Workshop, Lusaka, June 12, 2008.

[71] Mumbi, Interview.

[72] Daniel Young, "Is Clientelism at Work in African Elections? A Study of Voting Behavior in Kenya and Zambia," Afrobarometer Working Paper no. 106 (April 2009), 1.

[73] Ibid., 4–8.

parties just so they can get goods from all four, then they vote as they wish at election time."[74]

The findings cast doubt on the claims by some scholars that clientelism is the glue that holds together political systems across Africa. Instead, they support a recent observation by Hicken with respect to Thailand that "to the extent that vote buying and selling (long features of Thai elections) continue to dictate how some voters cast their votes, some of the strategic coordination assumptions may not hold."[75] As in Zambia, voters in Thailand accept the gifts of many politicians and then choose one for whom to vote. Hicken's claim that "vote buying might not have a large effect on strategic voting"[76] equally describes voting patterns in Zambia's fragmented system.

The deleterious effects on economic policy making of constant exit and entry and a weak base were manifold. First, defections or dismissals from the ruling party contributed to high turnover in government as ministers were constantly circulating in and out of power. Second, both Presidents Chiluba and Mwanawasa reshuffled ministers to punish critics, build loyalty, and reward supporters.[77] As a consequence, policy making with respect to private sector expansion was often inconsistent, contradictory, and slow. On the one hand, presidents and ministers used their considerable power to interfere in existing policies, distorting them in an attempt to favor a potential client or clients. On the other hand, government officials refrained from enacting bold, ambitious new policies. Rather, they sought to preserve the status quo even when the status quo was inefficient or dangerous; unjust or inadequate. Without a stable coalition, members of the ruling party who served in government were loathe to change policies because they did not know who would gain and who would lose.[78] Similarly, vague party manifestos that lacked substantive policies or clear-cut ideological positions translated into inconsistent policy stances by opposition parties in parliament. The opposition failed to engage in sustained critiques of government for fear they would alienate potential supporters or become the objects of government harassment.[79] In the end, fragmentation undermined the ability of the ruling party to govern effectively and precluded efforts by opposition parties to offer alternative policy platforms or to hold

---

[74] Personal Communication, Zambian party official, Conference on the Constitutional Review Process sponsored by the Foundation for Democratic Process, Lusaka, June 5, 2008.

[75] Allen Hicken, *Building Party Systems in Developing Countries* (Cambridge: Cambridge University Press, 2009), 131.

[76] Ibid.

[77] Amos Malupenga and Brighton Phiri, "Levy Criticises Chiluba's Housing Scheme," *The Post*, 11 January 2005 and Confidential, Interview, Lusaka, June 4, 2008. See also, Christian von Soest, "How Does Neopatrimonialism Affect the African State? The Case of Tax Collection in Zambia," German Institute of Global and Area Studies, Working Papers no. 32 (November 2006): 9, accessed 5/1/2007, http://www.giga-hamburg.de.

[78] Lise Rakner, "The Pluralist Paradox: The Decline of Economic Interest Groups in Zambia in the 1990s," *Development and Change*, 32 (2001): 507–529.

[79] Kathy Sikombe, Program Coordinator, Friedrich Ebert Stiftung, Interview, Lusaka, 6/5/2008.

government accountable. Unfortunately, the democratic context in Zambia did little to mitigate the negative impact of party fragmentation.

The Quality of Democracy: Pluralism without Participation

Where parties are fragmented, social actors must rely on available democratic institutions to curtail the state's use of discretionary authority. Yet, the quality of democracy in Zambia worked against the capacity of civil society to hold government accountable in mutually reinforcing ways. First, the greater pluralism that emerged following Zambia's return to democracy made possible the formation of multiple civil society organizations, business associations, independent trade unions, national and international NGOs. Although these attested to the vibrancy of Zambian civil society, Rakner notes that their proliferation undermined their effectiveness: Multiple organizations with varying strengths and weaknesses replaced single, centralized organs that characterized the period of the one-party state.[80] With respect to groups such as business and labor that were most likely to influence, and be influenced by, economic policy, greater pluralism brought collective action problems that made coordination on policy responses difficult. Second, Zambia became more pluralistic but the legacy of authoritarianism persisted. Government encroachment on civil liberties frequently went unchecked; political rights were circumscribed; the use of executive power was excessive; and unwarranted disruption of the policy process by the government became a regular occurrence. These characteristics of governance in Zambia worsened considerably any coordination challenges introduced by greater pluralism. I discuss these two difficulties in turn.

The paradoxical effects of greater pluralism are starkly obvious when examining business and labor, the two interests with the greatest stake in the outcome of private sector development. Many market economies typically have business associations to represent the myriad interests of commerce, banking, agriculture, industry, or mining. Zambia is no different and a number of its associations have a long history in the country. For example, both the peak or apex association, the Zambia Association of Chambers of Commerce and Industry (ZACCI) and the sectoral association, Zambia National Farmers Union (ZNFU), can trace their origins to the colonial period. Under colonialism, their membership comprised settlers who lobbied the colonial government for distributional goods that would benefit their sector.[81]

After independence, business associations represented mainly the interests of white, commercial farmers in tobacco or cotton, growing indigenous businesses in manufacturing and tourism, or parastatals. For example, ZACCI members from the private sector also overlapped with the membership of the Zambia

---

[80] Rakner, "The Pluralist Paradox." Scott Taylor makes a similar point and also places part of the blame on the state as I do, see *Business and the State*, 55–99.

[81] Ellah Chemba, Economist, Research and Development Office, Zambia National Farmers' Union, Interview, Lusaka, 6/17/2005; Taylor, *Business and the State*, 57–58.

Federation of Employers (ZFE), which included the heads of parastatals. Associations enjoyed access to the government, but within the parameters defined by a heavily state-dominated economy.[82] Ironically, the adoption of economic and political reforms altered the role and the membership of these organizations. With the change of regime, government no longer urged businesses to join associations as in the past; rather the freedom of association produced free riding.[83] Although the government reduced the role of the state and sold SOEs, one commentator allowed that "Privatization made the private sector weak."[84]

As privatization proceeded, business associations and investors fragmented by size, race, and sector. Multiple business associations existed with overlapping constituencies. They often worked at cross purposes and competed with each other for donor funds, members, and government attention. Small and large farmers joined ZNFU; medium-sized, manufacturing companies joined the Zambia Association of Manufacturers (ZAM), foreigners in the hotel industry tended to join the Tourism Council of Zambia. In turn, ZACCI brought together many of these sectoral associations under one umbrella. At the same time, new organizations arose to represent emerging interests.[85]

The old and new organizations varied with regard to their capacity to represent their members' interests and their access to government. Most of the established organizations, particularly ZACCI and ZNFU, had paid staff and offices. According to the head of ZACCI, the association interacted regularly with the government; it was statutorily included on the board of the ZPA, and its members served in government positions.[86] External evaluations also supported these assessments. A 1996 report by the British government referred to ZACCI as an "effective lobbying group" but also noted that its capacity was limited and that its staff was comprised mostly of volunteers.[87]

Yet ZACCI and organizations such as ZFE, which had formed during the period of state intervention, also lost members, as the economy shifted and politics became more pluralistic. Sectors they formerly represented broke away, and new associations formed.[88] The new organizations reflected emerging sectors, but they faced great organizational challenges. For example, membership of a newer association such as the Zambia Indigenous Business Association (ZIBA) cut across and competed for the membership of the more established organizations, which left the new organization small and weak. Similarly, other associations such as Zambia Chamber of Small and Medium Business

---

[82] Taylor, *Business and the State*, 59–62.
[83] Chrispin Mazuba, Research Office, Zambia Federation of Employers, Lusaka, 6/13/2005.
[84] Kasumpa, Interview.
[85] Chisulo, Interview.
[86] Ibid.
[87] United Kingdom, British Development Division in Central Africa/Overseas Development Administration, "ODA Assistance to Promote the Private Sector in Zambia" (February 1996), 5.
[88] Mazuba, Interview.

Associations (ZCSMBA) and the Tourism Council lacked capacity and could not properly fund a permanent staff.[89]

Alongside the fragmentation among associations, investors in Zambia were divided by ethnicity, region, race, nationality, firm size, and sectoral interests. Except for South African investment into the retail sector, foreigners dominated export-oriented businesses such as mining. Zambians owned mostly small and medium-sized businesses in agro-industry, milling, food processing, services, and storage that catered to the domestic market.[90] Tourism and manufacturing were about equally divided between foreigners and Zambians.[91] Moreover, foreigners from the United Kingdom and South Africa were responsible for the majority of the new investment in the country. They made major investments in communications, tourism, and the retail market.

The purchase of Zambia's most valuable assets by foreigners provoked divisions between domestic and foreign investors, which often overlapped with racial differences between white and black investors. Some Zambians resented foreign control over key sectors. They believed that the government gave foreigners tax holidays as incentives to invest or allowed them to take a stake in companies without full payment. They felt that the rules were different for foreigners, which left Zambians at a disadvantage unless they had political connections.[92] Equally, some black Zambians perceived that white Zambians and foreigners had better access to capital. Black Zambians tried to express their grievances collectively by forming "empowerment associations" such as ZIBA and ZCSMBA.

As a consequence, some foreign investors avoided associations all together and preferred to work directly with ministers.[93] For issues related to investment, they participated in or consulted with the Zambia International Business Advisory Council (ZIBAC), a broad-based organization formed in 2002 to promote investment and to apply investment experiences from other parts of the world to Zambia. It comprised stakeholders from across the economy, donors, and foreign investment consultants.[94]

[89] Zambia Business Forum, Private Sector Development Reform Programme (PSDRP) Review, Fringilla Lodge, December 12–14, 2007, Main Report vol. 1, prepared by John Kasanga, Robert Sichinga, and Chiwana Musonda, mimeo.

[90] Darlene Miller, "Transition in the Post-apartheid Regional Workplace" in Edward Webster and Karl Von Holdt, eds., *Beyond the Apartheid Workplace: Studies in Transition* (Scottsville: University of Kwazulu-Natal Press, 2005), 243–265; Rolfe and Woodward, "Attracting Foreign Investment," 20.

[91] World Bank, "Zambia Privatization Review," 23.

[92] These statements are based on interviews with several Zambian businesses, see also Taylor, *Business and the State*, 79 and Yusuf Dodia, "Private Sector Development in Zambia," presentation given at the Private Sector and Aid for Trade – ITC Dialogue, Montreux, Switzerland, June 3–5, 2007, mimeo.

[93] Confidential, Interview with a foreign investor, Lusaka, June 2005.

[94] Edward Mulenga and Stanslous Ngosa, "ZIBAC conference acknowledges Zambia's Positive Economic Strides," *Times of Zambia*, 2005, no date, accessed 4/7/2009, http://www.times.co.zm.

The proliferation of organizations within the business sector, their inability to mobilize their members, policy differences, and the poor state of their finances undercut collective efforts to check opportunistic state discretion during the 1990s. Yet business was not the only participant in the relationship. In spite of the efforts to gain a voice with government, both foreign and domestic businesses reported that the government did not listen to them and showed a lackluster interest in strengthening institutional links with the private sector.[95] Nor was business the only actor within an interest in pressuring the government to favor the private sector. Donors repeatedly used their preferential access to the government to influence policy on privatization and to offer credit support, technical advice, and equipment.[96] Where persuasion and incentives failed, they withheld grants and loans until the government complied with their policy recommendations. Donors also directly worked with business to reduce fragmentation among business associations and to address the coordination problems. In 2002, major donors including the United States, the United Kingdom, and the Netherlands supported the formation of an umbrella organization, the Zambia Business Forum (ZBF).

The ZBF brought together about seven of the largest sectoral organizations including ZACCI, ZNFU, ZAM, Bankers' Association of Zambia (BAZ), Zambia National Tourism Council (ZNTC), the Chamber of Mines of Zambia, and ZCSMBA. Its purpose was to harmonize the different sectoral interests, present a collective voice by business in discussion with the government, and further the objectives of the Private Sector Development Reform Programme (PSDRP). Begun in 2004, this initiative aimed to promote growth through the passage of key macroeconomic and policy reforms. Agreed on by donors, business, and the government, the PSDRP sought to reduce interest rates, remove barriers to investment, and eliminate corruption. The ZBF and other groups sought to accomplish the objectives of the PSDRP by working through a new structure, the Zambia Business Council, which brought together private sector representatives from ZBF, donors, and the government and which was to be housed within the ministry of commerce, trade, and industry.[97]

Although agreement on the objectives of the PSDRP demonstrated a unity of purpose on the part of business, government, and donors, the ZBF did not build cohesion among business. First, not all business associations in Zambia were members of ZBF. Notably, despite being a founding member of ZBF, the peak association, ZACCI failed to pay its dues and was eventually excluded from the organization in early 2008. The formation of ZBF also inadvertently

---

[95] Chisulo, Interview, 6/17/2005; Mark O'Donnell, Managing Director, Union Gold Limited, Interview, Lusaka, 6/23/2005; see also Bräutigam et al., "Business Associations and Growth Coalitions 522–533.
[96] Fundanga and Mwaba, "Privatization of Public Enterprises," 8.
[97] Ibid.

splintered ZACCI as several sectoral groups formerly under the umbrella of ZACCI joined ZBF.[98]

Second, ZBF had difficulty harmonizing effectively the interests of the private sector because members disagreed over policy and they varied greatly in the degree of influence they wielded in ZBF and in the economy. For example, the positions of associations in tourism, manufacturing, and farming differed from that of the Bankers Association of Zambia over access to credit. Whereas the former associations preferred lower interest rates and easier terms of credit, the bankers' association argued for more stringent loan criteria. In addition, as the copper sector revived after 2000, the association for mining companies not only enjoyed privileged access to the government, but also its views increasingly prevailed in ZBF. As a review of the PSDRP claimed, the private sector presence in Zambia was "dominated by a small group of individuals," and ZBF did not reflect the diversity of the sector.[99]

Third, the review found that the regulations governing ZBF either did not exist or were vague. It was unclear who should serve and who should have voting rights on the Executive Committee and the Board of the ZBF. The review claimed that the organization was "bloated," lacked transparency, and was "slow to respond" to the interests of members, a position that some Zambian businesses also held.[100] Fourth, despite agreement on the need to institutionalize within government a body that would promote regular dialogue between government, donors, and business, the new Zambia Business Council got off to a slow start and, at any rate, was only designed to meet twice a year.[101]

Finally, donors themselves disagreed on measures to adopt when the Zambian government failed to meet their performance criteria, and this again provided opportunities for the government to bend the rules. Notably, Van der Heijden and Rakner assert that the "donor community" split in its approach to the MMD by the mid-1990s. Bilateral donors suspended balance of payments support to the government due to what they perceived as poor governance; nevertheless, the IFIs continued to provide sizable amounts of aid.[102] These challenges and limitations reduced the ability of donors as well as business groups effectively to influence government. They encouraged more powerful sectors or companies to pursue their interests individually with government officials. In doing so, they reinforced a personalistic and clientelistic style of politics, even though, as noted earlier, personal contacts had limited effectiveness.

If business still faced serious challenges in spite of the fact that it had donor support and stood to gain the most from liberal reforms, then trade unions

---

[98] Source is confidential.

[99] Zambia Business Forum, PSDRP Review, 21.

[100] Ibid., 8–11.

[101] Kasumpa, Interview.

[102] Hendrik van der Heijden, "Zambian Policy Making" in Steve Kayizzi-Mugerwa, ed., *Reforming Africa's Institutions: Ownership, Incentives, and Capabilities* (New York: United Nations University Press, 2003), 91–94 and Rakner, *Political and Economic Liberalisation*, 162–166.

faced even greater difficulties. They confronted internal as well as external threats to their ability to exercise influence.[103] Trade unions provided considerable support to the MMD in both the 1991 and 1996 elections, especially in the economically important Copperbelt. Yet, the effects of economic reform, internal differences, and changes to their legal status weakened trade unions during the 1990s. First, unions lost membership through retrenchments and increased casualization of labor brought by privatization. Union membership declined by a third between the 1980s and 2000. Second, the initial ambivalence of trade unions weakened resistance to implementation of privatization.[104] Internal dissent within the union movement over how to respond to the government's policy choices resulted in bitter contestation for leadership positions within ZCTU, disaffiliation by some unions from ZCTU, and the formation of a rival federation, the Federation of Free Trade Unions of Zambia (FFTUZ) in the mid-1990s.[105]

Third, the government abandoned policies that allowed only one union per sector in order to conform to recommendations by the International Labor Organization (ILO) on freedom of association. Already destabilized by the effects of reforms, trade unions soon splintered in major sectors of the economy and in public service, compromising efforts at presenting a unified front to business and government. The copper miners' union, one of the most powerful and largest unions in the country, split into two unions which sometimes worked against each other.[106]

Like business, trade unions had other civil society actors with whom they could forge alliances, and they also had some official channels through which they could seek to influence policy, but each of these had their limitations. The proliferation of faith-based groups and organizations focused on poverty, land, gender, water, HIV/AIDs, and other issues called attention to the vibrancy of civil society in Zambia. Their presence offered opportunities for trade unions to coordinate strategies of resistance against government policy. Like business associations and trade unions, they had offices and staff, and government consulted them on policy reforms. They contributed, for example, to the Fifth National Development Plan and participated in discussions on

---

[103] For greater detail on trade unions, see M. Anne Pitcher, "What has Happened to Organized Labor in Southern Africa?," *International Labor and Working Class History*, 72 (2007): 134–160.

[104] Not only was organized labor a part of the coalition that brought the MMD to power, but Miles Larmer (citing Mijere) suggests that mine workers associated decline in the copper sector with the sector's nationalization. These factors explain the initial ambivalence, see Miles Larmer, "Reaction and Resistance to Neo-liberalism in Zambia," *Review of African Political Economy*, 32, 103 (2005): 34 and Simutanyi, "The Politics of Structural Adjustment," 836.

[105] Akwetey and Kraus, "Trade Unions," 138.

[106] Mumbi, Interview and see Na, "Desist from Mudslinging, MUZ Advises New Miners' Union," *Times of Zambia*, 2005 and "MUZ, NUMAW Agree to Co-exist," *Times of Zambia*, 2005, accessed 2/19/2009, http://www.times.co.zm.

the new constitution in 2008 and 2009.[107] But contact with government was inconsistent and acrimonious; often their voices were trumped by those of the donors.

Moreover, as in Mozambique and South Africa, the creation of a Tripartite Consultative Labour Council (TCLC) encouraged consultation and dialogue among government, business, and labor and should have compensated for labor fragmentation. The TCLC did play an important role with respect to labor law reforms, the creation of health and safety standards in business, and the implementation of workplace practices to increase productivity, but it was ineffective at reducing unemployment or preventing casualization. Findings from an ILO report suggest that in addition to infrequent consultation among the TCLC partners, the divisions in the labor movement contributed to its ineffectiveness.[108] These findings cast additional light on the difficulties that organized and formal sector labor faced after the transition to multiparty politics.

As the discussion shows, greater pluralism following democratization complicated collective action and reduced, rather than enhanced, the ability of organizations to disable arbitrary and harmful government discretion. Even with the challenges, however, these organizations likely would have exercised greater influence had the quality of Zambia's democracy been better. Between 1991 and 2005, Freedom House scores averaged 3.9 for political rights and 3.87 for civil liberties. Admittedly, several features of Zambia's democracy were positive. It consistently held presidential and parliamentary elections every five years after 1991. President Chiluba's efforts to seek a third term were thwarted not only by civil society groups and the intervention of the High Court, but also by resistance within his own party. In 2008, the country held a special election without incident following the death in office of President Mwanawasa and most importantly, it had a change of the party in power in 2011. Electoral practices have improved over time suggesting that Zambians and their officials have "learned democracy" and that democratic electoral procedures are becoming more institutionalized.[109]

---

[107] Interviews with Civil Society for Poverty Reduction, the Jesuit Centre for Theological Reflection, the Land Alliance and other NGOs indicate extensive consultation on development plans and constitutional review but little substantive impact on policy and lack of power to hold government accountable.

[108] Toya Fashoyin, "The Contribution of Social Dialogue to Economic and Social Development in Zambia," Working Paper 6, InFocus Programme on Strengthening Social Dialogue, International Labour Office (January 2002), 21–22.

[109] See Leslie Anderson and Lawrence Dodd, *Learning Democracy: Citizen Engagement and Electoral Choice in Nicaragua, 1990–2001* (Chicago: University of Chicago Press, 2005). In their fascinating account of democracy in Nicaragua, Anderson and Dodd challenge common assumptions that learning how to be democratic takes a long time. For cumulative and positive impact of elections on the quality of democracy, see Staffan Lindberg, *Democracy and Elections in Africa* (Baltimore: Johns Hopkins University Press, 2006) and Staffan Lindberg, ed., *Democratization by Elections: A New Mode of Transition* (Baltimore: Johns Hopkins University Press, 2009).

However, Freedom House continued to classify Zambia as partly unfree up to 2008 for the following reasons. After 1991, the government did not consistently respect political rights and civil liberties; it harassed opposition party members, and intermittently disregarded the rule of law. At times, it trampled on the rights of the media and curtailed freedom and open expression. Although the adoption of constitutional reforms that disqualified Kaunda from running for the presidency in the 1996 election offered the most blatant evidence of the MMD's reliance on authoritarian practices (and its Freedom House scores increased correspondingly), vote rigging, the manipulation of electoral laws, the arrest and harassment of opposition leaders, and the inappropriate channeling of state resources in favor of incumbents also occurred after 1996.[110]

Undemocratic practices were not confined to election periods. Rather, they were evident in the treatment of critics, the failure to adopt or respect mechanisms of accountability, threats to opponents, brutal treatment by the police, and continued discrimination against women. In 2004, several NGOs were banned, and journalists were threatened with deportation for criticizing repeated delays in the constitutional review process by the MMD.[111] Additionally, the government adopted a number of laws designed to restrict the rights of workers and NGOs. Where opposition parties controlled local councils, the MMD accused them of forming parallel governments and charged them with sedition.[112]

As in many countries in Africa, the design of formal institutions has concentrated power in the presidency, and presidentialism has bred authoritarianism. Election by direct popular vote, broad powers of appointment, and centralization of fiscal policy granted presidents extensive discretion to interfere in policy making or in the electoral process if they desired to do so. These institutional mechanisms and the opportunistic ways in which Zambian presidents relied on them to dispense patronage or engage in corruption have encouraged scholars to depict Zambian governments as "neopatrimonial," "authoritarian," lacking in commitment, or experiencing a "partial reform syndrome."[113]

Presidentialism facilitates the use of discretionary authority, but the fluidity of the party system also complicates presidential rule. On the one hand, the party system makes the relationship between the executive and legislative branches less predictable.[114] On the other hand, the institutional arrangements allow

---

[110] David Simon, "Democracy Unrealized: Zambia's Third Republic under Frederick Chiluba" in Leonardo Villalón and Peter Von Doepp, eds., *The Fate of Africa's Democratic Experiments* (Bloomington: Indiana University Press, 2005), 199–220.

[111] Neo Simutanyi, "Challenges for 2005," *The Post*, January 2, 2005, 11.

[112] Freedom House, "Country Report: Zambia," 2008, accessed 4/23/2009, http://www.freedomhouse.org.

[113] See Handley, *Business and the State*, 236–241; Rakner, *Political and Economic Liberalisation*, 166–170; and van de Walle, *Politics of Permanent Crisis*.

[114] Scott Mainwaring, "Multipartism, Robust Federalism, and Presidentialism in Brazil" in Scott Mainwaring and Matthew Shugart, eds. *Presidentialism and Democracy in Latin America* (Cambridge: Cambridge University Press, 1995), 55–109.

the pursuit of particularistic and political agendas by members of parliament, who do not owe their position to the president and are not necessarily beholden to the ruling party.[115] The election of members of parliament using the first-past-the-post system in single-member constituencies coupled with the lack of party loyalty mitigated the formation of stable coalitions, bred particularism on the part of bureaucrats as well as legislators, reduced legislative support for presidential initiatives, and encouraged numerous challengers to the office of the presidency. Threats of departure and promises of return by elites connected to the ruling party, an unstable voter base, and a shrinking majority heightened executive insecurity.

Such situations encouraged successive presidents to engage in repeated bargaining and undemocratic acts, to stifle attempts at collective action designed to hold government accountable and to use patronage to poach opposition members from other parties in order to shore up their mandates. In response, both President Chiluba and President Mwanawasa engaged in what O'Dwyer has described in another context as "runaway state building" in order to reduce fragmentation. Under Mwanawasa, the executive branch had sixty-seven government members by 2006 – up from twenty-eight in Chiluba's first term, which was considered an all time high.[116] The president extended the power of appointment even to permanent secretaries. The power to appoint and dismiss ministers may have protected presidents, but it resulted in a constant rotation of personnel, which undermined governmental capacity. Presidents relied on authoritarian mechanisms to concentrate power in the office of the presidency because the party lacked sufficient discipline and organization to be trusted with the delegation of authority. Not surprisingly, these acts have decisively affected policy implementation.

The Impact of Party Politics and Democratic Quality on Reform: 1996–2008

How did Zambia's limited democracy and fragmented party politics affect the outcome of economic reform? What were the implications for the development of a market economy in Zambia and also for state formation? Unquestionably, the Zambian economy was transformed, which lends support to my claim that the adoption of formal institutional arrangements consistent with private sector creation played an important role in the realization of reform. But governments in limited democracies with fragmented party systems also use their discretion opportunistically to build a base, reward cronies, repress opponents, or stymie threats to their power. The result is that private sector development

---

[115] Haggard, "Democratic Institutions," 129–139; Scott Mainwaring, "Presidentialism, Multipartism, and Democracy: The Difficult Combination," *Comparative Political Studies*, 26, 2 (1993): 198–228.

[116] Von Soest, "How Does Neopatrimonialism," 11.

often becomes ad hoc. Policies are manipulated or jettisoned to pursue populist agendas; they stall at a suboptimal status quo because governments fear the effects on real or potential supporters if they change them; they get subverted in response to the desires of cronies who may, or may not, deliver votes and funds to the party in power.

The administrations of Presidents Chiluba and Mwanawasa demonstrate the pathologies associated with fragmented party politics and limited democratic quality. Both administrations blended populism, cronyism, and authoritarian tactics to contain dissent and to attract support; both engaged in policy drift, stagnation and subversion but they did so to different degrees and directed their discretion to different purposes.

A major part of the Chiluba administration's repertoire for managing political and economic divisions consisted of derailing and hijacking the privatization process. Increased governmental interference into the ZPA is a case in point. It illustrates well an observation made by Kitschelt et al. on the exogenous impact of institutions when the interests of those who design them shift.[117] Elites greatly praised ZPA's independence when it was created and when there was unity on the objectives of economic reform. When support for reform deteriorated and the interests of elites changed, they began to curb the ZPA's independence. By 1996, interference in the privatization process by the ruling party intensified. The government overrode the authority of the ZPA to designate the method of sale and to oversee the privatization process. Privatization of parastatals or parts of parastatals was done "off the books" through special committees and according to irregular procedures.[118]

In tandem with its decision to rob the ZPA of its authority, the government directed the sale of assets to potential allies. President Chiluba no doubt sought personal gain from preying on the privatization of substantial assets such as Zambia Consolidated Copper Mines (ZCCM) as van Donge has argued,[119] but both President Chiluba and President Mwanawasa raided the privatization process to entice potential supporters with particularistic goods, to retain the support of powerful individuals, or to shape the process in the government's favor. The former did so to further aggrandize power; the latter, to build support in the wake of his election as a minority president. First, without the participation of the ZPA, the Chiluba administration divested small shops, farms, and council housing just prior to the general and presidential elections of 1996. Reminiscent of the sales of council houses in Britain during the 1980s, thousands of council houses and houses that comprised the assets of parastatals

---

[117] See Herbert Kitschelt, Zdenka Mansfeldova, Radoslaw Markowski, and Gábor Tóka, *Post-Communist Party Systems: Competition, Representation, and Inter-Party Cooperation* (Cambridge: Cambridge University Press, 1999), 11–12.

[118] Matale, Interview; Cruickshank, Interview.

[119] Jan Kees van Donge, "The Plundering of Zambian Resources by Frederick Chiluba and His Friends: A Case Study of the Interaction Between National Politics and the International Drive towards Good Governance," *African Affairs*, 108, 430 (2008): 69–90.

were "sold" at very low prices to their sitting tenants, many of whom were copper miners and other workers. Council houses were given to trade union officials and executives in the copper parastatal just around election time.[120] The divestiture had several consequences besides buying support for the president from new homeowners, especially on the Copperbelt. It directed the revenue from privatization to the office of the president rather than the ZPA and it robbed local councils of the rents they had formerly received from sitting tenants, thereby reducing their power and autonomy.[121]

Second, after establishing the government's central position in the divestment of housing, the Presidential Housing Initiative or PHI then reestablished the government's role as a participant in the residential construction sector. Announced before the local government elections of 1998, the ostensible purpose of the scheme was to build 4,000 new low-, medium-, and high-cost homes in Lusaka. An informal body, the PHI was never legally incorporated under the statutory authority of the National Housing Authority, which had jurisdiction over public housing initiatives. Instead, Richard Sakala, the press and public relations aide and a close confidante of President Chiluba, personally managed it on behalf of the president.[122] Revenue from sales to civil servants of existing public housing was supposed to fund the project. As with the sales of council houses, the policy intended to demonstrate the President's generosity and to purchase support for Chiluba from potential beneficiaries of the new homes.

Third, whether the procedure for the privatization of a parastatal was a "competitive tender" or a management buyout, the beneficiaries of the sales or giveaways of state assets in agriculture, manufacturing, or tourism, were increasingly individuals in government, potential supporters of the ruling party, or persons with connections to those in power. Zambian law allows for the purchase of firms by politicians and several of these purchases were even noted as such. The ZPA recorded the sales of at least sixteen parastatals to ministers and deputy ministers, members of parliament, and relatives of government officials prior to the 1996 elections. Officials at ZPA also observed that many deals were concluded without the participation of the ZPA and without transparency. For example, the former head of ZPA recollected that the government broke up 40,000 hectares of farmland outside of Lusaka into individual parcels and sold three-quarters of it to members of the government without ZPA involvement. Further, he recalled that the government did not even inform him of the sale of approximately thirty-two MBOs; instead he read about it in the newspaper.[123]

[120] Confidential, Interview, 6/20/2005; and Sikombe, Interview.
[121] Sikombe, Interview; John Milimo, "Social Impacts of Privatisation: Findings from a Qualitative Participatory Research Exercise," undertaken for the ZPA, field research by Mwiya Mwanavande and Nalishebo Katukula, Lusaka, May 2005, 2–3; David Simpson, "Local Authorities in Trouble," *Profit* (August 1997), 13.
[122] Reuben Phiri, "Chiluba Authorised Sakala to sign $17M Loan-Gov't," *The Post*, 01/08/2002, accessed March 11, 2009, http://www.LexisNexis.com.
[123] Matale, Interview.

Fourth, the president manipulated the sale of the copper mines and related assets just after the 1996 election. Due to a boycott by the opposition occasioned by the disqualification of their presidential candidate, President Chiluba won a landslide victory in the second election. Yet a high voter abstention rate in key provinces[124] and a looming succession crisis generated renewed efforts to use both continued control over parastatals and privatization for patronage. On the one hand, as long as it remained in state hands, ZCCM served as a classic example of the "partial reform syndrome."[125] Suppliers linked to cabinet ministers and high-level mine management sold goods to the parastatal at inflated prices in order to secure a substantial rent from the difference between their own purchase price and the sale price to the mines.[126]

On the other hand, as mine sales got underway, the president encroached on the work of the ZPA to direct the proceeds of privatization to his own supporters. Contravening key provisions of the Privatization Act, he personally appointed a Privatization Negotiating Team (PNT) to undertake the sale process. During the negotiating process, the PNT did not consult with the ZPA on the methods of sale, the bids received, and the awarding of contracts to buyers. In some cases, contracts were awarded to personal colleagues of the head of the PNT and/or the President of the country.[127]

In addition, despite criticism and resistance by the ZPA, the head of the PNT authorized the sale of Ndola Lime to a Belgian firm in which he had a business interest and that had little experience with lime production. The sale was concluded despite the fact that the ZPA had received higher bids from more experienced companies. After the deal eventually collapsed due to public outcry and the persistent refusal by ZPA to sanction the sale, allegations were made that President Chiluba had stood to benefit financially from the sale to the Belgian firm.[128] In total, US$140 million in revenue were alleged to have disappeared from the sales of copper and cobalt mines in the 1990s.[129] Following the failure of this and other sales, ZPA then reauthorized mine divestitures after Chiluba left office in 2001.

Changes to property rights laws also affected the implementation of privatization and related liberalization measures. It is true that several revisions in the Lands Act of 1995 were consistent with the implementation of a private

---

[124] Daniel Posner and David Simon, "Economic Conditions and Incumbent Support in Africa's New Democracies," *Comparative Political Studies*, 35, 3 (2002): 323–324. Posner and Simon demonstrate that along with the boycott economic conditions contributed to voter abstention. As I argue, subsequent actions by the president reinforce this claim.

[125] See Hellman, "Winners take All."

[126] Wilcliff Sakala, "Corruption Causes Concern," *Profit* (September 1997), 7.

[127] Cruickshank, Interview and see also Larmer, "Reaction and Resistance," 32–34.

[128] Reuben Phiri, "AAGM: President Levy Exposes More Evidence of Ex-President's Plunder," *The Post*, July 17, 2002, accessed 3/1/2009, LexisNexis.

[129] "Analysis of Zambia's World of Theft and Abuse of Public Resources," *Alexander's Gas and Oil Connections*, 7, 14 (July 12, 2002), accessed 4/25/2007, http://www.gasandoil.com/goc/

sector–driven economy and followed alterations to land laws enacted by other African governments during the 1990s. These included the conversion of existing customary land to leasehold tenure, procedures on land titling, extended leaseholds by foreigners, and the reliance on market forces to determine land values. Moreover, as in other countries, several aspects of the new land law maintained institutional arrangements that had existed since the colonial period such as the distinction between customary and state land and the administration of customary land by local chiefs.[130]

But central to the implementation of many provisions was the authority over land exercised by the president. This provision remained unchanged from the previous Land Act of 1975. Accordingly, all land "vests" in the president and he/she, or those appointed to act in his/her interest, have the right to alienate it. After meeting certain legal criteria, non-Zambians who wanted to obtain land leases could only do so subject to the personal approval of the president.[131] Second, those who held land under customary tenure were allowed to convert it to leasehold tenure with legal title as long as they received the authorization of the president, the consent of the chief, and approval of the local rural council to do so.[132] Third, land leased by local councils or subleased to others by local councils was surrendered to the president excepting land directly used by councils or covered by the Housing Act, chapter 194. While the terms of leases or subleases were left unchanged from previous acts, those rents collected from the leases or subleases were now given to the president rather than local councils, thereby facilitating his/her ability to interfere in housing provision.[133]

Finally, legislation failed to provide sufficient limits on the power of the president to interfere in land affairs.[134] Rather, the brevity and ambiguity of the act and the lack of accompanying regulations allowed government officials, especially the president and the ministry of lands, considerable discretion in interpreting and applying the law. In a context where the quality of democracy was limited, the latitude accorded to the president contributed to the ad hoc nature of private sector creation in Zambia.

Unlike his predecessor, President Mwanawasa claimed to be against personal enrichment and supported investigations into corruption when he attained power in 2001. Notably he allowed the judicial branch to strip

news/nta22869.htm; Andrew Sardanis, Businessman and Former CEO of Meridian Bank, Interview, Chaminuka, 6/8/2008 and Lusaka, 6/13/2008.

[130] Zambia, "The Lands Act," Government of Zambia, Act No. 29, September 13, 1995; Michelo Hansungule, Patricia Feeney, and Robin Palmer, "Report on Land Tenure Insecurity on the Zambian Copperbelt," Oxfam GB in Zambia (November 1998 – Electronic Version with maps created 2004), 20; Henry Machina, Zambia Land Alliance, Interview, Lusaka, 6/11/2008.

[131] Zambia, "The Lands Act," Part II, Section 3.

[132] Ibid., Part II, Section 8.

[133] Ibid., Part II, Section 6.

[134] Adams, Martin, "Land Tenure Policy and Practice in Zambia: Issues Relating to the Development of the Agricultural Sector," DCP/ZAM/018/2002/, Draft (2003), 9.

Chiluba of his immunity and sanctioned the prosecution of Chiluba's closest supporters. Richard Sakala was indicted and convicted of illegal acts while administering the PHI.[135] Moreover, several economic policy choices made by the Mwanawasa administration signaled a greater responsiveness to increasingly well-orchestrated domestic and international demands and a greater willingness to abide by the rules than had occurred under the Chiluba administration. Under these circumstances, it is pertinent to ask whether some uses of state discretion to interfere in the privatization process might have been more justifiable, more akin to those strategic compromises that more liberal democracies achieve and that Chapter 6 on South Africa will examine. Unfortunately, the policy approach was inconsistent and used in tandem with cronyism and repression. These strategies worked in combination to influence the trajectory of reform over time.

The embrace of populism and developmentalism by the Mwanawasa administration attests to the more effective role played by civil society in holding the regime accountable as well as the government's concern to consolidate power in the wake of the 2001 elections. The government offered free primary schooling to woo back a population hard hit by structural adjustment policies. The Mwanawasa government was also more responsive to small and medium-size businesses after the previous government had largely marginalized them. It encouraged local councils (which had become among the worst paid in Africa) to form joint ventures with private companies to supply services to local residents. It reintroduced subsidies for pesticides and subsidized half of the cost of fertilizer purchase for small and medium farmers. For the poorest farmers, it provided a fertilizer and seed packet to each household. With the passage of the Zambian Development Agency Act (ZDAA) in 2006, the government established a broad-based policy and organizational approach to private sector development.[136] The act included a special development fund to offer financial aid and investment information to micro and small businesses, rural enterprises, and organizations engaged in education or skills training. The measures brought Zambia more into line with other countries such as Mozambique and South Africa that gave support to indigenous investors and suggested also that the government was trying to diversify the economy away from its dependence on copper.

Populist measures extended to private sector development. Even though the government sold approximately 90 percent of the total number of the state's assets and allowed foreign investment in its most important sector, copper, privatization stalled after 2002. Most of the remaining parastatals such as Tanzania Zambia Railways Limited (Tazara), Tazama Pipeline, the electricity parastatal, Zesco, Zambia State Insurance Corporation (ZSIC), and Zambia National Building Society were retained by the state until the end of the Mwanawasa

---

[135] Phiri, "Chiluba Authorised."
[136] Zambia, Zambia Development Agency Act (ZDAA), no. 11 of 2006 (January 24, 2006).

administration.[137] Many of these parastatatals were concentrated in strategic sectors, such as utilities, and they had very large, well-organized workforces. In 2006, parastatals employed 49,000 workers or about 10 percent of the formal sector workforce. Average earnings in the parastatal sector were the highest in Zambia, nearly three times as high as a job in the private sector.[138] Rather than privatize them, the government decided to commercialize them. Where it sought strategic partners in the private sector, it retained a majority share. With respect to the Zambia National Commercial Bank (Zanaco), for example, the government allowed the Dutch-owned bank, Rabobank, only to purchase a minority share in 2007.[139]

As it might have in a liberal democracy, sustained public outcry over the proposed privatization of these assets likely encouraged the government to stall privatization in order to quell dissent and retain support. Although divisions continued to plague the trade union movement, union militancy rose over privatization, wages, and government restrictions on union rights after 2000. The unions also joined with other popular organizations such as churches and anti-poverty groups to challenge government on issues of broader significance to Zambians such as the constitution, press freedom, and democracy.[140] Alongside union and popular expressions of disapproval with government policy, opposition politicians and parties attracted support by campaigning against foreign purchases of SOEs.[141] Some members of parliament used their positions to hold ministers accountable for their actions, to inform the public about policy changes, and to highlight abuses. These efforts included questioning ministers about privatization deals.[142]

Collectively, these efforts and resulting policy changes suggest that the government was more accountable than it had been previously. As is frequently the case, however, the adoption of populism was perfectly compatible with more opportunistic uses of the state's discretionary authority. These were brought to bear on economic policy. With respect to the retention of parastatals for example, even though sales were cancelled in response to public outcry, critics allege that parastatals provided a reliable source of funding for MMD politicians during elections.[143] As one study conducted for the ZPA asserted, "the government can and does often go to parastatal companies to borrow things

[137] Robb Stewart, "Four Zamtel Bidders Shortlisted in Privatization," *The Wall Street Journal Online*, 1/13/2010, accessed 1/29/2009, http://online.wsj.com/article/SB126337615790627633.html.

[138] Zambia, Central Statistical Office, "Formal Sector Employment and Earnings Inquiry Report," 2006: 3–5.

[139] The Banda administration has shifted course again and sold 75 percent of Zamtel in 2010.

[140] Akwetey and Kraus, "Trade Unions," 147.

[141] Chifuwe, "Privatization Will Be," and Larmer and Fraser, "Of Cabbages and King Cobra," 611–637.

[142] See for example Zambia, National Assembly, Debates-Thursday, April 5, 2007, 2, accessed June 7, 2007 www.parliament.gov.zm.

[143] Sources from business and academia wish to remain confidential.

like fertilizer and money in order to give out to people. This is especially the case near political elections."[144]

Retention of parastatals allowed President Mwanawasa's administration to rely on state procurement contracts to build alliances with powerful private investors, a strategy that President Kaunda previously employed and one that was popular in stable party systems such as Mozambique and South Africa. In Zambia's case, capricious uses of power were evident in the awarding of contracts, the selective bailouts of failing firms, and shady business deals. The administration overlooked abuses by civil servants who used their offices to rent seek. For example, the auditor-general found that the Patents and Companies Registration Office was signing procurement contracts with private companies for building materials, fire extinguishers, and air conditioners without tender authority and that these materials could not be produced on inspection. Liquidations provided another revenue stream for those in government employment. For example, liquidators of Zambezi Sawmills appear to have asset stripped without any government oversight. In addition, employees at the Food Reserve Agency, which was supposed to manage reserve grain stocks in Lusaka, were having multiple meetings so they could collect the per diem allowed under Zambian law. Last, government officials had received advances that were not repaid.[145]

Finally, the government halted sales in order to thwart its enemies. Several sources alleged that the president stopped the privatization of Maamba Collieries because one of his political rivals, Hakainde Hachilema, was connected to one of the companies in the consortium favored to win the bid.[146] Hachilema formed his own party, the UPND, in 1998; he challenged Mwanawasa in the 2006 presidential race and placed third behind Michael Sata.

Beyond direct interference in the privatization process, the government also continued its strategy of disabling economic opponents and consolidating power. Although the Tripartite Consultative Labour Council met quarterly to discuss matters of importance to government, unions, and employers, trade unionists and observers reported that government regularly scorned its recommendations.[147] The government and investors ignored collective bargaining agreements, and unions continued to face increasing casualization and lax enforcement of health and safety regulations. Cowing to investors, the

---

[144] John Milimo, "Social Impacts of Privatisation," 5.

[145] Zambia, National Assembly, Public Accounts Committee, "Report of the Public Accounts Committee on the Report of the Auditor-General on the Accounts of Parastatal Bodies for 2004 for the Fifth Session of the Ninth National Assembly appointed by Resolution of the House on 20th January 2006."

[146] Kingsley Kaswende, "Govt Stops Sale of Maamba Collieries," *The Post*, October 10, 2006, accessed 3/11/2009, http://www.LexisNexis.com.

[147] Mumbi, Interview; Kathy Sikombe, Programme Coordinator, Friedrich Ebert Stiftung, Interview, June 5, 2008.

government tabled an Industrial Relations Act in 2008 that gave increased power to Labor Commissions to oversee union finances and membership; to withdraw union recognition; and to limit the power of unions to negotiate with companies.[148]

Trade unions bore the brunt of government caprice, but investors were not immune to the vacillating policy choices of the Mwanawasa administration. The ability of business to navigate these changes varied with the fiscal strength of the sector. For example, when copper prices rose dramatically after 2005, the administration sought to revise the favorable tax concessions it had granted to mining companies when copper prices were low. After failing to renegotiate these with individual companies, it unilaterally announced a new tax structure in the 2008 budget that increased corporate income taxes and royalty rates. It created a variable profit tax rate and a graduated windfall tax. Although admittedly the earlier arrangements had been highly favorable to the companies, the 2008 reforms were introduced with little collective input from business. Following resistance from mine owners and donors coupled with a drop in copper prices owing to the global financial crisis in 2008, Mwanawasa's successor, Rupiah Banda, scrapped several elements of the reform and retained the increases in the profit tax rate, corporate income tax, and royalty rates.[149]

Fraser interprets the imposition of a more stringent tax code for private mining operations as evidence that "African governments and parliament ultimately retain some autonomy, some legalistic sovereignty"[150] – an observation that usefully contrasts with persistent claims in the literature regarding the power of donors. Yet, the shifting stances of the government and the opposition during the debate over the tax changes underscore again the highly fragmented nature of party politics in Zambia. Not only did the government change its position several times – bowing first to popular opinion and then giving in to mine owners – so also did the main opposition party, the PF. After arguing in favor of the new tax regime, the leader of the party changed his mind on the revisions. Neither party had a solid base either with owners or with mine workers.

A similar pattern of opportunistic decision making by government materialized in other sectors. Whereas the ZDAA appeared to support indigenous investors, for example, it also provoked other concerns by the private sector. First, the government stalled on the creation of the authority charged to carry

[148] Mumbi, interview.
[149] Alastair Fraser, "Introduction: Boom and Bust on the Zambian Copperbelt" in Alastair Fraser and Miles Larmer, eds., *Zambia, Mining, and Neoliberalism: Boom and Bust on the Globalized Copperbelt* (New York: Palgrave Macmillan, 2010), 19–22; Christopher Adam and Anthony Simpasa, "The Economics of the Copper Price Boom in Zambia," in Alastair Fraser and Miles Larmer, eds., *Zambia, Mining, and Neoliberalism: Boom and Bust on the Globalized Copperbelt* (New York: Palgrave Macmillan, 2010), 77–82.
[150] Fraser, "Introduction," 19.

out the provisions of the act and did not create it until a year and a half after its passage.[151] Second, critics argued that the act arbitrarily restricted the qualifications for fiscal incentives to those investments that were over US$500,000 and in officially designated priority sectors (mostly manufacturing but also floriculture, horticulture, and education). For nonpriority sectors, it set the bar even higher at a minimum investment of US$10 million, which one observer described as "against all principles to attract investment" because of the high threshold for qualification. Although the government consulted with the private sector on this provision, it then overlooked the recommendations made by business.[152]

Most importantly, the ZDAA continued government efforts to centralize power in the executive branch. The act merged, revised, and repealed the provisions of several previous acts such as the Export Development Act, the Export Processing Zones Act, the Investment Act, the Small Enterprises Development Act, and the Privatisation Act.[153] Since the government had privatized a majority of Zambia's parastatals and had moved beyond a transitional economy by that date, it would be incorrect to interpret the repeal of these acts as reneging by the government on its commitment to create a private sector–driven economy. Instead, it should be seen as a reconfiguration of the government's discretionary authority to cope with the internal distributional conflicts that emerged with the growth of the market.

Principally, ZDAA undermined the statutory independence of the ZPA by shifting oversight of the ZPA to the executive branch. It eliminated the requirement that the agency report to parliament on privatization matters and increased the role of cabinet ministries in the agency's governance and functions. Instead of a board that included twelve representatives from three government ministries as in the former ZPA, the expanded sixteen-member board included representatives from eight government ministries. Unlike the ZPA board, the ZDAA board did not explicitly include trade union representatives or church officials. Rather it mostly preferenced organizations or individuals interested in business, be they small-scale enterprises or civil society organizations "involved in or interested in commerce and industry." The minister of trade and industry was responsible for appointing the chair and vice-chair of the board giving directions to the board and working with the board.[154]

---

[151] Statement by the chairperson of the Private Sector Development Association cited by the Zambia Development Authority, June 13, 2007, accessed 3/13/2009, http://www.zda.org.zm.

[152] Jean José Villa Chacón, Attaché, Private Sector Development and Civil Society, European Union, Interview, Lusaka, 6/10/2008 and see ZDAA, part VIII, section 56.

[153] The repeal of the Privatisation Act was to take effect once the Minister of Trade and Industry deemed that all pending activities of the ZPA were concluded. See ZDAA, section 84, subsection 2.

[154] ZDAA, section 6.

Last, the property rights regime, which was critical to the security of both rural households and private commercial enterprises, was not revised. Despite soliciting broad input from civil society on proposed revisions, the 1995 Lands Act continued to exist as did the substantial powers it accorded to the president on land issues. A draft land policy of 2006 preserved the ambiguity and broad, central government discretion expressed in the previous law and draft policy. As the Zambia Land Alliance, a leading advocate for land rights in Zambia observed, the draft land policy still did "not provide any guidelines on how [to] strengthen (the) customary land system."[155] Further, the ZLA pointed out that the second draft land policy continued to lack clarity regarding what was considered state land and whether national parks and forests were considered state or customary land. Like the previous policy, it promoted titling for land under customary tenure, while failing to address and clarify multiple and complex titling procedures in urban areas.[156]

The adoption of populist reforms, the reliance on different forms of patronage, and the retention of power in the executive branch did not reflect a ruling party that rested on a well-defined base and that acted in a democratic fashion. Rather, they were associated with a government that had authoritarian tendencies and that was subject to the vicissitudes of volatile constituencies. These conditions produced inconsistent and opportunistic policy choices that negatively impacted both the pace and the outcome of private sector development.

Conclusion

By 2005, Zambia had privatized around 260 state companies – a clear indication that it had moved beyond motivationally credible commitment.[157] As the policy intended and as institutional theorists expect, individual firm performance now depends on global processes and on decisions made by private boards of directors, individual managers, and even shareholders. Moreover, the institutional design of the privatization program delegated to the ZPA some leverage to challenge executive encroachment and to continue the policy in spite of serious challenges to its authority.

In theory, the transfer of ownership from the state to the private sector should have acted to disable discretion if only for the reason that private individuals now control decisions that the state used to make. Yet, Zambia's privatization process illustrates why sales of firms are an insufficient proxy for determining a commitment that is credible in the imperative sense. It suggests that where reforms interact with partisan fragmentation and shifting coalitions, vulnerable governments will opportunistically interfere in the reform process to build

---

[155] Zambia Land Alliance (ZLA), "Land Policy Options for Development and Poverty Reduction" (January 2008), 11.
[156] Ibid., 11–13.
[157] Cruickshank, Interview, and ZPA, "Status Report," 1.

or maintain support. Repeated, arbitrary intervention by the executive in the selection of assets to be privatized, the valuation of those assets, the allocation of land, and new investment projects became a hallmark of private sector development in Zambia from the mid-1990s. The purpose was not only to satisfy the rent seeking ambitions of leaders, but more importantly, to provide an extensive source of political patronage for a ruling party that was uncertain about its base of support and needed to rely on gifts, bribes, and populist gimmicks in order to attract it.

Ironically, the formal recognition of private property rights and the sales of state assets to the private sector as well as democratization contributed to the separation between state and the economy that neo-liberal proponents advocate. Trade unions became autonomous from the state and divided in their tactics and preferences. Civil society organizations populated the political landscape. Moreover, although the low quality of Zambia's democracy limited the degree to which the private sector could act independently of capricious interference; nevertheless, businesses could and did ignore politics in order to focus on production and trade.[158] However, the constant tinkering by successive administrations with the constitution, electoral laws, labor and private sector regulations in order to unsettle any potential opponents not only distorted the outcome of reforms but also contributed to a "hollowing out" of government. Alongside the enactment of neo-liberal prescriptions, undemocratic practices, and transient party politics weakened the state in Zambia.

Whereas the particular configuration of interests and the specifics of their responses differ, other states such as Mali and Malawi displayed characteristics similar to those of Zambia. In Madagascar, too, where the privatization program accelerated after 2000, a similar pattern emerged. The adoption of institutional arrangements spurred economic reform, but fluid party politics and the limited quality of democracy shaped its trajectory. By contrast, the combination of limited democracy and stable party politics resulted in a different pattern of economic and political change as the following chapter details in the case of Mozambique.

---

[158] O'Donnell, interview.

5

Stable Parties, Limited Democracy, and Partisan Private Sector Development

Mozambique

The starting point for the privatization of the Mozambican economy was much worse than that of Zambia. A seventeen-year war that concluded in 1992 had left the economy in a shambles. Infrastructure had deteriorated, many state firms were destroyed or not working, and the salaries of thousands of state workers were in arrears. State capacity in areas such as regulatory enforcement or technical expertise was low. The political environment was also discouraging. The two main parties that participated in the first democratic elections in 1994 were the belligerents in the war, and they brought many of their former grievances into the postwar settlement. The peace accord constructed a political system that relied on institutional means such as the rule of law, but also extra institutional mechanisms such as bargaining and threats to avoid damaging stalemates or a resurgence of conflict.[1]

The experience of conflict, a fragile state, a failing economy, and a hostile political setting – these factors indicated to most observers that the privatization process would be protracted and conflictual; that its impact would lack credibility, and that its consequences would prolong political instability. Yet, not only did Mozambique sell a percentage of state firms comparable to that of Zambia, but also its imperative credibility score was higher than Zambia's. It sustained positive growth rates over more than a decade and attracted significant amounts of new investment. Particularly noteworthy was that the government relied on private sector development to rebuild state capacity.

In contrast to Zambia, the government in Mozambique consciously crafted the institutions of economic change to allow the broad use of state discretion with respect to the management of private property rights and the growth of

---

[1] Carrie Manning, "Assessing Adaptation to Democratic Politics in Mozambique: The Case of Frelimo" in Leonardo Villalón and Peter VonDoepp, eds., *The Fate of Africa's Democratic Experiments: Elites and Institutions* (Bloomington: Indiana University Press, 2005), 238–240.

a private sector. In so doing, the government was able to strengthen the power
of the ruling party over the course of the privatization process. Although distributional conflicts surfaced during implementation as they did in Zambia,
a disciplined and experienced ruling party in a relatively stable two-party
system sustained its base throughout the process. Uses of patronage, corruption, and a lack of transparency were elements of the strategy as they were in
Zambia's limited democracy, but also the leadership appealed to party loyalty
or appeased its base with club goods. In effect, the government used privatization to reinvigorate the networks that formed the constitutive elements of the
ruling party. It took advantage of the process to create interests with a stake in
private sector development.

The chapter describes the configuration of the private sector, the patterns
and sources of investment, and the distributional impact of the shift to a market economy. It explores the institutional arrangements associated with private
sector creation, the properties of the party system, and characteristics of its
democracy. It will then explain how a stable party system and a limited democratic environment molded the trajectory of economic reform. Finally, it will
analyze the implications of the interaction of economic policy and politics for
the development of capitalism in countries with political systems similar to
that of Mozambique.

Privatization in Mozambique

As in Zambia, the privatization process in Mozambique resulted in its transformation from a largely state-run economy to one dominated by the private
sector. By 2002, the Mozambican government had sold approximately 1,200
SOEs, or the majority of its assets, to the private sector. Ninety percent of these
assets were small and medium companies bought by nationals. About half of the
companies sold were in industry, tourism, and commerce whereas agriculture
and agro-processing accounted for a little more than 10 percent of the total.

As they did in Zambia, domestic investors bought the majority of the total
number of companies that were privatized, but foreign investors accounted
for only about half the total value of assets sold in Mozambique in contrast to
just over eight percent of the value of those sold in Zambia. Foreigners wholly
or partially purchased approximately twenty-six parastatals out of a total of
one hundred fifteen companies under the authority of the Technical Unit for
Restructuring Enterprises, which was responsible for handling the divestment
or restructuring of the largest companies. Purchases occurred in sectors such
as food and beverage, construction, telecommunications, minerals, railways,
and tourism.[2]

---

[2] Mozambique, Ministry of Planning and Finance, Technical Unit for Enterprise Restructuring
(UTRE) "Privatisation in Mozambique: 1998 – Consolidating the Gains," no. 5 (March 1998),
Lista dos Investidores, 1–2.

Alongside the sales of parastatals, Mozambique attracted more than US$14 billion in proposed and actual investment between 1990 and 2007. The investment included the completion of two aluminum-smelting plants at a total cost of about US$2 billion. Other mega-projects with foreign participation were a titanium dioxide mining and processing project worth about US$500 million, the exploration of mineral resources such as natural gas and coal; the development of ecotourism; steel mills and smelting plants, and the proposed construction of a refinery near the port of Nacala.[3] This latter project was projected to cost US$6 billion and was negotiated in 2007 but had made little progress by 2010.[4]

As in Zambia, foreign investors focused on sectors that had the potential to generate considerable returns through sales in global markets or through the development of niche markets such as tourism. Several characteristics of foreign investment are worth highlighting. First, although there were more than one hundred proposed projects each year, only a few of the projects involved sizable capital outlays. In any given year, two or three mega-projects accounted for between 30 and 90 percent of the total value of proposed investments. Otherwise, most proposed projects were small or medium-sized projects involving investments of less than US$1 million. Second, mega-projects in Mozambique broadened the tax base, provided skills training and employment, and increased exports.[5] With the exception of sugar processing, however, they did not foster upstream and downstream linkages with Mozambican businesses nor did they generate large increases in employment.[6] There is no direct correlation between large capital outlays and the number of jobs an investment generates. For example, the US$6 billion refinery project was expected to generate 470 jobs, whereas a US$44 million investment in a tourist development was expected to provide employment for 1,200 workers. On the other hand, a number of investments of less than US$1 million in agriculture, agro-processing, and industry were expected to generate employment for more than 400 workers per project.

---

[3] Lourenço Sambo, Head of Research Division, Centro de Promoção de Investimentos (CPI), Personal communication, Maputo, Mozambique, 8/1/2003; Mozambique, Centro de Promoção de Investimentos (CPI), "Tabelas dos Anos de 2002–2007" (2008), mimeo, and see http://www.mozbusiness.gov.mz. Figure includes pledged and committed foreign and direct investment, grants, and loans. It may underestimate investment in Mozambique, however, as it does not include projects that are negotiated without the help of the Center for Investment Promotion.

[4] "Mozambique Threatens to Cancel Nacala Oil Refinery," *Club of Mozambique*, August 20, 2010, accessed 4/28/2011, http://www.clubofmozambique.com.

[5] Dianna Games "Mozambique: The Business View, Results of a Survey on the Business Environment and Investment Climate," Business Leadership South Africa, Occasional paper number 4 (November 2007), 10–11.

[6] Carlos Castel-Branco, "Mega Projectos e Estrategia de Desenvolvimento: Notas para um Debate," Outubro 2002, 6–7, accessed 2/5/2009, http://www.iese.ac.mz/lib/cncb/Mega_projectos_Moz_texto.pdf.

Third, despite the differences in the value and expected employment of the proposed projects, an examination of all projects since 2003 suggests that they were evenly spread across a number of sectors such as agriculture, tourism, and industry rather than concentrated in one sector.[7] Unlike Zambia where most large capital outlays of foreign investment went to copper and related mining projects after 2000, mega-projects in Mozambique were in diverse sectors: They included telecommunications, transport, tourism, and energy. Small and medium investments included industry, tourism, agriculture, construction, and the retail sector. Last, as opposed to the late 1990s where private monopolies initially replaced state monopolies following privatization, limited competition characterized the formal Mozambican economy, particularly in banking, telecommunications, construction, coal, textiles, and food and beverages by 2007. In tourism and agricultural processing (especially cotton, cashew, and sugar cane), the competition ranged from moderate to extensive.

Since the mid 1990s, the most consistent investors were from South Africa, the United Kingdom, and Portugal. The value of South African investments grew steadily from US$26 million in 2003 to US$82 million of projected investment in 2007. South African companies dominated the tourism sector and invested in approximately 93 out of 126 projects between 2003 and 2007. They also directed their investments equally toward agriculture and industry with 31 projects and 37 projects, respectively, in these two sectors. Moreover, via subsidiaries in Mauritius, South African companies invested in steel- and metal-making factories and the cellular telephone industry.

British investors focused on tourism, agriculture, and agro-industry with a total of thirty-four projects. British investment grew steadily after the turn of the century and was projected to be US$92 million in 2007. In total, British investment between 2003 and 2007 equalled about US$159 million. By contrast, Portugal averaged around US$15 million in investments per year. The majority of projects were in industry followed by agriculture and tourism. The most important Portuguese investments during this time period were two hotels in Maputo worth around US$1 million each, a US$4 million investment in a business that supplied medical technology, and an agricultural project in Sofala province.[8]

Mozambique also attracted investors from other African countries besides South Africa and from other continents besides Europe. Investment from Kenya, Mauritius, Zimbabwe, Tanzania, and Malawi financed projects in tourism, industry, and agriculture throughout the country. China, India, and Brazil had a growing presence. In 2007, China proposed to invest US$45 million to construct a cement factory in Maputo, which, when completed was expected to employ 300 workers. Several public sector railways companies in India were jointly rehabilitating and managing railway lines in the center of the

[7] Mozambique, CPI, "Tabelas dos Anos."
[8] Ibid.

country in partnership with Mozambique's public ports and railways company, CFM. Along with Brazilian, British, and Australian firms, Indian companies were also investing in Mozambique's vast coal reserves.⁹ Owing to the extent of Mozambique's coal deposits, investment in this sector likely will dwarf all prior investments in a few years.

Like Zambia, Mozambique had a small stock exchange where the majority of the sixteen listed companies were owned by foreigners or by the state. These included large public companies in telecommunications, insurance, and hydrocarbons, a foreign-owned brewery, several banks, and a major cement manufacturing company. The government structured initial public offerings on the stock exchange to favor domestic investors and encouraged them to purchase shares. Regardless of the origin of the investor, however, most observers have expressed disappointment in the stock market. It has grown since its initial launch in 1999, but it has not become a viable capital market.¹⁰

Several features of the emerging market economy in Mozambique distinguish it from that of Zambia. First, domestic capital was visible in nearly every divestiture or new investment from telecommunications and transport to banking and agriculture. As in Zambia, domestic investors were concentrated in small and medium-sized companies in the retail sector; however, they also participated in larger ventures in transport, banking, agriculture, and industry either alone or alongside foreign investors. In joint ventures with foreigners, their interests varied from 1 percent to more than 50 percent.

Although not as divided as those in Zambia, national investors exhibited sectoral and ideological differences over the direction of the economy and experienced rivalries in the struggle to gain and retain lucrative assets. They had diverse racial and ethnic backgrounds, and their business experience varied from minimal to extensive. Some companies such as João Ferreira dos Santos, Grupo Entreposto, or Gani Comercial had their origins during the colonial period when Portuguese investors or Indian traders established large concessionary companies in agriculture or carved out a niche in retail or wholesale trade. Having survived the war and the socialist period, these companies expanded, contracted, or collapsed following the shift to a private sector economy.¹¹

⁹ World Bank, "Project Appraisal Document on a Proposed Credit in the Amount of SDR 7.6 million (US$110 million) to the Republic of Mozambique for the Beira Railway Project," Transport Sector, Country Department 2, Africa Region (November 9, 2004) and Sanjay Dutta, "Coal India Secures Two Blocks in Mozambique," *The Times of India*, December 26, 2009, accessed 4/26/2011, http://articles.timesofindia.indiatimes.com/2009-12-26/india-business/28075390_1_cil-mozambique-government-equity-in-overseas-mines.
¹⁰ "Major National Firms Listed on Maputo Stock Exchange," *The Mozambican Investor*, 126, February 17, 2009, accessed 3/1/2009, http://www.clubofmozambique.com; Jennifer Piesse and Bruce Hearn, "Barriers to the Development of Small Stock Markets: A Case Study of Swaziland and Mozambique," *Journal of International Development*, 22, 7 (2009): 1018–1037.
¹¹ M. Anne Pitcher, "Sobreviver a Transição: O Legado das Antigas Empresas Coloniais em Moçambique," *Análise Social*, xxxviii, 168 (2003): 793–820.

Importantly, domestic investors with extensive links to the ruling party, Frelimo, which has been in power since 1975, received or purchased parastatals and new ventures from tourism to finance. They consisted of party members who either moved from politics into business or, like the current and previous presidents of Mozambique, employed their networks in the political arena to engineer expansion into the market economy. In addition to heads of state, these politically well connected businessmen and women included former first ladies, former prime ministers, members of the military, heads of parastatals, and veterans of the armed struggle. They were represented across a wide range of sectors including banking, tourism, trade, industry, and agriculture, in large as well as small, private firms.[12]

A second feature of the privatization process was the degree to which the state retained or acquired a majority shareholding in electricity, telecommunications, airlines, ports, and railways and minority interests in a host of other businesses from sugar and cotton companies to natural gas and coal exploration (see Table 5.1). As of 2008, the government held interests in more than one hundred companies and participated as a minority or majority shareholder in most of the top twenty-five companies in Mozambique.[13] Unlike Zambia, where the government reneged on its decision to privatize large parastatals or began only recently to engage in joint ventures with foreign investors in limited sectors of the economy, the Mozambican government consciously adopted a strategy of maintaining a state presence in the economy from the beginning of the process.

Rather than outright sales of its largest parastatals, the government formed joint ventures with national and foreign private investors in agriculture, industry, energy, mineral resources, banking, and insurance. These companies were restructured to operate according to market principles and to generate profits and rebranded as "public companies."[14] Moreover, public companies were "rationalized" and commercialized in order to compete more effectively in national and regional market economies. Public companies invested in other economic sectors producing a complex web of interlocking directorships, cross-shareholdings, and strategic alliances.[15] CFM formed public–private partnerships with foreign investors to rehabilitate the rail lines; to establish

---

[12] Material based on data from Mozambique, *Boletim da República, Série III*, selected years.

[13] Criteria for selection of the top companies in Mozambique include revenue growth, return on equity, liquidity, revenue per employee, see KPMG, *100 Maiores Empresas*, 21, 68–71; Mozambique, Instituto de Gestão das Participações do Estado (IGEPE), "Empresas com Participações do Estado," mimeo, 2010. In 2008, IGEPE was responsible for 135 companies. Some public enterprises such as Mozambique Electricity and Mozambique Ports and Railways fall under the responsibility of the ministry of finance and sector ministries. The actual number in this group is unknown.

[14] KPMG, *100 Maiores Empresas*.

[15] M. Anne Pitcher, *Transforming Mozambique*, 140–178 and "Conditions, Commitments and the Politics of Restructuring in Africa," *Comparative Politics*, 36, 4 (2004): 279–398.

TABLE 5.1. *Mozambique: Companies in the Top Twenty-Five with Shares Held by the State*

Rank	Name of Company	Sector	State Share (%)
1	Mozal	Industry	3.9
2	MCEL	Communications	26.0
3	Petromoc	Energy	100.0
4	Hidroelectrica de Cahora Bassa	Energy	85.0
6	Electricidade de Moçambique	Energy	100.0
7	Cervejas de Moçambique	Food and Beverage	1.8
8	Mozambique Transmission Company	Energy	33.3
9	Banco International de Moç[a]	Banking and Leasing	26.4
10	Sasol Petroleum Temane[b]	Energy	25.0
12	Telecomunicações de Moçambique	Communications	100.0
13	Linhas Aereas de Moçambique	Transport	91.2
14	Cimentos de Moçambique	Industry	11.9
16	CFM	Transport	100.0
17	Coca-Cola SABCO	Food and Beverage	28.8
23	Co. Moç. de Hidrocarbonetos	Energy	20.0
24	Petromoc e Sasol	Energy	51.0

[a] 4.95% is via the National Institute of Social Security; 4.15% via Mozambique Insurance Company.

[b] State shares via National Hydrocarbons Company.

Source: Author's Compilation from KPMG, *100 Maiores Empresas de Moçambique*, XI Edição, Ranking das Maiores Empresas 2008 (Maputo: Boom, 2009) and Mozambique, Instituto de Gestão das Participações do Estado, "Empresas com Participações do Estado," 2010, mimeo.

new container terminals; and to upgrade port facilities in the south, center, and north of the country. It took a stake in eleven different companies all of which were directly or indirectly linked to ports and railways operation.[16]

In addition to maintaining a presence in former parastatals, the government contributed to new investment projects such as Mozambique Cellular (MCEL), a nationwide cellular telephone network that was a public–public partnership between the publicly owned telephone company, Mozambique Telecommunications (TDM), and the government agency responsible for managing state assets. MCEL was the fourth largest company in Mozambique with regard to the volume of business transacted in 2006. Along with foreign investors, the government had a stake in emerging coal, natural gas, oil, and biofuels projects.[17]

[16] World Bank, "Project Appraisal Document."

[17] African Development Bank and Organisation of Economic Cooperation and Development, "Mozambique," *African Economic Outlook* (2008), 463 and Adam Welz, "Ethanol's African Land Grab," *Mother Jones*, March/April 2009, accessed 2/7/2010, http://motherjones.com/print/21671.

The Distributional Consequences of Reform

The aggregate results from economic reform were more positive in Mozambique than in Zambia. First, the country experienced economic growth both earlier and at a higher rate than Zambia did. From a rate of −5 percent at the end of the war in 1992, the growth rate jumped to nearly 9 percent the following year. Although the increase could be ascribed simply to the war's end, high growth rates have been sustained for nearly two decades, which suggests that economic reform, not just recovery from conflict was the cause.[18] Annual growth rates averaged 8 percent from 1993 to 2000. By contrast, Zambia's annual growth rate was zero from 1992 to 2000. From 2001 to 2006, Zambia's annual growth rate averaged 5 percent, but Mozambique's was higher still at 8.5 percent annually.[19]

Second, just as the sales of state assets and new investment were cross-sectoral, so also was Mozambique's growth. Unlike Zambia, where growth was largely confined to the copper sector after 2001, almost every sector in Mozambique such as transport and communications, agriculture, industry, energy, tourism, construction, and finance recorded increases after 1993. Manufacturing, transport, and communications saw the highest growth as measured by their share of GDP, whereas traditional sectors such as agriculture grew more slowly.[20]

Third, cross-sectoral growth contributed to broad-based poverty reduction, although to what extent is the subject of debate. Seventy percent of the population lived below the poverty line in 1997; the number had dropped to 54 percent by 2003 according to the World Bank. One prominent critic argues, however, that World Bank calculations for 2003 underestimate the cost of the food basket consumed by people near the poverty line. The number of those living below the poverty lines was closer to 63 percent or about 11.7 million people, a difference of 1.7 million.[21] Both calculations show greater decreases in rural than in urban areas.[22] Maternal and infant mortality have also declined. Nevertheless, Mozambique only ranked 172 out of 182 countries on the Human Development Index in 2007. Comparatively Zambia did eight points better with a ranking of 164.[23]

Despite impressive aggregate results, the outcome of the privatization process had a differential impact on different segments of the population, which

---

[18] Unicef–Mozambique and Government of Mozambique, *Childhood Poverty in Mozambique: A Situation and Trends Analysis* (Maputo: Unicef, 2006), 37.

[19] World Bank, *World Development Indicators*.

[20] African Development Bank, "Mozambique," 392–394.

[21] Joe Hanlon, "Is Poverty Decreasing in Mozambique," Instituto de Estudos Sociais e Económicos (IESE), Maputo 1 (September 9, 2007), 9–10.

[22] World Bank, *Beating the Odds: Sustaining Inclusion in Mozambique's Growing Economy*, Summary (Washington, D.C.: World Bank, 2008), 4; Hanlon, "Is Poverty Decreasing," 10.

[23] United Nations Development Program (UNDP), *Human Development Report, 2009*, Summary (New York: UNDP, 2009), 12.

engendered conflicts in Mozambique as it did in Zambia. Alongside growth, inequality increased, sparking tensions between the haves and the have-nots. The Gini coefficient was .42 in 2002–2003 but an even higher .52 in the capital of Maputo.[24] The rise of inequality there appears paradoxical because Maputo was the largest recipient of investment in the country. An influx of migrants from poorer parts of the country also cannot explain the increase because population growth in the capital has only averaged about 1.2 percent per year since the 1990s. By contrast, the province in which the capital is located has experienced a 50 percent increase in population since 1997. The nearby city of Matola accounts for 55 percent of the province's total population.[25]

A likely explanation for the high inequality in the capital is that most of the upper and middle classes were residing in Maputo city, whereas poor and vulnerable groups lived in high-density settlements on the outskirts.[26] Calculating the exact size and composition of socioeconomic groups in Maputo is difficult since much of the scholarship on these groups has largely been impressionistic. If we consider access to a computer and Internet usage as indicators of the upper class, then the recent census calculates that approximately 38,000 to 60,000 people or 3 to 5 percent of the total population in the city of 1.1 million people fit into this category.[27] The pattern of higher inequality in the capital is replicated in other cities and towns in the rest of the country.[28]

Beyond the numbers, visible disparities distinguish the housing and lifestyles of the wealthy versus the poor (with the "middle class" falling somewhere between these two extremes). Gated communities for the elite have mushroomed along the coast of the city. Wealthy Mozambicans and foreigners have refurbished homes in the attractive residential neighborhoods within the heart of the city and fortified their properties with walls and private security. Shopping malls, stylish boutiques, hairdressers, hotels, and restaurants have also multiplied since the adoption of reforms.

By contrast, surveys find that around 80 percent of Mozambicans live on less than $2.00 a day.[29] Squatter settlements with houses made of mud or cane occupy the margins of urban areas throughout the country. Like many in the rural areas, the poorest of the poor in cities do not have electricity or running water. And like the rural areas, the urban poor mostly rely on the informal economy to survive and to supply their needs. Six million economically active

[24] Channing Arndt, Robert James, and Kenneth Simler, "Has Economic Growth in Mozambique Been Pro-Poor?," *Journal of African Economies*, 15, 4 (2006): 582–583.
[25] AIM, "Mozambique: Sharp Population Growth in Maputo Province" (April 24, 2009), allAfrica. com, accessed on 6/17/2009, http://allafrica.com/stories/printable/200904240893.html.
[26] Arndt et al., "Has Economic Growth?," 583–584.
[27] Mozambique, Instituto Nacional de Estatística, III Recenseamento Geral da População, 2007, accessed 4/26/2009, http://www.ine.gov.mz/censo.
[28] Hanlon, "Is Poverty Decreasing?"
[29] João C. G. Pereira, "'Antes o "diabo" Conhecido do Que Um "anjo" Desconhecido': As Limitações do Voto Económico Na Reeleição do Partido Frelimo," *Análise Social*, XLIII, 2 (2008): 430.

Mozambicans work in the informal sector in rural areas; a little more than 1.5 million people participate in the urban informal economy selling everything from food to electronics within densely populated settlements.[30]

Contributing to the divergent lifestyles and growing number of informal sector workers are the job losses experienced by the formal sector owing to privatization and rationalization of the workforce. Out of a total available labor force of a little more than 9 million, the formal sector employed approximately 360,000 workers by 2008, indicating that the market for formal sector jobs had stagnated since the early 1990s in spite of population growth and increased investment.[31] As in Zambia, total numbers of trade unionists also declined as the transition to a market economy progressed during the 1990s. Of those employed in formal sector, wage labor jobs, approximately 140,000 workers belonged to one of about twenty national trade unions in the country.[32]

In response to losses of jobs and benefits, trade unionists in the formal sector organized frequent protests during the early phases of privatization. Land conflicts in the most productive and populated areas of the country intensified as smallholders competed with large agribusinesses for land and labor.[33] In addition, during the mid 1990s, domestic industrialists in the newly privatized cashew sector, to name but one example, protested vigorously at the liberalization of duties on exports of raw cashew. Liberalization resulted in the export of most of Mozambique's raw cashews to India for processing, rather than the domestic processing of raw cashews. The drop in a supply that had already sharply decreased owing to the civil war left 8,500 workers and the newly privatized industry without sufficient cashews to process.[34]

Furthermore, like their counterparts in Zambia, domestic investors in Mozambique faced difficulties with restricted access to bank loans, high interest rates, unfair competition, complex tax and licensing regimes, and a lack of skilled labor. Many of the larger, better capitalized, foreign-owned firms

[30] Mozambique, Instituto Nacional de Estatística, "O Sector Informal em Moçambique: Resultados do Primeiro Inquérito Nacional (2004/5)," Maputo (Agosto 28, 2006), 84.

[31] Calculated from Ministry of Planning and Development, National Directorate of Policy Studies and Analysis and World Bank, Poverty and Economic Management Department, Africa Region, "Job Creation in Mozambique: Is Labor Law Reform the Answer?" (November 2006), 15; Mozambique, INE, "O Sector Informal."

[32] This figure is compiled from data on trade unions furnished by Alexandre Munguambe, Secretário Geral, and Boaventura Mondlane, Secretário do CCS para Administração e Finanças, Organização dos Trabalhadores de Moçambique (OTM), Interview, Maputo, 5/26/2008 and Edward Webster, Geoffrey Wood, Beata Mtyingizana, and Michael Brookes, "Residual Unionism and Renewal: Organized Labour in Mozambique," *Journal of Industrial Relations*, 48 (2006): 262.

[33] See M. Anne Pitcher, "Forgetting from Above and Memory from Below: Strategies of Legitimation and Struggle in Postsocialist Mozambique," *Africa*, 76, 1 (2006): 88–112.

[34] Joe Hanlon, "Power Without Responsibility: The World Bank and Mozambican Cashew Nuts," *Review of African Political Economy*, 83 (2000): 29–45 and Pitcher, *Transforming Mozambique*, 225–233.

were able to overcome these challenges by accessing donor or private funding, hiring expatriate workers, and partnering with the state, but they complained about the obstacles to investment and production in Mozambique's business environment, too.[35] Although surveys point to marked improvements in the business environment over time, they also underscore the presence of bureaucratic delays, centralization, and corruption. In a national survey conducted in 2004, 51 percent of respondents claimed they had paid a bribe in the preceding year.[36] The police force accounted for most of the petty corruption, whereas the incidence of large-scale corruption appeared to be low.[37]

As in Zambia, a limited democracy provided the political context in which private sector development took place. The Mozambican government periodically resorted to authoritarian measures to constrain popular responses to privatization or circumvented existing rules to favor some participants in the process over others. Intimidation and violence against journalists by state officials and the security forces circumscribed media oversight and facilitated abuses of state discretion. Police brutality against members of the opposition or protesters stifled open and vigorous debate, and a poorly functioning judiciary precluded the defense of civil liberties and political rights.[38]

Yet, where Mozambique differed markedly from Zambia was in the logic of party politics. Unlike Zambia, the two top parties in Mozambique had both the capacity and the motivation to reproduce themselves over time. A stable party system characterized by relatively entrenched party loyalties helps to explain the objectives behind state discretion during the process of privatization. The ruling party used its discretion selectively and deliberately to favor its base and to engineer what I label partisan private sector development. To protect formal sector workers, it softened the harshest effects of privatization through protective labor laws and maintained a state presence in strategic sectors of the economy where employment of workers was sizable. It directed divestitures toward party loyalists and cemented alliances between supporters and other private investors. Although internal factions existed and had to be managed carefully, the process reaped considerable political benefits: It reinvigorated the party in power and strengthened state capacity.

---

[35] Mozambique, Ministry of Planning and Development, National Directorate of Studies and Policy Analysis, "Enterprise Development in Mozambique: Results Based on Manufacturing Surveys Conducted in 2002 and 2006," Discussion Papers, no. 33E (October 2006, revised January 2007); Jim LaFleur, *Economist*, Confederation of Business Associations (CTA), Interview, Maputo, 5/21/2008 and 5/30/2008.

[36] Unicef–Mozambique, *Childhood Poverty*, 62.

[37] Transparency International, "National Integrity System (NIS) Country Study Report Mozambique 2006/7," written and researched by Marcelo Mosse, Nelson Manjate, and Edson Cortez (2007), 7.

[38] Freedom House, "Mozambique Country Report (2008)," accessed 2/10/2010, http://www. freedomhouse.org. A fuller discussion of limited democracy in Mozambique takes place later.

Explaining Reform Outcomes I: Institutional Design

The Mozambican government set the institutional foundations for a private sector economy before the signing of the 1992 peace accord and the country's first multiparty elections of 1994. As I have argued elsewhere, the shift not only recognized the direct and indirect aid to the government's opponents by Western interests but also reflected piecemeal efforts to erode socialism by the small remaining private sector in Mozambique.[39] In 1984, the government established an office to attract foreign investment and set the conditions under which foreigners could invest. By 1987, it offered incentives such as special tax breaks and customs duty reductions on imports to encourage domestic investment in private sector undertakings. Two years later, it withdrew restrictions on the accumulation of capital and the employment of workers by members of Frelimo, freeing them up to participate in the market economy if they so wished.

While continuing to assert that all land belonged to the state, the new constitution of 1990 acknowledged private property rights for the first time since independence. Subsequent legislation detailed the procedures for the privatization of large versus small assets, established a framework for privatization, designated agencies to handle the process, and listed those state assets slated for divestiture. The government reinforced a constitutional provision to aid the development of national capital by favoring domestic investors in a number of ways. It allowed domestic investors to put down a smaller share of the total purchase price of a company than foreign investors and gave them more time than foreigners to complete their purchase. For larger companies, it reserved part of the shares for management and workers of the company if they had worked there for at least five years. It provided tax breaks for nationals at a lower threshold of investment than foreigners. Furthermore, the government offered support for particular projects that contributed to the training or growth of domestic entrepreneurs.

The government complemented its legislative efforts by creating a privatization agency within the ministry of planning and finance to handle the privatization of large and medium-sized companies. Within the ministries of agriculture and industry and commerce, the government established additional units to undertake the privatization of smaller state assets. To advise foreign as well as domestic investors, furthermore, the government replaced the Foreign Investment Promotion Agency with the Center for Investment Promotion in 1993.[40]

Given that the institutional design for a private sector was already underway even before the country became democratic, it seems reasonable to ask whether its creation and initial implementation by a government that was still authoritarian made a difference to the subsequent development of the private

---

[39] Pitcher, "Sobreviver a Transição."
[40] For additional details on the process, see Pitcher, *Transforming Mozambique*, 124–138.

sector. Did the existence of an authoritarian regime affect the content of the legislation or the pace of sales? Did it determine who the beneficiaries were or how the losers were treated?

Regime type did not greatly influence the content of legislation or the pace of privatization before the democratic transition of 1994, but the continuity of the ruling party affected the process and the beneficiaries of privatization after the elections. First, many of the reasons that motivated other countries to undergo privatization in the early 1990s also drove the decision in Mozambique, regardless of regime type. The failure of state firms, demands from private sector actors, the fall of the Soviet Union, and conditions on aid by multi- and bilateral donors heavily influenced the adoption of sweeping institutional and organizational changes. Second, the content of the new rules adopted by the Mozambican government reflected the diffusion of neo-liberal norms by donors and technocrats, rather than the effects of regime type, and they were norms that Frelimo's opponent, Renamo, also favored.[41] Under donor guidance, the government created a privatization agency, passed laws on divestiture of parastatals, created an investment center, and revised the constitution in order to acknowledge individual property rights. It concluded trade agreements just as other countries did.

Third, as a practical matter, the conclusion of the war, negotiations over the peace accord, and preparations for the first democratic elections precluded the consistent implementation of economic policy between 1990 and 1994. Under the circumstances, foreign investors were reluctant to purchase companies and the government was not yet equipped to undertake the privatization of major parastatals. Macroeconomic conditions were highly unstable; and basic inputs such as credit, electricity, water, and primary materials were either unavailable or in short supply.

Because the incumbent regime was victorious in the elections, however, ex ante decisions made a difference ex post with regard to the beneficiaries, the pace, and the institutional qualities of privatization. Regarding beneficiaries, the adoption of legislation prior to 1994 signaled to the existing domestic private sector and interested foreign companies that the government had abandoned socialism and was committed to the creation of a private sector–driven economy. Because the government had already constructed much of the institutional framework for privatization, it was able rapidly to enact it after victory, without having to confront challenges either from its own party in parliament or from the opposition.

Furthermore, the government created an interest group with a stake in privatization that was connected to the ruling party. Although major assets were

[41] Bruce Kogut and J. Muir Macpherson, "The Decision to Privatize: Economists and the Construction of Ideas and Policies" in Beth Simmons, Frank Dobbin, and Geoffrey Garrett, eds., *The Global Diffusion of Markets and Democracy* (Cambridge: Cambridge University Press, 2008), 104–140.

not privatized until after the elections, around 369 small and medium-sized companies in agriculture, industry, construction, and commerce were sold between 1989 and 1994.[42] Besides liquidating those companies that had collapsed, the government divested firms to the small existing private sector, emerging Mozambican entrepreneurs, foreigners, and members of Frelimo. By creating beneficiaries among staunch party loyalists, the government neutralized insider resistance to privatization and minimized the chances of a policy reversal. After the elections, this group in particular would become invaluable to advancing the privatization process and tying private sector interests to the interests of the ruling party. In advance of the elections, then, an authoritarian government was beginning to build a political and economic base of support that linked party loyalists as well as a small private sector to the outcome of its economic policies.

In a setting where the party in power continued in office following the transition, economy policy choices reflected its partisan considerations and authoritarian inclinations. The privatization of state assets was both highly centralized and hierarchical. The highest echelons of state authority exercised the order to privatize, which several lower layers of the state bureaucracy then carried out. Unlike Zambia, where the privatization agency was an independent agency, the agency in Mozambique depended on prime ministerial and ministerial authorization to identify and sell state assets, especially large and medium-sized enterprises. With regard to the sale of large enterprises, the prime minister was legally empowered to create the privatization commission that evaluated bidders and their proposals. Moreover, the privatization law of 1993 stipulated very clearly that for purchases greater than US$10 million, only the Council of Ministers could authorize the sale. By contrast, specialized units within the respective ministries handled sales of smaller state firms in industry or agriculture.[43]

Centralized state control over the privatization of the country's most important assets ensured that the ruling party would exercise substantial influence over how and to whom companies would be sold. The government used this authority to champion the interests of the party and direct assets to the party faithful. Additional legislation reinforced the continuing presence of the state and the favoritism toward partisan players, even as it advanced the institutions required for a market economy. For example, the 1997 land law served multiple political objectives. It acknowledged property rights and welcomed the expansion of commercial agriculture, while protecting rural smallholders and the interests of the state and the party.

---

[42] Mozambique, UTRE, "Privatisation in Mozambique," 1 (1995), 2–3; Mozambique, Ministry of Agriculture, Unit for the Restructuring of Agricultural Enterprises, "Mapa das empresas alienadas no Ministério da Agricultura em 23.05.95" (1995); Mozambique, *Boletim da República*, I–III Série, 1989–1995.

[43] Mozambique, UTRE, "Privatisation in Mozambique," 1 (1995), 2.

To reduce opposition to policy change inside the party and to maintain state control over land, the government circumscribed rights to private property by continuing to assert legally in the 1997 land law that all land belonged to the state just as it had during the socialist period and in the revised constitution of 1990. Instead of freehold property, the property rights established in the rural areas consisted of concessionary arrangements with companies or individuals that gave them leasehold rights from thirty to fifty years, renewable for an additional fifty years.[44] While the long concessionary period enhanced security of tenure for commercial landholders, equally the law acknowledged communal land rights in rural areas in order to strengthen the rights of communities vis-à-vis investors seeking to acquire land. Although there is much discretion in the law regarding who in the community may assert these rights and under what conditions, the attention to communal land rights sought to assuage indigenous smallholder interests, especially those in the center and north of the country where historically the party had encountered resistance.[45] Except in the south and far north of the country, smallholders do not constitute a sizable share of the party's base, but the history of conflict in the country demonstrates that no party can afford to alienate them.

Just as the government sought to adopt a land law that would recognize private property rights without disaffecting rural smallholders, likewise, it revised existing labor laws without losing the support of one of its most loyal allies, organized labor. To be certain, the government severely reduced the benefits it once accorded to formal sector workers under socialism, severed the institutional links to organized labor it once had, and drastically reduced the labor force prior to privatization. However, for the small percentage of formal sector workers who remained following privatization the labor law afforded considerable job security particularly for those workers in large firms.[46]

Lastly, the government institutionalized the state's remaining presence in the economy. With the bulk of privatization complete by 2001, the government formed a new agency, IGEPE, the Institute for the Management of State Shareholdings, which was responsible not only for managing the state's assets in approximately 135 companies as of 2008, but also for pursuing additional restructuring of these firms in consultation with other ministries.[47] Together with those public companies such as the ports and railways company and

---

[44] Mozambique, Assembleia da República, Lei no. 19/97 (October 1, 1997) and Decreto-lei 69/98 (December 1998).

[45] Ibid.

[46] Mozambique, Assembleia da República, *Lei do Trabalho*, Lei no. 8/98 (July 20, 1998), revised, Lei no. 23/2007 (August 1, 2007). Subsequent revisions to the law in 2007 are consistent with the previous claim.

[47] Mozambique, Institute for the Management of State Participation, "Corporate Governance in State-Owned Enterprises in Mozambique," Powerpoint Presentation by Daniel Tembe, Executive Chairman, IGEPE, May 27–28, 2009. The total number of state enterprises exceeds this total as not all remaining SOEs were included under the umbrella of IGEPE.

the electricity company, the firms in the state's portfolio fulfilled a number of political and economic objectives. Some, such as TDM, were profitable and employed large workforces and managers who likely supported Frelimo. Others such as Mozambique Airways were symbols of national pride; or currently or potentially lucrative such as Cahora Bassa Dam or Mozambique Petroleum. Retaining an interest in these companies afforded protection to the base of the party and secured revenue for the state.

Key features of the reform process support conventional scholarly opinion that the presence of donors and the diffusion of neo-liberal ideas acted as important influences on the economic transition in Mozambique, as they did in many other countries in Africa, Latin America, or Eastern Europe. However, the continuity of the party in power was brought to bear on the substance, pace, and beneficiaries of the privatization program. The party that won the elections was the same party that declared Marxism-Leninism in 1977 and created the one-party state. In sharp contrast to Zambia where a new party initiated sweeping economic reforms, Frelimo had a quarter century of experience running the government.

But Frelimo's previous experience would have mattered less and may even have been a liability if the political context had been different. If the party system had been more fragmented as in the case of Zambia or the context more democratic as in the South African case, then the outcome of privatization might have been more inconsistent or more subject to compromise as, respectively, they were in those cases. What made a critical difference to the trajectory of privatization in Mozambique was that the ruling party operated in a context where party stability was high and where democracy was limited. The ruling party relied on that context to facilitate an alliance between party loyalists and emerging capital, to coopt organized labor, and to mute political dissent.

Explaining Reform Outcomes II: Party Politics and Limited Democracy

Although many parties participated in national and municipal elections up to 2009, the number of effective parties in the Assembly of the Republic (Mozambique's national parliament) and in the electorate was two. In comparison with the average for political parties in Africa, electoral and seat volatility in Mozambique was low. Shifts from one party to the other between 1994 and 2004 were infrequent; where movement occurred, it was from Renamo to Frelimo. Nevertheless, the formation of the Mozambique Democratic Movement (MDM) by former Renamo supporters and several smaller parties in 2008 demonstrated that the durability of the party system cannot be assumed. In Mozambique, the cleavages defined by the period of violent struggle may have diminished and new divisions may replace them in the future. To be consistent with the other cases, I mainly focus on the period from the 1990s until 2005, although I refer also to the 2009 elections where appropriate.

Party Organization

Frelimo and Renamo were opponents during the lengthy conflict that took place in Mozambique from the 1980s until 1992. These same parties faced each other consistently in elections after 1994, and together they dominated parliament. Both benefited from provisions on public financing of elections and direct budget support to members of parliament written into the 1992 Peace Accord. Parties were tax exempt and enjoyed free coverage and equal time by the media during electoral campaigns.[48]

The opposition party, Renamo, typified in many ways the stereotype described in scholarly accounts of African political parties. It was dominated by a "big man," Afonso Dhlakama, who was also Renamo's leader when the party was an armed rebel movement. Like many strongmen, Dhlakama's interaction with the ruling party and his management of his own party could be unpredictable and arbitrary. If he could not gain an advantage through formal institutional channels such as the courts or parliament, he and his top aides were not averse to the use of informal mechanisms such as boycotts or rumors to pressure the ruling party.[49] Dhlakama himself selected those who occupied top positions in the party, and he was inclined to favor personal loyalty over competence. He dismissed or sidelined those whom he perceived as threats to his power even if they attracted supporters to the party or proved to be skillful politicians.[50]

The tactic of eliminating rivals who threaten the big man tends to undermine party cohesion and predictably, Renamo has shown increasing signs of fragmentation, particularly since 2004. Defections from the party have risen in recent years as potential successors to Dhlakama have either left or been expelled from the party, taking their followers with them.[51] Moreover, local party structures were weak. In several areas of the country, Renamo's presence was "little more than a flag on someone's house" as Giovanni Carbone has

---

[48] Bruno Speck provides a detailed account of the laws and loopholes regarding public financing of campaigns and politicians in Mozambique. See "Political Finance in Mozambique," a report based on desk research and a field mission in Mozambique in November 2004, mimeo, São Paulo (December 2004). For example, public funding provided US$150,000 to each of the five presidential candidates in 2004. Laws have since been revised to exclude candidates who are seeking funds for personal use.

[49] Carrie Manning, "Conflict Management and Elite Habituation in Post-war Democracy: The Case of Mozambique," *Comparative Politics*, 35, 1 (2002): 63–84.

[50] Mozambique News Agency, "Crisis in Renamo: Raul Domingos Suspended," AIM Reports, no. 187, 11 July 2000; Giovanni Carbone, "Emerging Pluralist Politics in Mozambique: The Frelimo-Renamo Party System," Crisis States Programme, Development Research Centre, London School of Economics, Working Paper no. 23 (March 2003), 14.

[51] Recent departures occurred in connection with the formation of the Mozambique Democratic Movement prior to the 2009 elections, see AIM News, "Renamo Members Drift Towards Daviz Simango" March 5, 2009; and Sérgio Chichava, "MDM: A New Political Force in Mozambique?" *Domingo*, "Reflectindo sobre Moçambique," May 2, 2010, accessed 11/6/2010, http://comunidademocambicana.blogspot.com/2010/05/sugestao-para-leitura-mdm-new-political.html.

observed.[52] It was also chronically short of money relative to the resources that Frelimo had at its disposal.

Yet there were a number of ways in which Renamo differed organizationally and ideologically from the fluid or inchoate parties of Zambia. First, Renamo's existence as an armed insurgent group prior to its transformation into a political party gave it deeper historical roots in the country. Whatever reputation Renamo may have garnered during the conflict, the longevity of the movement and the party over a period of thirty years demonstrated its organizational stability. Second, personnel who served the political and military wings of the movement continued into the period of multiparty politics. They brought experience to the party and contributed to its cohesion in and out of parliament. These included several former commanders such as Herminio Morais, Arlindo Maqueval, Ossufo Momade, now general secretary of the party; and Fernando Mazanga, the party's national spokesperson.[53] Third, although Renamo's stronghold was among rural populations and traditional authorities (chiefs) located in the center of Mozambique, it was able to develop and articulate a national agenda, unlike many opposition parties in Zambia. It had an election manifesto, a party flag, a symbol, and a motto. It held rallies and ran nationwide electoral campaigns in each of the national elections from 1994.[54] It consistently challenged Frelimo policies on the stump, in parliament, and in the media. Finally, as the major opposition party, Renamo had a shadow cabinet that paralleled the existing administration. Where Renamo perceived gaps in the existing government, it also created additional shadow ministries such as the ministry for traditional authorities.[55]

Like Renamo, Frelimo brought the discipline garnered from years of combat during the liberation struggle and the civil conflict into the era of multiparty democracy. Yet, its organizational capacities outmatched those of Renamo. Having governed the country since 1975 and having been elected four times since the country democratized in 1994 (most recently in 2009), Frelimo was a skilled, experienced party where internal disagreements rarely became public and party loyalty among its nearly 1.5 million members was strong. As with many former liberation movements in Africa, the foundation of loyalty to the party for the longest serving members was grounded in a shared history of colonial oppression and armed struggle for independence. It was reinforced for older and newer members through memories and social networks; participation in local party organizations; and involvement in meetings, congresses, and

[52] Giovanni Carbone, "Continuidade Na Renovação? Ten years of Multiparty Politics in Mozambique: Roots, Evolution, and Stabilization of the Frelimo-Renamo Party System," *Journal of Modern African Studies*, 43, 3 (2005): 431 and see Manning, "Elite Habituation," 71.
[53] See Renamo Web site, accessed 11/8/2010, http://www.renamo.org.mz.
[54] See Michel Cahen's compelling account of Renamo's initial campaign, *Os Outros: Um historiador em Moçambique* (Basel: P. Schlettwein Publishing, 2004).
[55] For information on the current shadow cabinet, see Renamo Web site.

training sessions. And finally, loyalty was rooted in self-preservation – for party membership has brought political and economic rewards.

Party structures reinforced the loyalty of party supporters by binding them to one another from the local to the national level. Organized initially according to the principles of democratic centralism, the party's organization was modified to accommodate the shift to electoral democracy. Each level of the party organization drew its members from the previous level. About 88,000 party cells constituted the base of the party. These cells were in factories, neighborhoods, or small villages as they were during the period of the one-party state. From cells, the next level of party organization was the circle of which there were 3,525. Beyond circles, the party had 376 larger zones organized across the country.[56]

Directives and guidelines for the functioning of party members, their cells, circles, and zones emanated from party statutes and also the party congresses, which took place every five or six years. Party statutes, which are revised from time to time, expressed the rights and duties of members. They tied individuals structurally to the organization by stating that party members were expected to belong to cells. The statutes also detailed obligations to the consolidation of democracy in Mozambique (and hence to the party's continuity in power) by admonishing members to conduct themselves responsibly during election campaigns and by requiring them to vote. They bestowed upon a specially selected Party Verification Commission the power to uphold the ethics of the party and to administer disciplinary action against members who failed to behave in accordance with party rules.

The 1, 326 delegates to the party's ninth congress in 2006 were dedicated party members who served in government; worked for the party; or occupied prominent positions in business, academia, and the civil service. Consistent with the larger transformation that Mozambique has undergone over the past two decades, the socioeconomic profiles of congress delegates have changed. After more than a decade of reform, few were peasants and workers as in the past, rather the majority were career civil servants, state employees, politicians, or party members. Twenty-one percent of delegates worked for the party. Only 15 percent of delegates were in Frelimo during the struggle for independence meaning that a new generation of party supporters dominated the party congresses.[57]

Delegates discussed issues of central importance to the party and voted for the 180 members of the Central Committee (CC) of the party. They implemented the decisions taken at the Congress and approved the general rules, regulations, and reports of the party. The CC oversaw and planned party

---

[56] Frelimo, Departamento de mobilização e propaganda, "Relatório do CC ao 9o Congresso," *Boletim de Célula*, 1, Fevereiro, 2007, 4.

[57] Joe Hanlon, "Frelimo Is Now the Party of the Bureaucracy," "Mozambique News Reports and Clippings," Mozambique, 102, 11/17/2006.

activities between elections and congresses, instructing the various levels of the party on their duties and how to carry them out. Since the CC only met once or twice a year, however, they chose from among their members an eight-person secretariat that coordinated the work of the CC. Members of the CC also chose the party's Political Commission, which was the locus of decision making in the party and its most powerful body. Composed of seventeen members, it included the president of the party who was also president of the country, the general secretary, and members elected from the CC. The head of Frelimo in parliament was also a nonvoting member of the Political Commission.

The commission met once a month, and its work was multifaceted. Taking into account the deliberations at the congress, it developed the party's policy agenda and prioritized the objectives of the party. It expressed the party's values and enforced its statutes. It coordinated the activities of the party, oversaw the training of party members, disseminated information about the party, and recruited new members. Since the party was also ruling the country, the commission coordinated policy initiatives with the party in government and in parliament.[58]

Policy coordination and communication between the party and its representatives in the government and parliament were greatly facilitated by the fact that members of government were intimately acquainted with how the party functioned. The number of years that members of government served the party provided a striking contrast with Zambia, where members of government had less experience either in parliament or in party organizations. By contrast, members of the ruling party in Mozambique who served in government had moved through the ranks of the party. They had directed cells and zones and served on the Central Committee and the Political Commission, gaining experience and demonstrating their loyalty at each stage of their political careers. Many had government experience as district administrators or provincial governors before serving in central government.

Parties in the Electorate

Party success does not simply depend on the loyalty of card-carrying members but also on getting out the vote. Mozambique's closed list, proportional representation system facilitated the development of stable party identities among voters, though it did not guarantee them. Members of parliament were chosen from eleven multimember constituencies corresponding to the country's provinces. In addition, two members of parliament were in single member districts that represented Mozambican communities living abroad. Until 2004, parties had to obtain at least 5 percent of the votes in order to gain a seat in parliament. Although the threshold did not discourage the participation of smaller

---

[58] Frelimo, "Estatutos," Aprovados pelo 9 Congresso, n.d., see especially Capitulo V., and Frelimo, "Inovações introduzidas pelo 9o Congresso nos Estatutos do Partido," *Boletim de Célula*, 13–15.

TABLE 5.2. *Mozambique Election Results: Presidency and Assembly of the Republic*

Presidency	Assembly of the Republic		
	Frelimo	Renamo[a]	Third Party
1994 Joaquim Chissano (F)	129	112	9
1999 Joaquim Chissano (F)	133	117	
2004 Armando Guebuza (F)	160	90	
2009 Armando Guebuza (F)	191	51	8

[a] Renamo formed a coalition in 1999 and 2004 with ten and eleven smaller parties, respectively. In 1999 these smaller parties held eighteen seats. In 2004, the number held by the smaller parties is unclear.

Source: EISA, "Mozambique: Election Archive."

parties (thirty-two participated in the first elections); it did reduce significantly their chances of capturing seats as few parties got close to crossing it. At 10 percent, voter volatility is low in Mozambique and its ENPP of 1.90 offers further indication that a two-party system prevailed. In 1994 and 2009, a third-party captured seats; otherwise, most of the votes between 1994 and 2009 went to Frelimo or Renamo. Renamo formed coalitions with smaller parties in both 1999 and 2004 to improve its chances of capturing seats, but these coalitions had little impact on its overall vote share.[59]

Mozambique has held four elections following the transition to democracy. Election results in Table 5.2 illustrate the relative stability of the two parties and their comparable seat shares in parliament up until 2004. Recent results reflect the increasing dominance of Frelimo and correspondingly the decline of Renamo. Frelimo has captured the presidency and a majority of seats in the National Assembly in all four elections.

As in many other countries, the respective parties dominated particular regions. Frelimo regularly captured most of the seats in the southern part of the country whereas Renamo's stronghold was in the central provinces of Manica, Sofala, and Zambezia. Ethno-regional loyalties linked to these areas were insufficient to explain voting patterns, however, as a number of cross-cutting cleavages and alliances muddied the picture. Up to 2009, the ruling party increasingly attracted urban support in heavily populated, northern provinces such as Nampula and Zambezia that otherwise showed strong rural support for Renamo. The largely rural, northern province of Cabo Delgado, which served as Frelimo's base when it was a revolutionary movement, has also strongly backed the party since 1994, but even here Renamo managed to capture between 15 and 30 percent of the seats at each election.[60]

[59] See Electoral Institute for the Sustainability of Democracy in Africa (EISA), "Mozambique: Election Archive," accessed 5/30/2011, http://www.eisa.org.za/WEP/mozelectarchive.htm.
[60] Ibid.

Data from public opinion surveys and on voter turnout reinforce the pattern observed in the electoral results and they serve as reminders that party stability cannot be taken for granted. Overall responses to a question on voter closeness to parties by the Afrobarometer survey are consistent with what we would expect to find in a system where parties are stable, but they underscore a decreasing trend in support for Renamo. In 2005, 82 percent of respondents said they felt close to a political party, and the majority of respondents said it was Frelimo. In 2008, 72 percent of respondents still felt close to a political party: 65 percent of them felt close to Frelimo and only 3 percent felt close to Renamo. The disproportionately high number of responses in favor of Frelimo might be owed to the misperception among respondents in 2005 and 2008 that the surveyors were from the government, but the responses still suggest that support for Renamo has waned.[61]

Unfortunately "feeling close" to or trusting a party has not translated into turnout for either party at election time. Although both Frelimo and Renamo sought to broaden their bases after 1994, voter turnout in Mozambique has declined with each successive election.[62] For national elections, voter turnout fell from 77 percent of registered voters in 1994 to 68 percent in 1999 to 36 percent in 2004 before rising to 44 percent in the 2009 national elections.[63] In the 1999 elections, the decline disproportionately affected the Frelimo candidate, Joaquim Chissano, who was nearly unseated in his bid for reelection as president. About two million registered voters stayed away from the polls. President Chissano received 300,000 fewer votes than in 1994, whereas the opposition leader gained about half a million votes. Chissano was able to eke out a four-point win but analysts widely suspected fraud and cast doubt on the credibility of the results.[64]

In 2004, both presidential candidates lost votes as voters stayed away from the polls. While the total number of votes received by Frelimo's presidential candidate, Armando Guebuza, declined by about 15 percent over 1999, he still won a decisive victory with 64 percent of the votes cast. On the other hand, Dhlakama's total number of votes plummeted by more than 50 percent.[65] In 2009, turnout improved slightly but this time, the ruling party candidate, Armando Guebuza, won a landslide. He garnered 75 percent of the vote

---

[61] Afrobarometer Survey Findings, " Mozambique, 2005," Afrobarometer Survey Findings, "Summary of Results: Round Four, Afrobarometer Survey in Mozambique, 2008," Compiled by Carlos Shenga and Amilcar Pereira, Afrobarometer Survey, Round 4, 2008, see answers to question 100, accessed 11/2/2010, http://www.afrobarometer.org.

[62] Michel Cahen, "Mozambique: L'instabilité comme gouvernance?," *Politique Africaine*, 80 (2000): 118.

[63] EISA, "Mozambique: Election archive."

[64] Cahen, "Mozambique," 119–122.

[65] Anne Pitcher, "Les élections générales de 2004 au Mozambique: Choix, conséquences et perspectives," *Politique Africaine*, 98 (2005): 152; Luis de Brito, "Uma Nota sobre Voto, Abstenção e Fraude em Moçambique," Instituto de Estudos Sociais e Económicos, Discussion paper 4 (2008), 6–10.

in his bid for reelection. By contrast, the main opposition party saw its share of the vote collapse.

These results underscore the increasing fragmentation of Renamo and serve as a reminder that party system stability or fluidity is a dynamic process. Three intertwining reasons explain the shifting dynamics in Mozambique's contemporary party system. First, the formation of a new party undercut support for Renamo. The significance of the party lies not in its ability to offer an alternative to the two-party system but that it has the capacity to replace Renamo.[66] In 2008, Dhlakama failed to renominate Daviz Simango to represent Renamo in the Beira mayoral race. Simango is the well-known son of a controversial liberation leader, and in 1992 he founded a smaller opposition party, the National Convention Party, but he was elected as the mayor of Beira in 2003 on the Renamo ticket.[67] As mayor he was both popular and successful, and the electorate had every expectation that Dhlakama would nominate him again in 2008. When that did not occur, Simango responded to Dhlakama's rebuff by winning the mayoral race as an independent candidate.

In advance of the 2009 national elections, Simango formed a new opposition party, the MDM, which encouraged defections from a Renamo-led coalition of smaller parties that had formed to contest the 2004 elections. Yet disagreements among coalition partners over the leadership of the coalition in parliament and the appeal of a new party exposed Renamo's undemocratic treatment of its partners and destabilized the coalition prior to the 2009 elections.[68] The party not only managed to entice away part of the Renamo leadership and former coalition partners, but also Simango captured nearly 9 percent of the presidential vote.[69] The party received a little more than 3 percent of the vote for parliament and likely would have received a higher share had it been able to run in all provinces of the country. Prior to the election, the draconian application by the National Elections Commission of rules on party list registration disqualified the party's candidates in all but three provinces.[70]

The divisions within and beyond Renamo underscore a second and related obstacle faced by the major opposition party: the lack of effective and credible leadership. Renamo's leader, Afonso Dhlakama, has now lost four presidential elections and his reliance on informal bargaining and intimidation to get

[66] Michel Cahen, "Resistência Nacional Moçambicana, de la victoire à la déroute? Pluripartisme sans pluralisme et hégémonie sans stabilite," *Sociétés politiques comparées*, 17 (2009): 79–81.

[67] AIM, "Renamo no Longer Supporting Daviz Simango," *Club of Mozambique*, accessed 8/11/2011, http://www.clubofmozambique.com/solutions1/sectionnews.php?secao=mozambiq ue&id=12747&tipo=one.

[68] "Mozambique: Attempt to Overturn Renamo Decision Rejected," allAfrica.com, May 6, 2009, accessed 5/7/2009, http://allafrica.com/stories/200905061011.html.

[69] EISA, "Mozambique: 2009 Presidential Election Results," updated January 2010, accessed 2/8/2010, http://www.eisa.org.za/WEP/moz2009results1.htm.

[70] EISA, "Mozambique: 2009 Assembly of the Republic National Results," updated January 2010, accessed 8/10/2011, http://www.eisa.org.za/WEP/moz2009results2.htm.

what he wants is becoming increasingly counterproductive. Whereas in the past his allegations of fraud or threats of returning to war may have galvanized Frelimo to compromise with him, by 2004 his actions worked to discourage voters from going to the polls in support of the opposition. Moreover, his habit of removing anyone within the party who competes with his authority has deprived the party of competent, committed cadres.[71] In addition, his failure to secure financial resources beyond meager public funds, token fees paid by party members, and a few private donations has hindered the party's ability to woo voters.[72]

Third, Frelimo has more tools at its disposal than Renamo, and it has used them to weaken its main rival. Since the election of a new party leader in 2002, Frelimo has focused its energy on tackling low voter turnout, reinvigorating party loyalties, and refining its message to incorporate themes of nationalism, poverty reduction, the elimination of corruption, and bureaucratic inefficiency.[73] Prior to the 2004 elections, it made concerted efforts to increase voter registration and the CC complemented these efforts with several intraparty initiatives. It expanded the membership of party organs, and the rights and obligations of party members at the ninth party congress. Revised party statutes emphasized the importance for party members to register other voters, to disseminate the party's message more broadly, to mobilize Frelimo voters at election time, and to cast their own votes. The statutes clarified the roles of the various organs of the party and those individuals who served in these positions. Last, the CC strengthened the powers of disciplinary bodies within the party.[74]

The party devoted equal attention to finances. Like other parties in Mozambique, Frelimo initially received donor funding for the first election, but this funding declined soon after. As in South Africa, public funding is available for all parties in Mozambique but its allocation in proportion to the vote share gained in the previous election benefits the ruling party. In comparison with other parties, the ruling party has disproportionately benefited from additional sources of funding such as individual and corporate donations and rents. It received approximately US$1.5 million annually from party members and accepted contributions from private companies, several of which were run by prominent members of the party. It hosted fundraising events in urban and rural areas to seek contributions from businesses and individual members. It also used rents from buildings owned by the party to fund campaign costs.[75]

[71] Cahen, "Resistência Nacional Moçambicana," 44–81.
[72] Speck, "Political Finance in Mozambique," n.p.
[73] de Brito, "Uma Nota," 8.
[74] Frelimo, "Inovações introduzidas," 13–15.
[75] Speck, "Political Finance in Mozambique," and Centro de Integridade Publica, "Curiosidades sobre o financiamento politico em Moçambique" (October 27, 2006).

Securing revenue accompanied efforts by President Guebuza to promote loyalists and to discourage deviations from the party line. The rise of the Guebuza administration since 2004 has signaled a return to greater party discipline, rewards for party loyalty, the increased presence of party headquarters in towns and cities, and tighter controls over the party's base. These tactics were characteristic of the party under former President Samora Machel following independence,[76] and Frelimo's victory in the 2009 elections demonstrates their continued utility in the era of electoral politics. Additionally, the ruling party engaged in egregious vote tampering in key opposition areas, stuffing ballot boxes and disqualifying votes on the flimsiest of excuses.[77] As Manning observes, the ruling party's "subtle, but effective manipulation of the legal institutions that govern elections" such as the Constitutional Council and the National Elections Commission worked to sustain Frelimo's political hegemony, but so also did its control over many of the country's economic assets.[78]

Parties and Economic Policy

Frelimo's growing dominance of the political space in Mozambique coupled with worrying declines in voter turnout direct attention not only to the capacity of parties to attract voters but also to the content of party policy. In contrast to the vacillating and vague policy content of Zambia's fluid party system, the policy messages by the two parties in Mozambique – like those in Ghana or South Africa – were more consistent over time. As in these countries, the two parties in Mozambique demonstrated programmatic differences in several issue areas, thereby challenging claims by some scholars of Africa that parties in Africa are mostly "personalistic." During the period of conflict, the two parties held sharply divergent views regarding the value of customary practices, the importance of traditional authorities, the role of the state, and the existence of a market economy. After independence, Frelimo formerly denounced customary practices as obscurantist and abolished the formal role of traditional authorities, whereas Renamo professed to embrace tradition and collaborated with traditional authorities to prosecute the war. In the postwar period, Frelimo expressed appreciation for the country's multicultural heritage and has formally assigned traditional authorities a role in the country's local administration. By contrast, Renamo sought to "restore communities to the centre of our national life" and to recognize the role of traditional authorities as a "central mechanism of dialogue between the state and civil society."[79]

---

[76] Paul Fauvet, Editor and Journalist, Mozambique Information Agency, Interview, Maputo, 5/27/2008.

[77] Joe Hanlon, ed., "2009 Elections," *Mozambique Political Process Bulletin*, no. 33 (6 October (sic) [November] 2009), see also http://www.elections2009.cip.org.mz.

[78] Carrie Manning, "Mozambique's Slide into One Party Rule," *Journal of Democracy*, 21, 2 (2010), 154.

[79] Renamo, "Main Renamo Policy Guidelines," mimeo, 2004.

Where the policy differences between the two parties narrowed was with regard to economic policy.[80] Private ownership, a market economy, and the reduction of state intervention constituted the core of Renamo's economic alternative to Frelimo's centrally planned economy during the conflict. Once the ruling party adopted the main tenets of neo-liberalism, Renamo's message lost power. Similar to Frelimo, Renamo's party manifesto called for foreign investment, improvements in infrastructure, job creation, poverty reduction, and even a limited role for the state in the pursuit of development objectives.[81] Even though Renamo has criticized "capitalismo selvagem" (savage capitalism), regional asymmetries, corruption, social injustice, and inequality, most of these themes historically have been associated with Frelimo, and they resonate equally well with Frelimo's base.[82]

Yet, declines in voter turnout and recurrent protest suggest that Frelimo has not entirely avoided the paradoxes that Renamo confronted in the changed economic environment. In the following sections, I examine how the party that implemented capitalism has dealt with the distributional consequences of reform. Here, as in Zambia, the limited quality of democracy has provided the context in which policy implementation has taken place.

Quality of Democracy

As in Zambia, the transition to multiparty democracy fostered the emergence of greater pluralism in Mozambique. In 2006, the country had 4,853 nonprofit organizations, which included international and domestic nongovernmental organizations, trade unions, business associations, and political parties. Over half of them were religious, and approximately one-quarter of them were political. Nearly half of the political nonprofits formed after Mozambique became democratic in 1994. The work of religious nonprofits stretched from proselytization to health care, education, and theater, while political groups focused on law, partisan advocacy, and political recruitment. Like their counterparts in Zambia, many of these organizations were small and weak. They had few resources or infrastructure, they lacked staff, and most of them depended on funds from foreign countries in order to operate.[83]

Constituting a small, but nevertheless important, fraction of the total were those nonprofits that focused primarily on business, commercial, and trade union activities, which are the most relevant with respect to this study.[84] The

---

[80] See Pereira, "Antes o 'diabo' Conhecido," 419–442.

[81] Renamo, "Main Renamo Policy Guidelines," mimeo, 2004.

[82] Armindo Milaco, "Intervenção Antes da Ordem do Dia," speech by Renamo member of parliament (Cabo Delgado) to Assembly of the Republic, date unknown, accessed 5/9/2009, http://www.renamo.org.mz.

[83] Mozambique, Institute of National Statistics (INE), "As Instituições Sem Fins Lucrativos em Moçambique: Resultados do Primeiro Censo Nacional (2004/5)," Maputo (Agosto 28, 2006), 46–48.

[84] Mozambique, INE, "As Instituições Sem Fins," 73.

number and variety of business associations has mushroomed over the last fifteen years consistent with the growth of nearly 32,000 businesses in the country.[85] They ranged from sectoral associations for the cashew industry, the hotel sector, or sugar producers; agricultural cooperatives; identity-based organizations for women or small business; and a number of peak associations for commerce, industry, or agriculture. In response to the proliferation of so many associations with divergent constituencies, private investors formed an umbrella organization in the 1990s with support from USAID. The Confederation of Economic Associations (CTA) sought to harmonize the views of sixty-three different business associations and to improve the business environment. These associations represented approximately 7,000 to 10,000 members.[86] Like the ZBF, the CTA included under its umbrella associations that represented large as well as small companies, foreign and national investors, commerce, agriculture, and industry.

CTA's actions offered an innovative twist on classic collective action problems delineated by Mancur Olson. Since donors underwrote the founding of the CTA, and supplied and funded part of the technical staff, they influenced its policy positions. Yet, donors (particularly the largest funder of CTA, USAID), tended to entertain more orthodox economic views than many of CTA's members.[87] Whereas donors pressured the government for freer trade or greater competition, actual businesses in Mozambique lobbied for greater protection, duties on imports of products that competed with domestic industry, and subsidies. According to the representative of a large peak association for commerce and industry, the "business environment" that donors had in mind when they lobbied government was an abstract, idealized one, not the reality that many businesses confronted.[88] The result was that the CTA existed in a creative tension between pleasing donors, representing the views of its own members, and cooperating with government.

An added complexity concerned the different relationships that domestic and foreign investors had with government. Many of CTA's members were domestic investors who were strongly nationalistic and pro-Frelimo. They adhered to a strict definition of who constituted a domestic investor (born in Mozambique and capital is Mozambican). These members felt that foreigners were better financed and got the support of their own governments so consequently they favored a larger, more proactive role for the Mozambican government than donors. Additionally, they looked to the government for preferential treatment in the sale of state assets, the supply of credit, incentives

[85] Mozambique, INE, "Censo de Empresas: Estatisticas Oficiais" (2002), Table 5, n.p.
[86] Confederação das Assõçiacões Económicas de Moçambique (CTA), "Estatutos," March 21, 2005; Jim LaFleur.
[87] Tim Born, Private Sector Enabling Environment Office, U.S. Agency for International Development, Interview, Maputo, 5/28/2008; Graeme White, President, Associaçao Comercial e Industrial de Sofala (ACIS), Interview, Maputo, 5/28/2008.
[88] White, Interview.

for investment, and the formation of partnerships in new undertakings. By contrast, those who adhered to more orthodox positions argued that preferential treatment of domestic investors did not yield a better business environment for all, and it discouraged foreign investors.[89]

These issues constituted points of difference within the business sector and between businesses and donors. The ensuing factions were a constituent element of the greater pluralism brought by democratization as they were in Zambia. Moreover, as in Zambia, the lack of a consistent message from the business community gave the government opportunities to choose the policy options that best served its own interests. But two significant differences distinguished the business environment in the two countries, and they can be explained by the respective differences in systems of party competition. First, because the ruling party was more internally unified than that of Zambia, it was more able to manage the factions and to build a relationship with business and donors. Second, extensive linkages and movement between the party, the state, business, and the donor community produced more coherent and consistent policy implementation than in Zambia. These results support Schneider's findings in Latin America that closer relations between the state and business improve policy coordination.[90]

More than was the case in Zambia, business associations in Mozambique had to contend with organized labor. Organized labor was historically the base of Frelimo, and about 68 percent of formal sector workers belonged to trade unions that were brought together under a single confederation, the Organization of Mozambican Workers (OTM) during the era of the one-party state.[91] Organized by and dependent on Frelimo since the early 1980s, OTM received considerable benefits for its members in exchange for its loyalty to the ruling party.

When Frelimo severed its formal connections with organized labor in 1991 to prepare for multiparty democracy, the trade union movement confronted new opportunities and challenges brought by political and economic transition. Regarding the opportunities, democratization opened up spaces for unions to express their grievances, to engage in the right to strike, and to access the media in order to convey their opinions on working conditions and wages. The government's decision to conform with ILO guidelines on freedom of association allowed the formation of rival unions to that of OTM and gave workers the right to choose whether to belong to a union or not. Greater pluralism facilitated more extensive cross-national coordination and information exchanges with unions in South Africa and Zambia and greater collaboration between unions and nascent associations for workers in the informal sector.[92]

---

[89] Born, Interview.
[90] Schneider, *Business Politics and the State.*
[91] Ana Maria Antónia Rocha da Fonseca Lopes, *Os Empresários da Construção Civil e as Relações de Trabalho: Estratégias e Desafios (1991–2004)* (Maputo: Imprensa Universitária, 2006), 56.
[92] M. Anne Pitcher, "What Has Happened to Organized Labor in Southern Africa?," *International Labor and Working Class History*, 72 (2007): 151–155.

Democratization and the growth of capitalism also introduced significant organizational, financial, and administrative hurdles for organized labor. First, policy changes allowing the formation of rival unions prompted the withdrawal of unions from OTM. Owing to "ideological differences," three unions representing construction, timber, and mining; the hotel industry; and transport workers withdrew from the OTM to form an alternative union, the National Confederation of Free and Independent Unions of Mozambique (CONSILMO), which was legally recognized in 1998. A fourth union representing private security workers joined in 2002.[93] The fragmentation caused by the formation of CONSILMO initially weakened union bargaining power as the unions exchanged recriminations rather than presenting a united front to government. However, in recent years the two confederations have worked more closely together to negotiate better working conditions, benefits, and wages with government and the private sector.[94]

Of those approximately 360,000 workers who were in the formal sector in 2008, about 40 percent were represented by trade unions. Formal sector workers were organized under the umbrella of either OTM or CONSILMO. OTM included fifteen unions totaling about 110,000 members, whereas CONSILMO contained four unions with a total membership of about 30,000. The combined figures indicated a significant recovery from a low of 89,000 registered workers in 2000, but it still represented a decline of 60,000 registered workers from 1990. A unionization rate of 40 percent suggests an improvement from a low of 36 percent in 2002, but it represented a sharp decrease from 1990.[95]

Second, like many organizations in Mozambique, trade unions faced considerable financial and organizational hurdles. Although they claimed to be nationally representative, most of their members were concentrated primarily in the capital of Maputo. Most trade unions did not have the resources to extend their coverage across the country and to stay in touch regularly with their members. Their offices lacked basic equipment and their officials were poorly paid.[96] One trade union official from the ports and railways union, which was one of the largest trade unions in the country, remarked that during sectoral negotiations, the union could not afford to bring officials from the rest of the country to participate. Thus, when consultations took place over wages or working conditions, representatives from the center and the north of the country often were not there.[97]

---

[93] For general information on Consilmo, see their Web site, accessed 5/10/2009, http://www.consilmo.org.mz.

[94] Fonseca Lopes, *Os Empresários*, 49–51.

[95] Figures calculated from Fonseca Lopes, *Os Empresários*.

[96] Raul Sango, General Secretary, Sindicato Nacional dos Trabalhadores dos Portos e Caminhos de Ferro, Interview, Maputo, 5/29/2008. There are some exceptions to this general picture such as the sugar workers' union, Sintia, which is well equipped. I thank Lars Buur for pointing this out. I expect unions in the coal sector to become stronger as demand for coal rises.

[97] Sango, Interview.

Third, the bargaining process became more complex with the transition to a market economy. To establish a minimum wage per sector, trade union representatives negotiated with the private sector via a tripartite negotiating forum such as the one in Zambia. Once they concluded these negotiations, trade unions had to bargain with individual firms to set wages for employees in those firms. The process was difficult and protracted because sectors contained vastly different kinds of work within them. For example, the transport sector included railroad and port workers but also *tchovas* (people who pull or push carts in the city), and one minimum wage was established for all of them. Trade union officials were then expected to negotiate different levels of remuneration for different levels of skill and education with each firm. These demands on their time and their expertise expanded at the same time that they confronted critical shortages of personnel and financing.[98]

Finally, as jobs in Mozambique's state sector declined without a corresponding increase in formal, private sector jobs, the percentage of the economically active population in the informal sector accelerated. About 75 percent of the economically active population of a little more than 9 million people were in the informal sector (including agriculture), whereas approximately 4 percent were in the formal sector by 2006.[99] With the exception of informal market workers around the capital who formed an association with the help of one of the main labor unions, most workers in the informal sector were not represented by trade unions so they were not part of official negotiations. Moreover, most of the country's 120,000 public civil servants, who constituted about one-third of the workforce, were prohibited from belonging to trade unions. A large informal sector along with government restrictions on the rights of public civil servants to organize thus undercut the power of labor to challenge government effectively.[100]

The changes reduced labor's membership, weakened its organizational ability and altered union-government interaction. In this respect, the Mozambique case shares some parallels with union-government interactions in Latin America following transitions there. As Murillo states, "When labor-based parties implement market-oriented reforms, allied union leaders are willing to collaborate despite the uncertainty and distress of their constituencies due to their loyalty to long-term allies. Loyal union leaders are predisposed to collaborate and can expect some concessions in return."[101] Similarly, in Mozambique, union leaders and rank-and-file members in OTM continued to vote for the ruling party despite their formal break in 1991. The explanation for their allegiance did not stem simply from a "reflexive loyalty" to Frelimo owing to their historic

[98] Ibid.
[99] Mozambique, "O Sector Informal," 84.
[100] Munguambe and Mondlane, Interview.
[101] Victoria Murillo, "From Populism to Neoliberalism: Labor Unions and Market Reforms in Latin America," *World Politics*, 52 (January 2000): 151.

association nor from the failure of the main opposition party, Renamo, to build support among workers. Rather, it was rooted in the electoral power that formal sector workers exerted in urban areas where most formal sector workers were located. Their votes for Frelimo affected the outcome of national and municipal elections. In return they gained concessions on wages, job security, and the privatization of large, strategic enterprises, which ultimately shaped the trajectory of private sector development in the country.

Nongovernmental organizations, business, and unions do not exhaust the competition for influence with government. The role of donors in Mozambique's private sector development has been pervasive, and their behavior exemplifies well James Ferguson's observation that governance in Africa has been "outsourced" to a hodgepodge of nonstate actors.[102] Donors have been active in Mozambique since the conflict in the 1980s. By 2008, the country had nineteen "Program Aid Partners" who provided general budget support (equal to about half of the budget) and project aid, while two, the United States and Japan, only provided project aid. Those who provided general budget support included the World Bank, the European Commission, most Western European countries, and Canada.[103] As was the case with Zambia, their presence in Mozambique was paradoxical. They both contributed to, and detracted from, the democratic process. They financed the initial elections, and helped rebuild the country. They provided technical and financial support in areas where the government lacked capacity from education to health care to infrastructure. They also held the government accountable for its commitments. With the formation over the last decade of sector-wide approaches and sector working groups on health, education, the private sector and other important areas, their dialogue with the government increased, and they harmonized their positions around specific policy goals. Through the use of common funds contributed by donors to particular sectors, donors were better able to coordinate their support, thus enabling government to pursue important objectives such as poverty reduction and HIV/AIDS prevention and treatment.[104]

Donor presence and participation contributed to a more plural society; however, their lack of accountability also circumscribed democracy. The formation of sector-wide approaches and working groups, for example, further institutionalized donor access to government officials. Sector working groups improved policy coordination, but they constituted another layer of governance in a country that was already bureaucratically complex. The individuals who occupied this layer were accountable to constituents who were not

[102] Ferguson, *Global Shadows*, 38–42.
[103] African Development Bank, "Mozambique," 462. Direct budget support has been favored over project aid since 2005; AIM, "Mozambique: Donors Reconfirm Budget Support for 2009," September 18, 2008, accessed 1/6/2009, http://allafrica.com/stories/printable/200809190058.html.
[104] Unicef–Mozambique, *Childhood Poverty*, 65–69.

Mozambicans. They advanced policy goals based on priorities set by donors and supported by research conducted and funded by donors. Broader civil society in Mozambique rarely participated in, nor did it oversee, the decision-making process that informed donor goals established for the country.

Donors also exercised a disproportionate influence on business owing to their preferences for a liberal market economy. Donor funding supported CTA, and individual donors, especially USAID, influenced CTA's policy positions. The two groups also met frequently as CTA was included in meetings of the private sector working group, one of the most active of the donor driven working groups. While they did not determine it, donors helped to set the agenda of this group, and they influenced who got invited to the meetings.[105] In a poor country, then, a more pluralistic environment was compromised by the formation of complex semigovernmental structures, unclear mechanisms of accountability, and the greater financial power of donors.

The limited quality of democracy in Mozambique compounded the challenges brought by greater pluralism as it did in Zambia. Until 2010, Freedom House scores averaged 3 for Political Rights and around 4 for civil liberties for over a decade. Several factors explain why Mozambique had lower (better) scores than Zambia for political rights and higher (worse) scores than Zambia for civil liberties. Mozambique has held regular presidential and parliamentary elections since 1994. The government also extended the electoral process to the selection of mayors and assemblies in forty-three larger municipalities. In 2007, parliament passed a law on the direct election of provincial assemblies, which were held concurrently with the national elections in October 2009.[106]

Furthermore, the decision by former President Joaquim Chissano to step down voluntarily after two elected terms in office set an important precedent for leadership turnover in the party and the government. Mozambique appeared to be institutionalizing two-term limits for the presidency and avoiding the conflict that ensued in Zambia when President Chiluba attempted to run for a third term. Mozambique's semipresidential system restricted opportunistic uses of executive authority more than in Zambia. In addition, members of parliament in the ruling party and the opposition have used their positions to express their disagreement with decisions taken by the party in government and to force government to modify its policy stance in certain instances. Beyond the institutional limits, Frelimo 's powerful Political Commission and Central Committee, both of which contain prominent members of parliament, also serve to check presidential and executive authority.[107]

---

[105] U.S. Agency for International Development/Mozambique Trade and Investment Project (TIP), Private Sector Working Group (PSWG) Meetings, Trade Sub-Committee, see Minutes of Meetings from 2005 to 2009, accessed 2/10/2010, http://www.tipmoz.com/pswg-minutes.

[106] Mozambique, Assembly of the Republic, Lei no. 10/2007, May 28, 2007: Mozambique, *Boletim da República*, 20 Suplemento, June 5, 2007. The law on direct election of provincial assemblies has 207 articles.

[107] The overlap between powerful members of the party and MPs continues following the 2009 elections. On the role of Frelimo in parliament, see Manning, "Assessing Adaptation," 232–236;

Although institutional checks within Mozambique's political system curbed capricious behavior by a single unitary actor, they were insufficient to prevent authoritarian responses if the power of the party was threatened. The alignment of interests in favor of Frelimo and the resources at its disposal as an incumbent were simply too great. Electoral observer organizations have documented irregularities at almost every election since 1994. During the 2004 campaign, for example, supporters of the ruling party in some parts of the country harassed and intimidated members of the opposition party. Opposition supporters were arrested on trumped up charges and held for days at a time. Over the two days of the elections, some domestic election observers and opposition party polling agents were unable to receive accreditation so that they could observe the voting at some 12,807 polling stations. After the polls closed, more than 5.5 percent of votes cast were not counted in the final tally owing to a variety of "mistakes" on individual ballot papers – and lost, stolen, or falsified records of results. Software for computer tabulation of the votes failed; members of the national election commission also prevented observers from witnessing the final tally.[108] Following the election, violent clashes between the two main parties over the results left twelve people dead and forty-seven people wounded. Most analysts agree that the recovery of lost and stolen ballots would not have affected the outcome of the election; nevertheless, the irregularities and violence explain why Freedom House continues to classify Mozambique as partly unfree.[109]

Mozambique's Freedom House ranking for civil liberties was worse than its ranking for political rights and worse than that of Zambia. First, the ruling party dominated access to information and curtailed freedom of the press. Some journalists who were too critical of the government lost their lives, received death threats, or were subject to lawsuits for libel. As a result, most journalists engaged in strict self-censorship. Second, bureaucratic agencies showed little accountability. Ordinary Mozambicans could not depend on either the security forces or the judicial system for protection or redress in the event of violent crimes, which have sharply increased in the last decade. Corruption and bureaucratic inefficiency pervaded the police force and the judiciary. Last, although the Mozambican parliament adopted a very progressive family law in 2004 guaranteeing equal rights to women with regard to property rights, inheritance law, assets within marriage, and the division of assets following

Efforts by Renamo to use parliament to challenge government have declined following the recent elections as they seem to be fighting mostly amongst themselves. The strength of the new party is yet to be determined.

[108] For a detailed account of election irregularities as they were occurring, see AWEPA, "Mozambique Political Process Bulletin," election e-mail special issues 29–39 (December 19, 2004–February 17, 2005), http://www.mozambique.mz/awepa/issues.htm .

[109] See Pitcher on irregularities in the 2004 election, "Les élections générales"; Freedom House scores on Mozambique in 2010 were reversed. The country now has a 4 for Political Rights and a 3 for Civil Liberties. For an explanation, see Manning, "Mozambique's Slide."

divorce, the rights of women still remained fully to be realized.[110] In many rural areas, women were still denied property rights and men continued to control household assets. Far fewer females than males had a secondary school education, while households where the only adult was a female were among the poorest in the country. Violence against women was common, and few perpetrators were ever punished.[111]

The Effects of Party Politics and Democratic Quality on Reform

Just as party fragmentation and limited democracy shaped the responses to conflicts by the ruling party in Zambia, the stability of the party system and limited democracy contributed to how the ruling party in Mozambique dealt with the effects of reform there. Where necessary, the ruling party used its discretionary power in a deliberate way to favor constituencies that were loyal to the party and to marginalize those that were not loyal. It counted on established party networks and alliances to cultivate support for reform among donors, business, and workers. Relying partially on donor aid, it rewarded party stalwarts with private and club goods over the course of the privatization process. It adopted institutional mechanisms to channel grievances along carefully controlled pathways of dispute resolution. When such approaches proved insufficient, the government relied on corruption, secrecy, and repression to stifle opposition.

Among workers, the transition to a private sector–driven economy engendered broad social conflicts over loss of jobs and benefits, low wages, and increased job insecurity owing to the growing use of casual labor. Workers voiced their discontent through strikes, protests, the media, and formally sanctioned channels of communication. Between 1995 and 2004, approximately 494 legally recognized strikes took place. Eighty percent of these occurred prior to 2001 when the majority of state assets were sold. More than 50 percent of the total number of strikes took place in manufacturing and construction, where the majority of formal sector jobs were and where the transition produced the highest number of salaries in arrears, reductions in benefits, job losses, and increasing casualization of labor.[112]

Given that Frelimo was formerly a Marxist-Leninist party, there is considerable overlap between union and Frelimo membership. The government has responded to the negative effects of privatization on formal sector labor

---

[110] Freedom House, "Country Report: Mozambique," 2008, accessed 2/10/2010. http://www.freedomhouse.org.

[111] International Federation for Human Rights, *Women's Rights in Mozambique: Duty to End Illegal Practices*, May 2007. n° 474/2, UNHCR Refworld, accessed 5/5/2009, http://www.unhcr.org/refworld/docid/46f146890.html.

[112] Fonseca Lopes, *Os Empresários,* 54. This figure may underestimate the total number of strikes as it is only a count of legally recognized strikes.

by combining cooperation, cooptation, and resistance to retain their support. First, it tried to direct investment toward towns and cities, where most formal sector workers lived. While the pattern of investment during the colonial and early independence periods partially dictated the choice of location, the ruling party also consciously targeted investment to areas where its base was located such as the southern provinces; or to provinces such as Nampula and Tete that demonstrated economic potential but were potentially swing provinces, and urban areas throughout the country with the exception of Beira, an opposition stronghold. With the aid of donors and nongovernmental organizations, the government also delivered public goods such as infrastructure, universal education, health care, and loans to districts to finance local development projects that enhanced food security, improved infrastructure, or created jobs.[113] These initiatives conformed to broader government policy goals and benefited those beyond the party, but also they supported and extended the party's base.

Second, members of government tried to cultivate good personal relations with organized labor, causing one donor to complain that labor's influence was disproportionate to its numbers.[114] According to the leader of OTM, general strikes in Mozambique were rare and dialogue was productive because the channels of communication with government were open. The OTM felt that it could express its concerns to parliament and that it had a good working relationship with the other confederation, CONSILMO, and with the ministry of labor.[115] The ruling party brought former trade union leaders into government as illustrated by the example of Soares Nhaca, a former trade union leader who formerly served in several government positions such as deputy minister of labor and minister of agriculture.

Third, the government cooperated with organized labor to formulate legislation on employment contracts, conditions of service, and benefits. Previous and current labor laws were considered favorable to labor. The 1998 labor law restricted the use of fixed-term contracts in order to prevent firms from hiring workers and then dismissing them when the contract expired. Instead, it protected permanent employees by providing a high degree of employment security and by imposing high costs for firing workers. Moreover, the law required authorization from the ministry of labor to hire foreign workers. A revised labor law passed in 2007 relaxed some of the provisions regarding the hiring of expatriates and workers on fixed-term contracts, but it continued to provide employment security for permanent employees. Additionally, a provision in the new law allocated a period of fifteen years before caps on severance pay, reductions in the number of annual holidays, and more flexible

[113] The loan scheme is connected to protracted initiatives to decentralize administration, see Mozambique, Conselho de Ministros, *Regulamento da Lei do Órgãos Locais do Estado*, Decreto 11/2005, Boletim da República, 23, 1 Série (June 10, 2005).
[114] Born, Interview.
[115] Munguambe and Mondlane, Interview.

hiring and firing practices would take effect.[116] Owing to these protections for permanent employees who tend to be unionized and to have more skills, Mozambique scored poorly on the "employing workers" category in the World Bank's "Doing Business" index.[117] But the laws reflect the country's socialist past and the support base of the ruling party.

Fourth, the government adopted formal mechanisms in order to resolve conflicts between business and labor. The tripartite organization, the Consultative Labor Council (CCT), hosted regular meetings among government, labor, and the private sector to negotiate wages, working conditions, revisions to the labor law, and pending or existing grievances. The CCT was not simply a forum at which the government solicited the perspectives of capital and labor; rather it was a body where differences between employers and workers were openly debated with the goal of informing policy and mediating conflicts. For example, the private sector and organized labor resolved differences over the proposed changes to the labor law in 2005 via the CCT. The revised labor legislation reflected the influence and interests of both participants.[118]

Organized labor did not gain all it desired in the legislation, but the secretary general of OTM reported that the experience was "very positive" for labor. More recently, organized labor and business representatives reached consensus via the CCT on minimum salaries for nine economic sectors in Mozambique. The government participated as an observer. Thus, the CCT in Mozambique appeared to be more dynamic than the one in Zambia, but as the next chapter will show, it was institutionally weaker than its counterpart in South Africa.[119]

Fifth, where contestation was particularly acute, the government made limited tactical concessions. It rapidly responded to a spontaneous and explosive transport strike in February 2008, not just because the protesters were consumers but also because they were urban workers challenging the government less than a year before the national elections. The government agreed to subsidize the cost of transport to avoid raising fares, sacked the transport minister, and brought the OTM into negotiations to resolve the high cost of public transportation.[120]

But there were limits to the government's accommodation of labor, particularly labor militancy. The government has remained committed to the creation of a private sector–driven economy and has overseen the retrenchment and casualization of thousands of workers. Even in public enterprises such as CFM where the state was still present, jobs were cut in the interest of greater rationalization and efficiency. Moreover, government resisted the spread of trade

[116] Mozambique, Assembleia da República, *Lei do Trabalho*, Lei no. 23/2007 (August 1, 2007).
[117] The World Bank has recently dropped this category from the indicators.
[118] Munguambe and Mondlane, Interview; LaFleur, Interview.
[119] Munguambe and Mondlane, Interview.
[120] Fauvet, Interview; Munguambe and Mondlane, Interview.

unions in the public sector. Most of the country's 120,000 public employees were not in trade unions and the government repeatedly stalled on discussion of this issue with the two confederations. Since public sector employees comprise nearly one-third of formal sector workers, their ability to pressure the government has been limited.[121] Finally, the government sought to depoliticize its critics in labor through a masterful blend of rhetoric and threats. While government members continued to invoke the name of Samora Machel to show their solidarity with workers and to address issues of concern to workers such as poverty or development, they rarely appeared at Mayday parades and have clearly indicated that the future lies with capital.[122]

To maintain its base among workers, Frelimo has been able to reference its past as a liberation movement and a socialist government, but that same past should have hobbled efforts to attract support from investors. After all, this was the party that said "down with capitalism." Why didn't the emerging private sector gravitate to the opposition party, Renamo, which had a pro-capitalist rhetoric during the war and which campaigned in favor of a market economy during the elections? Following the peace accord, Renamo sought to diversify its base beyond its locus of operations during the war. In fact, the leader of Renamo nearly won the 1999 presidential elections.[123] Yet, business did not ally with Renamo nor did the party consistently cultivate business the way that the New Patriotic Party in Ghana did when the ruling National Democratic Congress was implementing privatization there. Part of the failure lies with the internal dynamics of Renamo, first, the concentration of power in the person of Dhlakama and, second, a lack of organizational and financial capacity – two difficulties that so often plague opposition parties in Africa. But Renamo's fatal contradiction was that many of its supporters were amongst the poorest and most marginalized in the country. Its base was located in areas where the private sector was slow to emerge in the postwar period.[124]

By contrast, the party that used to embrace Marxism-Leninism created the private sector, populated it with loyalists, and then worked energetically to cultivate a productive relationship with it. The relationships were formal and informal, collective and individual. Besides its inclusion in CCT, the peak association for business, CTA, sponsored regional and national private sector conferences attended by government officials to identify existing barriers to trade, investment, growth, and productivity. Moreover, the government regularly solicited the opinion of the organization on trade agreements, customs procedures, skills training, sector-specific policies, and licensing requirements.[125]

---

[121] Munguambe and Mondlane, Interview.
[122] Pitcher, "Forgetting from Above," 88–112.
[123] Cahen, "Mozambique," 118.
[124] Cahen, "Mozambique," 129–130.
[125] To access their newsletters, go to their Web site, accessed 11/8/2010, http://www.cta.org.mz.

Rather than constituting an autonomous sphere independent of the government, CTA and the government were interwoven. One representative of CTA described it as a "cobweb" where the linkages between the state and business were so interconnected they could not be disentangled.[126] CTA's member associations in banking, tourism, commerce, and manufacturing contained powerful supporters of the party. They had useful knowledge of how the government worked, but they were also people whose loyalty to Frelimo was without question. The former president of CTA, Salimo Abdula, was even in business with President Guebuza, who was elected in 2004.[127] These linkages allowed for the synchronization of state, ruling party, and business interests in the most profitable sectors of the economy.

Beyond those formal venues for interaction between the government and CTA, the government offered financial support to the private sector. It established funds and incentive schemes for small and medium domestic investors and pushed development corridors and free trade zones to attract foreigners. It actively promoted public–private partnerships and joint ventures among the state, foreign, and indigenous investors. Furthermore, it worked closely with investors of large mega-projects in aluminum, titanium, coal, and oil refining as well as in the sugar sector.[128] It reinforced these efforts through vigorous campaigns to market capitalism as much as it propagated socialism after 1977.

Finally, after a decade of sales, liquidations, and new investment, a new privatization law in 2003 revised, clarified, and simplified existing legislation particularly with regard to the bidding process for purchases of SOEs. The law restated the government's commitment to a private sector–driven economy and detailed an agenda for privatizing existing firms in sectors from energy to aviation. Furthermore, it anticipated greater use of the stock market to offer shares in existing companies.[129]

These initiatives have created a close association between government and business that has led to greater policy coordination and an increasingly business friendly environment. Again, as the Latin American experience suggests, such relationships not only provide stability to the economy but also strengthen the state.[130] They have fostered mutual dependence between the ruling party and business. In return for funds, contracts, and favors, the ruling party has sought and secured donations from business at election time. In a recent survey, 21 percent of those businesses interviewed replied that they had made contributions to political parties during elections. Although it is not clear to which party they

[126] LaFleur, Interview.

[127] Francisco Carmona, "Guebuza entra na Vodacom," *Savana*, March 9, 2007.

[128] Games, "Mozambique: The Business View," 10–11, and on sugar, see Lars Buur with Carlota Mondlane and Obede Baloi, "Strategic Privatisation: Rehabilitating the Mozambican Sugar Industry," *Review of African Political Economy*, 38, 128 (2011): 235–256.

[129] International Financial Law Review, "Mozambique: Legal Market Overview," *IFLR 1000*, 2006, p. 701, accessed 2/7/2010, http://www.iflr.1000.com/jurisdiction/86/Mozambique.html.

[130] Schneider, *Business Politics and the State*.

contributed, just over half of those interviewed stated that they contributed financially in return for "good relations" or "economic advantages," which suggests that many of the contributions went to the ruling party.[131]

Last, although Mozambique's aid dependency gave donors a great deal of leverage, this was also the case in Zambia. The two countries were the largest aid recipients in Africa, yet they employed different approaches to donors. First, in Zambia the donor community disagreed on measures to adopt when the government failed to meet its performance criteria. Whereas bilateral donors suspended balance of payments support due to what they perceived as poor governance in the mid 1990s, the IFIs continued to provide sizable amounts of aid.[132] Lack of coordination reduced oversight and allowed the government to play donors off against each other, but also it produced policy stalemates and incoherence.

By contrast, the Mozambican government took advantage of diverse views on development within the donor community to build support for its own privatization strategy. Its cooperation and coordination with donors parallel successful efforts by several African governments in the 1990s to lobby donors to grant debt relief, which Callaghy has highlighted in his work.[133] In Mozambique, the government worked hard to understand the objectives of nineteen donors, and developed close personal and professional relationships with them. This reduced the marginalization or fragmentation that is characteristic of many aid-dependent countries. Although the formation of sector working groups offered donors new mechanisms to influence government policy, the degree to which they controlled the government was questionable. First, donors shifted the balance of grants and loans from project aid to general budget support, which allowed the government to exercise a greater role in the determination of the country's priorities. Second, because donors spent a relatively brief period in Mozambique, bureaucrats and government officials were in a stronger position to convince donors to accept their points of view or their approaches to governance. The stable party system strengthened the government's position vis-à-vis donors because senior government officials rose through the ranks of the party and were seasoned politicians. Owing to the slower rate of turnover in the party leadership – in contrast to the ruling party in Zambia – government officials had years of experience working with donors. For example, the previous prime minister and minister of finance, Luisa

---

[131] Mozambique, Ministério da Função Pública, Unidade Técnica da Reforma do Sector Pública, "Pesquisa Nacional sobre Governação e Corrupção," prepared by Austral Consultoria e Projectos, (2005), 99–101.

[132] Hendrik van der Heijden, "Zambian Policy Making," 91–94.

[133] Thomas Callaghy, "Networks and Governance in Africa: Innovation in the Debt Regime" in Thomas Callaghy, Ronald Kassimir, and Robert Latham, eds., *Intervention and Transnationalism in Africa: Global-Local Networks of Power* (Cambridge: Cambridge University Press, 2001), 128–136, 141–144.

Diogo, was a trained economist who was the World Bank's Program Officer in Mozambique for two years in the 1990s. She developed good personal and professional relationships with Bank staff.

Third, because Mozambique has been an economic success story, donors have tolerated continued state intervention in the economy, the capture of the privatization process by supporters of the ruling party, high-profile scandals, and widespread petty corruption. Central and local state authorities have abused their authority to engage in dubious land allocations to foreigners, transactions that lacked transparency, and sales of assets at highly discounted prices. Criminal activities and corruption have risen.[134]

Donors have denounced these abuses and crimes without withdrawing aid. They differed on the seriousness of the problem and how to combat it, which made it easier for the government to continue the practices and to receive aid. Several Scandinavian countries supported projects to increase government transparency and accountability and threatened to withhold aid if corruption was not addressed. Other donors, such as the World Bank, condemned the more egregious incidences of corruption while sustaining generous levels of financial support.[135]

In response to donor complaints, the Mozambican government passed an anticorruption law in 2004, established an Ombudsman's office, adopted an anticorruption strategy for 2006–2010, and has an Administrative Tribunal, which audits government financial record keeping. Although the tribunal has become more active in recent years, these other institutions are still weak, and it remains to be seen whether they will be effective at controlling continued state and ruling party interaction, particularly in the business world.[136]

The ways in which the government designed the initial institutional arrangements of privatization and then managed those distributional conflicts arising from economic reforms has implications for the kind of capitalism that has developed in Mozambique. In a country with a stable party system and where the quality of democracy has been limited, private sector creation has followed

---

[134] Joe Hanlon, "Mozambique's Banking Crisis," *Moçambique On-line*, English version of an article published in *Metical* 1073, September 17, 2001, accessed 8/3/2002, http://www.mol.co.mz/noticias/metical/2001/en010917.html; Carlos Castel-Branco, Christopher Cramer, and Degol Hailu, "Privatization and Economic Strategy in Mozambique," UNU/WIDER, Discussion Paper 2001/64 (August 2001), 4–8; AIM, "Mozambique: Fraud Alleged by Coca-Cola Under Investigation Says Bank" (April 2, 2005), accessed 2/10/2010, http://allafrica.com/stories/200504040445.html and "Mozambique Bank 'Stole' from Coca Cola Account," *Savana* (April 4, 2005), posted by *Afrol News*, http://www.afrol.com/articles/16050.

[135] Transparency International, "National Integrity," 73–77; for a pessimistic assessment of the effects of corruption, low voter turnout, Frelimo dominance and other areas of concern in Mozambique, and the contribution of aid, see Tony Vaux, Amandio Mavela, João Pereira, and Jennifer Stuttle, "Strategic Conflict Assessment: Mozambique," prepared for the U.K. donor team in Mozambique (April 2006); "'Disappointing' Performance Means No Extra Budget Support," *Mozambique Political Process Bulletin*, 39 (June 10, 2009) and see rest of issue.

[136] Transparency International, "National Integrity."

partisan affiliations. The government relied on conscious and selective uses of its discretionary authority to facilitate the accumulation of capital by members of the ruling party and to tie together the objectives of the state and the private sector. The result is that the privatization process created interests with a stake in an emerging private sector economy, but they are dependent on the state for survival. Moreover, the party has used the privatization process to consolidate its power and to build legitimacy for the state among investors. Although they exist, factions within the party have been tightly controlled. Under the leadership of President Guebuza, the ruling party has redoubled efforts to revive and extend its base and to use the state to provide club goods to supporters and to deliver selected public goods to a larger population. Where those initiatives have been ineffective, repression and corruption have become reliable substitutes.

Conclusion

In Mozambique, the ruling party responded to distributional pressures by cultivating supporters for the institutions that had been adopted, moving the initial commitment closer to one that was "credible in the imperative sense." The sales of firms to private investors, the creation of business associations, funds for investors, new regulatory agencies, and the discourse of the market illustrate the growing presence of the private sector in Mozambique. However, the privatization process took place within parameters largely determined by Frelimo, which encroached on political rights and civil liberties to achieve its objectives. The economy remains fragile and only a small elite has benefited from the transition, but the process has also revitalized the state. Since the starting point for private sector creation was a quasi-failed state weakened by conflict and economic crisis, this is quite a feat. It suggests that for some countries, privatization has not "hollowed out" the state, but "filled it in." It has facilitated the efforts of ruling parties to build new constituencies and to enhance state capacity.[137]

Key to this outcome was not only the creation of institutions but also loyal players who gave national leaders the courage to defend costly policy initiatives in return for a stake in the new arrangements. Looking at the rest of Africa, Mozambique is not the only case where the presence of a stable party system and a limited democracy shaped the government's approach to reform. As Chapter 3 discussed, President Rawlings of Ghana also tried to channel

---

[137] Further, it indicates that state capacity may be endogenous to the content of the reform process, thus challenging criticisms that states in Africa were too "weak" to implement structural adjustment or weakened by it ex post facto, see Arthur Goldsmith, "Foreign Aid and State Administrative Capability in Africa" in Nicolas van de Walle, Nicole Ball, and Vijaya Ramachandran, eds., *Beyond Structural Adjustment: The Institutional Context of African Development* (New York: Palgrave Macmillan, 2001); in another context, see MacLeod, *Downsizing the State*, 25–31.

the benefits of privatization to his supporters in order to remain in power. In that case, however, the strengths and bases of the two major parties were more evenly balanced, and the political environment gradually offered better opportunities for the electorate to scrutinize the actions of the ruling party. The electorate rejected the NDC rule in the 2000 elections, and it ceded power to the NPP. As its rival did, the NPP relied on the state to deliver club goods to its main constituency of support, business.[138] Faced with the effects of the global economic crisis, voters opted for the "welfarism" of the NDC by 2008.[139]

A similar approach to that of Mozambique characterized the privatization process in Tanzania where a formerly socialist, incumbent party survived the transition to democracy and to a market economy largely by sheltering its base from the harshest effects of privatization and also cultivating interests with a stake in the new arrangements (but the transition occurred too late to be included in our sample).[140] These cases suggest that where major parties are able to reproduce themselves over time and where democracy is limited, partisan private sector development usually follows.

---

[138] Handley, *Business and the State*, 172–206. As with Zambia, Handley refers to the Ghanaian state in the 1990s as "neo-patrimonial," but this masks the very real differences in their party systems.

[139] In opting for the alternation of parties in power, voters also contributed to the consolidation of democracy in Ghana. See Whitfield, "Change for a Better Ghana."

[140] Tanzania initially adopted a privatization approach similar to Zambia's but has recently favored Mozambique's dirigiste and partisan approach, see Stefano Ponte, "The Politics of Ownership: Tanzanian Coffee Policy in the Age of Liberal Reformism," *African Affairs*, 103, 413 (2004): 615–633. Namibia's recent privatization efforts are also "partisan."

6

Stable Parties, Liberal Democracy, and Strategic Compromise

South Africa

The South African economy differs markedly from those of Zambia and Mozambique in many respects. Its GDP of US$283 billion in 2007 dwarfed most other economies in Sub-Saharan Africa. Per capita income for this nation of 48 million people averaged US$4,770 in 2007, while those of Mozambique and Zambia were US$310 and US$700 per capita, respectively. South Africa dominated regional trade among the group of countries that are members of the Southern African Development Community.[1] In addition, South African investment in Mozambique and Zambia consistently ranks among the top with regard to the number and value of investments. Its influence on the other two cases is therefore considerable.

Unlike the other two countries, the private sector dominated South Africa's economy at the time of the transition to parliamentary democracy. Whereas the state sector in South Africa was important, its contribution to the GDP was only 14 percent. Moreover, the government's decision to commit to structural adjustment cannot be traced to a severe crisis in the parastatal sector, as was the case with the other countries. Although global trends and interests influenced the economic policy choices of South Africa's new democratic government after 1994, the adoption of a neo-liberal agenda did not derive from donor dependence, nor was it linked to the pressures of conditionality.[2]

Owing to these and other differences, South Africa is often treated as an exception in the scholarly literature on Sub-Saharan Africa. Single case studies of the country are common and rarely are comparisons made with other countries on the continent. Differential treatment of South Africa by much of

---

[1] World Bank, World Development Indicators, and Global Development Finance, World databank.

[2] J. J. Hentz, "The Two Faces of Privatization: Political and Economic Logics in Transitional South Africa," *The Journal of Modern African Studies*, 38, 2 (2000): 203–223.

the current scholarship on economic reform, however, has meant that those characteristics that it shares with other countries in Sub-Saharan Africa are often overlooked. South Africa has high rates of unemployment and poverty. Estimated to be about 50 percent of the population, South Africa's poor live on less than US$2.00 a day as do the poor in Mozambique and elsewhere. Much of the population lacks consistent access to an adequate income and lives in chronically unstable conditions with uncertain guarantees of services, security, shelter, and clothing. Similar to Zambia and Mozambique, South Africa's working population faces a highly volatile job market with significant differences in earnings and benefits according to the gender, race, occupation, and skill level of the worker.[3] Colonialism and apartheid have bequeathed an authoritarian legacy to the democratic government in South Africa that other countries in the region also confront.

Yet, in spite of its repressive past, South Africa serves as an exemplar of high-quality democratization. It is a country where popular participation is encouraged and governmental accountability is expected. Given that our other two cases fall short in this regard, the inclusion of South Africa in comparative study offers lessons for other countries to follow. South Africa is representative of those cases in Africa (Mauritius and Cape Verde are the other two) where motivational commitment to private sector creation during the 1990s was high, but where the process unfolded in a country that was a liberal democracy with a stable party system. As in Mozambique, preferences of stakeholders acting within a stable party system influenced the properties of the reforms. In contrast to Mozambique, however, South Africa's democratic context allowed well-organized actors with opposing positions to contest the government's choices within and beyond the ruling party. In response, the government often employed contingent uses of discretionary authority to resolve distributional conflicts. Such uses of state discretion produced strategic compromises that modified but did not dismantle institutional arrangements.

This chapter will examine the impact of the privatization process in South Africa and assess the contestation among different coalitions that arose as a result of it. It will describe the institutional reforms adopted by the government and explain why these were reconfigured by the turn of the century. It will explain how stable party politics and the features of South Africa's liberal democracy interacted to produce policy outcomes marked by strategic compromises.

---

[3] Percentage is based on 14 rands per day as the poverty line or US$2 per day at an exchange rate of 7 rands to the dollar. This exchange rate is used throughout the chapter. On measurements of poverty, see Mark Swilling, John Van Breda, Albert Van Zyl, and Firoz Khan, "Economic Policymaking in a Developmental State: Review of the South African Government's Poverty and Development Approaches, 1994–2004," *Economic Policy & Poverty Alleviation Report Series*, Research Reports 4 & 5 (2004): 1–157; Miriam Altman, "A Review of Labour Markets in South Africa: Wage Trends and Dynamics," Human Sciences Research Council, October 2005, 5.

Privatization and Restructuring in the New South Africa

Institutional Change after Apartheid

Similar to transitional moments in many other countries, the shift to multiparty democracy in South Africa occurred in the midst of an economic recession.[4] Although the South African economy did not reach the high levels of debt or inflation that many other countries did, nevertheless, nearly every sector from manufacturing to mining had experienced declines between 1989 and 1993.[5] Per capita income, savings, and investment had deteriorated after 1980. While actual rates of unemployment were highly disputed, most estimates placed it at somewhere between 20 and 30 percent, with another 40 to 45 percent of the economically active population estimated to be in the informal sector. With a Gini coefficient of .68 in the 1990s, South Africa had the highest inequality in the world. Forty percent of the population earned less than 4 percent of the country's annual income while the richest 10 percent earned 51 percent of the wealth.[6]

Unlike governments in Zambia and Mozambique, the newly democratic government of South Africa did not inherit a largely state-run economy dominated by parastatals. Rather, its task was to respond to a black majority against whom the apartheid state, with the overt and covert collusion of the dominant private sector, had engaged in systematic discrimination in the provision of basic services, skills training, and opportunities for capital accumulation and employment. As Elisabeth Jean Wood has argued, South Africa under apartheid was an "oligarchic society" where "economic elites relied on nonmarket regulation of labor by the state for the realization of incomes superior to those possible under more liberal, market-based arrangements."[7] Mostly white investors took advantage of draconian legislation, a coercive state apparatus, and government subsidies to realize the geographical and racial concentration of capital. With the exception of the gold and diamond mines, which were located in rural areas, most of the productive assets were concentrated in spaces populated by whites, while black townships and homeland areas lacked services or a substantial manufacturing

---

[4] My use of the terms "privatization" and "restructuring" is meant to distinguish between the whole or partial sale of an SOE to a private company in the former case and the commercialization and corporatization of parastatals or publicly run services in the latter case. Critics are correct that restructuring and commercialization have had serious distributional consequences but incorrect when they suggest that there is no difference among the methods.

[5] Adam Habib and Vishnu Padayachee, "Economic Policy and Power Relations in South Africa's Transition to Democracy," *World Development*, 28, 2 (2000): 246.

[6] Hein Marais, *South Africa Limits to Change: The Political Economy of Transition* (New York: Zed Books and Cape Town, University of Cape Town Press, 1998), 102–106; Habib and Padayachee, "Economic Policy," 246.

[7] Elisabeth Wood, "An Insurgent Path to Democracy: Popular Mobilization, Economic Interests, and Regime Transition in South Africa and El Salvador," *Comparative Political Studies*, 34, 8 (2001): 867.

base. Most firms were white owned, whereas the majority of potential or existing indigenous investors, like their counterparts in Mozambique and Zambia, had little access to capital and limited business experience.

Popular and sustained mobilization together with international pressure against the apartheid regime forced a transition to democracy by 1994. Elected with a convincing mandate to transform the material circumstances of the black majority, the government stripped away the remaining vestiges of discriminatory legislation. In their place, the government laid the foundation for an inclusive and participatory democracy. It recognized political rights and civil liberties that were consistent with those in established, industrialized, liberal democracies.

But if the reconfiguration of political institutions serves as an illustration of "critical juncture," "breakdown," or "punctuated equilibrium," the same could not be said of economic reforms. Structurally, these were less dramatic and more incremental. The government assumed power during a historical moment that favored market solutions to cyclical economic problems such as budget deficits, low productivity, lack of competitiveness, and slow growth. The shift to the private sector, the reduction of state intervention, financial deregulation, and greater trade integration by developed, industrialized countries and some developing countries had already led to the expansion of global capital flows, the reorganization of commercial distribution networks, more flexible labor markets, and growing consumerism by the time of South Africa's transition.[8] The global dominance of liberal prescriptions and the presence of a powerful private sector within South Africa largely foreclosed the adoption of socialism or even nationalization in order to solve entrenched inequality or long-standing deprivation, despite the fact that ANC leaders and policy documents had championed the redistribution of the country's wealth and part of the ANC's own base strongly supported such choices.[9] Instead, by 1996, the government had moved in a decidedly neo-liberal direction with the adoption of the Growth, Employment and Redistribution strategy. GEAR and associated legislation aimed to privatize state assets, liberalize trade, attract foreign investment, streamline the bureaucracy, restructure public services, and introduce fee-for-service plans in the utilities sector.

State-owned enterprises, which numbered about three hundred, were a minority of the total number of businesses in South Africa, but they were responsible for about 55 percent of fixed capital assets at the peak of state intervention in the mid 1980s.[10] Under apartheid, parastatals furnished employment

---

[8] Michael Storpor, "Lived Effects of the Contemporary Economy: Globalization, Inequality and Consumer Society" in Jean Comaroff and John Comaroff, eds., *Millennial Capitalism and the Culture of Neoliberalism* (Durham, N.C.: Duke University Press, 2001), 88–124.

[9] Antoinette Handley, *Business and the State*, 62–94; Habib and Padayachee, "Economic Policy," 245.

[10] Afeikhena Jerome, "Privatisation and Regulation in South Africa. An Evaluation," prepared for 3rd International Conference on Pro-Poor Regulation and Competition: Issues, Policies, and Practices, Cape Town, South Africa, mimeo September 7–9, 2004, 6; Reg Rumney, "Overview of Progress

for about one-third of the economically active, white wage earners and around 12 to 16 percent of the so-called nonwhite wage earners.[11] The apartheid government divested a few SOEs and adopted other features of neo-liberalism in the 1980s and early 1990s, but its commitment was erratic owing to political instability.[12] It was left to the ANC to make a high motivational commitment to divestiture by "layering" reforms onto existing market institutions.[13]

Following the identification and valuation of several parastatals by the Department of Public Enterprises (DPE), privatization proceeded to attract investors and to generate revenue for the state. Transactions included the sale of six broadcasting stations, state-run resorts, a forestry company, and several airports. Partial privatization of South African Airways (later renationalized) and of the four largest SOEs – Denel, Transnet, Telkom, and Eskom – also occurred. With respect to these four, the government divested some noncore assets but retained a majority interest in the remaining core enterprises. It corporatized and unbundled some operations, brought in strategic partners and reserved shares for Black Economic Empowerment (BEE) investors, or rather, those investors from historically disadvantaged groups in South Africa.[14]

Besides selling state assets, the government also opted for partnerships with the private sector, notably in the area of service delivery at the local level. In 1998, with the support of the U.S. Agency for International Development, it created a not-for-profit company called the Municipal Infrastructure Investment Unit to give technical and financial help to municipal authorities seeking to form partnerships with the private sector. The purpose of these partnerships (referred to as municipal service partnerships) was to create, improve, and extend public services such as water, electricity, garbage collection, sanitation, and public transport.[15] They included build, operate, and transfer schemes; management contracts; and fixed-term concessions that varied from five to

to Date" in BusinessMap Foundation, *Restructuring 2004: A Change of Pace* (Johannesburg: BusinessMap Foundation, 2004), 3, accessed 1/6/2006, http://www.businessmap.org.za.

[11] Merle Lipton cited by Laurence Harris, "Nationalisation and the Mixed Economy" in Graham Howe and Pieter Le Roux, eds., *Transforming the Economy: Policy Options for South Africa* (Durban: Indicator Project, University of Natal and Institute for Social Development, University of Western Cape, 1992), 37.

[12] Rudolf Gouws, "The Costs of State Intervention" in Howe and le Roux, eds., *Transforming the Economy*, 25–34. ISCOR, the Iron and Steel Corporation, was sold in 1989 and see Hentz, "The Two Faces of Privatisation."

[13] On the distinction between incremental and abrupt institutional change and different kinds of incremental change, see Mahoney and Thelen, "*A Theory*" 1–37.

[14] Reg Rumney, "Calculating the Worth of SOEs" in BusinessMap Foundation, *Restructuring*, 19. BEE and other legislation use a broad definition of "black" and include those groups previously classified by the apartheid government as Indian, Coloured, or African. Except where indicated, I use a broad definition of black.

[15] Monhla Hlahla, "The Municipal Infrastructure Investment Unit: The Government's PPP-Enabling Strategy," *Development Southern Africa*, 16, 4 (1999): 567.

thirty years; or alternatively, some form of corporatization. By 2004, local authorities had entered into approximately forty municipal service partnerships across the country, about half of which were focused on water and sanitation provision.[16]

In clearly demarcated zones of larger urban areas, municipal authorities and the private sector established more comprehensive public–private partnerships. Referred to by Murray as "entrepreneurial modes of urban governance,"[17] their ostensible goal was enhanced security, "urban revitalization," or, more grandly, building a "world class city." Yet the instruments to accomplish these goals largely rested on market principles. The schemes shared control over urban management and service provision between elected or appointed city planners and stakeholders such as property owners and privately run management consultancy firms. They employed the language of neo-liberalism such as efficiency, competition, rationalization, deregulation, and decentralization to justify their growth. To realize the design of the schemes, private firms and the management companies with whom they contracted relied on various Business Improvement District (BID) models pioneered in the United States and Canada and then adopted by other cities across the world in the 1980s and 1990s. According to Murray,

BIDs are officially-sanctioned, administrative entities that enable property-owners and business enterprises in a defined geographical area of the city to levy additional "assessments" and to use these funds to collectively contribute to the maintenance, development, and promotion of their commercial district in whatever ways they deem appropriate.[18]

Johannesburg's adoption of the BID model was altered to the more politically neutral appellation, City Improvement District (CID) and enacted into law with the passage of the City Improvement District Act no. 12 of 1997. The act sanctioned the formation of CIDs under circumstances where 51 percent of the property owners agreed to its creation and it recognized management agencies for CIDs. The agencies included property owners and at least one representative from the municipal council.[19] The cities of Cape Town and Durban followed suit. In 2000, Cape Town adopted the CID model to cultivate its image as a "world class city" and to become more competitive in global tourist markets. By 2007, fourteen districts operated within the city.[20] Moreover, the private sector extended the CID model to residential areas (Residential

---

[16] Kevin Allan, "Post-Consolidation in the Municipal Sphere: Increased Opportunities for Investment" in BusinessMap Foundation, *Restructuring*, 31–37, accessed 1/6/2006, http://www.businessmap.org.za.

[17] Martin Murray, *City of Extremes: The Spatial Politics of Johannesburg* (Durham, N.C.: Duke University Press, 2011), 246.

[18] Ibid., 258.

[19] Ibid., 259.

[20] Faranak Miraftab, "Governing Post Apartheid Spatiality: Implementing City Improvement Districts in Cape Town," *Antipode*, 39, 4 (2007): 602–626.

Improvement Districts). From the gentrification of once derelict housing to the provision of security cameras, private firms undertook key roles in the development and surveillance of urban space.

The Characteristics of Investors and Investment

Parastatal sales and public–private partnerships for municipal services attracted foreign and domestic investors, including large transnational corporations and newly formed consortia within South Africa. Purchases of SOEs were about evenly split between domestic and foreign buyers. Foreign investors became strategic equity partners in telecommunications, the defense industry, and the transport sector, whereas they fully purchased tourist resorts. Former South African multinationals that became legally registered in the United Kingdom after 1994 such as SABMiller, Old Mutual, and AngloAmerican were also important sources of investment in the existing private sector, but investment from the United Kingdom extended beyond those companies with a previous history in South Africa.

British and French firms participated in public–private partnerships in water and sanitation across South Africa. Denel, South Africa's defense parastatal, also sold a 51 percent stake in a unit that manufactured engine components and serviced helicopter engines to Turbomeca, a French company, while the South African government retained a golden share through the appointment of one director. German investors, purchased 70 percent of the optronics division of Denel.[21] Furthermore, Swissair purchased 20 percent of South African Airways, which the government later reacquired when Swissair filed for bankruptcy.[22]

American companies also showed an interest in the South African market. Forever Resorts purchased eight holiday resorts and the U.S. telephone giant, AT&T formed a consortium with Telekom Malaysia called Thintana Communications to purchase 30 percent of Telkom in 1997. The US$1.2 billion payment for Telkom accounted for one-third of the total value of revenue received from privatization in South Africa. The government gave Telkom exclusive rights to operate a virtual monopoly in the fixed line telecommunications sector for five years, and it allowed the majority partner in the consortium, AT&T, to make most of the key management decisions with little government oversight.[23]

---

[21] South Africa, Department of Public Enterprises, "Joint Media Release by Denel and Turbomeca to Create New Company," May 2002, posted on DPE Web site, accessed 9/12/2009, http://www.dpe.gov.za/home.php?id=152.

[22] South Africa, Department of Public Enterprises, "SAA Reacquisition of 20% Shares Held by Swissair," accessed 9/21/2009, http://www.dpe.gov.za.

[23] Robert Horwitz and Willie Currie, "Another Instance Where Privatization Trumped Liberalization: The Politics of Telecommunications Reform in South Africa – A Ten-Year Retrospective," *Telecommunications Policy*, 31 (2007): 446–462.

In total, South Africa attracted around US$29 billion in foreign direct investment between 1996 and 2007, but most of it did not go to the purchase of parastatals. FDI by German, British, and American investors was also directed at the acquisition of existing private firms and the creation of new businesses. Manufacturing (both basic industries and cyclical consumer goods) and resources (oil and steel followed by mining after 2000) accounted for the largest shares of foreign investment. The automobile sector saw substantial investment from the United States, Germany, and Japan, whereas investors from the United Kingdom, particularly those firms formerly domiciled in South Africa such as AngloAmerican have continued to invest in resources and basic industries such as forestry and paper products. Telecommunications was also a significant source of foreign investment owing to the sale of Telkom to the Thintana consortium in 1997. This was reversed when Thintana divested in 2004, two years after its exclusivity clause expired.[24]

As opposed to greenfield investments, mergers and acquisitions constituted a third to nearly a half of foreign direct investment – a percentage of investment into mergers and acquisitions that is higher in South Africa than it is in those countries such as Egypt and India with which South Africa is typically compared. According to some analysts, the unbundling of South Africa's tightly controlled, vertically structured conglomerates laid the foundation for the peak in mergers and acquisitions activity by the end of the 1990s.[25] Foreign and domestic investors were drawn to an already well-developed corporate sector, sophisticated existing financial and capital markets, and established networks of domestic investors.[26] Others have argued, however, that pessimistic risk assessments of the South African business environment explain the preference for mergers and acquisitions.[27] If this is the case, the biases about risk levels that plague other African countries also affect assessments in South Africa.

Foreign and established domestic companies in South Africa (particularly those formerly registered in South Africa that moved to the United Kingdom) were the major beneficiaries from privatization and new investment opportunities in South Africa. In addition, most privatization and partnership deals allocated a percentage of equity to black-owned companies or employees as part of the government's Black Economic Empowerment strategy, later renamed Broad-Based Black Economic Empowerment (B-BBEE), which directed incentives, opportunities, and investment to previously disadvantaged groups.

[24] Andrea Goldstein, *Regional Integration, FDI and Competitiveness in Southern Africa* (Paris: OECD, 2004)Jonathan Leape and Lynne Thomas with Reg Rumney and Michel Hanouch, "Foreign Direct Investment in Africa," Regional Trade Facilitation Program (RTFP), Occasional Research Paper 1, October 2005 , 5–17; World Bank, *World databank* selected years.

[25] Neo Chabane, Andrea Goldstein, and Simon Roberts, "The Changing Face and Strategies of Big Business in South Africa: More than a Decade of Political Democracy," *Industrial and Corporate Change*, 15, 3 (2006): 555.

[26] Leape et al., "Foreign Direct Investment in Africa," 5–6.

[27] Mark Swilling et al., "Economic Policymaking," n.p.

Included in full or partial privatizations to black investors were six South African Broadcasting Corporation (SABC) stations, two forestry companies, Sun Air, a small percentage of MTN, the cellular telephone network, and shares of Telkom. Both Transnet and Eskom divested noncore enterprises to BEE firms or to new parastatals that complied with empowerment goals.

BEE firms also participated in public–private partnerships and the management of city improvement districts. In the divestiture of Telkom, for example, the government offered BEE investors a 20 percent discount on the initial share price with promises of additional shares if they retained their shares for a minimum of two years. Furthermore, when Thintana divested from Telkom in 2004, it sold its 30 percent stake to a combination of domestic and foreign institutional investors and BEE firms.[28] With respect to the creation of CIDs in Johannesburg, a single subsidiary of a BEE company administered funds collected from property owners and oversaw the direction and organization of CIDs in twenty-three districts. Their responsibilities included marketing the concept and the appeal of CIDs to the business community and managing the mundane but necessary details of urban life such as garbage collection and law and order.[29]

As in Mozambique, the politically well-connected derived considerable benefits from the government's initiatives. Former political prisoners and exiles with links to the ANC occupied seats on directors' boards or received financing from the state to acquire equity in new and existing companies. Established private conglomerates such as Sanlam, Old Mutual, and ABSA also backed business ventures by those with political power in return for influence with the ruling party. Even party organs such as the ANC Youth League and civic organizations joined the corporate community.[30]

Union federations and individual trade unions established holding companies to make targeted investments in a diverse range of companies from minerals to media. Many used their political linkages to leverage their involvement in diverse economic undertakings.[31] For example, the Congress of South African

[28] Horwitz and Currie, "Another Instance," 457–459.

[29] Murray, *City of Extremes*, 260–265; see also Kagiso Trust Investments, Annual Report 2009.

[30] "Malema's choice: show his grit or stick to rhetoric" *Business Report*, 10/7/2008, Business Report online, accessed 10/15/2009, http://www.busrep.co.za/index.php?fSectionId=553&fArticleId=4647364; Elke Zuern, "Continuity in Contradiction? The Prospects for a National Civic Movement in a Democratic State: SANCO and the ANC in Post-Apartheid South Africa," study commissioned for project entitled *Globalisation, Marginalisation & New Social Movements in post-Apartheid South Africa*, a joint project between the Centre for Civil Society and the School of Development Studies, University of KwaZulu-Natal (2004), 11–13; Ngobeni, "How Arms Dealers Pampered Sanco, *Mail and Guardian*, April 8, 2005.

[31] Some union officials found holding companies to be problematic for the labor movement although they also recognized that some had delivered benefits for members, see Petrus Mashishi, Former President, South African Municipal Workers' Union (SAMWU), Johannesburg, Interview, 12/9/2009 and Jane Barrett, Policy Research Office, South Africa Transport and Allied Workers' Union (SATAWU), Interview, Johannesburg, Interview, 12/8/2009.

Trade Unions (COSATU), one of the partners in the tripartite alliance (a formal partnership negotiated with the ANC and the South African Communist Party (SACP) to build political unity) had a number of investments. COSATU formed its own investment arm, Kopano ke Matla in 1996 and it had shares in manufacturing, finance, Internet technology, housing, and tourism. A year later, nine COSATU-affiliated unions founded Union Alliance Holdings, in partnership with unions affiliated with the third largest trade union federation, the National Council of Trade Unions, and New African Investments Limited, a company belonging to Cyril Ramaphosa, a prominent member of the ANC and former leader of COSATU. Its holdings extended into media, insurance, and finance.[32]

Black beneficiaries of privatization, partnerships, and empowerment deals extended beyond political elites or those organizations close to the Alliance. They included entrepreneurs who, in spite of discriminatory legislation, had worked in those economic spaces unseen or ignored by the apartheid state. They later took advantage of the relaxation of regulations to build businesses and accumulate capital.[33] Following the transition, they relied on the opportunities occasioned by the scrapping of apartheid as well as legislation targeting the historically disadvantaged to raise capital, to invest in existing or new businesses, to accept management positions, and to join company boards. In addition, public funding mechanisms such as the National Empowerment Fund, the Industrial Development Corporation, and the Development Bank of Southern Africa have been critical to the growth of black capitalists.[34]

Policy Outcomes and Political Contestation

By 2004, the government had received just over US$3.3 billion from the full or partial sale of approximately twenty-six former parastatals making South Africa the top performer in Africa with respect to proceeds from sales and average sale value per transaction.[35] The inclusion of the private sector in the delivery of formerly public services such as water, electricity, sanitation, and security had expanded significantly. Yet, contrary to scholarly expectations, these results did not bring widespread benefits. Early theories on privatization assumed that the process would produce short-term costs on an identifiable

---

[32] Okechukwu Iheduru, "Organised Labour, Globalisation and Economic Reform: Union Investment Companies in South Africa," *Transformation: Critical Perspectives on Southern Africa*, 46 (2001): 10–11; no author, "Union Alliance Holdings, (Pty) Ltd., Johannesburg, Gauteng, South Africa," accessed 10/30/2009, http://www.mbendi.com/orgs/cp6l.htm. Union Alliance Holdings is now defunct.

[33] Sipho Maseko, "From Pavement Entrepreneurs to Stock Exchange Capitalists: The Case of the South African Black Business Class." Thesis, D.Phil., School of Government, University of the Western Cape, Bellville, 2000.

[34] South Africa, Ministry [sic] of Public Enterprises, "A Summary of the Policy Framework for an Accelerated Agenda towards the Restructuring of State-Owned Enterprises," Policy Framework, August 2000, 65–68.

[35] Berthélemy et al., *Privatisation in Sub-Saharan Africa*, 35 and World Bank, "Privatization Database, 1988–1999" and "Privatization Database, 2000–2008."

group of "losers" such as parastatal directors and employees, whereas a larger, more diverse group of beneficiaries such as entrepreneurs and consumers would only gain in the long term. According to this logic, the challenge for policymakers was to sustain the policy in the face of distributional conflicts long enough for privatization's more diffuse benefits to emerge. The suggested policy recommendation that followed was for the state to remain sufficiently insulated from pressures in order to carry out the reforms, preferably by creating statutorily autonomous, technocratic change teams who acted free from political interference.[36]

The pattern of privatization in South Africa offers weak support for the assumptions by conventional claims regarding the diffuse benefits of privatization. Instead, economic reform in South Africa concentrated benefits on a select few, while dispersing costs among South Africa's largely poor population, a pattern that closely paralleled those observed in Argentina, Mexico, and Chile by MacLeod and Schamis.[37] Despite claims by some analysts that South Africa would experience a postapartheid dividend owing to a rash of capital inflows, investment and growth were erratic during the 1990s and early 2000s. Foreign direct investment increased dramatically following the transition, but fluctuated after 2000. The postapartheid period witnessed a reversal of the negative growth rates of 1989–1992, but growth rates for the period from 1994 to 2001 only averaged around 3 percent. From 2002 to 2007, they improved to nearly 5 percent before being affected by the global economic downturn.[38]

Foreign investors took advantage of parastatal sales and public–private partnerships, while domestic beneficiaries were many of the same established businesses that enjoyed privileges under apartheid. In addition, postapartheid economic policies contributed to a growing urban black middle class in South Africa. Using measures of living standards, rather than income and expenditure, the percentage of total middle-class households grew from 23 to 26 percent of all households between 1998 and 2006. This increase was highest in urban areas, where 65 percent of the population live, and highest among Africans and so-called Coloureds, who witnessed an increase respectively from 15 to 22 percent and 41 to 48 percent of households joining the middle class. The numbers of African households with a middle-class standard of living was estimated to be approximately two million people in 2006. Its projected growth was expected to reach about 5 million by 2016.[39]

[36] See contributions to Stephan Haggard and Robert R. Kaufman, eds., *The Politics of Economic Adjustment: International Constraints, Distributive Conflicts, and the State* (Princeton, N.J.: Princeton University Press, 1995); and Adam Przeworski, *Democracy and the Market: Political and Economic Reforms in Eastern Europe and Latin America* (New York: Cambridge University Press, 1991).

[37] MacLeod, Downsizing the State; Schamis, Re-Forming the State.

[38] International Monetary Fund, "International Financial Statistics – South Africa," 1990–2007.

[39] Unlike surveys based on household income and expenditure, which may overestimate the size of the middle class owing to unreported income, this estimate classifies households according

The growth of a black middle class, especially among Africans, constitutes a significant achievement by the democratic government, but it has occurred alongside worsening inequality. The percentage of income accounted for by the wealthiest (and mostly white) 20 percent of the population increased from 70 to 80 percent by 2005. While increases in inequality are not statistically significant for the rural areas, they have been marked in urban areas. Between 1995 and 2005, the Gini coefficient for urban areas increased from .59 to .69. The data are mixed on whether the contributing factor to increases in inequality among Africans in particular is owed to greater affluence among black South Africans because rural to urban migration accelerated at the same time. As in Mozambique, the arrival of migrants who were unable to find stable, wage-paying jobs in the cities swelled the ranks of the poor.[40]

Even if the global recession explains the loss of one million jobs in 2009, the government's economic policies did little to alleviate unemployment in the decade following the transition. Most of the proceeds from privatization were spent on recapitalization.[41] After the transition, nearly every sector in the South African economy shed full-time jobs, reclassified labor, or reorganized work to make it more "flexible" and efficient.[42] By 2005, approximately 40 percent of the economically active population were unemployed.[43] Public employment as a percentage of total employment contracted from 15 percent in 1995 to 9 percent of the workforce by 2004. Parastatals alone accounted for about 5 percent of the nonagricultural, formal sector workforce by 2006–2007. Even the top four SOEs – Denel, Transnet, Eskom, and Telcom – shed approximately

---

to sources of lighting, cooking, sanitation, and water in the house; the type of construction; and whether the household has a telephone. See South Africa, Statistics South Africa, *Profiling South African Middle Class Households: 1998–2006*, report O3–03–01, authored by Mosidi S. Nhlapo and Barbara A. Anderson (Pretoria: Statistics South Africa, 2009) and South Africa, Statistics South Africa, *Changes in Standard of Living among Population Groups in South Africa: 1998–2006*, authored by Barbara A. Anderson and Mosidi S. Nhlapo (Pretoria: Statistics South Africa, 2010). Even though this approach is conservative, its findings might still be considered controversial. For example, by this criteria, trade unionists would be considered middle class, which many would reject.

[40] Haroon Bhorat, Carlene van der Westhuizen, and Toughedah Jacobs, "Income and Non-Income Inequality in Post-Apartheid South Africa: What Are the Drivers and Possible Policy Interventions?," Development Policy Research Unit, DPRU Working Paper 09/138, August 2009, 10–14. For a more detailed analysis of inequality in South Africa, see Jeremy Seekings and Nicoli Nattrass, *Class, Race, and Inequality in South Africa* (New Haven, Conn.: Yale University Press, 2005).

[41] Reg Rumney, "Overview of Progress to Date," 2.

[42] See the contributions to Edward Webster and Karl Von Holdt, eds., *Beyond the Apartheid Workplace: Studies in Transition* (Scottsville, South Africa: University of Kwazulu-Natal Press, 2005).

[43] Calculations based on Karl von Holdt and Edward Webster, "Work Restructuring and the Crisis of Social Reproduction: A Southern Perspective" in Webster and von Holdt, *Beyond the Apartheid Workplace*, 28–29.

30,000 jobs in the last decade as they sought out strategic equity partners, or corporatized their operations.[44]

Changes in the global organization of production have altered the nature of work in the private sector by replacing formal sector positions with informal sector jobs. As in Zambia and Mozambique, the reduction and reclassification of employment meant that formal sector wage labor jobs constituted a minority of total jobs after 2000. According to Webster and Von Holdt, the majority of South Africa's economically active population of 21 million had access to work in which wages, job security, and safety were highly variable. Of this number, a little less than a third or 6.8 million had full-time work, while another 5.3 million were employed as temporary, part-time, or casual workers, partly in and partly out of the formal sector, or they had informal work.[45]

Poor service delivery dealt another blow to a population rendered vulnerable by low wage work or lack of work. Although the inclusion of the private sector in services such as electricity, water, waste removal, and sanitation increased their availability in selected areas of the country, segments of the population continued to go without because they were unable to pay for service provision or services had failed to materialize. This situation prevailed through 2008 despite efforts by the central government to improve service delivery by replacing unresponsive or incompetent local councilors, and providing a set quota of water and electricity for free.[46] The development of CIDs appeared to address the problem of service provision through privatization, but most CIDs concentrated resources, security, and services in those areas that could afford to pay, while leaving poor and marginal areas to fend for themselves.

The diffuse costs of privatization produced sustained resistance to reforms from different quarters. Trade unions with extensive experience in the antiapartheid struggle and strong links to the ruling party challenged the sale of SOEs. In poorer areas, nationally and locally organized antiprivatization groups forcefully lobbied the government to abandon public–private partnerships (PPPs) that delivered essential services in favor of public providers. They used multiple channels of access to express their demands including parliament, labor councils, the media, and demonstrations. Resistance was also spontaneous,

[44] Miriam Altman, "Employment Scenarios to 2024," Human Sciences Research Council (August 2007), 18; South Africa, Department of Public Enterprises, "Press Briefing on the Strategic IMCC Lekgotla on the Restructuring of State Assets," 1999, accessed 3/28/2007, http://www.dpe.gov.za; Ebrahim-Khalil Hassen and Mawethu Vilana, "Accelerated Delivery and Worker Security," *Indicator*, 7, 4 (December 2000): 12–17.

[45] Von Holdt and Webster, "Work Restructuring," 28–29, and see Pitcher, "What Has Happened."

[46] Susan Booysen, "Beyond the Ballot and the Brick: Continuous Dual Repertoires in the Politics of Attaining Service Delivery in South Africa?" in Anne McLennan and Barry Munslow, eds., *The Politics of Service Delivery* (Johannesburg: Wits University Press, 2009): 104–136.

uncoordinated, antidemocratic, and violent. In 2008, xenophobic violence against immigrants was at least partially a result of the increased use of casual, immigrant labor by private sector employers.[47]

The response of the ruling party has been no less complex. It has been conciliatory as well as obstructionist in the face of pressure. But over time, the coalitions comprising the ruling party and the liberal institutions that typified South Africa's democracy facilitated policy compromise in those situations where distributional conflicts were high. The compromise was epitomized by the suspension of privatization less than a decade after it had been adopted. Instead, the government shifted the emphasis of economic reforms in favor of greater state involvement. Although PPPs continued in selected urban locales, state-funded public works programs assumed greater significance. Rationalization and commercialization of parastatals were preferenced over privatization; restructuring was favored rather than outright divestiture. The change was not merely semantic as some critics alleged; instead, I argue that it constituted a "strategic compromise" by the government in response to distributional conflicts arising from the early impact of privatization. As forthcoming sections will show, the design of institutional arrangements adopted by the state to undertake reform help to explain why compromise was possible, but the nature of party politics and the quality of democracy demonstrate why compromise was necessary.

Contingent Discretion and Institutional Layering

Largely unexplored in much of the controversy regarding privatization and restructuring in South Africa are the particular features of the motivational commitment that the government made to neo-liberal economic reform. Unlike the Zambian and Mozambican economies, the South African economy already contained the principal institutions of a capitalist economy such as private property rights; mechanisms for buying, selling, and exchanging goods; a capital market; and a market for labor, hence its relatively high score for motivational commitment. In the past, rules and regulations that governed these arrangements were designed to benefit a privileged minority, and they were manipulated by the apartheid state to enforce racially discriminatory policies.

The terms and the timing of the negotiated transition produced not their replacement but their reform, such that the institutional framework after 1994 reflected the capitalist development and state formation that had gone before. Under apartheid, large parastatals in electricity and telecommunications had intricate linkages with private foreign and domestic companies via supply chains and partnerships. After the democratic transition, these existing institutional arrangements would set the parameters within which debate would take place and conflicts would be resolved. They thus offer a compelling illustration of the effects of institutional path dependence.

---

[47] Patrick Craven, National Spokesperson, COSATU, Interview, Johannesburg, 12/9/2009.

That existing institutions indicated the direction in which the South African economy would travel, however, did not eliminate entirely the government's ability to determine the route. First, as Jack Knight observes, institutions exist in a dynamic tension with those constituencies affected by them. They structure preferences. At the same time, moments of political transition change preferences and power relations, which may reshape institutions.[48] Second, the new government abolished some existing institutional arrangements and devised new ones, which, in turn, also altered preferences. The government stripped rules and regulations of their racially discriminatory provisions, *and* it supported private property rights, promoted free trade, restructured service delivery, favored PPPs, and embarked on spatial development initiatives. As a consequence, the government engaged with three broad groups: those mostly white interests that had benefited from the previous arrangements; those who had been harmed by those arrangements such as trade unions or urban squatters; and, finally, those who stood to gain or lose from the implementation of new frameworks.

Third, a critical point often overlooked by scholars and by government officials is that previous institutional arrangements provided for a highly centralized, interventionist state. As much apartheid era legislation indicates, the state intervened excessively to determine who had access to which property rights, to control labor, to redistribute wealth, to provide social assistance, and to support or deny capital accumulation. State procurement contracts and jobs in the public sector were key elements in the quest for Afrikaner economic empowerment. State contracts and subsidies helped to produce increases in the share of Afrikaner capital in finance, industry, and commerce by the early 1960s.[49] Whites occupied 39 percent of the jobs in the public service (excluding the homelands) and controlled the majority of the top management positions as late as 1990. Within the public sector, state corporations and parastatals provided employment for approximately 400,000 people.[50] SOEs also served as vital downstream and upstream linkages with the private sector.

Since the transition, the ruling party has not only tackled the constraints and opportunities afforded by existing institutions of capitalism but also recognized the magnitude and limits of state power with respect to realizing policy change. Much of the policy directed at SOEs in the last fifteen years demonstrates a process of institutional learning, a coming to grips with the breadth of the South African state. Many of the institutional reforms that the ANC initially undertook anticipated that such learning would occur. They gave state officials the opportunity to exercise discretion in their interpretation, to shift

---

[48] Knight, *Institutions and Social Conflict*, 183–185.
[49] Chabane et al., "The Changing Face," 551.
[50] Louis Picard, *The State of the State: Institutional Transformation, Capacity and Political Change in South Africa* (Johannesburg: Wits University Press, 2005), 68, 74.

policies in response to challenges arising from their implementation, and to centralize power as they gained experience.

The agencies and institutions associated with privatization offer ample evidence of such a process at work. Although decisions to restructure, rather than privatize, state firms suggest that the state reneged on its commitment, in fact, the provisions of many initial policies were deliberately ambiguous. Legislation reflected the uncertainty about policy consequences that might be expected from inexperienced state officials. Moreover, other state actors often checked those agencies designated to carry out intended policies. The frequent reorganization of departments such as the Department of Trade and Industry or the DPE demonstrates that as learning occurred and priorities changed, the government reconfigured government agencies in line with shifting preferences.

How has regulatory flexibility affected the substance of reforms? Over the course of the 1990s, the government recognized the limits of the market economy to correct the injustices of the past and increasingly relied on state enterprises and state procurement contracts to build black equity, pursue affirmative action, forge linkages with historically disadvantaged firms, train black managers, and create employment. At the same time, the government sustained and extended linkages between parastatals and private capital that previous governments had established. Parastatals did not previously and do not now operate in isolation from the rest of the economy; instead they interact and intertwine with existing private firms.[51]

The direction of economic policy illustrates the inherent tensions in the ANC's efforts to reconfigure the relationship between state and capital. This is evident in the many bills passed over the last decade and a half. Adopted in 1994, the White Paper on the Reconstruction and Development Program (RDP) was praised by supporters for its inclusive and developmentalist language, its focus on workers' rights, and its call for more participatory mechanisms. The RDP was agnostic with regard to SOEs or privatization. It noted that parastatals were a product of the "skewed policies" pursued by the apartheid government and that some could be sold to finance the RDP. It also remarked that "They are being made to be more efficient" in order to play a developmental role. But it left open the question of their future form and bequeathed further discussion to "stakeholders."[52]

Despite its title, the National Framework Agreement on the Restructuring of State Assets signed between the government and organized labor in early 1996 shed little additional light on the substance of SOE reform. It was circumspect

---

[51] Nancy Clark, "South African State Corporations: 'The Death Knell of Economic Colonialism?,'" *Journal of Southern African Studies*, 14, 1 (1987): 99–122.

[52] South Africa, Parliament of the Republic of South Africa, "White Paper on Reconstruction and Development," Cape Town, November 15, 1994, Notice no. 1954, WPJ/1 994, *Government Gazette*, 353, 16085, November 23, 1994.

about what methods the government would adopt in order to restructure and cautious in its assessment of the benefits of privatization. Like the RDP, it was critical of the role played by state institutions under apartheid. It anticipated that reform would "address the apartheid legacy and promote employment and service delivery to people who were disadvantaged."[53] Yet how that would be accomplished and by what method the document did not say.

Formulated with little input from Alliance partners,[54] GEAR adopted an explicitly neo-liberal approach to the economy. Yet here again the document left room for interpretation. Whereas it announced the state's intention to reform public enterprises, it avoided use of the word, "privatization," and it granted the state broad discretion with regard to the direction reform would take. It referred to the restructuring of state assets but understood the approach to consist of a number of options including divestiture, the acquisition of a strategic equity partner, or a PPP with the retention of a majority interest by the state. GEAR mentioned the use of cost-recovery approaches in public services through the adoption of PPPs as a means for the government to save money but provided no specific details on the features of such PPPs. The only sales of state assets that GEAR specifically mentioned were those of six SABC stations and the search for a strategic equity partner for Telkom.[55]

Just as the language of policy documents was deliberately vague, so also were the roles and responsibilities of those agencies entrusted with the power to privatize. Unlike many other countries with high motivational commitments to privatization including Zambia and Mozambique, the South African government never established an independent or even semiautonomous agency dedicated to the privatization of its SOEs. When the Office of Public Enterprises was created in 1994, it did not act as a stand-alone agency with such a mandate. After the office was upgraded to a department in 1999, its role was more clearly defined, yet its autonomy to privatize was circumscribed. The DPE coordinated the process, but it worked closely with key ministries such as finance, labor, trade, and industry and sectoral departments such as minerals and energy, transport, and defense to develop appropriate strategies for the state sector be it privatization, restructuring or regulating specific firms.

The mandate of the DPE entailed not only the inclusion of private sector actors or the restructuring of parastatals to realize greater efficiencies, but also oversight of South Africa's nine largest parastatals including Denel, Transnet, Telkom, and Eskom. The overlap of functions created a potential conflict of interest between DPE's responsibility to privatize and its duty to act in the best interest of parastatals, their employees, and the government. Over the course of the privatization and restructuring process, the conflict became evident in the

---

[53] South Africa, "National Framework Agreement on the Restructuring of State Assets," approved February 7, 1996.

[54] Craven, Interview.

[55] South Africa, Department of Finance, "Growth, Employment and Redistribution."

DPE's struggles to balance contradictory economic, social, and developmental objectives.

Intertwining responsibilities among departments and paradoxical objectives soon produced "ambiguities and bottlenecks" as a DPE strategy document recognized,[56] but simultaneously it made possible a reliance on contingent uses of authority to realize strategic compromises. The most striking compromise was that ten years after the passage of GEAR, privatization in the narrow sense had not been fully realized. Sales were limited and took place very slowly. Approximately 26 SOEs out of 300 or just 9 percent of state assets were sold by 2005. SOEs still comprised 44 percent of fixed capital assets and contributed 14 percent to the GDP.[57] Tellingly, the government retained all or most of the shares in large parastatals such as electricity supply and generation, defense manufacture, telecommunications, and transport services. Rather than sell these to the private sector, it reconfigured them in order to pursue closer relationships with private investors and to rationalize operations.[58] Although its intention was clearly different, this approach paralleled that adopted by the apartheid state when it originally created parastatals such as Escom (now Eskom, the electricity parastatal) and Iscor (the iron and steel parastatal) in the 1920s and 1930s.[59]

Many critics have asserted that commercialization and corporatization of SOEs have effectively accomplished the same ends as privatization. They point to the reduction of jobs in the state sector, the impact of cost-recovery approaches on the poor, and the increased casualization of labor that has followed the "rationalization" of the workforce in some sectors.[60] Moreover, the number and intensity of distributional conflicts indicate that the strategy generated its share of losers and skeptics from business as well as labor.

Yet, to elide the distinction between privatization and restructuring is to overlook how different stakeholders in SOEs, the tripartite alliance, and civil society used their access to the state to redirect the strategy after 2000. Although the government was certainly keen to avoid the conflicts that accompany use of the term "privatization" by referring instead to "restructuring," the preference was not simply a rhetorical one. The dynamics of the party system and the vitality of its democracy gave those with a vested interest in maintaining a role for the state multiple avenues to articulate their positions and to veto policy

---

[56] South Africa, Department of Public Enterprises, "A Summary of the Policy Framework for an Accelerated Agenda for the Restructuring of State-owned Enterprises" (August 2000), 19.

[57] Jerome, "Privatisation and Regulation," 6 and Rumney, "Overview of Progress," 3.

[58] Leape et al., "Foreign Direct Investment," 14–17.

[59] See Nancy Clark, "South African State Corporations" on these parastatals under apartheid.

[60] See especially work by David McDonald and John Pape, eds., *Cost Recovery and the Crisis of Service Delivery in South Africa* (London: Zed Press and Pretoria: HSRC Publishers, 2002); and Patrick Bond ed., *Unsustainable South Africa: Environment, Development, and Social Protest* (Durban: University of Kwazulu-Natal Press, 2002).

change. To use the language of Streeck and Thelen, after 2000, the government "layered" a new reform strategy that accorded a greater role for the state, parastatals, and public works onto a previous set of regulations favoring the private sector.[61]

Stable Party Politics and Liberal Democracy

Because the government designed a broad, vague mandate for the DPE and ambiguous legislation on privatization, it was able to construct a strategic compromise without appearing to renege on its commitments. The stability of the party system and the nature of liberal democracy in South Africa explain why the government adjusted structural adjustment. Like Mozambique, South Africa had a relatively stable party system where parties had identifiable constituencies of support and endured between elections. At 13 percent and 2.11, respectively, seat volatility and the effective number of parliamentary parties was low, despite having a system of proportional representation and parliamentary government. According to the Afrobarometer survey, a majority of respondents stated they felt close to two parties in South Africa as they did in other stable party systems.[62] But another feature of South Africa distinguished it from the cases of Zambia and Mozambique that I have previously examined. Like Cape Verde or Mauritius, South Africa's liberal democracy offered frequent opportunities for parties, their supporters, and other organized interests to contribute to debate, to articulate diverse preferences, and openly to challenge governmental priorities. I illustrate these features by using V.O. Key's framework to explore party organization in South Africa, the party system and the electorate, and the party in government.

Party Organization
The discussion of party organization and orientation in South Africa is largely a discussion about the ANC, owing to its command of the political arena for nearly two decades. The ruling party shared a number of similarities with its counterpart in Mozambique. Both have served continuously in office since the advent of multiparty democracy in 1994. Both were liberation movements that engaged in protracted armed struggles to bring about change in their respective

---

[61] Wolfgang Streeck and Kathleen Thelen, "Introduction: Institutional Change in Advanced Industrial Economies" in Streeck and Thelen, eds., *Beyond Continuity: Institutional Change in Advanced Industrial Economies*, (Oxford: Oxford University Press, 2005), 22–24, and see also Mahoney and Thelen, "A Theory" 14–18.

[62] Afrobarometer Survey Findings, "Summary of Results: Round Three, Afrobarometer Survey in South Africa, 2006," compiled by Citizen Surveys and Institute for Democracy in South Africa, Afrobarometer Survey, Round 3, 2006, accessed 12/18/2011, http://www.afrobarometer.org.

countries. Like its Frelimo counterpart, the leadership of the ANC considered the party to be a mass-based party. According to Lodge, "It remains an orthodoxy within the ANC that the organization is not merely a political party but remains a liberation movement."[63]

The organization of the party followed the principles of democratic centralism, which Frelimo also embraced. This structure built loyalty to the party and fostered discipline. It also concentrated policy making at the apex of the party and reduced opportunities for internal debate except during the national conference. Each successive level of the ANC drew its membership from the previous level; conversely, lower levels were expected to implement decisions taken by higher levels of the party. The ANC had four committees at the branch, regional, provincial, and national level, each of which was elected at the annual general meeting or conference associated with that level. The branch was the lowest level of the party structure and since 2001, it has coincided with the boundaries of municipal wards.[64] Approximately 90 percent of those delegates at the National Conference who voted for the National Executive Committee (NEC) were representatives of branch executive committees and were elected at branch general meetings. the remaining 10 percent of delegates came from provincial executive committees, the ANC women's league and the youth league.[65]

As was the case with the Frelimo congress, the ANC National Conference met every five years. The 4,000 delegates who convened at the conference, voted on the officers of the party such as president, deputy president, treasurer and the remaining members of the NEC. Like much of the Frelimo leadership, many in the eighty-six-member NEC had a long history of loyalty and service to the ANC. They had shared experiences of being in exile, prison, or underground during the apartheid period. Many were active in the trade union movement, the civics, and/or the South African Communist Party (SACP). Younger members may have had parents who were active in the ANC during the struggle against apartheid.

Delegates to the National Conference debated the party's manifesto, rules, and the annual program, but the NEC implemented party policies and managed the party in-between conferences. It oversaw the work of lower levels of the party, appointed committees, issued reports, and created the party lists for elections within the party and for government. It also supervised the activities of the youth and women's leagues and managed the party's assets. In addition, members of the NEC and the National Working Committee, which engaged in agenda setting for the cabinet and parliament, served in the executive branch

---

[63] Tom Lodge, "The ANC and the Development of Party Politics in Modern South Africa," *Journal of Modern African Studies*, 42, 2 (2004): 215.

[64] Ibid., 191.

[65] African National Congress, "African National Congress Constitution," accessed 8/11/2010, http://www.anc.org.za/show.php?doc=./ancdocs/history/const/const2002.html.

of government.[66] Despite institutional safeguards, the structure tended to reinforce control over policymaking *and* party unity at the top, as was the case with Frelimo.

The ANC differed from Frelimo with respect to the profile of the delegates to the national conference, the nature of their respective bases, and the political context in which the two parties operated. First, despite having a population that was over twice as large as that of Mozambique, a smaller percentage of South African voters claimed to be card-carrying members of the ANC. Prior to the 2007 conference, the party had more than 620,000 members and around 2,694 branches in "good standing."[67] By contrast, Frelimo boasted of having 1.5 million members. Like most parties in Africa, membership in the ANC ebbed and flowed: It rose before significant events such as party conferences and elections and fell when these events concluded. Persistent poverty also meant that membership dues were often in arrears.

Whereas delegates to Frelimo's party congresses were increasingly educated and urban, delegates to the ANC's national conference in 2007 were largely from rural areas. These areas were overrepresented in relation to the total population and the percentage of voters for the ANC from each province. Delegates from the more rural Eastern Cape, for example, accounted for 22 percent of the total number of delegates to the national conference even though the Eastern Cape only contributed 16.6 percent of the vote for the ANC in 2004. By contrast, more populous urban areas such as Gauteng and Western Cape contributed only 8.7 and 5.4 percent of the delegates, respectively.[68] These opposing trends should have favored the continuation in power of President Mbeki since Eastern Cape is the home base of Mbeki (as well as the birthplace of the ANC) and it was overrepresented at the conference. By contrast, urban interests, which were the strongest critics of Mbeki's economic policy, the centralization of power in the presidency, and efforts to stifle debate, were underrepresented.

Yet, delegates to the fifty-second annual conference in 2007 voted to replace Mbeki with Jacob Zuma as leader of the party. Nine months later, Mbeki resigned from office following a vote by the NEC to recall him.[69] These results and the means by which they were accomplished suggest that, in contrast with Mozambique's ruling party where succession crises were handled with greater

[66] Ibid. and see Joel Barkan, "South Africa: Emerging Legislature or Rubber Stamp?" in Joel Barkan, ed., *Legislative Power in Emerging Democracies* (Boulder: Lynne Rienner, 2009), 209.

[67] Institute for Democracy in South Africa (IDASA), Political Information and Monitoring Service (PIMS), compiled by Jonathan Faull with assistance from Pamela Masiko-Kambala, "Reading the ANC's National Membership Audit, *ePoliticsSA*, 4 (2007): n.p. Accessed 1/11/2008. http://www.idasa.org.

[68] Ibid.

[69] Roger Southall, "Zunami! The Context of the 2009 Election" in Roger Southall and John Daniel, eds., *Zunami: The 2009 South African Elections* (Johannesburg: Jacana Media and The Konrad Adenauer Foundation, 2009), 4.

secrecy, there was greater contestation within the ANC and the party was more accountable to its members and the general public. Two factors explain why. First, the nature and timing of South Africa's transition produced more liberal democratic institutions in the country as a whole, which shaped and influenced the organization of the ANC and those of the opposition parties. Whether through the media, protests, special councils or commissions, there were more opportunities to participate and more resources available to contest policies or the leadership in South Africa than in Mozambique or Zambia.

Second, COSATU and the SACP took advantage of their inclusion in the tripartite alliance to demand accountability from the ANC. They did not exert influence by casting votes as a bloc at the national conference. Rather, each partner represented important constituencies that complemented and overlapped with those of the ANC. The SACP had approximately 30,000 to 50,000 members and was active in the townships, whereas COSATU represented around 60 percent of organized labor or nearly 2 million people, one-third of whom were in the public sector.[70] Prominent members of the ANC were also members of COSATU and/or the SACP. A number of former or current government officials or NEC members such as Jeremy Cronin, Rob Davies, Alec Erwin, Barbara Hogan, Blade Nzimande, Ebrahim Patel, and Jeff Radebe were members of all three or at least two out of the three Alliance partners. Their relationship with the ANC was a dynamic and fluid one: Whether partners were close or distant depended on the personalities involved and the issues at hand. Partners wore several hats and represented conflicting tendencies within the Alliance.

Overlapping memberships of several distinct political identities explain the evident tensions that have arisen in the party over privatization, restructuring, entrepreneurialism, employment, and poverty. Both the SACP and COSATU actively lobbied government to revisit its economic policy. They joined social movements to engage in demonstrations and support strikes; to criticize the government; and to argue that established capital did not fully acknowledge the legacy of apartheid. Having been marginalized from major decisions within the ruling party beginning with the adoption of GEAR, COSATU and the SACP then helped to oust Mbeki.[71] In 2009, the two organizations were strategically placed to influence the new government. Nearly 100 of the SACP's most experienced and disciplined members, including nearly all of its leadership, served in the Zuma administration.

Despite their resistance to what has been dubbed the "imperial Presidency,"[72] the show of strength by the Alliance partners should not be overemphasized.

---

[70] Lodge, "The ANC," 199 suggests the SACP had 50,000 members; Pillay states it was only 30,000, see Devan Pillay, "Cosatu, Alliances and Working Class Politics" in Sakela Buhlungu, ed., *Trade Unions and Democracy: Cosatu Workers' Political Attitudes in South Africa* (Cape Town: HSRC, 2006), 183. On COSATU, see Buhlungu, "Introduction: COSATU and the First Ten Years of Democratic Transition in South Africa" in Buhlungu, ed., *Trade Unions and Democracy*, 8–9.

[71] Craven, Interview.

[72] See Editorial, *Business Day*, September 21, 2009.

Both COSATU and the SACP serve the party, "it is the ANC that rules, not the Alliance."[73] As Darracq has observed, different constituencies linked to the party are most effective when the leadership is divided.[74] Otherwise, under the Mbeki administration, Alliance partners disciplined members and dismissed militants from their ranks whom they thought were over-zealous in their efforts to challenge privatization. Along with the Communist Youth League and the ANC Youth League, they condemned ultra-leftism and avoided coalitions with progressive social movements to challenge privatization.[75]

The SACP has very much acted as the junior partner since 1994. Although its leadership was experienced, competent, and disciplined, the number of rank-and-file members declined and members were too poor to pay dues, leaving the party in precarious financial health. Aware that its survival in the face of global neo-liberalism was anachronistic, it largely obeyed the wishes of the ANC government. By contrast, the size of COSATU's membership and its dispersion across the country gave the trade federation formidable power, but like other trade unions that are associated with political parties such as those in Argentina or Mexico, it displayed structural vulnerabilities in its relationship with the ANC. Nearly two decades of ANC rule suggest that COSATU, like the SACP, was reluctant to adopt positions that were strongly opposed to the party for fear that it would be dropped from the Alliance. Moreover, union leaders who joined government often changed their interests, and they advised former colleagues in the union to soften their positions. COSATU therefore engaged in a delicate balancing act between responding to the demands of its members and sustaining loyalty to the ruling party.[76]

Whereas critics to the left of the party were often linked to the ANC via the Alliance, those to the right of the party joined the opposition. In comparison with the ANC, most opposition parties were poorly funded, less representative, and had smaller memberships. Some, like the Inkatha Freedom Party (IFP), commanded mostly regional support; many were unable or unwilling to move beyond narrowly based appeals to gain members. Nationally, most posed little threat to the ANC but several of them did have features that are worth highlighting. First, at least two of the opposition parties, the Democratic Alliance (DA) and the IFP, had identifiable bases of support and survived from election to election. Their survival contrasts markedly with fragmented opposition parties in countries such as Zambia, Benin, Mali, and Kenya. Second, policy positions

---

[73] Ivor Sarakinsky, Academic Director, School of Public and Development Management, University of the Witwatersrand, Johannesburg, Interview, 12/4/2009.

[74] Vincent Darracq, "Being a 'Movement of the People' and a Governing Party: Study of the African National Congress Mass Character," *Journal of Southern African Studies*, 34, 2 (2008): 439.

[75] Devan Pillay, "COSATU, the SACP and the ANC post-Polokwane: Looking Left but Does It Feel Right?" *Labour, Capital and Society*, 41, 2 (2008): 4–37.

[76] Sakhela Buhlungu, Department of Sociology, University of Johannesburg, Interview, Johannesburg, 12/2/2009.

of the opposition parties supported market solutions and favored the private sector to a greater extent than the ANC. Third, the opposition tried to hold the ANC accountable: parliamentary representatives of the DA consistently challenged the ANC in the national parliament. Just as important, the DA recently captured both the Cape Town metropolitan area and the provincial level government of the Western Cape.[77] These victories indicate that the ANC did not completely monopolize political space in South Africa.

The most important opposition party, the DA was the heir to the Progressive Party, a liberal party that formed in the 1950s in opposition to racial discrimination. It subsequently became the Progressive Federal Party in the 1970s. Consistent with its liberal values, it vigorously opposed the tricameral Constitution of 1983 on the grounds that it continued to entrench racial discrimination. Although it has undergone several name changes, mergers, and alliances since the transition, the DA has steadily gained seats in national and provincial parliamentary elections since 1999 (then called the Democratic Party).[78]

With a national presence, the DA was the largest opposition party in parliament after 1999 until the present. It had a shadow cabinet and presented itself as an "alternative government, rather than just another opposition party."[79] It was particularly outspoken on the issues of crime, corruption, and excesses of state power and relished its watchdog role. On economic policy, it was firmly pro-market and has criticized the ANC for being too slow to privatize.[80] Unlike the ANC, where members of parliament had little input into party policymaking, MPs in the DA largely shaped party policy along with elected officials at the provincial and municipal levels who were represented on its Federal Council.[81] The linkages between MPs, policy, and the party's Federal Council built loyalty to the party by elected officials and unified the party's message.

The remaining parties of note, including the IFP whose origins date back to the apartheid period, or the newest party, the Congress of the People (COPE), did not receive a significant share of the vote in the 2009 elections. IFP remained a regional party based in Kwazulu-Natal (KZN). Its total vote share dropped by 15 percent between 2004 and 2009, largely owing to a shift of support from the IFP to the ANC in KZN. The explanation for the shift is likely due to the fact that the ANC's choice for President, Jacob Zuma, shared the same ethnic

[77] Zwelethu Jolobe, "The Democratic Alliance: Consolidating the Official Opposition" in Roger Southall and John Daniel, eds., *Zunami: The 2009 South African Elections* (Johannesburg: Jacana Media and The Konrad Adenauer Foundation, 2009), 131–146.
[78] Ibid.
[79] Susan Booysen, "The Democratic Alliance: Progress and Pitfalls" in Jessica Piombo and Lia Nijzink, eds., *Electoral Politics in South Africa: Assessing the First Democratic Decade* (New York: Palgrave, 2005), 137.
[80] Kimberley Lanegran, "South Africa's 1999 Election: Consolidating a Dominant Party System," *Africa Today*, 48, 2 (2001): 81–102.
[81] Tom Lodge, "The Future of South Africa's Party System," *Journal of Democracy*, 17,3 (2006): 159.

background as most of the residents in KZN, where ethnic identity is quite salient.[82]

Last, only a year old in 2009, COPE was largely composed of Mbeki loyalists (minus Mbeki) who broke away from the ANC after his recall by the NEC. Its finances were weak and its structure was fluid. Despite its youth, it established a national presence in the 2009 elections, campaigning in every province and eventually capturing 7.4 percent of the national vote. Dismissively referred to as the "Black DA" by the ANC and constrained by its association with Mbeki supporters, COPE constituted the first plausible national alternative to the ANC. Positioned to the right of the ANC, it tried to appeal to a broad, nonracial mix of voters by embracing social democracy, a progressive civil rights agenda, and a mixed economy. Like other parties, it called attention to corruption and lack of accountability within the ANC and issued vague assurances that it would respect the rule of law. Beset by internal differences, weak finances, and aggressive counterattacks by the ANC, COPE nevertheless managed to become one of the top three opposition parties in the country.[83] Current discussions regarding a possible merger with the Democratic Alliance may bring it the added stability and visibility it requires to challenge the ANC effectively.

Attracting Votes
In spite of the evident disagreements among the ANC, organized labor, the poor, and the marginalized over privatization, casualization, cost recovery, and other economic policies, most voters have not punished the ANC in the national elections, either by voting for other parties or by staying away from the polls. Since 1994, South Africa has had three elections at regular intervals and two successful (albeit contentious) changes of presidential leadership. Over the course of all four elections, the ANC has garnered approximately 66 percent of the national vote on average. Even with the formation of a breakaway party during the 2009 elections, the ANC managed to gain 65.9 percent of the national vote with a turnout of 77 percent.[84]

After the ANC, the DA obtained the second largest share of the national vote in the 2009 elections with 16.7 percent as opposed to 12.4 percent of the vote in 2004. In Western Cape, it won a relative majority of votes (49 percent) for the National Assembly and an absolute majority of votes in the provincial

---

[82] Suzanne Francis, "The IFP Campaign: Indlovu Ayisindwa Kwasbaphambili!" in Roger Southall and John Daniel, *Zunami: The 2009 South African Elections* (Johannesburg: Jacana Media and The Konrad Adenauer Foundation, 2009), 147–161.

[83] Susan Booysen, "Congress of the People: Between Foothold of Hope and Slippery Slope" in Roger Southall and John Daniel, eds., *Zunami: The 2009 South African Elections* (Johannesburg: Jacana Media and The Konrad Adenauer Foundation, 2009), 85–113.

[84] South Africa, Independent Electoral Commission, Results Reports, 2009, accessed 12/28/2009, http://www.elections.org.za/NPEPWStaticReports/reports/.

elections, taking votes from the ANC in both cases. These victories reflect a growing disenchantment with the ANC among so-called colored and white voters in that region. The improvement in vote share over 2004 suggests that the DA was becoming more effective at getting its message out to voters in this province.

How did the ANC get votes in most of the country for the fourth consecutive election? Conventional explanations point to weaknesses of the opposition, the wealth of the ruling party, and reflexive loyalty to the ANC by voters. I would like to consider a fourth reason, positive retrospective as well as prospective evaluations of the economy and their own particular economic circumstances by the black middle class and urban workers, ironically, the very groups that were most vocal in their criticism of government policies. With respect to the first reason, some claim that the flaws in the positions and campaigns of the opposition parties explain why voters continued to support the ANC. The DA had the support of established business, but its pockets were not deep enough to produce sophisticated ads that targeted particular groups of voters. The DA also did not figure out how, or whether, to court black voters at the national level.[85]

Second, as the incumbent party, the ANC had access to substantial funds to pay for its electoral campaigns. Similar to Mozambique, public funds for elections were allocated according to the percentage of votes gained in the previous election, which of course gave great advantages to the ruling party. Public funding was well managed and transparent, whereas sources and amounts of donations from private businesses, the trade unions, and even parastatals were more opaque.[86] Contributions were greater than private donations in Mozambique or Zambia. In South Africa, the absence of laws on donations to parties meant that parties raised money with little accountability to the general public or other organs of the state. Unfortunately, few political parties were calling for more transparency in electoral funding so the source of private donations remained a secret.[87]

Because it was the ruling party, the ANC had access to broader sources of financing than the opposition parties. It accepted contributions from wings of the party such as the ANCYL, Alliance partners, corporate capital, and individuals. In the 2004 elections, voluntary disclosure of contributions from the private sector revealed a pattern of campaign contributions that mimicked that of the United States. Big business donated heavily to the elections and typically the incumbent benefited from the contributions. Big business invested a larger

---

[85] Barry Bearak, "South African Party Leader Shrugs Off Suspicions," *New York Times*, April 18, 2009: Sean Jacobs, "Slim Pickings in South African Poll," *Guardian.co.uk*, April 22, 2009, accessed 5/6/2009, http://www.guardian.co.uk/commentisfree/2009/apr/22/south-african-elections.

[86] Sarakinsky, Interview.

[87] n.a, "South Africa: The Richest Party wins a Wealth of Votes," April 21, 2009, accessed 9/28/2009, http://www.allAfrica.com.

proportion of its contributions in the party that it believed would win, but also it funded opposition parties, either according to a formula similar to that of public funding – or according to its own preferences.[88] Large firms supported parties that had little chance of winning for three reasons: first, they wanted to support democracy; second, they shared an ideological affinity to particular parties (notably the DA in the South African case); or, third, they were hedging their bets.[89]

The sources of some donations to the ANC and other parties reveal influence peddling by private companies and parastatals.[90] In one instance both the ANC and the DA were accused of accepting large cash donations from a mining magnate, who was under investigation for share price fixing, tax evasion, and other shady dealings at the time of his murder in 2005. While the DA claimed to have returned the money to avoid further involvement with the estate of the controversial businessman, the ANC has so far resisted.[91] In two other instances, donations from parastatals in the oil sector and in electricity allegedly were channeled to the ANC through companies with close ties to the ruling party.[92] These cases illustrate the complex relationships that parastatals and private firms have with the ruling party.

Third, some observers claim that despite continuing hardship for many, the vote for the ANC stemmed from "reflexive loyalty": Allegiance to the party trumped economic voting in spite of poor economic outcomes. Shared beliefs and common identities do shape loyalty to the ANC and party allegiance helps to explain vote choice as it tends to do in other countries where party identification is strong.[93] The ANC is credited with the collapse of apartheid, liberation, and the advent of democracy. Many older, black voters have supported the ANC all their lives, from the time when the movement was banned to the present day. For those who did not have direct experience of the ANC's efforts against apartheid, the ANC occupies a prominent role in the official history and its political dominance crowds out the voices of other parties in political discourse.

---

[88] Ivor Sarakinsky, "Political Party Finance in South Africa: Disclosure Versus Secrecy," *Democratization*, 14, 1 (2007): 121.

[89] Sarakinsky, Interview.

[90] Roger Southall, "The ANC for Sale? Money, Morality and Business in South Africa," *Review of African Political Economy*, 35, 116 (2008): 281–299.

[91] South African Press Association, "ANC 'Must Repay Kebble Millions,'" *News24South Africa*, March 11, 2004, accessed 10/1/2009, http://www.news24.com/Content/SouthAfrica/News/1059/.

[92] Stefans Brümmer, Sam Sole, and Wisani Wa Ka Ngobeni, "The ANC's Oilgate," *Mail and Guardian*, May 3, 2005; Stefans Brümmer, "ANC to Exit Eskom Deals," *Mail and Guardian*, February 15, 2008 and "Chancellor House," *Mail and Guardian*, November 27–December 12, 2009, 6.

[93] José María Maravall and Adam Przeworski, "Political Reactions to the Economy: The Spanish Experience" in Susan Stokes, ed., *Public Support for Market Reforms in New Democracies* (Cambridge: Cambridge University Press, 2001), 35–76.

Yet, opposition weakness, greater access to funding by the ruling party, or reflexive loyalty by voters only partially explain why voters supported the ANC. A fourth reason had to do with the economy. The ANC's economic policy has been highly criticized but until 2008 when the global financial crisis hit, the ANC's economic strategy was producing around 5 percent growth per year and contributing to the expansion of the black middle class. Although polling data are only suggestive at this point, positive retrospective and prospective economic evaluations appeared to play a role in support for the ruling party at the last election.

With the striking exception of responses from the Western Cape, which was won by the DA, responses to polling data indicate that South Africans experienced some economic improvements, evaluated them positively, and expected them to continue. Asked by Afrobarometer whether economic and living conditions had improved in the last twelve months, between 27 and 47 percent of respondents from all provinces except Western Cape said they had gotten better or much better. In Western Cape, only 16 percent of those surveyed responded that both economic and living conditions had improved. Asked if they expected economic and living conditions to improve in the next twelve months, respondents' answers ranged from a high of 59 percent in Mpumalanga province who expected them to be better or much better to 40 percent in Northern Cape. Western Cape was again an outlier with only 23 percent of respondents indicating that conditions would be better or much better over the next 12 months.[94] Additional research is required, but these responses indicate that voters supported the party that contributed to their own and the country's well-being. Their expectations that conditions for themselves and the country would improve in the future likely also influenced them to cast their vote for the ANC.

More detailed data on the organized working class support the claim that voters combine retrospective and prospective assessments to determine their vote for the ANC. Longitudinal data on the attitudes of a sample of rank-and-file members of COSATU indicates that the percentage of those who stated that they would vote for the ANC has remained remarkably consistent and remarkably high since 1994. Of those surveyed (around 655 in 2004), 75 percent in 1994 and 2000 and 73 percent in 2004 said that they intended to vote for the ANC in national elections.[95] Panel data collected between 1994 and 2004 indicates that the ANC met many of the expectations of workers regarding

---

[94] Afrobarometer Survey Findings, "Summary of Results: Round Four, Afrobarometer Survey in South Africa," compiled by Citizen Surveys, Afrobarometer Survey, Round 4, 2008, accessed 12/18/2011, http://www.afrobarometer.org. I averaged together responses to questions on past living and economic conditions and future economic and living conditions.

[95] Sakhela Buhlungu, Roger Southall, and Edward Webster, "Conclusion: COSATU and the Democratic Transformation of South Africa" in Buhlungu, ed., *Trade Unions and Democracy: COSATU Workers' Political Attitudes in South Africa.* (Cape Town: Human Sciences Research Council, 2006), 205.

the provision of services such as water, electricity, telephone access, and skills training.[96] Pillay argues that "worker support for the ANC is not based on blind loyalty but on real improvements in workers' living conditions and the *expectation* of further improvements."[97] Furthermore, interviews with union members at the electricity parastatal, Eskom, suggest that workers supported Zuma (and therefore the ANC) in 2009 not only because they believed he might be more responsive to the demands of the marginalized, but also because he was "socially conservative."[98] His populist appeals to tradition and his overtures to traditional leaders resonated with their own cultural values.[99]

The leadership of the ruling party, however, has had difficulty reconciling economic demands for jobs and benefits by workers with the demands by middle-class business owners who seek flexible labor laws in order to secure higher profits in the private sector. The 2009 elections appeared to tip the balance in the party toward COSATU, the SACP, new social movements, and assorted leftist groups. They viewed the downfall of Mbeki as a victory for participatory democracy and a people's defeat of neo-liberalism. Although Zuma's commitment to the left's agenda is questionable, the replacement of Mbeki raised expectations (and fears) within and without the party that leaders could be held accountable, that interests influenced policymaking and implementation, and that parliament could exercise some control over the executive.[100]

The Party in Government

After 1994, the policies of the ruling party reflected the heterogeneous interests that constituted its base. Efforts to support business, encourage investment, promote free trade, and foster regional integration acknowledged the institutional legacy of the South African economy and the realities of the global environment. They anticipated also a growing entrepreneurialism among historically disadvantaged groups. The formation of holding and investment companies, even among COSATU affiliates and the Youth League, has confirmed this expectation.

As future sections will show, facilitating the maintenance and expansion of the private sector did not exhaust the ANC's policy options. After 2000, the party in government equally relied on contingent uses of discretionary authority to align more effectively the interests of two core constituencies: trade unionists and

---

[96] Sakhela Buhlungu, *A Paradox of Victory: COSATU and the Democratic Transformation in South Africa* (Durban: University of KwaZulu-Natal Press, 2010), 75. A majority of workers noted that increases in wages did NOT meet their expectations which helps to explain protests and discontent around restructuring.

[97] Devan Pillay, "COSATU, Alliances," 180.

[98] Alexander Beresford, "Comrades 'Back on Track' The Durability of the Tripartite Alliance in South Africa," *African Affairs*, 108, 432 (2009): 406.

[99] Ibid., 391–412.

[100] Patrick Craven, Interview; Petrus Mashishi, Interview.

the black middle class, notably black investors and managers. Interventionism became a strategic compromise, a response to preferences initially articulated by the ANC's alliance partners, the SACP and COSATU, but also accepted by middle-class ANC members, that to survive as a movement and to progress as a country the state had to broaden its policy agenda.[101] Public works projects, procurement policies, state-driven investment companies, the deployment of ANC cadres into business, and control over parastatals were the tools used to generate employment and promote capital accumulation. South Africa's political dynamics drove the compromise, but equally the institutional outlets afforded by South Africa's liberal democracy made compromise possible.

Liberal Democracy in an Era of Restructuring

Institutional Checks and Balances on Economic Policy Choice
The legacy of apartheid left a highly centralized state, which the continuity in power by a strong, stable party tends to reinforce. Not surprisingly then, the style of economic policy implementation replicates patterns found in former one-party states such as Mexico or in limited democracies such as Mozambique. The South African government has demonstrated marked tendencies to concentrate power and has relied on parastatals to do so. As the Mexican government did when it privatized, the government actively cultivated some constituencies and marginalized others. Political elites used the process to secure alliances with organized labor or alternatively, with established businesses.[102]

Still, we have to consider whether the social movements, consumer protests, and media criticism generated by the privatization process and the government's subsequent decision to halt outright sales, to shift to restructuring, and to foster public works would have occurred in a more limited democracy. The answer is "no." In comparison with Zambia and Mozambique, South Africa's more democratic institutions expanded opportunities for interests to express their preferences. Checks and balances coupled with a vibrant, organized civil society allowed contestation, facilitated negotiation, and fostered accountability. Over time, conflict and consultation produced policy compromises without overturning the initial reform.[103]

Many political and structural challenges impeded the effective use of checks and balances following the transition, but no formal institution was moribund, including the South African parliament. Under Mbeki, parliament did not exercise effective oversight of executive functions and activities.[104] Yet parliamentary

[101] Roger Southall, "The ANC and Black Capitalism in South Africa," *Review of African Political Economy*, 31, 100 (2004): 313–328.
[102] Hector Schamis, "Distributional Coalitions and the Politics of Economic Reform in Latin America," *World Politics*, 51, 2 (1999): 236–268
[103] Hellman, "Winners Take All" and see also Frye, *Building States and Markets*, 70–104.
[104] Tim Hughes, "The South African Parliament's Failed Moment," in M. A. Mohammed Salih, *African Parliaments: Between Governance and Government* (New York: Palgrave Macmillan, 2005), 225–246.

portfolio and select committees charged with reviewing government activities such as procurement and housing did launch aggressive inquiries into governmental business. Committees also acted as information and lobbying conduits between constituents or interest groups and ministers. Consider the proposed privatization of Transnet, an SOE that is responsible for South Africa's transport freight; rail, port, and pipeline infrastructure and management. Proposals to privatize Transnet became the subject of political contestation in 2000. When negotiations concluded, Transnet was corporatized but remained a parastatal with the South African government as the sole shareholder. A new parastatal was created for urban passenger road and rail transport, and several noncore enterprises were sold.

Two actors working together played key roles convincing the cabinet not to privatize: the South African Transport and Allied Workers' Union (SATAWU) and the parliamentary portfolio committee.[105] The union's campaign to stop the privatization of Transnet had three elements: an information campaign, lobbying, and mobilization. First, it engaged in detailed research to expose the risks of privatization and to identify the potential rewards of retaining and restructuring several Transnet services rather than privatizing them. Second, the union not only lobbied the relevant ministers, but also sought out members of parliament who would listen to its concerns. Although the extent to which portfolio committees act effectively varies, it was fortunate that the parliamentary portfolio committee for transport was under the leadership of Jeremy Cronin. Cronin, an SACP member, was both an experienced and knowledgeable member of parliament, and he was sympathetic to the arguments of the trade union. His position on the committee enabled him to articulate the union's interests and to question ministers about the privatization strategy. Last, the union mobilized its members to defend their interests through several day-long stoppages, although union officials stressed that these never became explosive.

The three-pronged strategy, which included members of parliament in important roles, contributed to the government's eventual decision to create a new parastatal for road transport and to retain Transnet as a restructured public company.[106] Reflecting on this achievement, a trade unionist observed that portfolio committees were becoming "more responsive and less timid in their approach."[107] Members of parliament were asserting greater independence from the presidency and portfolio committees were more likely to challenge ministers, especially if interests such as labor or business pressured them.[108] These claims

[105] Barrett, Interview; South Africa, Department of Transport, Keynote address at the launch of Passenger Rail Agency of South Africa by Mr. Jeff Radebe, MP, Minister of Transport, Park Station, Johannesburg, March 20, 2009, accessed 12/26/2009, http://www.info.gov.za/speeches/2009/09032409451003.htm.

[106] Barrett, Interview.

[107] Barrett, Interview.

[108] Barrett, Interview.

are consistent with those of Joel Barkan, who found that committees chaired by skilled, talented politicians who enjoyed the support and respect of other members of parliament were more effective. Those such as finance, justice, and transport, which handled with a great deal of legislation tended to have greater capacity. In addition, committees that had a staff and a space in which to meet were more effective than those that did not.[109] Should committees enhance their capabilities, they may be subject to more targeted appeals by particular constituencies such as business or voters in the future.

Efforts to shape policy or demand accountability were not limited to portfolio and standing committees. Consistent with the rule of law, the auditor general's (AG) office monitored the financial performance of government departments, investigated alleged abuses of government funds, and oversaw potential conflicts of interest by public sector employees. It worked with the judiciary and the Standing Committee on Public Accounts to pursue cases of wrongdoing. Where wrongdoings were egregious, the public accounts committee or the AG referred the more serious cases to the judiciary for prosecution. In some cases, greater transparency was sufficient to secure compliance with the law. In 2006, for example, the AG disclosed that thousands of government employees had business interests despite conflict of interest legislation prohibiting such associations.[110] Several public sector officials resigned positions in companies to avoid running afoul of the law. Following the disclosure, documented linkages between the public sector and business subsequently declined suggesting that the AG's efforts had been effective.[111]

Bargaining and negotiation were equally built into the political system through the creation of agencies such as the National Economic Development and Labour Council (Nedlac) or labor mediation boards, though these were not as active during the Mbeki administration as unions hoped. Informal instruments such as persuasion and struggle were sometimes employed to modify the policy. Where efforts to persuade became outright dissent, the government largely tolerated it; and the government allowed the media openly to criticize job losses, inefficiency, crony capitalism and the power of white business. The activities of numerous think tanks, advocacy groups, research units, and watchdog organizations from across the ideological spectrum attest to the vibrant pluralism that exists in South Africa, which is a critical component of any democratic society.

---

[109] Barkan, "South Africa: Emerging Legislature," 216–218.

[110] Gary Pienaar, "Procurement Corruption," *New Agenda*, 31 (August 2008): n.p., reprinted by Idasa online, accessed 1/5/2012, http://idasa.krazyboyz.co.za/countries/output/procurement_corruption/.

[111] South Africa, Auditor General, "Report of the Auditor-General to Parliament on a Performance Audit of Entities That Are Connected with Government Employees and Doing Business with National Departments," RP 242/2008 (August 2008), 11, Table 1.

Civil Society I: Privatization and Its Critics

Owing to the high quality of South Africa's democracy, civil society actors enjoyed the political space to compete against each other and against the state to win concessions.[112] Many opponents of privatization such as trade unions, civic associations, various ad hoc groups, and newly formed social movements drew on substantial financial and organizational resources to confront local and national state agencies or firms that cut benefits or jobs. With regard to labor unions organized under the umbrella of COSATU, high rates of unionization, a high degree of organization, negotiating skills and experience, and their affiliation with the ruling party gave them greater opportunities to influence reform. This finding is consistent with claims by other scholars on the determinants of an effective response by labor to privatization.[113]

Raul Madrid's study of responses to economic reform in Latin America by labor unions demonstrates that the "breadth and depth" of reforms can also shape the extent of trade union opposition and the subsequent response by the state. Reforms such as trade liberalization have a targeted impact. They affect those firms that may have to compete with less expensive imports and thus tend to evoke a response from a limited number of trade unions, which poses a collective action problem for labor. By contrast, reforms such as pension or labor law reform are more likely to be resisted effectively by unions because they impact larger numbers of people.[114] In the South African case, the response to cost-recovery schemes reinforces Madrid's claim. Because service sector reforms exacted high and widespread costs, they provoked an equally broad response by, and beyond, the labor movement and one that the government found difficult to ignore.

About 40 percent of South Africa's formal sector workers are members of trade unions and the majority of these belong to COSATU-affiliated unions. COSATU had a long and commendable history of resistance to apartheid and many of its affiliates were active participants in the debates around privatization. Along with other trade unions, COSATU relied on formal and informal mechanisms to exert influence on government. Begun just after the transition, the corporatist style arrangement, Nedlac, brought together government, labor, business, and various community groups to advise government on development, trade, monetary, financial, labor, and social policies. Deliberations within Nedlac influenced the development of labor policies, but it was less effective with respect to broader macroeconomic and trade policies or those with ramifications for the larger South African economy. The Mbeki

---

[112] South Africa averaged 1.08 for Political Rights and 2.08 for Civil Liberties from 1994 to 2005 according to Freedom House, "Historical and Comparative Data."

[113] See especially Victoria Murillo, "From Populism to Neoliberalism: Labor Unions and Market Reforms in Latin America," *World Politics*, 52 (January 2000): 135–174.

[114] Raul Madrid, "Labouring against Neoliberalism: Unions and Patterns of Reform in Latin America," *Journal of Latin American Studies* 35, 1 (2003): 61.

administration largely excluded it from policymaking and only recently has its consultative role resumed.[115]

Business and labor developed a more streamlined, bilateral forum in 2000 consisting of twelve representatives each from organized labor and business. The Millennium Labor Council (MLC) addressed working conditions of mutual concern to the two parties including job creation, poverty, HIV/AIDS, labor productivity, and other issues that did not necessarily require a policy stance by government to be resolved.[116] MLC was meant to be an arena for discussion; its findings and positions were used to inform Nedlac.[117]

As members of the Alliance, COSATU and the SACP initially worked with the government to fashion the RDP in 1994, but their marginalization from policy decisions by the Mbeki administration after 1999 encouraged them to rely on additional tactics to express their disagreements with government. These included industrial action, mass protests, efforts to expand membership to casual workers, and public relations campaigns. They sought and received favorable media coverage particularly from the *Mail and Guardian*; and they appealed to members of parliament to represent their interests.

Most industrial action focused on salary increases, but protests against privatization, cost-recovery schemes, casualization, and retrenchments also explain the frequency, timing, and intensity of strikes, including unauthorized wildcat strikes. Strikes and protests have surged and receded over time. In 1997, one year after the adoption of GEAR, strike action and lockouts reached a peak of 1,324 incidents but began dropping the following year. From 2000, strike action averaged about 75 incidents per year. The creation of a dispute mediation board after 1997 and increased use of bargaining via Nedlac likely contributed to the decline in incidents after 1997,[118] but the causes and the timing of incidents is also related to calculations by COSATU and its affiliated unions regarding their potential to impact government policy in a democratic context. COSATU relied on labor action and protests strategically to increase pressure on the government to respond to its demands without being disloyal. These actions influenced government decisions to rethink privatization after 2000.[119]

Cost-recovery measures generated the most sustained resistance against privatization both because they affected social groups such as consumers and because they spawned the formation of movements beyond organized labor as Madrid's study predicts. Although the inclusion of the private sector in the provision of electricity or water produced increases in the availability of services in

[115] Sarakinsky, Interview; Craven, Interview; see Gregory Houston, Ian Liebenberg, and William Dichaba, "Interest Group Participation in the National Economic and Development Council" in Gregory Houston, ed., *Public Participation in Democratic Governance in South Africa* (Pretoria: HSRC, 2001), 17–82.
[116] Craven, Interview.
[117] Millennium Labour Council, "The Launch," accessed 10/22/2010, http://www.mlc.org.za.
[118] South Africa, Ministry of Labour, Labour Force Surveys, 1996–2008.
[119] Mashishi Interview; Craven Interview: Barrett Interview.

some areas, it also resulted in the cessation of services in the event that citizens lacked the ability to pay. In 2001, about 35 percent of the respondents to a random, stratified, public opinion survey of over 2,500 people reported that they either could not pay for services or had to cut back on other necessities in order to pay for them. Estimates indicated that approximately 20 million low-income and lower-middle-income households had water or electricity services discontinued for failure to pay.[120]

Cost increases associated with the commercialization of local services ignited intense resistance in many of those local municipalities where they occurred. Where COSATU and the SACP stopped short of an open break with the Alliance over privatization and public–private partnerships, other groups stepped into the breach to defy governmental policy. Many of them organized under the umbrella of the Anti-Privatization Forum (APF), founded in 2000. The APF had twenty-seven affiliates that mobilized the unemployed and underemployed to criticize the privatization of state assets, the injustice of cost-recovery solutions for essential utilities such as water, sanitation, and electricity, and the reduction of rights at the workplace.[121] APF's message often drew parallels between what it perceived as ANC favoritism toward corporate capital and the global hegemony of neo-liberalism.

The APF offered socialist or social democratic alternatives to privatization. A loose, decentralized, heterogeneous movement, whose affiliates were largely based in black townships and inner city areas of Gauteng province, the APF was one of the few organizations that represented the poor and vulnerable. It formed linkages with international nongovernmental organizations such as War on Want in order to build support, but it was largely driven by a diverse group of domestic actors with backgrounds in politics, the trade union movement, local community activism, and academia. Its actions included workshops for activists, public information and awareness raising campaigns, and mass protests. After nearly a decade of political activism, the APF has been eclipsed by less ideological, smaller community organizations that attack poor service delivery by local government and criticize the lavish lifestyles of municipal councilors.[122]

Civil Society II – Business and Management

The grievances of those who lost jobs or had to pay higher fees for electricity or water following restructuring have been well publicized and have evoked

[120] McDonald and Pape, *Cost Recovery*, 162–167.
[121] Patrick Bond, with George Dor, Becky Himlin, and Greg Ruiters, "Eco-Social Injustice for Working-Class Communities: The Making and unmaking of Neoliberal Infrastructure Policy" in Patrick Bond ed., *Unsustainable South Africa: Environment, Development and Social Protest* (Scottsville: University of Kwazulu-Natal Press, 2002), 185–254 and R. Ballard, Adam Habib, Imraan Valodia, and Elke Zuern, "Globalization, Marginalization and Contemporary Social Movements in South Africa," *African Affairs*, 104, 417 (2005): 615–634.
[122] Trevor Ngwane, Soweto Electricity Crisis Committee, Interview, Johannesburg, 12/1/2009.

responses from diverse quarters, but in a largely private sector–driven economy, they were not the only actors using democratic institutions to shift policy. Across the class divide was the highly concentrated, better financed, business class. Many of the divisions within business that were discussed with regard to Zambia and Mozambique also characterized business in South Africa. Interests splintered along racial, sectoral, and policy lines; major differences existed between black and white business people; between large established business and small and medium emerging entrepreneurs; between those who favored greater liberalization and those who desired more protection; and between manufacturing and minerals, or energy and agriculture. These differences gave the South African government room to maneuver: It played interests off against each other, formed temporary coalitions with one or a few groups, and balanced competing claims.[123]

Depending on their size and importance to the South African economy, businesses relied on formal and informal arrangements to influence policy and to hold government accountable. Via their associations, both established and emerging businesses participated in Nedlac or the Millenium Labor Council, voiced support for GEAR, and criticized the slow pace of privatization in the 1990s.[124] Just as communities and organized labor relied on several channels to exercise influence, business used the media, their associations, and opposition parties to subject privatization deals to scrutiny and to demand a reduction in government concentration.[125]

Even prior to the transition, established big business used its dominant economic position, organizational skills, and global networks to encourage the ANC government to pursue neo-liberal economic reforms, but also it became adept over the course of the 1990s at convincing the government of its commitment to deracializing the workplace. Sanlam, Old Mutual, and Anglo American financed black economic empowerment deals and appointed promising black entrepreneurs or the politically well connected to their boards. Figures from the 2004 elections suggest that Anglo-Vaal Mining, Sanlam, and Anglo-Gold contributed financially both to the ruling party and the opposition and thus "bought" access to politicians as much as business in more developed capitalist countries does.[126] To show their commitment to a "new" South Africa, many of these large companies also established trusts and financed projects to promote education, skills development, or sustainable communities in disadvantaged

---

[123] Nicoli Nattrass and Jeremy Seekings, "State, Business and Growth in Post-Apartheid South Africa," Research Programme Consortium for Improving Institutions for Pro-Poor Growth," Discussion Paper Series 34 (January 2010), 37–51.

[124] Handley, *Business and the State*, 76–85. Nattrass and Seekings note that by the mid-1990s, big business found Nedlac an ineffective forum in which to advance their interests and preferred alternative channels to influence government, see "State, Business and Growth," 42–46.

[125] No author, "Crying for Freedom," *Financial Mail* (March 23, 2001), 42–44

[126] Sarakinsky, "Political Party Finance"; Southall, "The ANC for Sale?," 286.

areas.[127] At the same time, some large firms hedged their bets on the future of South Africa by shifting assets elsewhere.

Besides participating in formally constituted bargaining fora or directing funds to political parties, businesses joined think tanks, advocacy groups, and business associations to exercise leverage on government. Peak associations such as the South African Chamber of Commerce and Industry, which represented around 20,000 mostly small and medium businesses, or Afrikaanse Handleinstituut (AHI), which historically represented Afrikaner business, have retained their pretransition identities and advocated on behalf of their members' interests. By contrast, the historically white, sectoral business association, the Chamber of Mines, became deracialized and worked closely with government on matters pertaining to the mining sector. Powerful groups such as Anglo American and Rembrandt influenced policy debates either by sponsoring studies of the economy and/or by joining councils overseen by the president.[128]

Occupying a space within the business community were black managers and business owners. But that space was a shifting one. On the one hand, black managers and business owners were part of the previously disadvantaged and, as such, supported economic empowerment initiatives. On the other hand, they shared the economic interests of established, historically white, businesses. Many of them had strong links to the ANC leadership, and they moved between government and business. They relied on their political connections or their ties to established business to expand their business interests. Equally, they exercised influence through black business associations such as the National African Chamber of Commerce, the Foundation for African Business and Consumer Services, the Black Business Council, or the Black Management Forum (BMF).

Black business associations voiced diverse concerns on a range of issues from labor laws to the tax regime, but their major focus was on BEE goals. By the mid-1990s, organizations such as BMF were disappointed with the results of early SOE sales and schemes to create black investor groups.[129] Given the lack of capital and relatively low skills base of black businesses, these associations pressured government to extend BEE beyond equity creation to include the expansion of blacks in management positions, skills development, procurement policies favoring black firms, and increased government support for existing black-owned firms. The new B-BBEE approach and scorecard in 2003

---

[127] The most prominent of these efforts is the "Business Trust," a partnership between big business and government engaged in skills training, job creation, small and medium business development, and other pro-business initiatives. One hundred forty companies have contributed 1.2 billion rands or US$170 million since its founding in 1999, see "Business Trust," accessed 2/11/2011, http://www.btrust.org.za.

[128] Chabane et al., "The Changing Face," 567–572.

[129] Tembakazi Mnyaka, Deputy President, Black Management Forum, Interview, Johannesburg, 12/6/2009.

addressed many of their criticisms, but they continued to seek opportunities that would benefit and support black investors and managers.[130]

In 2003, a merger of business associations aimed to strengthen the influence of the private sector by bringing together under one umbrella sixty-one existing associations, representing established and emerging businesses, black and white business owners and managers, small and large firms from tourism to mining. Business Unity South Africa (BUSA), combined the economic power of established white capital with the political influence of black business. It included BMF, AHI, and the South African Chamber of Commerce and Industry, formerly an association with only white members. Major companies such as Sanlam, Nedbank, and Sasol joined the new peak association. BUSA's officers came from diverse socioeconomic, political, and business backgrounds. In addition to having business acumen, several officers had experience in government. They served on Nedlac, participated in commissions on black economic empowerment, or worked for the South African Reserve Bank. Others had legal, financial, or academic backgrounds and some were members of the ANC.[131]

BUSA tried to lobby government with one voice on issues of concern to business, but tensions within the group were evident almost from its inception. On the one hand, it supported empowerment initiatives, skills development, and poverty alleviation. Member associations such as BMF favored these objectives, because BMF represented managers from historically disadvantaged backgrounds, who were employed by parastatals and private companies. On the other hand, consistent with the interests of many business owners, BUSA was committed to an "enabling environment for business." It favored free trade, lower interest rates, labor law reform, and enterprise development for small and medium firms. These goals were not incompatible, but disagreements arose around the organization's priorities as well as the means by which it selected its representatives. These divisions culminated in the withdrawal of several black business associations in July of 2011.[132] Although BUSA has survived the departure of these associations, the split has weakened attempts to present a united front to government and exposed the historical racial and occupational faultlines within South Africa.

Despite tensions and divisions, what have been the results of efforts by business to shape government policy since the transition? Handley notes that, in spite of its historically racial exclusivity, big business had a "substantial impact" on economic policy. In particular, fears of a "radically redistributionist" approach by the ANC never came to pass.[133] The evidence presented here on privatization lends further support to her claim. The government struck compromises on

[130] Ibid.
[131] Business Unity South Africa, see profiles of members, accessed 1/27/2011 on http://www.BUSA. org.za.
[132] Michael Bleby, "BMF Quits BUSA over 'Opposition to Change,'" *Business Day*, July 5, 2011, 1.
[133] Handley, *Business and the State*, 63, 92.

privatization, but no large-scale nationalizations took place as in Mozambique following independence and no property was seized in the name of "indigenization" or "Africanization." Rather, the government welcomed private sector participation in spatial development initiatives, cost-recovery schemes, CIDs, and RIDs.

Handley owes the success of business, particularly historically white, big business, not only to the market, but also to "its autonomy and strength," to its relative distance from the party in power.[134] The autonomy of the business class now seems in doubt. Party leaders and the business class hardly constitute an "epistemic community," but a relatively stable party system has allowed business to forge relationships with party notables without the challenges associated with shifting party loyalties encountered in Zambia. Increasing global integration and the government's poor financial health initially prompted the relationship; however, the growing black middle class and the movement between business and politics as a result of the ANC's deployment tactics and empowerment initiatives helped to sustain it. Indeed, the ANC borrowed from the playbook of the former authoritarian government in Mexico by institutionalizing closer ties between the party and business, capturing business in the process.

These ties appeared to strengthen with the creation of the Progressive Business Forum by the ANC in 2006. Depending on the size of the business and the number of membership benefits desired by a prospective member, businesses paid fees that ranged from US$430 to US$8500 in order to be members. In exchange, they received the chance to "network" with government officials, to mingle with government at specially arranged functions, and to have one-on-one meetings with ministers.[135] These opportunities contributed to the party's finances at the same time that they encouraged more informal exchanges between government officials and business leaders.

Moreover, the influence of the private sector may have derived from its strength, but it also depended on the quality of South Africa's democracy. Business influence rested on the freedoms afforded by the democratic process, freedoms which business did little to secure under apartheid but from which it benefited after the transition. The right to organize into associations, the right to use the media, the right to support political parties or pressure parliamentarians, the reliance on informal and personal contacts with government, and finally the right to move assets out of the country – all of these rights gave business diverse tactics with which to bargain with government. These are not readily available in limited democracies. Ironically, what tempered business

[134] Ibid., 95.
[135] Wisani wa ka Ngobeni and Dumisane Lubisi, "ANC Ministers For Sale," *Sunday Times*, February 29, 2007; Sipho Khumalo, "ANC Offers Business Owners Connections," *The Mercury*, August 13, 2008; and the Web site of the ANC, accessed 11/23/2009, http://www.anc.org.za.

influence was the same thing that tempers it in other democracies – greater pluralism. The democratic moment produced a multiplicity of associations and multiple channels by which business could express its wishes to government. But the same pluralism that allowed business to form linkages with others or to lobby government also gave other organizations such as trade unions or social movements the space to influence those in power. The policy compromises that emerged as a result of these varied pressures illustrates these characteristics of democracy rather well.

Politics and Policy Compromise: 2000–2009

Under conditions where institutions favoring a private sector–driven, market economy already existed, the presence of a stable party system and liberal democracy made possible the layering of new rules and regulations onto existing arrangements. As in Mozambique, responses by the ruling party to distributional conflicts by established capital, labor, the black middle class, and social movements were deliberate and strategic. The ANC preferred solutions that addressed the contradictory demands of key constituencies in the party – the black middle class and organized labor. A more democratic environment encouraged greater government accountability than that which existed in Zambia or Mozambique, and it influenced the government to pursue policy compromises that balanced conflicting demands. The compromises blended liberalization and restructuring with policy revisions that increased government investment in public works projects, expanded empowerment initiatives to support black managers and owners, and used parastatals to drive job creation. The layering of these policy revisions onto existing institutional arrangements appeared to be small changes, but institutionalists observe that small changes may significantly impact institutional arrangements over time.[136]

As in many cases of institutional change, the layering of policy revisions preceded the official acknowledgment of the shift. Whereas the DPE sought to reduce the financial burden of SOEs on the state in the 1990s, it began to stress social as well as economic imperatives after 2000. Alongside conventional neoliberal objectives, the policy framework emphasized the contribution of SOEs to employment creation, the provision of public goods, and empowerment.[137] Policies issued by other ministries on skills development, empowerment, and competition complemented the DPE's approach.

As distributional pressures mounted and their own grasp of the state's extensive reach expanded, the government adopted more aggressive measures to address the legacy of apartheid. The joining of social and economic objectives surfaced clearly in the government's development program, the Accelerated and Shared Growth Initiative for South Africa (ASGISA), which was launched in 2003/2004

---

[136] Mahoney and Thelen, "A Theory," 16–17.
[137] South Africa, Department of Public Enterprises, "A Summary," 7–8.

and adopted as a national strategy in 2006. ASGISA was as much a blueprint for what the government would do as it was an inventory of what the government had already done. It continued to promote efficiency, growth, liberalization, and competition, but it blended these themes with a strategy to reduce poverty, generate employment, increase skills, and strengthen state capacity.[138]

At the heart of ASGISA was a revised approach to Black Economic Empowerment, a policy goal repeatedly expressed but inconsistently pursued after 1994. Initially, BEE comprised a varied set of regulatory initiatives and funding mechanisms aimed at redressing the country's legacy of systematic economic marginalization of the black majority. Its goals were to reverse the long-standing patterns of racial discrimination with respect to employment, land tenure, and ownership; to support small and medium-sized businesses belonging to previously disadvantaged groups; to encourage and finance the purchase by black investors of equity stakes in existing companies; and to build a workforce that reflected the demographic makeup of the country.[139]

By the turn of the century, critics from the growing black middle class, the trade union movement, and assorted national and community-based organizations charged that policy initiatives had focused too narrowly on ownership at the expense of skills training or a more representative workforce in both senior management and entry-level positions. Among the groups that drove the policy revisions, Black Management Forum observed that owing to the weakness of the earlier legislation, black South Africans were merely "fronting" for companies that wanted to comply with the rules. They had no real power nor did they acquire substantial equity in the firms they "owned."[140] Tellingly, companies in which blacks owned more than 25 percent of the total equity comprised less than 2 percent of the assets listed on the Johannesburg stock exchange (JSE) a decade after the transition.[141]

In response, the government replaced the narrow, ad hoc approach of the 1990s with more comprehensive legislation, the Broad-Based Black Economic Empowerment Act of 2003. The revised policy included provisions to promote black ownership and produce a workforce that was more representative of the population of South Africa as it had done before. But it went beyond the previous act by mandating that a detailed set of criteria with respect to black economic empowerment would govern eligibility for government issued licences or authorizations, preferential procurement, parastatal sales, or partnerships with the private sector. The application of "codes of good practice"

---

[138] South Africa, The Presidency, "Accelerated and Shared Growth Initiative for South Africa (ASGISA) – A Summary," n.d., accessed 1/10/2010, http://www.info.gov.za/asgisa.

[139] Southall, "The ANC and Black Capitalism"; Roger Tangri and Roger Southall, "The Politics of Black Economic Empowerment in South Africa," *Journal of Southern African Studies*, 34, 3 (2008): 699–716.

[140] Mnyaka, Interview.

[141] Tangri and Southall, "The Politics of Black Economic Empowerment," 700.

was expected to secure the expanded objectives of the act in rural and urban areas. These included the promotion of skills development, greater managerial control, expanded ownership, and increased access to land, infrastructure, and other commodities by previously disadvantaged South Africans.[142]

The codes assigned points to companies for achieving empowerment goals in areas from the subcontracting of business to black-owned enterprises to investment in empowerment firms by established businesses. Companies with a turnover of less than US$700,000 were generally exempt from compliance, whereas those with a turnover of more than US$700,000 were expected to comply with a certain number of elements on the scorecard depending on their size. Any company that did business with the government had to address each element of the scorecard. After 2007, the government introduced detailed codes and charters regarding the requirements for compliance in each sector. It also initiated legislation that specifically targeted small and medium enterprises in particular product areas.[143]

Formerly, the neo-liberal project was the centerpiece of the government's economic strategy: BEE was one of the justifications for privatization of parastatals, but it was not the only, nor even the most important justification for sales. With the passage of ASGISA and B-BBEE, a more complex and deliberate approach emerged whereby the government blended neo-liberalism with developmentalism to foster empowerment and to align the interests of the established private sector with those of the state. The strategy continued to recognize the importance of the private sector, but it revived the state's active role in the economy. There are numerous examples apparent across financial, manufacturing, mining, agricultural, and public service sectors that address different aspects of the revised strategy including labor creation and the expansion of black ownership. Here I explore the roles of five linked and cross-cutting components: SOEs, preferential procurement for black companies, public asset management, public–private partnerships, and the expanded public works program.

First, SOEs were no longer targeted for divestiture under the new strategy, rather they became one of its cornerstones. According to the director-general of public enterprises, the government gave the DPE "the challenging task of ensuring that state-owned enterprises (SOE) reporting to it played a more significant role in the growth and development of the South African economy."[144] Parastatals directly overseen by DPE were expected to contribute to the goals of ASGISA, B-BBEE, and related legislation on procurement,

[142] South Africa, Department of Trade and Industry, "Broad-Based Black Economic Empowerment Act," 53 (2003), accessed 6/13/2007, http://www.dti.gov.za/bee/BEEAct-2003–2004.pdf.

[143] African Development Bank and Organization for Economic Cooperation and Development, "South Africa," *African Economic Outlook* (Paris: OECD Publishing, 2007), 497; Vula Mthimkhulu, "New Deal in the Offing for SMMEs," *Enterprise* (May 2008), 10–18.

[144] South Africa, Department of Public Enterprises, "Analysis of the Performance of State Owned Enterprises During the Period 2003/4–2007/8," n.d., 5.

skills, and competition policy. These goals were reiterated in the DPE's strategic plan for 2009–2012.[145] To back up its rhetoric, the government allocated about 25 percent of total public expenditure for use by parastatals on road and rail improvement, power generation and distribution, and other infrastructure.[146]

By the middle of the decade, SOEs had expanded management positions, increased employment for the historically disadvantaged, and fostered downstream and upstream linkages with BEE firms to comply with new procurement guidelines favoring such firms.[147] With respect to employment, five of the largest SOEs –Alexkor, Denel, Eskom, Transnet, and Telkom – employed 136,000 people and accounted for 1.2 percent of total formal sector employment.[148] Most SOEs had met government targets with regard to employment equity for blacks, women, and persons with disabilities.[149]

Black South Africans occupied a majority of management positions in SOEs and 70 percent of black graduates from universities worked initially in the public sector. Slightly over half of black South Africans earning at least R8,000 a month were employed by the state or an SOE.[150] These results highlight the vital contribution of SOEs to the creation of a black middle class, particularly the upper end of the middle class. They help to explain why a share of the black middle class voted for the ANC and why the ANC rethought its approach to privatization. Parastatals did a great deal of heavy lifting for B-BBEE and for the party's base. They were not only the largest employers of organized, formal sector workers but also entry points for managers into the upper echelons of the economy. By preserving parastatals, the ruling party reduced contestation among two of its most vocal supporters and critics – the black middle class and trade unions.

The degree to which individual SOEs met government targets for empowerment, skills training, and procurement varied. By 2009, Eskom had exceeded the targets it had set for 2010. Eskom had a total number of 37,857 employees: 69 percent of managers were black, and 35 percent were female. With these figures, Eskom had nearly met its 2010 employment equity targets of 65 percent blacks and 40 percent females in management. Eskom engaged in skills training for engineers and artisans and established linkages with small and medium

---

[145] South Africa, Department of Public Enterprises, "Strategic Plan, 2009–2012," accessed 12/28/2009, http://www.dpe.gov.za.
[146] Ronald Quist, Corina Certan, and Jerome Dendura, "Republic of South Africa. Public Expenditure and Financial Accountability," Public Financial Management Performance Assessment Report, Final Report (September 2008).
[147] See South Africa, "Preferential Procurement Policy Framework Act," Act 5 (2000).
[148] M. Walker and L. Farisani, "SOEs back up 'developmental state,'" *South African Labour Bulletin*, 29, 5 (October 2005), 18.
[149] South Africa, Department of Public Enterprises, "Analysis of the Performance," 18.
[150] Altman, A Review of Labour Markets," 14–15; Market Tree Consultancy, "Facts and Statistics," accessed 8/9/2009, http://www.markettree.co.za/fact_desc.html.

empowerment firms to supply additional electricity generating capacity, which was desperately needed.[151] Like Eskom, Transnet sought to meet empowerment targets such as employment equity and skills training. Transnet had 48,000 employees in 2008, making it the largest employer in South Africa. Seventy-four percent of its workforce was black; however, whites still outnumbered blacks in management positions, and females comprised only 18 percent of the workforce.[152]

Second, consistent with the objectives of the Preferential Procurement regulations of 2000, the public sector and parastatals were expected to consider and award tenders for subcontracted work to firms owned by historically disadvantaged individuals. They were encouraged (but not required), to preference locally owned businesses, small and medium firms, enterprises in rural areas, and those where the award of a contract would create jobs or develop skills.[153] SOEs such as Eskom and Transnet in particular were core nodal points in the creation of networks of suppliers from small and medium empowerment firms. Transnet spent US$1.6 billion on the purchase of supplies and locally assembled locomotives from small and medium-sized private sector firms.[154]

Preferential procurement to companies meeting the criteria in the codes of good practice helped to fulfill the goals of ASGISA and B-BBEE by tying together the interests of the public and the private sectors. Where the state was a partner on a project, strict procurement guidelines mandated the inclusion of historically disadvantaged firms. Because the requirements "cascade down public sector supply chains,"[155] many private firms had to conform to the procurement regulations in order to do business. Yet, calculations of the costs of complying with them suggest they are very high and the private sector has expressed concerns about the effect on competitiveness.[156] In interviews, the high cost of compliance emerged as one of the major complaints by Chambers of Commerce representing foreign investors from different countries.[157] For those BEE firms that received contracts, however, the existence of the regulations increased their chances of survival in a highly competitive market.

Third, linkages between the private and the public sector were fostered through the government's asset management fund, the Public Investment

[151] Eskom, "Eskom Annual Report," 2009, accessed 12/13/2009, http://www.eskom.co.za/annreport09/ar_2009/business_employment_equity.htm.
[152] Transnet, "Transnet Annual Report, 2009," accessed 12/13/2009, http://www.transnet.co.za.
[153] South Africa, "Preferential Procurement Policy Framework Act," Act 5, 2000.
[154] Transnet, "Transnet Annual Report, 2009."
[155] Anthony M. Butler, "Black Economic Empowerment since 1994" in Ian Shapiro and Kahreen Tebeau, eds., *After Apartheid: Reinventing South Africa* (Charlottesville: University of Virginia Press, 2010), 16–17.
[156] OECD, "South Africa Economic Assessment," *Economic Surveys*, 2008/15 (July 2008), 52.
[157] Centre for Development and Enterprise, "Can Black Economic Empowerment Drive New Growth?," *CDE in Depth*, 4 (January 2007). Reference to interviews with investors by Christian Rogerson, Professor, School of Geography, University of Witswatersrand, Interview, Johannesburg, 12/1/2009.

Corporation (PIC). The PIC is the heir to the Public Investment Commission, which was created in 1911 after South Africa became independent. Relaunched as the Public Investment Corporation in 2005, it was financed primarily by assets from the government employees pension fund. With assets of over US$130 billion, it was said to be "one of the largest investment managers on the African continent" and "one of the largest asset bases in the country."[158] It controlled about 9 percent of market share on the JSE and its institutional weight was sufficiently powerful that it was able to force Sasol, in which it held nearly a 14 percent share, to appoint a black South African woman to the Sasol board for the first time.[159]

Managed by a board that answered to the ministry of finance, PIC sought market-based returns on low-risk, long-term investments in order to fund pensions for retired government employees. To realize these goals, it invested alongside private capital in large infrastructure projects, property development, strategic sectors of the economy, and new investment ventures at home and abroad. Its investments included shopping malls and retail outlets in suburbs and townships, airports, office complexes in South Africa, and infrastructural projects in the rest of Africa. A small percentage of its total allocation targeted domestic projects that created jobs or fostered empowerment.[160]

Fourth, the government's effort to align the interests of big business with its own priorities was reflected in large-scale public–private partnerships. Although it seems to have slowed down the formation of PPPs in local service delivery owing to consumer protests,[161] it has energetically pursued imaginative partnerships with the private sector including the construction of five stadia and the refurbishment of existing sports facilities for the World Cup at a cost of about US$1.4 billion.[162]

The PPP project that most embodied the government's complex economic and political goals was the Gautrain. It is a high-speed passenger rail link of 80 kilometers that snakes its way both above and below ground through the northern suburbs of Johannesburg on its route to Midrand and Pretoria. Critics have questioned the government's claim that the link between Johannesburg and Pretoria is vital to the economic development of Gauteng,[163] but these criticisms underestimate the contribution of this project to the amalgamation of public and private interests. At a cost of US$3.6 billion, the Gautrain was

[158] Public Investment Corporation, "Annual Report 08," 2008, 1, 4.
[159] Heather Formby, "Sasol Yields to Big Stick," *Business Times, Sunday Times*, May 12, 2004, 1.
[160] Public Investment Corporation, "Annual Report 08," 6–7, 34–42.
[161] Aymeric Blanc and Cédric Ghesquières, "Decentralisation and the Free Basic Water Policy in South Africa: What Role for the Private Sector?," Working Paper 25, Agence Française de Développement, September 2006, 8.
[162] Peter Alegi, "'A Nation To Be Reckoned With': The Politics of World Cup Stadium Construction in Cape Town and Durban, South Africa," *African Studies*, 67, 3 (2008): 416.
[163] Janis Van Der Westhuizen, "Glitz, Glamour and the Gautrain: Mega-Projects as Political Symbols," *Politikon*, 34, 3 (2007): 333–351.

one of the largest construction projects ever in Africa. Begun in 2006, it was a PPP between the Gauteng Municipal government and a consortium of private sector firms known as the Bombela Concession Company. The consortium was awarded a twenty-year concession to design, partially finance, build, operate, and transfer the railway though as is often the case with PPPs, the government shouldered most of the risk.[164]

The composition of the concessionaire adhered to B-BBEE regulations. It consisted of six foreign and domestic firms; one of the latter firms, the Strategic Partners Group (SPG), was explicitly designated as a BEE company with a 25 percent shareholding.[165] SPG was formed in 2002 largely for the purpose of participating in the Gautrain investment, and it included a number of interests that were politically valuable to the ANC. Individual shareholders included former or current members of the Black Economic Empowerment Commission, the Black Management Forum, and the Black Business Council, who had business experience in both the public and private sector. Corporate shareholders included Black Management Forum Investment, the investment arm of BMF; Dyambu Holdings, a women's investment group; the Alexandra Chamber of Commerce; several community trusts; and holding companies started by the individual shareholders.[166]

One of the other domestic investors, the J and J Group was equally interesting, particularly because it reflected so well several core constituents of the ANC's political base. It included among its 200,000 shareholders, a coalition of nongovernmental organizations; SACCAWU, the South African Catering and Commercial Workers Union, a union with over 100,000 members; and Masincazelane, a social investment trust belonging to the South African Communist Party.[167]

Furthermore, in accordance with the expanded objectives of B-BBEE, the Gautrain project subcontracted or procured goods from approximately 350 new or existing empowerment firms. The total value of procurement was estimated at around US$460 million. Many of the materials used to build the train were sourced locally. In addition, construction of the Gautrain promoted skills training and employed unionized workers. The project generated just over 11,700 direct, local jobs by 2008. The development of retail services at the sites of stations was also underway.[168]

PPPs such as the Gautrain or stadium building are unlike those that consumers protested against in the service sector. In services, the rate hikes implemented by PPPs imposed costs on a vulnerable group of consumers who previously had

[164] Ibid., 342–344; Gautrain, accessed 6/10/2011, http://www.gautrain.co.za.

[165] Gautrain, accessed 6/10/2011, http://www.gautrain.co.za.

[166] Strategic Partners Group PTY Ltd., "Company Profile," n.d., accessed June 4, 2011, http://www.gautrain.co.za/contents/background/spg_profile.pdf.

[167] J and J Group, 2011, accessed 6/10/2011, http://www.jandjgroup.com/about.aspx.

[168] Gautrain Management Agency, "Socio-economic Development Progress," 2008, accessed 6/10/2011, http://www.gautrain.co.za/contents/brochures/sed_brochure_final_print.pdf.

received those services for no or reduced fees, if they had them at all. By contrast, greenfield investments such as the Gautrain occurred in areas that the public did not view as essential services or where consumers did not yet exist, hence protests regarding private sector inclusion were minimal. An analogous example would be the creation of city improvement districts or CIDS. Partnerships between local government and private management companies to provide security, collect garbage, or engage in city building took place in spaces where labor was neither organized nor concentrated and where affected consumers actually preferred the private alternative. Although the inclusion of the private sector in urban management represented a significant departure from conventional approaches to local governance and undercut both the responsibilities and accountability of democratically elected representatives, resistance to CIDS was sporadic. Similarly, resistance to the Gautrain was slight. Consequently, the national government has not had to compromise on CIDs, the Gautrain, or similar PPPs as it did with respect to the privatization of parastatals.

These approaches demonstrate the state's commitment to the promotion of a black middle class through the expansion of ownership, managerial positions, and investment opportunities. The projects joined government policy choices to the future development of established and emerging private businesses. Equally, these projects aimed to generate employment, especially for unionized workers. The fifth initiative supported by government, the Expanded Public Works Program (EPWP), moved in a slightly different direction by tackling South Africa's unemployment problem. The EPWP linked the enhanced provision of electricity, water, sanitation, and roads to job opportunities for the unemployed or "discouraged work seekers" especially youth, women, and the disabled. The EPWP sought to reduce the costs borne by those who were subject to higher rates for utilities; or by those who have lost, or never obtained, jobs due to retrenchments or casualization.[169]

The EPWP was administered by all levels of government and included the participation of SOEs and the private sector. It offered skills training; financial support to small and medium enterprises; labor intensive, temporary jobs, primarily in sectors such as infrastructure and construction; and financial aid for projects contributing to sustainable livelihoods in rural areas.[170] It provided employment opportunities for around 1.6 million people in its first five years. This figure exceeded the original government target of creating one million "work opportunities" over five years. Regarding higher-quality, full-time work, however, only 550,915 person-years of employment were created. Wage rates varied considerably among the sectors that provided employment. In some cases, the wages offered were below estimated cost-of-living expenses and did

[169] Human Sciences Research Council (HSRC) with Rutgers University, "Mid-Term Review of the Expanded Public Works Programme: Synthesis Report," October 2007, 10–11.

[170] South Africa, Department of Public Works, "Expanded Public Works Programme Five Year Report, 2004/5–2008/9: Reaching the One Million Target," 2009, 15–25.

not keep pace with the rate of inflation. Phase II of the project from 2009 to 2014 anticipates the creation of a further 4.5 million work opportunities or approximately 2 million full-time jobs.[171]

The trajectory of institutional change and continuity in South Africa since 1994 serves as a reminder that institutions and the interests they generate are frequently path dependent. Powerful established business interests, an interventionist state intertwined with the private sector, and an international environment that favored liberal approaches to economic policy constituted the parameters within which the ANC negotiated compromises around its economic objectives. Over time, the government's policy adjusted from privatization to corporatization and commercialization. It shifted from a rather vague idea of BEE to concrete guidelines for the enforcement of B-BBEE. It moved from private sector–driven cost recovery approaches to public sector–driven public works and investment projects. These shifts cast light on the flexibility built into institutional frameworks adopted by the government after 1994. The design allowed government officials to reshape decisions as they acquired experience and gained control over the South African state.

Conclusion

Contestation over economic policy became a standard feature of South African politics after the transition. In response, the government neither subverted existing institutional arrangements that provided for a private sector–driven economy nor turned a blind eye to the complaints of historically disadvantaged groups in the country. Rather, it relied on contingent uses of discretionary authority to forge compromises in the state and private sectors. It opted for commercialization, restructuring, and the use of affirmative action legislation to bolster the position of black South African investors and managers in new and existing companies. It built relationships with labor and with capital. This compromise joined the interests of white business to those of black capital and the ruling party in order to expand opportunities for those who had experienced discrimination under apartheid. SOEs were expected to serve the goals of the government's affirmative action policy by hiring black managers, privileging black-owned firms in their procurement policies, partnering with BEE firms, and broadening black ownership through sales of shares.[172] The government made SOEs more efficient and more globally competitive, but also it relied on them to provide managerial experience and secure jobs for black university graduates. Alongside other initiatives to foster black empowerment, SOEs became a critical component in the efforts to build a black middle class.

[171] Ibid., 110, 138.
[172] Jeff Radebe, Minister of Public Enterprises, "Black Economic Empowerment," speech, Johannesburg, April 2, 2003.

Although contingent uses of discretionary authority modified the initial policy framework, the compromises allowed the ruling party to maintain stability, to appease partisans, and to realize several of its major economic objectives, notably the pursuit of restructuring alongside black economic empowerment. Interestingly, stable party systems in more liberal and capitalist democracies in Africa have embraced compromise, too. Countries such as Botswana and Mauritius were slow to implement privatization and have made a number of policy revisions since they initially formulated their strategies. These countries did not have as large a state sector as their neighbors nor were they as dependent on donors for grants and loans. But the pushing and hauling of interests also explains why these governments have resorted to contingent uses of authority to forge compromise: Their constituents are holding them accountable beyond the polling booth. Consequently, the trajectory of private sector development in high-quality democracies with stable party systems reflects government efforts carefully to weave new rules into the patterns of existing institutional arrangements.

7

Conclusion: Rules, Politics, and Discretion

Some scholars have praised the commitment of African governments to the privatization of state-owned assets and declared them successful reformers, whereas others have bemoaned the capture of market reforms by aggrandizing states or condemned the unsuitability of neo-liberal strategies for poor countries. At the heart of the debate about the implementation and outcome of private sector development lie significant questions about how much and what kind of commitments states have made to transform their economies. To answer these questions, this book operationalized Kenneth Shepsle's distinction between a motivationally credible commitment and a commitment that is credible in the imperative sense. Conceptually dividing these two aspects of commitment differentiates the moment when governments choose to establish limits to their discretionary authority by adopting new formal institutions from that moment at a future time when structures, rules, and interests act to constrain the state's ability to act arbitrarily. The distinction recognizes the dynamic, temporal, and processual aspects of an institutional reform as significant as privatization.

Assessing Credible Commitments

Reinforcing the theoretical insights offered by the literature on institutions, this book argued that formal institutional arrangements, not governmental reputation or investor beliefs, should constitute the starting point for determining whether governments in developing countries made motivationally credible commitments to build market economies. To isolate that moment when states committed to private sector creation or expansion, I systematically disaggregated key dimensions of the reform process in twenty-seven African countries and identified which formal rules and agencies they adopted. The index revealed that even when the decision to reform was executed in the midst of crisis or driven by exogenous actors such as the World Bank, governments did not embrace a uniform, standard package of neo-liberal prescriptions. Rather, the constitutional revisions, laws, decrees, regulations, and agencies that African governments adopted to withdraw from their economies and create private sectors reflected balanced considerations by states regarding their historical legacies, ideas, and capacities and subtle accommodations to existing and potential partisan coalitions. These results show that institutional choices made by governments in Africa to reform their economies appear neither more, nor less, formulaic than those made by other transitional countries.

Did countries that made very high or high commitments to expand their private sectors follow through with their policy intentions and actually sell SOEs? In most studies of privatization, sales of SOEs are the hallmark of a successful privatization policy. Although it is relatively easy to commit to a balanced budget (and consequently easy to backtrack on the commitment), making and sustaining a commitment to sell SOEs can be politically and economically difficult for some governments. Three reasons explain why. First, even if international financial institutions and donors underwrite the cost of valuing companies, setting up agencies, training technocrats, supporting indigenous capital, and retrenching workers, governments may fear the distributional consequences of selling SOEs. Workers or managers of those SOEs that are offered for sale may try to sabotage or thwart the process. Better financed, more skilled foreign companies may purchase larger, potentially more profitable SOEs, thereby sowing resentment among indigenous capitalists, who often lack the capital or the experience of their foreign competitors. Consumers may challenge price hikes for electricity, transport, and water that follow from private sector participation in service delivery.

Second, although governments frequently shed a heavy debt burden when they privatize, they lose access to sources of pork or patronage such as management positions or procurement contracts for party loyalists. They also sell potential club goods such as jobs and benefits for trade unions, and public goods such as electricity or water for consumers. Such readily available means to dispense favors or welfare are not as easily secured after parastatals are sold; hence, governments hesitate to divest them.

Third, unlike other structural adjustment policies such as balancing the budget or adopting a floating exchange rate, the cost of reneging on the sale of a company or the granting of private property rights is high, especially if it occurs suddenly. Even if the government that reverses course is not the one that implemented the policies in the first place, nevertheless, backtracking on private sector creation has severe consequences. The world economy is now largely liberal: Country leaders face material and moral costs if they do not conform. Most other institutional arrangements that countries have implemented such as regional trade agreements, international conventions on export quotas or subsidies, and dispute mediation mechanisms are predicated on the acceptance of liberal economic principles. The completion of a privatization process structures individual and firm preferences, such that an abrupt reversal is likely to produce explosive conflicts.[1]

For all of these reasons, governments may hesitate to sell productive assets. For these same reasons, moreover, if sales do occur, they should serve as good indicators of commitments that are credible in the imperative sense. This book urges caution, however, about relying on sales of parastatals as indicators of imperatively credible commitments. The study did find a moderate, positive, and statistically significant relationship between motivational commitment and sales of state assets; the association strengthened when a clear outlier, South Africa, was removed. If motivational commitment was low, then governments did not sell their parastatals as in the cases of Burkina Faso, Zimbabwe, or São Tomé and Principe illustrate. Where motivational commitment was high as it was in the cases of Cape Verde, Mali, or Uganda, then sales were correspondingly high. But as Chapter 2 demonstrated, some countries were selling firms without having made high or very high motivational commitments to privatization, whereas another group scored high or very high with respect to motivational commitment but did not sell firms commensurate with that commitment.

These findings on the relationship between motivational commitments to privatization and the sales of state companies have implications for the study of formal institutions and economic reform in Africa and elsewhere. First, contrary to the conventional wisdom, a subset of African governments did take formal institutions seriously. They followed the rules that they enacted and preferences changed in response to new rules. Disaggregating the data demonstrated that where levels of commitment were high, sales were commensurate with the level of commitment, particularly in those cases where governments had significant assets to sell. When governments such as Ghana, Mozambique, Tanzania, and Mali formally recognized new institutional arrangements, they implemented them.

Second, with respect to those cases that deviate from the general trend, observers should revisit the conclusions they draw from parastatal sales (or the lack thereof). For example, when sales are low, the explanation might not be that a government has reneged on an initial commitment, but rather that it simply has *not* adopted the requisite rules to proceed with the divestment of parastatals. Alternatively, high sales figures may lead researchers to overestimate the extent to which governments have actually adopted new rules and regulations. Where sales occur in spite of the partial adoption of rules (as in the cases of Guinea or Kenya), governments likely are selling or giving firms to cronies in the absence of the rule of law. These results call attention to structural constraints or distributional challenges that may be arising earlier in

---

[1] Much has been said about the effects of such institutional reversals as the literature on "critical junctures" and "punctuated equilibria" attest. On more gradual institutional displacement, however, see Mahoney and Thelen, "A Theory," 16.

the policy process, long before sales occur. Paying attention to these obstacles would further enrich our theoretical understanding of the complexity of institutional change.

Third, there are instances where a government has the machinery in place to engage in the privatization process but where sales fall short. In these cases, the explanation may indeed conform to the prevailing wisdom on African countries, which is that their formal institutions are merely a façade; the "real" business of governing takes place in smoke-filled rooms or on the veranda. Experienced students of Africa can recite numerous examples where African governments fail to honor their obligations owing to avarice, incompetence, or a lack of capacity, but as the book has argued, governments have confronted legitimate distributional challenges to the extension of private sector–driven economies, which prevented them from fully realizing policy reforms even after they made motivational commitments.

To gauge more comprehensively the effectiveness of institutional arrangements after they were adopted or revised, the book moved beyond sales to assess key elements of private sector expansion. It developed an index that evaluated the degree to which institutional developments in twenty-seven cases approximated commitments that were "credible in the imperative sense."[2] The index incorporated sales into a broader category that captured the percentage of the state sector that had been privatized or restructured (commercialized, corporatized, or a pubic–private partnership). It included evaluations of trade and financial sector policy, the effectiveness of the regulatory environment for business, and the extent to which governments acknowledged and enforced property rights. To further facilitate cross-national comparisons, the index included an evaluation of utility restructuring, since utilities are common to every country. Last, building on scholarly research that highlights the importance of state–business relations, the index assessed the relationship between government and business in African countries.[3]

Together with the data on motivational commitment, the index on the institutional effectiveness of laws, regulations, policies, and guidelines promulgated by states in the 1990s brings greater conceptual clarity to our understanding of institutional change and credible commitments. It makes possible a more systematic analysis of economic transformation in Africa and facilitates comparative study with other developing areas. Positively and strongly correlated with the index on motivational commitments, it casts critical light on the relationship between the institutional architecture erected by governments and its effectiveness at a later point in time. Those governments that revised land laws, guaranteed property rights in their constitutions, promoted investment, and adopted privatization agencies were more likely to have sold state enterprises, reformed their infrastructure and utilities, and concluded a formal relationship

---

[2] Shepsle, "Discretion, Institutions."
[3] See Schneider, *Business Politics and the State*; Handley, *Business and the State*.

with the business sector. Those governments that failed to establish agencies or revise laws in favor of greater private property rights correspondingly failed to demonstrate effective financial, commercial, and private sector institutions at a later moment in time.[4]

The Political Dynamics of Institutional Development

The quantitative and qualitative findings substantiate many of the claims by historical and rational choice institutionalists regarding the pace and character of institutional development.[5] First, they demonstrate that the adoption of new formal institutions, even in cases where countries have a reputation for ignoring formal rules, can contribute to broader, multifaceted processes of transformation over time. As North asserts, the "institutional framework dictates the opportunity set that defines the kind of organizations that will come into existence but also creates the incentives that will shape the kind of knowledge and skills that the organizations will invest in."[6] In the particular case of private sector creation, where attracting investors, rehabilitating firms, creating partnerships, and inculcating habits of ownership and entrepreneurialism have long time horizons, institutional development has been subject to contestation, compromise, subterfuge, and even reversals. Reforms may be slow when powerful coalitions benefit from the status quo; they may accelerate when those same agents anticipate lucrative opportunities that may arise from change.

Second, the uneven pace and the contradictory character of the process call attention to the ways in which political dynamics molded patterns of privatization in particular locales in Africa just as they did in Latin America or East and Central Europe. To illustrate this, the book examined cases where democratic regimes adopted all or most of the institutions typically associated with a private sector economy such as property rights and investment laws (i.e., they made very high or high motivational commitments to privatization). One of the major contributions of the study is to demonstrate that trajectories of private sector development depend on differences in the quality of democracy and the nature of the party system. Whether a democracy is liberal or limited, whether a country's party system is fragmented or stable, influences the extent to which the stakeholders in the process leverage the new rules to balance the power of the state. They affect how the government responds to distributional

---

[4] As Chapter 2 explained, Botswana, Mauritius, and Namibia already had many of the institutions associated with private sector driven economies (as did South Africa) but did not fully embrace sales of SOEs. However, they adopted or strengthened other institutions typically associated with market economies, thus their credible commitment scores were very high.

[5] See especially Knight, *Institutions and Social Conflict*; Wolfgang Streeck and Kathleen Thelen, *Beyond Continuity: Institutional Change in Advanced Industrial Economies* (Oxford: Oxford University Press, 2005); Mahoney and Thelen, eds., *Explaining Institutional Change*.

[6] Douglass North, "Five Propositions about Institutional Change" in Jack Knight and Itai Sened, eds., *Explaining Social Institutions* (Ann Arbor: University of Michigan Press, 1995), 20.

conflicts that arise during implementation and whether it will sustain, bend, or break rules in order to manage contestation.

Chapter 3 explored the theoretical dimensions of this claim and demonstrated its generalizability with examples from nine cases. Chapters 4 through 6 offered more refined case studies of each pattern. The analysis isolated three patterns exhibited by African democracies that made high or very high motivational commitments to economic reform. In the first pattern, where the quality of democracy was limited and the party system was characterized by high volatility, ruling parties resorted to opportunistic uses of discretion to preserve their power and deter defections from the party. Without a stable opposition to check or question their authority and without robust democratic institutions through which diverse constituencies could express their discontent, insecure rulers capriciously manipulated the privatization process to solve short-term political problems. These uses of discretion generated outcomes that diverged from those anticipated by economic theory. The pace of reform was often inconsistent and erratic. Policy drift was noticeable and private sector development became ad hoc.

Beyond this first pattern, the book distinguishes and explains additional pathways of reform. As with the first pattern, the second pattern contains cases where ruling parties also restricted political and civil liberties to realize their goals, but the logic of party system competition was more stable. The combination of a limited democracy and a stable party system brought advantages and disadvantages. In contrast to the first pattern, more stable opposition parties were in a position to criticize policy content or the manner in which governments implemented policy. The opposition constituted a viable alternative to the ruling party for voters also. However, in limited democracies, ruling parties often trampled on political rights and employed their discretionary authority deliberately to design and implement economic reform in a manner consistent with the interests of their base. Ruling parties often relied on the machinery of the state to benefit party loyalists who were (or were becoming) entrepreneurs, trade unionists, or rural producers. Since these constituencies were relatively stable, the pace of privatization and restructuring was more consistent but its outcome reflected the preferences of the partisan coalitions that underpinned the party in power.

The third pattern delineated cases of liberal democracies with stable party systems. Governments were more careful about adopting commitments that might provoke distributional conflicts. They hedged their bets by relying on vague language in laws and statutes that they could reinterpret at a later date. During the implementation process, they relied on contingent uses of their discretionary authority to modify and adjust specific policy components to satisfy their base or the larger general population. These adjustments did not mean that governments reneged on their commitments. Rather they suggest that governments were struggling to deal with the conflicts among distributional interests occasioned by the policy reform and allowed by the more liberal democratic context. Consistent with the institutional arrangements the ruling party adopted, economic reform occurred, but it was marked by strategic compromises in order to manage contestation and sustain the policy.

Extending Cross-National Comparisons

In order to underscore the empirical support for the argument, I return briefly to the cases discussed in previous chapters. Where motivational commitment is high, the explanation for the varied trajectories withstands cross-national comparison. As Chapter 4 showed in the case of Zambia, even though the institutional design of the privatization program gave the Zambia Privatisation Agency leverage to challenge executive encroachment and to continue the privatization process, the reform process reflected the volatility that characterized party politics. Early negative results from privatization contributed to declining public support for the policy by 1995. These outcomes, combined with other divisions in Zambia, encouraged defections from the ruling party and exacerbated factions within it. But the causal arrow also points in the other direction. In Zambia, the party system was marked by high fluidity. Threatened with electoral loss due to departures of party members and voter discontent, successive Zambian presidents then capriciously interfered in the implementation of economic reform to shore up party support. The pace slowed, policy drift ensued, and private sector development assumed an improvisational character.

Other countries replicate the pattern of fluid party politics and limited democracy exhibited by the Zambian case. Like that of Zambia, governments in Mali and Malawi made high motivational commitments to privatization and, by 2005, had sold over 50 percent of their SOEs. The extent to which their commitments to privatization were credible in the imperative sense was consistent with their degree of motivational commitment. They liberalized trade, reformed their banking sectors, adopted infrastructural reforms, established a regulatory framework for business, and fostered formal institutional relationships between business and government. In Malawi, as in Zambia, part of the initial motivation for privatization reflected the exigencies of party politics. One of the reasons the UDF embraced privatization following the transition to democracy was to undermine control over state enterprises by the previous ruling party just as the MMD had done in Zambia.[7] In the ensuing years, Malawian governments remained committed to reform but party fragmentation and the demands of democratic politics left weak governing coalitions with bare majorities confronting highly contentious interests. As a result, presidents either raided privatization to satisfy particular constituencies, as was the case with the UDF or delayed it for fear of negative electoral consequences as the DPP government under Mutharika did. When critics accused the government

---

[7] VonDoepp, "Institutions," 175–198.

of corruption, insider trading, and the low valuation of assets, or when protests erupted over expected job losses from divestitures, privatization was suspended and sales of major utilities were temporarily halted.[8]

In Mali, like Zambia, a new government that came to power following multiparty elections moved quickly to enact institutional arrangements conducive to privatization. Yet, resistance by vested interests, the involvement of multiple government agencies, and the slow pace of decision making hindered the identification, valuation, and sale of SOEs.[9] The World Bank reported that a project it financed to foster private sector development and to strengthen government agencies associated with privatization (including the Bureau of Public Enterprises) made only limited progress owing to "protracted political crisis," changes of the cabinet, and "internal political issues which diverted government attention."[10] One critic contrasted the relative ease with which Mali's authoritarian government enacted early privatization and liberalization measures to the difficulties encountered after Mali democratized in 1991, but the challenges did not arise simply with the shift to a more democratic form of government.[11] Defections and factions within the ruling coalition, student unrest, and a boycott by opposition parties of the 1997 presidential election thwarted the process during the mid 1990s. Fragmentation of the party system, as much as a limited democracy, contributed to the difficulties and delays with economic reform.

Like those in the first pattern, countries in the second pattern were limited democracies, but their party systems were more cohesive. With respect to the representative case illustrated by Mozambique, Chapter 5 showed that stable party loyalties helped to shape the design and implementation of privatization. Of course, the paralysis of many state firms owing to a long period of violent conflict undercut dissent from organized labor, but also the ruling party built ownership of the policy by offering its support base a stake in the process. It passed regulations designed to foster the growth of domestic capital and to protect labor; it joined the interests of foreign investors to those of the state by forming public–private partnerships. It also intertwined the state and party in a new way by allocating former state enterprises to party stalwarts. When

---

[8] Malawi, Privatisation Commission, "Executive Director's Report-2001," by Dye Mawindo, Executive Director, Privatisation Commission, 2001, accessed 11/11/2006, http://www.privatisationmalawi.org., Bertelsmann Transformation Index, "Malawi Country Report," 9; Raphael Thenthani, "Malawi's President Halts Privatization of State Owned Telecom Company," AP Worldstream, August 6, 2005, accessed 3/8/2008, http://www.highbeam.com/doc/1P1-111891148.html.

[9] Shantayanan Devarajan, "Mali" in Shantayanan Devarajan, David Dollar, and Torgny Holmgren, eds., Aid and Reform in Africa (Washington, D.C.: World Bank, 2001), 227–286.

[10] World Bank, "Implementation Completion Report (IDA – 24320) on a Loan/Credit/Grant in the Amount of US$ Million to the (sic) Mali for a (sic) Private Sector Assistance," Report no. 25275, Private Sector group, Africa region (December 30, 2002), 13.

[11] Devarajan, "Mali," 262–263.

challenged by the opposition or protestors, it relied on repression, manipulation, or cooptation to sustain "partisan privatization."

Ghana and the Seychelles were also in the quadrant of countries that made high motivational commitments to privatization, had stable party systems, and were governed by limited democracies during the period under study. Regardless of the alternation in power of two parties in Ghana, successive ruling parties relied on the state and party loyalties to shape the privatization process in a manner consistent with their political traditions and with their base of support. In the 1990s, the NDC under Rawlings paralleled that of Frelimo in Mozambique: It consciously designed and implemented privatization policies to benefit the NDC. Faced with challenges to its authority, the government resorted to many of the illiberal practices it had once relied on as an authoritarian, civil–military regime, allocating companies to party supporters, creating business associations sympathetic to its interests, and isolating those interests believed to be associated with the opposition.[12] Since the 1990s, competitive elections, greater transparency, and alternations of the party in power have improved the quality of democracy and served gradually to distance Ghana from Mozambique, but a stable pattern of party system competition has influenced the character of capitalism in that country. Each party sustained the commitment to the creation of a private sector–driven economy, but in power, each party tweaked policies and used mechanisms of the state to benefit a loyal base of support. In Ghana, like Mozambique, the process has been distinguished by policy consistency, but the development of the private sector has a partisan character.

Much the same could be said for the Seychelles. A series of small islands populated by 81,000 people, the Seychelles has a growing reputation as an offshore banking and business facility. Owing to constitutional guarantees regarding the protection of property rights, few restrictions on the right to buy and sell land, an investment promotion act, and the creation of the Seychelles International Business Authority to attract offshore business, the Seychelles demonstrated high motivational commitment in the 1990s. But alongside its commitment to facilitating global capital flows through the provision of offshore services, the Seychelles Progressive People's Front, which has ruled continuously since the first elections in 1993, tightly controlled any changes to the public sector. No privatization law was passed in the 1990s, and no agency created to handle the privatization of assets such as the state bank, several supermarkets, utilities, and selected companies in fishing and agriculture. Although the government partially privatized the state tuna company, several hotels, and a timber business, the public sector continued to account for about 40 percent of employment as late as 2009.[13] Like Frelimo, the SPPF is the same

---

[12] Opoku, *The Politics of Government-Business Relations in Ghana*, 150–159.
[13] African Economic Outlook, "Seychelles," 2009, accessed 1/18/2010, http://www.africaneconomic outlook.org/en/countries/eastafrica/seychelles; International Monetary Fund, "Review of Financial Sector Regulation and Supervision-Seychelles" (October 2004).

party that declared socialism in Seychelles in the 1970s, and it has remained in power almost continuously since then, managing the reform process in a manner that serves the interests of the party. From 2002, a new party, the Seychelles National Party, challenged the SPPF at the polls by capturing more than a third of the seats in parliament and retaining those seats in 2007.[14] The growth of a viable party in the Seychelles may potentially check the power of the SPPF, but should the SNP gain power, it is likely that it will be just as partisan in the allocation of rewards to its supporters.

With respect to the third and last pattern, South Africa is viewed as a model of liberal democracy on the continent, but it is also a case where an incumbent party in a relatively stable party system has largely monopolized the levers of power and avenues of debate. The ANC's performance over the course of the 1990s demonstrated a growing merger of the party and the state, the centralization of power in the executive as opposed to the legislative branch' and as Mattes has observed "draconian central party control over legislators" that has only recently been challenged.[15] These characteristics suggest that a plausible explanation for the government's decision to favor restructuring and commercialization over outright divestiture to private sector actors was simply that it could. It faced no serious challenge at the polls and thus it could revise agreements if it wished. A similar situation exists in Botswana where the ruling Botswana Congress Party has enjoyed a comfortable majority since the 1960s and has faced few electoral threats until recently. Moreover, as in Mozambique, even members of the ANC who are highly critical of the party will still vote for it.

Yet this reason only partly explains why the ANC would make a high motivational commitment to privatization and then compromise on one of its most salient features – the sale of SOEs to the private sector. A more convincing claim must take into account that South Africa is more democratic than either Zambia or Mozambique. An ideologically well-defined and stable configuration of interests exists in South Africa, and these interests directly affect unity within the ruling party. In a country where whites own 69 percent of assets, one of the major economic challenges facing the ruling party has been to reconcile the interests and aspirations of established (or white) big business, the aspiring black middle class, highly organized formal sector workers, and those who constitute the most vulnerable and disadvantaged sectors of society but have no regular access to work. Organized interests enjoy extensive formal and informal channels of access to the government – from personal relationships to inclusion in formal councils – and they use it to shape and direct policy.

---

[14] Consortium for Elections and Political Process Strengthening, "Election Guide: Seychelles," Presidential and Legislative Results, 1998–2007, accessed 2/17/2010, http://www.election guide.org.

[15] Robert Mattes, "Democracy without People: Political Institutions and Citizenship in the New South Africa," Afrobarometer Working Paper, no. 82, 2007, 30.

Besides unemployment and antiprivatization conflicts occasioned by government efforts to privatize local services such as water and electricity, the challenges faced by BEE companies help to explain why the South African government has privatized fewer state firms, proceeded very slowly with sales of state assets, and shifted in favor of restructuring local service delivery. The numbers of black businesses have now multiplied considerably beyond those prominent ANC loyalists who benefited from early empowerment deals, yet BEE firms still only controlled around 4 percent of the firms listed on the JSE in 2008.[16] The difficulties that historically disadvantaged groups have experienced capturing greater equity may explain why government divested only the noncore assets of the largest SOEs such as Transnet and Eskom and why it shifted to restructuring rather than privatization by the beginning of the millennium. The government divested only 9 percent of the total number of SOEs in South Africa. Since 2002, there have been few sales of SOEs: Major assets such as its ports, railways, aerospace industry, electricity, and telecommunications have not been sold.[17] Instead, the government turned to SOEs in order to shore up black capital and management through procurement projects directed at BEE firms, to form linkages with smaller suppliers via preferential procurement policies, to train managers from historically disadvantaged backgrounds, to provide employment, and to better control the pursuit of employment equity.

The groups that sought to influence economic policy had intersecting as well as conflicting interests: The task of the government was to align and control them to maintain the ruling party's cohesion, to retain support at the polls, and to formulate policy. As the contentious party congress at Polokwane in 2007 and the formation of a new opposition party in 2008 demonstrated, the ANC has confronted formidable challenges with respect to these tasks. Not only the structure of the party and the nature of the tripartite alliance but also ideological differences fractured the party leadership leading to the ouster of Thabo Mbeki and his replacement by Jacob Zuma as general secretary. Surprisingly, these internal divisions and the birth of a breakaway party did little to undermine voter support for the ANC in the 2009 elections. What the crisis within the party demonstrated best is that the state of democracy and the status of party politics in South Africa remain contested and dynamic.

The challenges faced by the South African government and the reliance on strategic compromises in response to distributional conflicts seem to characterize well the approaches to economic reform by liberal democracies in Africa with stable party systems. This pattern of piecemeal reform and compromise

[16] Vusi Mona and Keri Harvey, "The New Black Randlords," *Enterprise*, July 2008, 22.
[17] See South Africa, Ministry [sic] of Public Enterprises, "A Summary of the Policy Framework for an Accelerated Agenda for the Restructuring of State-Owned Enterprises," Policy Framework, August 2000, see also, BusinessMap Foundation, *Restructuring*.

deserves much greater attention by researchers who have tended to overlook the formidable challenges faced by responsive governments in poor countries. In Mauritius, for example, what looks like a highly fragmented party system is actually an institutionalized form of compromise: Over the last few decades, the parties repeatedly have formed coalitions in an effort to collectively solve the country's challenges. And like the ANC, ruling parties in Mauritius have been slow to privatize out of concern for the negative costs of divestiture on employment and fear of foreign dominance. Most parties in Mauritius endeavor to maintain institutional relationships with business while at the same time avoiding distributional conflicts generated by labor or consumers.[18]

In Cape Verde, another case that fits the pattern, two stable political parties have alternated in power since Cape Verde became democratic. The shift to a market economy followed the transition to multiparty rule in 1991. Owing to the dominance of the state sector and the poor condition of many parastatals, the pace has been faster and privatization has been more extensive than in Mauritius or South Africa. Following the pattern in these other countries, negotiation between the parties and compromises with bases of support have been features of the process in Cape Verde. The PAICV (African Party for the Independence of Cape Verde), which instituted socialism following the end of Portuguese colonialism in 1975, was unseated in 1991 by the Movement for Democracy (MPD). Aided by the World Bank, the MPD made a high motivational commitment to privatization, sold most of the country's parastatals, and attracted foreign investment during the 1990s.[19] Returned to power after 2001, the PAICV continued to extend the market economy, but also it maintained its leftist orientation by seeking to alleviate poverty, reduce unemployment, and finance development projects.[20] The receipt of remittances from Cape Verdean migrants to Europe and the United States likely mitigated the harsh effects of economic reform. Nevertheless, successive ruling parties in Cape Verde sought to minimize distributional conflicts around privatization by offering retrenchment packages to labor. Equally, governments relied on donors to rebuild ports and to realize the country's economic potential in the areas of tourism, oil production, and light industry. Like other liberal democracies with stable party systems in Africa, Cape Verdean governments honored their initial commitments. Where appropriate, they sought strategic compromises in order to appease supporters and to address broader concerns from civil society.

---

[18] Mistry, "Commentary," 551–569; Reshma Peerun, Sumil Bundoo, and Kheswar Jankee, "Mauritius" in Pradeep Mehta, ed., *Competition Regimes in the World: A Civil Society Report* (Jaipur: Consumer Unity and Trust Society in Association with International Network of Civil Society Organisations on Competition, 2006), 254–259.

[19] World Bank, Country Operations Division, Sahelian Department, Africa Region, "Republic of Cape Verde: Public Sector Reform and Capacity Building Project," Staff Appraisal Report, Report no. 12422-CV, January 7, 1994, p. 3.

[20] PAICV, "O que pretendemos," accessed 2/15/2010, http://www.paicv.cv.

Implications, Predictions, and Future Research

When structural adjustment was initially prescribed for Sub-Saharan African countries in the late 1980s and early 1990s, scholars expressed skepticism that it would ever be implemented. Because the new rules shifted the state's discretion over the economy to private sector actors, scholars feared that governments would either resist, owing to an unwillingness to relinquish the clientelistic networks they had built up during one-party rule, or they would manipulate the process such that its impact would be minimal.

This book has demonstrated that where African countries have adopted formal institutions designed to expand a private sector–driven economy, economic reform has been substantial. Private property rights as well as the conflicts associated with them have emerged; new forms of capitalist organization – from limited liability companies to public–private partnerships – have been established; labor laws have been aligned more closely with private sector interests. Changes in formal economic rules and regulations do shape preferences, provide incentives, alter behavior, and influence political and economic outcomes over time. Contrary to claims that African countries have ignored, flouted, or derailed formal rules in favor of informal, invisible, "shadow" institutions, African countries adhere to formal rules just as much or just as little as other countries that have made such changes. Thus, with respect to policy adoption and implementation, or the outcomes of privatization, few reasons remain for treating Africa as an exception to the patterns found elsewhere in the world.

Whereas the impact of reform has constrained, it has not disabled the uses of discretion by states. This book has argued that in order to understand the different uses of discretion and their effects on privatization in democratic contexts, scholars should be paying at least as much attention to the kind of democracy that is being established and the nature of the party system as to the implementation and outcome of economic reform. Acknowledging the roles that these two variables play in the divergent reform experiences of African democracies moves scholarly contributions beyond the attribution of patronage, personalism, corruption, and nepotism to the neo-patrimonial behavior of "big men" and their cronies who deliberately set out to partially reform their economies. Rather it directs analysis to the partisan coalitions that seek to influence policy choice and the political settings in which those coalitions are embedded. Research on the linkages among democracy, party politics, and economic policy choice is extensive for Latin America and Eurasia; hence, scholars of Africa will be able to draw on a rich body of existing scholarship.

Politicians, trade unions, business associations, social movements, and donors are visibly and formally participating in new forms of political engagement in many African countries. Although these groups have different levels of organizational capacity and enjoy varying levels of success in their endeavors, their impact on the development of institutions deserves to be taken seriously.

Given new life by the birth of multiparty politics, many groups play a vibrant role in political discussions with government, or they seek actively to challenge government policies through protests, sabotage, or support for opposition parties. As Habib has remarked, "robust political engagement" is vital to enhancing the democratic process.[21]

The different ways in which states use their discretion to respond to these pressures has important implications for the relationship between state and market and for assessments about political stability. We should expect to see opportunistic uses of executive power in those countries where the party system is volatile, where interests are fragmented and contentious, where the president is accorded much constitutional and informal power, and where democracy is limited. Vulnerable states that are confronted by unstable, fragmented interests within a weak party system are likely to plunder the privatization process to buy or maintain support for a fragile regime.

Under these circumstances, private sector development becomes a form of improvisation: Elites transfer material benefits (in the form of state enterprises, land, and procurement policies) to individuals in exchange for their support through a process that is nontransparent and arbitrary. Like other forms of patronage, the ostensible purpose of such transfers is to maintain alliances, curb defections from the ruling party, and curtail the appearance of new parties at election time. These arbitrary uses of state authority have a distortionary impact on the goals of privatization, but the greater danger may lie in the reciprocal effect this produces on the state. As state officials rely more on patronage than programmatic policies to speak to their constituents, the state may lose effectiveness and begin to "hollow out" or deteriorate over time.[22]

Alternatively, where disciplined, cohesive ruling parties build stable coalitions of support for reforms but in circumstances where democracy is circumscribed and limited, discretionary uses of authority by governments will have the character of purposeful intervention. Ruling parties in these countries respond to distributional pressures by dispensing patronage like their counterparts in the first pattern, but also they respond by intervening systematically in the privatization process to foster national capital, to control foreign investment, to build institutional relationships between the state and the emerging private sector, and, of course, to benefit the party. In contrast to fluid party systems, the time horizon of stable parties in limited democracies is more long term; the methods of intervention in the privatization process are more systematic and predictable, and government officials combine formal and informal approaches, material and ideological appeals, in their efforts to maintain dominance. Such intervention may cultivate and control support for reforms, but it comes at a

---

[21] Adam Habib, "Politics and Human-Oriented Development" in Raymond Parsons, ed., *Zumanomics: Which Way to Shared Prosperity in South Africa? Challenges for a New Government* (Johannesburg: Jacana Media, 2009), 169.

[22] See O'Dwyer, *Runaway State-Building*.

price. In a limited democracy, privatization designed to serve the interests of the ruling party may compromise further the development of mechanisms of democratic accountability.

If the victory of opposition parties in Ghana offers the antidote to attempts by a ruling party to use the state to survive, the continued presence of Frelimo in Mozambique calls attention to what stable parties in limited democracies may gain when they retain power. As the book has demonstrated, Mozambique presents a case where a state actually became stronger *because* it privatized. Contrary to the claims of those who stress the unsuitability of reforms in Africa, the Mozambique case suggests that even nearly failed states can design institutions and create coalitions that consolidate their authority, enhance their capability, and privatize their economies but they may do so in restricted democratic environments.

Lastly, we can expect that contingent uses of authority will be common features in cases where liberal democracies and stable party systems exist, particularly in developing countries where large segments of the population live near or below the poverty line. Here, governments are likely to respond to distributional conflicts arising from privatization by using their discretionary authority to bend but not break the rules, to find compromises, and to reach a consensus. Such uses of discretionary authority marginally adjust reforms to meet political and economic circumstances, while maintaining policy stability. In spite of the fact that liberal democracies offer institutional access to critics as well as supporters of liberal economic reform, in the long run, a more open society with stable parties is going to be the most conducive environment for private sector development.

In Africa, this third configuration presently characterizes only a handful of countries, but perhaps it will be the modal category one day. As transitional market economies across the world continue to experiment with different institutional arrangements, future work might examine more closely how partisan coalitions can encourage governments to balance more equitably the trade-off between rules and discretion. A balance between rules and discretion is a salient quality of credible commitment, but it is also an important feature of accountability, which is the foundation of truly democratic societies.

Appendix 1

Coding Scheme

Indicators of Motivational Commitments

Legislation (Total score = 0–12)

Property Rights – How extensive are constitutional constraints on arbitrary alterations to property rights?

0. Very limited; few or no constraints on ability of state to intervene into individual rights to possessions and property.
1. Limited; state has broad powers to intervene; few individual rights acknowledged.
2. Somewhat limited; individual rights are generally but vaguely acknowledged: restrictions on state power vague or not delineated.
3. Somewhat extensive; individual rights to property and possessions acknowledged; state powers to intervene restricted.
4. Very extensive; rights of individual to property and possessions clearly delineated; state powers to intervene very restricted.

Land Law – Is there an existing land law? Do people have a right to own title to their land or business? Who has the authority to allocate land? Does land act favor rights of certain groups over others? How restricted are the rights to buy/sell land?

0. Individual land tenure rights expressly forbidden by law.
1. Individual land tenure rights limited by law.
2. Individual and communal rights recognized but not clearly demarcated or protected by law.
3. Individual rights coexist with communal land rights by law.
4. Individual right to buy, own, sell, lease land regardless of gender, race, ethnic, racial, national background.

Privatization Regulations and Related Investment Codes – Does country have laws or decrees mandating the full or partial sale of state assets? How favorable are they to investors?

0. Very unfavorable; no privatization law or excessively restrictive law with extensive restrictions on nationality and type of investment; repatriation of profits.
1. Unfavorable; some restrictions on SOEs to be privatized and on nationality and type of investment, repatriation of profits.
2. Neither favorable nor unfavorable; legislation to privatize state assets exists but provides no clear indication of whether it is favorable or unfavorable to investors. Alternatively, country does not have regulations on the privatization of existing SOEs but does encourage investment by the private sector.
3. Favorable; welcoming to investors but some restrictions on type of investment or repatriation of profits.
4. Very favorable; few restrictions on assets to be privatized, nationality of investor, repatriation of profits, type of investment, sector for investment.

Agencies (Total score = 0–6)

Is there an actual agency mandated to undertake privatization? How involved are other branches/ministries of the government in this organization?

0. No agency exists to undertake privatization.
1. Agency exists, but has other responsibilities besides privatization, and is dependent on other government branches/ministries.
2. Agency exists, has mandate to undertake privatization, but is not independent from other government branches/ministries.
3. Agency exists, has mandate to undertake privatization and is statutorily independent from government.

Method of Sale – Are companies listed for sale, restructuring, and the like? Is it clear how they will be sold? Are companies advertising?

0. No list, no clear methods.
1. Selective list of companies and proposed method of sale is unclear.
2. Comprehensive list of companies for sale but proposed method of sale is unclear OR clear method of sale but selective list of companies.
3. Comprehensive list of companies for sale and proposed method of sale is clear.

Commitment Total Scores: *High ratings equal greater levels of motivational commitment; low ratings equal lower levels of motivational commitment. Highest Possible Total Score is 18 (Very High Motivational Commitment) and Lowest Possible Total Score is 0 (Low Motivational Commitment).*

Appendix 2

Coding Scheme

Indicators of Imperative Commitments

(6 point scale: 1 = lowest; 6 = highest; values of .5 are allowed)

1. Trade

Examines extent to which policy framework is conducive to cross-border trade by assessing tariffs and customs procedures

1. Average tariff is above 25 percent; many rates above 50 percent, no use of tariff bands; b. customs – endemic corruption, inconsistent and undocumented customs procedures.
2. Average tariff below 25 percent; many rates above 40 percent; more than five tariff bands; b. customs – widespread perception of corruption; slow collection of duties; some formal documentation of customs procedures but out of date and incomplete.
3. Average tariff below 20 percent; five or fewer bands; maximum band at 30 percent tariff; b. customs – frequent allegations of corruption; duty collection slow; procedures, regulations, and guidelines published, but need to be simplified.
4. Average tariff below 16 percent, four or fewer tariff bands, maximum band at 25 percent; b. customs – limited allegations of corruption; laws, regulations published and efforts to simplify; formal mechanisms for appealing customs.
5. Average tariff below 12 percent; three or fewer tariff bands, maximum band at 20 percent; customs – reputation for professionalism, few instances of corruption; speedy processing, laws are published, rationalized, simplified.
6. Average tariff rate less than 7 percent; maximum tariff rate 15 percent; customs – sound reputation for professionalism and integrity, speedy

resolution of appeals; laws, regulations, and guidelines published, simplified, rationalized.

2. Financial Sector

Examines depth, stability, and strength of the financial sector since access to finance is critical for business.

1. Banking sector very vulnerable to shocks; size and reach of financial markets is limited; payment and clearance systems highly underdeveloped.
2. Banking sector highly vulnerable to shocks in the medium term; size and reach of financial markets is limited and capital markets underdeveloped but improving; payment and clearance systems are underdeveloped.
3. Banking sector vulnerable to shocks in the medium term; size and reach of financial markets is underdeveloped but growing; payment and clearance systems are underdeveloped but functioning.
4. Banking sector vulnerable to shocks to some extent in the medium term; size and reach of financial markets is approaching adequate levels for economies of similar size and sophistication; payment and clearance systems are moderately developed and functional.
5. Banking sector resilient to shocks; size and reach of financial markets is good; payment and clearance systems are well developed.
6. Banking sector highly resilient to shocks; size and reach of financial markets is very good; payment and clearance systems demonstrate best practice.

3. Privatization and/or Restructuring of State-Owned Enterprises

The extent to which the parastatal sector has been privatized in those economies with previously large state sectors or restructured in those cases where the private sector was already dominant. Restructuring includes liberalization, commercialization, and rationalization.

1. No privatization or restructuring initiatives.
2. Less that 25 percent of state enterprises privatized or restructured.
3. Have privatized or restructured more than 25 percent of the state sector but less than 50 percent.
4. Have privatized or restructured more than 50 percent of the state sector but less than 75 percent.
5. Have privatized or restructured more than 75 percent of the state sector.
6. Have privatized or restructured 100 percent of state sector to standards and performance typical of advanced industrialized economies.

4. Infrastructure Reform

The ratings are calculated as the average of five infrastructure reform indicators covering electric power, railways, roads, telecommunications, water, and wastewater. The classification system used for these five indicators is detailed below.

1. No progress in commercialization and regulation, extensive government intervention.
2. Some progress in commercialization and regulation, but political interference continues.
3. Modest progress in commercialization and regulation; partial cost recovery but continuing political interference in some sectors.
4. Substantial progress in commercialization and regulation across sectors; operating costs recovered or fair degree of liberalization with some competition introduced.
5. Commercialization and decentralization, regulations enforced, institutional reforms; extensive liberalization of entry.
6. Effective regulation through an independent entity. Coherent regulatory and institutional framework to deal with tariffs, interconnection rules, licensing, concession fees and spectrum allocation. Consumer ombudsman function.

5. Business Regulatory Environment

Extent to which legal, regulatory, and policy environment helps or hinders private business. Particular focus on direct regulations of business activity, including factor markets.

1. Extensive bans on, or complex licensing of, investment. Extremely burdensome operational licensing systems, extensive labor market controls, private land ownership is illegal or severely curtailed.
2. Many bans on or complex licensing of investment. Burdensome operational licensing systems, very rigid labor market controls, private land ownership is curtailed.
3. Few bans on investment but complex licensing requirements. Moderately burdensome operational licensing systems, rigid labor market controls, private land ownership is permitted with few restrictions but in practice some businesses do not have formal title or use rights.
4. Licensing requirements for most activities eliminated or streamlined. Operational licensing systems impose few burdens on business, employment law reasonably flexible.
5. Very few bans on investment licensing requirements. Operational licensing systems impose only minimal burdens on business, employment law flexible.

6. Almost no bans on investment licensing requirements. Streamlined industry licensing systems, employment law provides high degree of flexibility.

6. Property Rights and Rule-Based Governance

Extent to which an effective legal system and rule-based governance structure facilitates private economic activity. Beyond the legal basis for secure property rights, the category examines the degree to which the legal and judicial system enforces impartial laws and the degree to which crime and violence hinder business activity.

1. Formal property rights are hardly recognized. Laws and regulations change frequently; the state is unable or unwilling to protect lives and property of its citizens
2. Enforcement of contracts and recognition of property rights depend largely on informal mechanisms. Laws and regulations are unpredictable; the state is ineffectual in protecting lives and property.
3. Property Rights protected by law, but institutions to enforce function poorly. Laws and regulations not arbitrarily changed but not publicly available; state provides some protection against crime and violence.
4. Property rights protected in practice and in theory. Laws and regulations not changed arbitrarily, mechanisms exist to resolve conflicts of rules; state able to protect lives and property of most citizens from crime and violence most of the time.
5. Property rights transparent and well protected. Laws and regulations determined through transparent processes; well functioning police force.
6. Each subrating in "5" is fully met; no signs of possible deterioration, widespread expectation of continued strong or improving performance.

7. Institutional Relationship with the Private Sector

Examines the kind of institutional relationship that exist between government and the private sector and the degree to which mechanisms exist for the private sector to influence policy.

1. Excluded; no competition law, no investment center, no regular meetings, weak or nonexistent business associations.
2. Somewhat excluded; intermittent and unreliable contact with government, no competition law, weak business associations, little government effort.

3. Neither included nor excluded; active business associations but no competition law, relationships are selective and limited, irregular meetings, and evidence of collusion between state and business.
4. Somewhat included; has competition law, active business associations, regular meetings but evidence of some collusive behavior.
5. Highly included; established business associations, investment center, dialogue between government and business, there is a formal relationship with the state and regular meetings.
6. Very highly included; business is actively and regularly consulted on major policy decisions, formal organizations include government and business, regular opportunities for business–government interaction, competition policy and investment center.

Sources for Categories, Guidelines, and Assessments

For the categories, guidelines, and scores assigned in categories 1, 2, 5, and 6, see World Bank, Institutional Development Association, "2005 IDA Resource Allocation Index (IRAI)," 2005, accessed 5/11/2009. http://web.worldbank. org/IDA/.

Note that the first release of these assessments was in 2004 in quintile format, and data do not appear to be available before that date. By 2006, the Bank began releasing individual scores for sixteen criteria as well as averages of these criteria clustered into four categories and the overall mean score for each country. The IRAI is based on Country Policy and Institutional Assessments scores calculated for each of the seventy-nine countries eligible for IDA assistance. In my dataset, five countries – Botswana, Mauritius, Namibia, Seychelles, and South Africa were not IDA eligible and therefore were not assessed by the World Bank. I relied on primary and secondary sources from those countries and comparisons with other countries to derive their scores.

Categories 3 and 4 and the guidelines followed to make the assessments were adapted from the transition indicators developed by the European Bank for Reconstruction and Development for evaluating the extent of transition to a market economy by countries in East and Central Europe after 1989 and up to 2008. The methodology can be found at http://www.ebrd.com/country/sector/econo/stats/timeth.htm.

The sources relied on to assign the values for each country in the dataset were the following: White and Bhatia, *Privatization in Africa*; Berthélemy et al., *Privatisation in Sub-Saharan Africa*; the World Bank, "Privatization Database" for 1988–1999; 2000–2008. Government reports and data on privatization from individual countries were also relied on to address gaps in existing data.

The guidelines for category 7 drew on the existing scholarly literature on the importance of the relationship between state and business for private sector development. Assessments for each country relied on primary and secondary sources on the relationship between state and business in individual African countries including the World Bank, newspaper articles, government Web sites, and business organizations. See especially te Velde, "Measuring State-Business Relations."

Appendix 3

Effective Number of Parliamentary Parties (ENPP) in Nine African Democracies c. 1990s–2000s

	ENPP
Cape Verde	
1991	1.7
1995	1.76
2001	2.07
2006	2.05
Average	1.9
Ghana	
1992	1.12
1996	1.87
2000	2.19
2004	2.1
2008	2.12
Average	1.88
Malawi	
1994	2.69
1999	2.66
2004	4.58
2009	2.49
Average	2.9
Mali	
1992	2.24
1997	1.31
2002	2.71
2007	1.63
Average	1.97
Mauritius	
1991	1.23
1995	1.21
2000	1.43
2005	2.09
Average	1.49

	ENPP
Mozambique	
1994	2.14
1999	1.99
2004	1.85
2009	1.6
Average	1.9
Seychelles	
1993	1.44
1998	1.27
2002	1.78
2007	1.78
Average	1.57
South Africa	
1994	2.21
1999	2.15
2004	1.97
2009	2.12
Average	2.11
Zambia	
1991	1.38
1996	1.31
2001	3
2006	2.87
Average	2.14

Notes: Several opposition parties boycotted Ghana's 1992 elections and Mali's 1997 elections. One opposition party boycotted Zambia's 1996 election.

Sources: Calculated using the spreadsheet and information supplied by Michael Gallagher, Indices.xls, accessed 7/19/2010, http://www.tcd.ie/Political_Science/staff/michael_gallagher/ElSystems/Docts/IndicesCalc.pdf and African Elections Database, accessed 2/9/2010, http://african elections.tripod.com.

Bibliography

Interviews

Barrett, Jane. Policy Research Office, South Africa Transport and Allied Workers' Union (SATAWU), Interview, Johannesburg, 12/8/2009.

Born, Tim. Private Sector Enabling Environment Office, U.S. Agency for International Development, Interview, Maputo, 5/28/2008.

Buhlungu, Sakhela. Department of Sociology, University of Johannesburg, Interview, Johannesburg, 2/12/2009.

Chacón, Jean José Villa. Attaché. Private Sector Development and Civil Society, European Union, Interview, Lusaka, 6/10/2008.

Chemba, Ellah. Economist, Research and Development Office, Zambia National Farmers Union, Interview, Lusaka, 6/17/ 2005.

Chisulo, Justin. Chief Executive, Zambian Association of Chambers of Commerce and Industry (ZACCI), Interview, Lusaka, 6/17/2005.

Craven, Patrick. National Spokesperson, COSATU, Interview, Johannesburg, 9/12/2009.

Cruickshank, Stuart. Acting Chief Executive Officer, Zambia Privatisation Agency, Interview, Lusaka, 6/14/2005.

Fauvet, Paul. Editor and Journalist, Mozambique Information Agency, Interview, Maputo. 5/27/2008.

Kasumpa, Glenam. Management Information Officer and Gibson Masumbu, Public Policy Research Officer, Zambia Business Forum, Interview, Lusaka, 6/14/2005.

LaFleur, Jim. Economist, Confederation of Business Associations (CTA), Interview, Maputo, 5/21/2008 and 5/30/2008.

Machina, Henry. Zambia Land Alliance, Interview, Lusaka, 6/11/2008.

Mahabane, Itumeleng. Managing Partner, Brunswick Group LLB, Interview, Johannesburg, 12/4/2009.

Mashishi, Petrus, Former President, South African Municipal Workers' Union, Interview, Johannesburg, 12/9/2009.

Masumbu, Gibson. Public Policy Research Officer, Zambia Business Forum, Interview, 6/13/2008.
Matale, James. Former Chief Executive Officer, ZPA, Interview, Lusaka, 6/12/ 2008.
Mazuba, Chrispin. Research Office, Zambian Federation of Employers, Interview, Lusaka, 6/13/2005.
Mnyaka, Tembakazi. Deputy President, Black Management Forum, Interview, Johannesburg, 6/12/2009.
Momba, J. C. Professor of Political Science, University of Zambia, Interview, 6/9/2008.
Mumbi, Steven. Director of Organization and Trade Union Development, Zambia Congress of Trade Unions – Regional Office, Interview, Lusaka, 6/4/2008.
Munguambe, Alexandre. Secretário Geral, and Boaventura Mondlane, Secretário do CCS para Administração e Finanças, Organização dos Trabalhadores de Moçambique (OTM), Interview, Maputo, 5/26/2008.
Museteka, Danny. Company Secretary, Zambeef, Interview, Lusaka, 6/22/2005.
Mweetwa, Jerome. Zambia Investment Centre, Interview, Lusaka, 6/13/2005
Ngwane, Trevor. Soweto Electricity Crisis Committee, Interview, Johannesburg, 12/1/2009.
O'Donnell, Mark. Managing Director, Union Gold Limited, Interview, Lusaka. 6/23/2005.
Rees, Rob. Provincial Organizer, South African Municipal Workers Union, Interview by Lorraine Coulter, Johannesburg, 7/20/2004.
Rogerson, Christian. Professor. School of Geography, University of Witswatersrand, Interview, Johannesburg, 12/1/2009.
Sambo, Lourenço. Head of Research Division, Centro de Promoção de Investimentos (CPI), Personal communication, Maputo, 8/1/2003.
Sango, Raul. General Secretary, Sindicato Nacional dos Trabalhadores dos Portos e Caminhos de Ferro, Interview, Maputo, 5/29/2008.
Sarakinsky, Ivor. Academic Director, School of Public and Development Management, University of the Witswatersrand, Johannesburg, Interview, 12/4/2009.
Sardanis, Andrew. Businessman and Former CEO of Meridian Bank, Interview, Chaminuka, 6/8/2008 and Lusaka, 6/13/2008.
Shepsle, Kenneth. Personal Communication, 1/18/2008.
Sikombe, Kathy. Program Coordinator, Friedrich Ebert Stiftung, Interview, Lusaka, 6/5/2008.
White, Graeme. President, Associação Comercial e Industrial de Sofala (ACIS), Interview, Maputo, 5/28/2008.

Government, Party and Other Primary Documents

African Elections Database. Accessed 2/9/2010. http://africanelections.tripod.com.
African National Congress. "African National Congress Constitution." Accessed 8/11/2010. http://www.anc.org.za/show.php?doc=./ancdocs/history/const/const2002.html.
    Web site. Accessed 1/23/2009. http://www.anc.org.za.
Afrobarometer Survey Findings. "Summary of Results: Malawi, Round Four, Afrobarometer Survey, 2008." Maxton Tsoka and Blessings Chinsinga. Afrobarometer survey, Round 4, 2008. Accessed 7/21/210. http://www.afrobarometer.org.
    "Summary of Results: Round Four, Afrobarometer Survey in Cape Verde, 2008." Compiled by Afro-Sondagem and Michigan State University. Afrobarometer Survey, Round 4, 2008. Accessed 7/21/2010. http://www.afrobarometer.org.

"Summary of Results: Round Four, Afrobarometer Survey in Mozambique, 2008." Compiled by Carlos Shenga and Amilcar Pereira. Afrobarometer Survey, Round 4, 2008. Accessed 7/21/2010. http://www.afrobarometer.org.

"Summary of Results: Round Three, Afrobarometer Survey in Ghana, 2005." Compiled by Edem Selormey, Joseph Asunka, and Daniel Armah-Attoh. Afrobarometer Survey, Round 3, 2005. Accessed 11/29/2007. http://www.afrobarometer.org.

"Summary of Results: Round Three, Afrobarometer Survey in Malawi, 2005." Compiled by Stanley Khaila and Catherine Mthinda. Afrobarometer Survey, Round 3, 2005. Accessed 7/21/2010. http://www.afrobarometer.org.

"Summary of Results: Round Three, Afrobarometer Survey in Mali, 2005." Compiled by Michigan State University. Afrobarometer Survey, Round 3, 2005. Accessed 11/29/2007. http://www.afrobarometer.org.

"Summary of Results: Round Three, Afrobarometer Survey in Mali, 2008." Compiled by Michigan State University. Afrobarometer Survey, Round 3, 2008. Accessed 7/21/2010. http://www.afrobarometer.org.

"Summary of Results: Round Three, Afrobarometer Survey in Mozambique, 2005." Compiled by João Pereira, Domingos de Rosário, Sandra Manuel, Carlos Shenga, and Eliana Namburete. Afrobarometer Survey, Round 3, 2005. Accessed 3/6/2008. http://www.afrobarometer.org

"Summary of Results: Round Three, Afrobarometer Survey in South Africa, 2006." Compiled by Citizen Surveys and Institute for Democracy in South Africa. Afrobarometer Survey, Round 3, 2006. Accessed 7/21/2010. http://www.afrobarometer.org.

"Summary of Results: Round Three Afrobarometer Survey in Zambia, 2005." Compiled by Peter Lolojih. Afrobarometer Survey, Round 3, 2005. Accessed 7/21/2010. http://www.afrobarometer.org.

Afrobarometer Survey Findings, Round 3, 2005 and Round 4, 2008, selected countries. Accessed 5/29/2011. http://www.afrobarometer.org.

"The Quality of Democracy and Governance in Cape Verde," 2005, Accessed 11/29/2007. http://www.afrobarometer.org.

Burkina Faso. "Le programme de privatisations au Burkina Faso." Accessed 4/20/2011. http://www.fdi.net/documents/WorldBank/databases/plink/burkina/burki.htm.

Cameroon. Ministere de L'Economie et des Finances. Commission Technique de Privatisation et de Liquidations. Accessed 4/10/2006. http://www.ctpl.cm.

Electoral Institute for the Sustainability of Democracy in Africa. "Mozambique: 2009 Presidential election results" (updated January 2010). Accessed 2/8/2010, www.eisa.org.za/WEP/moz2009results1.htm.

"Mozambique: 2009 Assembly of the Republic National Results" (updated January 2010). Accessed 8/10/2011, http://www.eisa.org.za/WEP/moz2009results2.htm.

"Mozambique: Election Archive." Accessed 5/30/2011. http://www.eisa.org.za/WEP/mozelectarchive.htm.

Frelimo. "Estatutos." Aprovados pelo 9 Congresso. n.d.

Frelimo. Departamento de mobilização e propaganda. Boletim de Célula. 1. Fevereiro, 2007.

Ghana, Divestiture Implementation Committee. "The Divestiture Program." Accessed 1/21/2010. http://www.dic.com.gh/info/faq.html.

International Monetary Fund. "International Financial Statistics – South Africa." 1990–2007.

"Review of Financial Sector Regulation and Supervision-Seychelles." October 2004.

"Strengthening Country Ownership of Fund-Supported Programs," Policy Development and Review Department. December 5, 2001.

Lesotho, Lesotho Privatisation Unit. "The Lesotho Privatisation Program." Privatization Link: Project Opportunities in Emerging Markets. February 3, 2000. Accessed 1/21/2010. http://www.fdi.net/documents/WorldBank/databases/plink/lesotho/pprogram.htm.

Malawi. National Assembly. Accessed 1/11/2010. http://www.parliament.gov.mw.

Malawi, Privatisation Commission. "Commissioners, 1996–2001." Accessed 11/11/2006. http://www.privatisationmalawi.org.

"Executive Director's Report – 2001." By Dye Mawindo, Executive Director, Privatisation Commission. 2001. Accessed 11/11/2006. http://www.privatisationmalawi.org.

Public Enterprises (Privatisation) Act, no. 7 of 1996. April 17, 1996. Accessed 5/26/2008. www.privatisationmalawi.org.

Mauritius, Republic of. Ministry of Telecommunications and Information Technology, "White Paper on the Telecommunications Sector: Fostering the Info-Communications Society." December 1997.

Mozambique, Assembleia da República. *Decreto-lei 69/98*. December 1998.

Lei no. 10/2007. May 28, 2007.

Lei no. 19/97. October 1, 1997.

Lei do Trabalho. Lei no. 8/98. July 20, 1998.

Lei do Trabalho. Lei no. 23/2007. August 1, 2007.

Mozambique. *Boletim da República*, Série III, 1992–2008.

Mozambique, Centro de Promoção de Investimentos. "Tabelas dos Anos de 2002–2007." Mimeo. 2008.

Mozambique, Conselho de Ministros. Regulamento da Lei do Órgãos Locais do Estado. Decreto 11, 2005.

Mozambique. Instituto de Gestão das Participações do Estado. "Empresas com Participações do Estado." Mimeo. 2010.

Institute for the Management of State Participation. "Corporate Governance in State-Owned Enterprises in Mozambique," Powerpoint Presentation by Daniel Tembe, Executive Chairman, IGEPE. May 27–28, 2009.

Instituto Nacional de Estatística. "III Recenseamento Geral da População." Accessed 4/26/2009. http://www.ine.gov.mz/censo_2007.

"As Instituições Sem Fins Lucrativos em Moçambique: Resultados do Primeiro Censo Nacional (2004/5)." Maputo. Agosto 28, 2006.

"O Sector Informal em Moçambique: Resultados do Primeiro Inquérito Nacional (2005)." Maputo. Agosto 28, 2006.

Ministry of Agriculture, Unit for the Restructuring of Agricultural Enterprises. "Mapa das empresas alienadas no Ministério da Agricultura em 23.05.95." 1995.

Ministry of Planning and Development. National Directorate of Policy Studies and Analysis. "Enterprise Development in Mozambique: Results Based on Manufacturing Surveys Conducted in 2002 and 2006." Discussion Papers, no. 33E. October 2006, revised January 2007.

Mozambique, Ministry of Planning and Development, National Directorate of Policy Studies and Analysis and World Bank, Poverty and Economic Management

Department, Africa Region. "Job Creation in Mozambique: Is Labor Law Reform the Answer?" November 2006.

Mozambique, Ministry of Planning and Finance, Technical Unit for Enterprise Restructuring (UTRE). "Privatisation in Mozambique." Nos. 1–5. March 1995–1998.

Mozambique. Ministério da Função Pública, Unidade Técnica da Reforma do Sector Pública. "Pesquisa Nacional sobre Governação e Corrupção." Prepared by Austral Consultoria e Projectos. 2005.

Namibia. The Constitution of the Republic of Namibia.

PAICV. "O que pretendemos." Accessed 2/15/2010. http://www.paicv.cv.

Radebe, Jeff, Minister of Public Enterprises. "Black Economic Empowerment." Speech, Johannesburg, 4/2/2003.

Renamo. "Main Renamo Policy Guidelines." Mimeo. 2004.

South Africa, Auditor General. "Report of the Auditor-General to Parliament on a performance audit of entities that are connected with government employees and doing business with national departments." RP 242/2008. August 2008.

South Africa, Department of Finance. "Growth, Employment and Redistribution: A Macroeconomic Strategy." 1996.

South Africa, Department of Public Enterprises. "Analysis of the Performance of State Owned Enterprises During the Period 2003/4–2007/8." n.d.

"A Summary of the Policy Framework for an Accelerated Agenda for the Restructuring of State-owned Enterprises" (August 2000), 19.

"Joint Media Release by Denel and Turbomeca to Create New Company." May 2002. Posted on DPE Web site 9/12/2009. http://www.dpe.gov.za/home.php?id=152.

"Press Briefing on the Strategic IMCC Lekgotla on the Restructuring of State Assets." 1999. Accessed 3/28/2007. http://www.dpe.gov.za.

"SAA Reacquisition of 20% Shares Held by Swissair." Accessed 9/21/2009. http://www.dpe.gov.za.

"Strategic Plan, 2009–2012." Accessed 12/28/2009. http://www.dpe.gov.za.

South Africa, Department of Public Works. "Expanded Public Works Programme Five Year Report, 2004/5–2008/9: Reaching the One Million Target." 2009.

South Africa, Department of Trade and Industry. "Broad-Based Black Economic Empowerment Act," 53 (2003). Accessed 6/13/2007. http://www.dti.gov.za/bee/BEEAct-2003–2004.pdf.

South Africa, Department of Transport. Keynote address at the launch of Passenger Rail Agency of South Africa (PRASA) by Mr. Jeff Radebe, MP Minister of Transport, Park Station, Johannesburg, 20 March 2009. Accessed 12/26/2009. http://www.info.gov.za/speeches/2009/09032409451003.htm.

"Medium Term Strategic Framework 2009–2012."

South Africa, Independent Electoral Commission, Results Reports. 2009. Accessed 12/28/2009. http://www.dti.gov.za/publications/mtsf09.pdfhttp://www.elections.org.za/NPEPWStaticReports/reports/.

South Africa, Ministry of Labour. Labour Force Surveys. 1996–2008.

South Africa, Ministry [sic] of Public Enterprises. "A Summary of the Policy Framework for an Accelerated Agenda for the Restructuring of State-Owned Enterprises," Policy Framework. August 2000.

South Africa, "National Framework Agreement on the Restructuring of State Assets." Approved 2/7/1996. Accessed 4/15/2004. http://www.gov.za/reports/1996/nfa.htm.

South Africa, Parliament of the Republic of South Africa. "White Paper on Reconstruction and Development." Cape Town. November 15, 1994. Notice no. 1954, WPJ/1 994, Government Gazette, 353, 16085. November 23, 1994.

South Africa. "Preferential Procurement Policy Framework Act." Act 5. 2000.

South Africa, Public Investment Corporation. Annual Report 08. 2008.

South Africa, Statistics South Africa. Profiling South African Middle Class Households: 1998–2006. Report O3–03–01. Authored by Mosidi S. Nhlapo and Barbara A. Anderson. Pretoria: Statistics South Africa, 2009.

   Changes in Standard of Living among Population Groups in South Africa: 1998–2006. Authored by Barbara A. Anderson and Mosidi S. Nhlapo. Pretoria: Statistics South Africa, 2010.

South Africa, The Presidency. "Accelerated and Shared Growth Initiative for South Africa (ASGISA) – A Summary." n.d. Accessed 1/10/2010. http://www.info.gov.za/asgisa.

South Africa. "Green Paper: National Strategic Planning" (September 2009).

United Kingdom, British Development Division in Central Africa/ Overseas Development Administration. "ODA Assistance to Promote the Private Sector in Zambia." February 1996.

United Nations Conference on Trade and Development (UNCTAD). "Country Fact Sheet: Zambia." World Investment Report 2009. Accessed 1/29/2010. http://www.unctad.org.

United Nations Development Program (UNDP). Human Development Report, 2009. Summary. New York: UNDP, 2009.

U.S. Agency for International Development/Mozambique Trade and Investment Project (TIP), Private Sector Working Group (PSWG) Meetings, Trade Sub-Committee, see Minutes of Meetings from 2005 to 2009. Accessed 2/10/2010. http://www.tipmoz.com/pswg-minutes.

World Bank, Country Operations Division, Sahelian Department, Africa Region. "Republic of Cape Verde: Public Sector Reform and Capacity Building Project." Staff Appraisal Report. Report no. 12422-CV (1/7/1994).

World Bank, International Development Association. "2005 International Development Association Resource Allocation Index." 2005. Accessed 5/11/2009. http://www.worldbank.org/IDA/.

World Bank. "Implementation Completion Report (IDA – 24320) on a Loan/Credit/Grant in the Amount of US$ Million to the (sic) Mali for a (sic) Private Sector Assistance." Report no. 25275Private Sector group, Africa region (December 30, 2002).

   "Moçambique Análise de Pobreza e Impacto Social Admissão e Retenção no Ensino Primário – o Impacto das Propinas Escolares." Relatório N° 29423-MZ. January 31, 2005.

World Bank, Operations Evaluations Department, Country Evaluation and Regional Relations. "Project Performance Assessment Report: Guinea." Report no. 27166 (October 31, 2003).

World Bank. "Privatization Database, 1988–1999." 1999. Accessed 11/4/2009. http://rru.worldbank.org/Privatization/.

   "Privatization Database, 2000–2008." 2008. Accessed 11/4/2009. http://rru.worldbank.org/privatization/.

   "Project Appraisal Document on a Proposed Credit in the Amount of SDR 7.6 million (US$110 million) to the Republic of Mozambique for the Beira Railway Project." Transport Sector, Country Department 2, Africa Region. November 9, 2004.

"The Role and Effectiveness of Development Assistance: Lessons from World Bank Experience." Research Paper, Development Economics Vice Presidency. 2002. Accessed 2/10/2007. http://econ.worldbank.org.

"Zambia Privatization Review: Facts, Assessment and Lessons." Report prepared at the request of the Minister of Finance and National Planning, Zambia. December 5, 2002.

World Development Indicators (WDI) and Global Development Finance (GDF), World databank. Accessed 11/22/2011. http://databank.worldbank.org.

Zambia Business Forum. Private Sector Development Reform Programme (PSDRP) Review, Fringilla Lodge, December 12–14, 2007), Main Report vol. 1. Prepared by John Kasanga, Robert Sichinga, and Chiwana Musonda. Mimeo.

Zambia, Central Statistical Office. "Formal Sector Employment and Earnings Inquiry Report." 2006.

Zambia, Electoral Commission of Zambia. "2008 Presidential Election: National Results Totals for 150 Constituencies" November 2, 2008.

"Election Results Index, Parliamentary Results, 1991–2006." Accessed 1/11/2009. http://www.elections.org.zm.

"General Elections 2006: Presidential-Constituency Result by Candidate." Mimeo, 2006.

Lusaka Stock Exchange. Accessed 2/6/2009. http://www.luse.co.zm.

Zambia, National Assembly, Public Accounts Committee. "Report of the Public Accounts Committee on the Report of the Auditor-General on the Accounts of Parastatal Bodies for 2004 for the Fifth Session of the Ninth National Assembly. Appointed by Resolution of the House on 20th January 2006."

Zambia, National Assembly, Debates – Thursday, April 5, 2007. Accessed 6/7/2007. http://www.parliament.gov.zm.

Zambia. Privatisation Act, 1992.

Zambia. "The Lands Act." Government of Zambia, Act No. 29. September 13, 1995.

Zambia, Zambia Development Agency Act (ZDAA), no. 11 of 2006. January 24, 2006.

Zambia, Zambia Privatisation Agency. "Privatisation Transactions Summary Sheets 1992–2005." Mimeo. 2005.

"Status Report as at 30th April, 2005." Mimeo. 2005.

Newspapers and Periodicals

Alexander's Gas and Oil Connections
allafrica.com
BBC News, United Kingdom
BuaNews, South Africa
Business Daily, Kenya
Business Day, South Africa
Business Report, South Africa
Club of Mozambique, Mozambique
Creamer Media's Mining Weekly, South Africa
Creamer Media's Engineering News, South Africa
Domingo, Mozambique
Enterprise, South Africa
Financial Mail, South Africa

Mail and Guardian, South Africa
Mail and Guardian Online, South Africa
Metical, Mozambique
Moçambique On-line, Mozambique
Mozambique Information Agency (AIM), Mozambique
Mozambique Political Process Bulletin, United Kingdom
New African, South Africa
New York Times, United States
Notícias, Mozambique
Profit, Zambia
Savana, Mozambique
The Chronicle, Malawi
The Mozambican Investor, Mozambique
The Post, Zambia
Sunday Times, South Africa
The Mercury, South Africa
Times of Zambia, Zambia
Xinhua General Overseas News Service, China
Zambia National Broadcasting Corporation, Zambia

Secondary Sources

Adam, Christopher and Anthony Simpasa. "The Economics of the Copper Price Boom
    in Zambia" in Alastair Fraser and Miles Larmer, eds., *Zambia, Mining, and
    Neoliberalism: Boom and Bust on the Globalized Copperbelt*. New York: Palgrave
    Macmillan, 2010: 59–90.
Adams, Martin. "Land Tenure Policy and Practice in Zambia: Issues Relating to the
    Development of the Agricultural Sector." Draft, DCP/ZAM/018/2002/. 2003.
Addison, Tony. "Do Donors Matter for Institutional Reform in Africa" in Steve
    Kayizzi-Mugerwa, ed., *Reforming Africa's Institutions: Ownership, Incentives, and
    Capabilities*. New York: United Nations University Press, 2003: 54–76.
African Development Bank and Organisation of Economic Cooperation and Development.
    "Mozambique." *African Economic Outlook*. Paris: OECD Publishing, 2008.
    "Seychelles." *African Economic Outlook*. Paris: OECD Publishing, 2009.
    Accessed 1/18/2010.http://www.africaneconomicoutlook.org/en/countries/eastafrica/
    seychelles.
    "South Africa." African Economic Outlook. Paris: OECD Publishing, 2007.
Ahiawordor, Stephens. "Issues and Dilemmas in Ghana's 2000 Elections" in Joseph
    Ayee, ed., *Deepening Democracy in Ghana: Politics of the 2000 Elections*, Vol. 1.
    Accra: Freedom Publications, 2001: 105–120.
Akwetey, Emmanuel and Jon Kraus. "Trade Unions, Development, and Democratization
    in Zambia: The Continuing Struggle" in Jon Kraus, ed., *Trade Unions and the
    Coming of Democracy in Africa*. New York: Palgrave Macmillan, 2007.
Alegi, Peter. "'A Nation To Be Reckoned With': The Politics of World Cup Stadium
    Construction in Cape Town and Durban, South Africa." *African Studies*, 67, 3
    (December 2008): 397–422.
Allan, Kevin. "Post-Consolidation in the Municipal Sphere – Increased Opportunities
    for Investment " in BusinessMap Foundation, Restructuring 2004: A Change of

Pace. Johannesburg: BusinessMap Foundation, 2004: 31–37. Accessed 1/6/2006. *http://www.businessmap.org.za*.

Allina-Pisano, Jessica. "Sub Rosa Resistance and the Politics of Economic Reform: Land Redistribution in the Post-Soviet Ukraine." *World Politics*, 56, 4 (2004): 554–581.

Altman, Miriam. "A Review of Labour Markets in South Africa: Wage Trends and Dynamics." Human Sciences Research Council. October 2005.

"Employment Scenarios to 2024." Human Sciences Research Council. August 2007.

Anderson, Leslie and Lawrence Dodd. Learning Democracy: Citizen Engagement and Electoral Choice in Nicaragua, 1990–2001. Chicago: University of Chicago Press, 2005.

Anti-Privatisation Forum. "Press Release: March for Free Basic and Clean Electricity." October 28, 2008.

Appiah-Kubi, Kojo. "State-Owned Enterprises and Privatization in Ghana." *Journal of Modern African Studies*, 39, 2 (2001): 197–229.

Archer, Ronald and Matthew Shugart. "The Unrealized Potential of Presidential Dominance in Colombia" in Scott Mainwaring and Matthew Shugart, eds., *Presidentialism and Democracy in Latin America*. Cambridge: Cambridge University Press, 1997: 110–159.

Ariyo, Ademola and Afeikhena Jerome. "Privatization in Africa: An Appraisal." *World Development*, 27, 1 (1999): 201–213.

Arndt, Channing, Robert James, and Kenneth Simler. "Has Economic Growth in Mozambique Been Pro-Poor?" *Journal of African Economies*, 15, 4 (2006): 571–602.

Asche, H, and U. Engel. *Negotiating Regions: Economic Partnership Agreements between the European Union and the African Regional Economic Communities*. Leipzig: Leipziger Universitätsverlag, 2008.

Ayee, Joseph, ed. *Deepening Democracy in Ghana: Politics of the 2000 Elections*, Vol. 1. Accra: Freedom Publications, 2001.

Ballard, R., Adam Habib, Imraan Valodia, and Elke Zuern. "Globalization, Marginalization and Contemporary Social Movements in South Africa." *African Affairs*, 104, 417 (2005): 615–634.

Banerjee, Sudeshna G. and Michael C. Munger. "Move to Markets? An Empirical Analysis of Privatization in Developing Countries." *Journal of International Development*, 16, 2 (2004): 213–240.

Barkan, Joel, ed. *Legislative Power in Emerging Democracies*. Boulder: Lynne Rienner, 2009.

"South Africa: Emerging Legislature or Rubber Stamp?" in Joel Barkan, ed., *Legislative Power in Emerging Democracies*. Boulder: Lynne Rienner, 2009: 205–229.

Barro, Robert J. "Recent Developments in the Theory of Rules Versus Discretion." *The Economic Journal* 96, Supplement: Conference Papers (1986): 23–37.

Bartlett, David. "Civil Society and Democracy: A Zambian Case Study." *Journal of Southern African Studies*, 26, 3 (September 2000): 429–446.

Bartolini, Stefano and Peter Mair. *Identity, Competition and Electoral Availability: The Stabilisation of European Electorates 1885–1985*. Cambridge: Cambridge University Press, 1990.

Basedau, Matthias. "Do Party Systems Matter for Democracy? A Comparative Study of 28 Sub-Saharan Countries?" in Matthias Basedau, Gero Erdmann, and Andreas Mehler, eds., *Votes, Money and Violence: Political Parties and Elections in Sub-*

Saharan Africa. Uppsala: Nordiska Afrikainstitutet and Scottsville: University of Kwazulu-Natal, 2007: 105–137.

Basedau, Matthias, Gero Erdmann, and Andreas Mehler. *Votes, Money and Violence: Political Parties and Elections in Sub-Saharan Africa*. Stockholm: Nordiska Afrikainstitutet; Scottsville: University of KwaZulu-Natal Press, 2007.

Bates, Robert. "Comment" in John Williamson, ed., *The Political Economy of Policy Reform*. Washington, D.C.: Institute for International Economics, 1993: 29–34.

"Political Reform" in Benno Ndulu, Stephen O'Connell, Robert Bates, and Paul Soludo, eds. *The Political Economy of Economic Growth in Africa, 1960–2000*, Vol. 1. New York: Cambridge University Press, 2008: 348–390.

Bates, Robert and Anne Krueger, eds. *Political and Economic Interactions in Economic Policy Reform: Evidence from Eight Countries*. Oxford: Blackwell Publishers, 1993.

Bates, Robert and Paul Collier. "The Politics and Economics of Policy Reform in Zambia" in Robert Bates and Anne Krueger, eds., *Political and Economic Interactions in Economic Policy Reform: Evidence from Eight Countries*. Oxford: Blackwell Publishers, 1993: 387–443.

Bayart, Jean-François, Stephen Ellis, and Béatrice Hibou. *The Criminalization of the State in Africa*. Oxford: International African Institute in association with James Currey, 1999.

Bennell, Paul. "Privatization in Sub-Saharan Africa: Progress and Prospects during the 1990s." *World Development*, 25, 11 (1997): 1785–1803.

Beresford, Alexander. "Comrades 'Back on Track'? The Durability of the Tripartite Alliance in South Africa." *African Affairs*, 108, 432 (2009): 391–412.

Bergamaschi, Isaline. "Mali: Patterns and Limits of Donor-Driven Ownership" in Lindsay Whitfield, ed., *The Politics of Aid: African Strategies for Dealing with Donors*. Oxford: Oxford University Press, 2009: 217–245.

Bermeo, Nancy. "Sacrifice, Sequence, and Strength in Successful Dual Transitions: Lessons from Spain." *The Journal of Politics*, 56, 3 (1994): 601–627.

Bertelsmann Transformation Index. "Malawi Country Report." BTI 2006. Accessed 7/9/2010. http://bti2006.bertelsmann-transformation-#index.de/fileadmin/pdf/en/2006/EasternAndSouthernAfrica/Malawi.pdf.

"Mali Country Report." BTI 2006. Accessed 7/7/2010. http://bti2006.bertelsmann-transformation-index.de/fileadmin/pdf/en/2006/WesternAndCentralAfrica/Mali.pdf.

"Mauritius Country Report." BTI 2006. Accessed August 1, 2010. http://bti2006.bertelsmann-transformation-index.de/fileadmin/pdf/en/2006/EasternAndSouthernAfrica/Mauritius.pdf.

"South Africa Country Report." BTI 2006. Accessed 7/18/2010. http://bti2006.bertelsmann-transformation-index.de/fileadmin/pdf/en/2006/EasternAndSouthernAfrica/SouthAfrica.pdf.

"Zambia Country Report." BTI 2006. Accessed 7/18/2010. http://bti2006.bertelsmann-transformation-index.de/fileadmin/pdf/en/2006/EasternAndSouthernAfrica/Zambia.pdf.

Berthélemy, Jean-Claude, Céline Kauffmann, Marie-Anne Valfort, and Lucia Wegner. *Privatisation in Sub-Saharan Africa: Where Do We Stand?* Paris: OECD, 2004.

Bessinger, Mark R. and Crawford Young, eds. *Beyond State Crisis? Postcolonial Africa and Post-Soviet Eurasia in Comparative Perspective*. Washington, D.C.: Woodrow Wilson Centre Press, 2002.

Bhorat, Haroon, Carlene van der Westhuizen, and Toughedah Jacobs. "Income and Non-Income Inequality in Post-Apartheid South Africa: What Are the Drivers and Possible Policy Interventions?" Development Policy Research Unit, DPRU Working Paper 09/138 (August 2009).

Bienen, Henry and Jeffrey Herbst. "The Relationship between Political and Economic Reform in Africa." *Comparative Politics*, 29, 1 (1996): 23–42.

Bilakila, Anastase Nzeza. "The Kinshasa Bargain" in Theodore Trefon, ed. *Reinventing Order in the Congo: How People in Kinshasa Respond to State Failure*. London: Zed Books, 2004: 20–32.

Bird, Graham. "The Effectiveness of Conditionality and the Political Economy of Policy Reform: Is It Simply a Matter of Political Will?" *The Journal of Policy Reform*, 2, 1 (1998): 89–113.

Blanc, Aymeric and Cédric Ghesquières. "Decentralisation and the Free Basic Water Policy in South Africa: What Role for the Private Sector?" Working Paper 25, Agence Française de Développement (2006): 8.

Bogaards, Matthijs. "Counting Parties and Identifying Dominant Party Systems in Africa." *European Journal of Political Research*, 43, 2 (2004): 173–197.

"Crafting Competitive Party Systems: Electoral Laws and the Opposition in Africa." *Democratization*, 7, 4 (2000): 163–190.

"Dominant Party Systems and Electoral Volatility in Africa: A Comment on Mozaffar and Scarritt." *Party Politics*, 14, 1 (2008): 113–130.

"Elections, Election Outcomes, and Democracy in Southern Africa." *Democratization*, 14, 1 (2007): 73–91.

"Electoral Systems, Party Systems, and Ethnicity in Africa" in Matthias Basedau, Gero Erdmann, and Andreas Mehler, eds., *Votes, Money and Violence: Political Parties and Elections in Sub-Saharan Africa*. Uppsala: Nordiska Afrikainstitutet and Scottsville: University of Kwazulu-Natal, 2007: 168–193.

Bond, Patrick, with George Dor, Becky Himlin, and Greg Ruiters. "Eco-Social Injustice for Working-Class Communities: The Making and Unmaking of Neoliberal Infrastructure Policy" in Patrick Bond ed., *Unsustainable South Africa: Environment, Development and Social Protest*. Durban: The University of Kwazulu-Natal Press, 2002: 184–254.

Bond, Patrick, ed. *Unsustainable South Africa: Environment, Development and Social Protest*. Durban: University of Kwazulu-Natal Press, 2002.

Boone, Catherine. *Political Topographies of the African State: Territorial Authority and Institutional Choice*. Cambridge: Cambridge University Press, 2003.

"State, Capital, and the Politics of Banking Reform in Sub-Saharan Africa." *Comparative Politics*, 37, 4 (July 2005): 401–420.

Booysen, Susan. "Beyond the Ballot and the Brick: Continuous Dual Repertoires in the Politics of Attaining Service Delivery in South Africa?" in Anne McLennan and Barry Munslow, eds., *The Politics of Service Delivery*. Johannesburg: Wits University Press, 2009: 104–136.

"Congress of the People: Between Foothold of Hope and Slippery Slope" in Roger Southall and John Daniel, eds., *Zunami: The 2009 South African Elections*. Johannesburg: Jacana Media and The Konrad Adenauer Foundation, 2009: 85–113.

"The Democratic Alliance: Progress and Pitfalls" in Jessica Piombo and Lia Nijzink, eds., *Electoral Politics in South Africa: Assessing the First Democratic Decade*. New York: Palgrave, 2005: 129–147.

Borner, Silvio, Aymo Brunetti, and Beatrice Weder. *Political Credibility and Economic Development*. New York: St. Martin's Press, 1995.

Bourdieu, P. and J. Coleman, eds. *Social Theory for Changing Societies*. Denver: Westview Press and New York: Russell Sage Foundation, 1991.

Brambor, Thomas, William Roberts Clark, and Matt Golder. "Are African Party Systems Different?" *Electoral Studies* 26, 2 (2007): 315–323.

Bratton, M., R. B. Mattes, and E. Gyimah-Boadi. *Public Opinion, Democracy, and Market Reform in Africa*. Cambridge: Cambridge University Press, 2005.

Bratton, Michael and Nicolas Van de Walle. *Democratic Experiments in Africa: Regime Transitions in Comparative Perspective*. Cambridge: Cambridge University Press, 1997.

Bräutigam, Deborah, Lise Rakner, and Scott Taylor. "Business Associations and Growth Coalitions in Sub-Saharan Africa." *Journal of Modern African Studies*, 40, 4 (2002): 519–547.

Broz, J. Lawrence. "Political System Transparency and Monetary Commitment Regimes." *International Organization, The Political Economy of Monetary Institutions*, 56, 4 (2002): 861–887.

Buhlungu, Sakhela. *A Paradox of Victory: COSATU and the Democratic Transformation in South Africa*. Durban: University of KwaZulu-Natal Press, 2010.

"Introduction: COSATU and the First Ten Years of Democratic Transition in South Africa" in Sakhela Buhlungu, ed., *Trade Unions and Democracy: Cosatu Workers' Political Attitudes in South Africa*. Cape Town: Human Sciences Research Council, 2006.

ed. *Trade Unions and Democracy: Cosatu Workers' Political Attitudes in South Africa*. Cape Town: Human Sciences Research Council, 2006.

Buhlungu, Sakhela, Roger Southall, and Edward Webster. "Conclusion: COSATU and the Democratic Transformation of South Africa" in Sakhela Buhlungu, ed., *Trade Unions and Democracy: Cosatu Workers' Political Attitudes in South Africa*. Cape Town: Human Sciences Research Council, 2006.

Business Unity South Africa. Accessed 1/27/2011. http://www.BUSA.org.za.

BusinessMap Foundation. *Restructuring 2004: A Change of Pace*. Johannesburg: BusinessMap Foundation, 2004. Accessed 6/1/2006. http://www.businessmap.org.za.

Butler, Anthony M. "Black Economic Empowerment since 1994" in Ian Shapiro and Kahreen Tebeau, eds., *After Apartheid: Reinventing South Africa*. Charlottesville: University of Virginia Press, 2010.

Buur, Lars with Carlota Mondlane and Obede Baloi. "Strategic Privatisation: Rehabilitating the Mozambican Sugar Industry." *Review of African Political Economy*, 38, 128 (2011): 235–256.

Cahen, Michel. "Mozambique: l'instabilité comme gouvernance?" *Politique Africaine*, 80 (2000): 111–135.

Os Outros: Um historiador em Moçambique. Basel: P. Schlettwein Publishing, 2004.

"Resistência Nacional Moçambicana, de la victoire à la déroute? Pluripartisme sans pluralisme et hégémonie sans stabilite." *Sociétés politiques comparées*, 17 (2009): 1–81.

Callaghy, Thomas. "Vision and Politics in the Transformation of the Global Political Economy: Lessons from the Second and Third Worlds" in Robert Slater, Barry Schutz, and Steven Dorr, eds., *Global Transformation and the Third World*. Boulder: Lynne Rienner, 1993: 161–257.

"Networks and Governance in Africa: Innovation in the Debt Regime" in Thomas Callaghy, Ronald Kassimir, and Robert Latham, eds., *Intervention and Transnationalism in Africa: Global-Local Networks of Power.* Cambridge: Cambridge University Press, 2001: 115–148.

Callaghy, Thomas M., Ronald Kassimir, and Robert Latham. *Intervention and Transnationalism in Africa: Global-Local Networks of Power.* Cambridge: Cambridge University Press, 2001.

Campbell, John. *Institutional Change and Globalization.* Princeton, N.J.: Princeton University Press, 2004.

Campbell, John and Ove Pedersen. "The Rise of Neoliberalism and Institutional Analysis" in John Campbell and Ove Pedersen, eds., *The Rise of Neoliberalism and Institutional Analysis.* Princeton, N.J.: Princeton University Press, 2001: 1–23.

eds. *The Rise of Neoliberalism and Institutional Analysis.* Princeton, N.J.: Princeton University Press, 2001.

Campos, Jose and Hadi Esfahani. "Credible Commitment and Success with Public Enterprise Reform." *World Development* 28, 2 (2000): 221–244.

Carbone, Giovanni. "Continuidade Na Renovação? Ten Years of Multiparty Politics in Mozambique: Roots, Evolution and Stabilisation of the Frelimo–Renamo Party System." *Journal of Modern African Studies,* 43, 3 (2005): 417–442.

"Emerging Pluralist Politics in Mozambique: The Frelimo-Renamo Party System," Crisis States Programme, Development Research Centre, London School of Economics, Working Paper no. 23 (March 2003).

"Political Parties and Party Systems in Africa: Themes and Research Perspectives." *World Political Science Review,* 3, 3 (2007): 1–29.

Castel-Branco, Carlos. "Mega Projectos e Estrategia de Desenvolvimento: Notas para um Debate." Outubro 2002. Accessed 2/5/2009a. http://www.iese.ac.mz/lib/cncb/Mega_projectos_Moz_texto.pdf.

Castel-Branco, Carlos, Christopher Cramer, and Degol Hailu. "Privatization and Economic Strategy in Mozambique." UNU/WIDER, Discussion Paper 2001/64, August 2001.

Centre for Development and Enterprise, "Can Black Economic Empowerment Drive New Growth?" CDE In Depth, 4 (January 2007).

Centro de Integridade Publica. "Curiosidades sobre o financiamento politico em Moçambique." 10/27/2006.

Chabane, Neo, Andrea Goldstein, and Simon Roberts, "The Changing Face and Strategies of Big Business in South Africa: More than a Decade of Political Democracy." *Industrial and Corporate Change,* 15, 3 (2006): 549–577.

Cheeseman, Nic and Marja Hinfelaar. "Parties, Platforms, and Political Mobilization: The Zambian Presidential Election of 2008." *African Affairs,* 109, 434 (2009): 51–76.

Chhibber, Ajay, R. Kyle Peters, and Barbara Yale, eds. *Reform and Growth: Evaluating the World Bank Experience.* Piscataway, N.J.: Transaction Publishers, 2006.

Chhibber, Pradeep *and* Ken Kollman. *The Formation of National Party Systems.* Princeton, N.J.: Princeton University Press, 2004.

Chikulo, Bornwell. "Corruption and Accumulation in Zambia" in Kempe Hope and Bornwell Chikulo, eds., *Corruption and Development in Africa: Lessons from Country-Case Studies.* New York: Palgrave, 2000: 161–182.

Clague, Christopher, ed. *Institutions and Economic Development: Growth and Governance in Less-Developed and Post-Socialist Countries*. Baltimore: Johns Hopkins University Press, 1997.

Clark, Nancy. "South African State Corporations: 'The Death Knell of Economic Colonialism?'" *Journal of Southern African Studies*, 14, 1 (1987): 99–122.

Collier, Paul. "Learning from Failure: The International Financial Institutions as Agencies of Restraint in Africa" in Andreas Schedler, Larry Diamond, and Marc F. Plattner, eds., *The Self-Restraining State: Power and Accountability in New Democracies*. Boulder: Lynne Rienner, 1999: 313–330.

Collier, Paul and Catherine Pattillo, eds. *Investment and Risk in Africa*. New York: St. Martin's Press, 2000.

Collier, Paul and Stephen O'Connell. "Opportunities and Choices" in Benno Ndulu, Stephen O'Connell, Robert Bates, and Paul Soludo, eds., *The Political Economy of Economic Growth in Africa, 1960–2000*, Vol. 1. New York: Cambridge University Press, 2008: 76–136.

Collier, Paul, V. L. Elliott, Håvard Hegre, Anke Hoeffler, Marta Reynal-Querol, and Nicholas Sambanis. *Breaking the Conflict Trap: Civil War and Development Policy*. Washington, D.C.: World Bank, 2003.

Confederação das Assõçiacões Económicas de Moçambique (CTA). "Estatutos." March 21, 2005.

Consortium for Elections and Political Process Strengthening, "Election Guide: Seychelles." Presidential and Legislative Results. 1998–2007. Accessed 2/17/2010. http:www.electionguide.org.

Coppedge, Michael. "Political Darwinism in Latin America's Lost Decade" in Larry Diamond and Richard Gunther, eds., *Political Parties and Democracy*. Baltimore: Johns Hopkins University Press, 2001: 173–205.

Craig, John. "Privatization and Indigenous Ownership in Africa." *Annals of Public and Cooperative Economics*, 73, 4 (2002): 559–576.

Dahl, Robert Alan. *Polyarchy; Participation and Opposition*. New Haven, Conn.: Yale University Press, 1971.

Dalton, Russell J., Ian McAllister, and Martin P. Wattenberg. "The Consequences of Partisan Dealignment" in Russell J. Dalton and Martin P. Wattenberg, eds. *Parties without Partisans: Political Change in Advanced Industrial Democracies*. Oxford: Oxford University Press, 2000: 37–63.

Dalton, Russell J. and Martin P. Wattenberg, eds. *Parties without Partisans: Political Change in Advanced Industrial Democracies*. Oxford: Oxford University Press, 2000.

Darracq, Vincent. "Being a 'Movement of the People' and a Governing Party: Study of the African National Congress Mass Character." *Journal of Southern African Studies*, 34, 2 (2008): 429–449.

de Brito, Luis. "Uma Nota sobre Voto, Abstenção e Fraude em Moçambique." Instituto de Estudos Sociais e Económicos, Discussion paper 4 (2008).

Devarajan, Shantayanan. "Mali" in Shantayanan Devarajan, David Dollar, and Torgny Holmgren, eds., *Aid and Reform in Africa*. Washington, D.C.: World Bank, 2001: 227–286.

Devarajan, Shantayanan, David Dollar, and Torgny Holmgren, eds. *Aid and Reform in Africa*. Washington, D.C.: World Bank, 2001.

Diamond, Larry. "Thinking about Hybrid Regimes." *Journal of Democracy*, 13, 2 (2002): 21–35.

Diamond, Larry and Richard Gunther. *Political Parties and Democracy*. Baltimore: Johns Hopkins University Press, 2001.

Diamond, Larry and Leonardo Morlino, eds. *Assessing the Quality of Democracy*. Baltimore: Johns Hopkins University Press, 2005.

Diamond, Larry, Jonathan Hartlyn, Juan Linz, and Seymour Martin Lipset, eds., *Democracy in Latin America*, 2nd ed. Boulder: Lynne Rienner, 1999.

Diermeier, Daniel, Joel Ericson, Timothy Frye, and Steven Lewis. "Credible Commitment and Property Rights: The Role of Strategic Interaction between Political and Economic Actors" in David Weimer, ed., *The Political Economy of Property Rights: Institutional Change and Credibility in the Reform of Centrally Planned Economies*. Cambridge: Cambridge University Press, 1997: 20–42.

Dijkstra, A. Geske. "The Effectiveness of Policy Conditionality: Eight Country Experiences." *Development and Change*, 33, 2 (2002): 307–334.

Dinavo, Jacques. *Privatization in Developing Countries: Its Impact on Economic Development and Democracy*. Westport: Praeger, 1995.

Dodd, Lawrence. *Coalitions in Parliamentary Government*. Princeton, N.J.: Princeton University Press, 1976.

Dodia, Yusuf. "Private Sector Development in Zambia." Presentation given at the Private Sector and Aid for Trade – ITC Dialogue, Montreux, Switzerland. Mimeo. June 3–5, 2007.

Dollar, David and Jakob Svensson, "What Explains the Success or Failure of Structural Adjustment Programs?" Policy Research Working Paper 1938, Macroeconomics and Growth, Development Research Group, World Bank (June 1998).

Dorman, Sara. "Post-Liberation Politics in Africa: Examining the Political Legacy of Struggle." *Third World Quarterly*, 27, 6 (2006): 1085–1101.

Electoral Institute for the Sustainability of Democracy in Africa (EISA). "Mozambique: Election Archive." Accessed 5/30/2011.http://www.eisa.org.za/WEP/mozelect archive.htm.

  "Mozambique: 2009 Assembly of the Republic National Results." Updated January 2010. Accessed 8/10/2011. http://www.eisa.org.za/WEP/moz2009results2.htm.

  "Mozambique: 2009 Presidential Election Results." Updated January 2010. Accessed 2/8/2010. http://www.eisa.org.za/WEP/moz2009results1.htm.

Elischer, Sebastian. "Measuring and Comparing Party Ideology in Nonindustrialized Societies: Taking Party Manifesto Research to Africa." GIGA German Institute of Global and Area Studies Working Paper 139 (June 2010).

Epstein, David, Robert Bates, Jack Goldstone, Ida Kristenson, and Sharyn O'Halloran. "Democratic Transitions." *American Journal of Political Science*, 50, 3 (2006): 551–569.

Erdmann, Gero. "Party Research: The Western European Bias and the 'African Labyrinth." *Democratization*, 11, 3 (2004): 63–87.

Erdmann, Gero and Matthias Basedau. "Party Systems in Africa: Problems of Categorizing and Explaining Party Systems." *Journal of Contemporary African Studies*, 26, 3 (2008): 241–258.

Eskom. "Eskom Annual Report." 2009. Accessed 12/13/2009. http://www.eskom.co.za/annreport09/ar_2009/business_employment_equity.htm.

European Bank for Reconstruction and Development. "Transition Indicators Methodology." Accessed 1/9/2008. www.ebrd.com/country/sector/econo/stats/timeth.htm.

Faruqee, Rashid. "Nigeria: Ownership Abandoned" in Ishrat Husain and Rashid Faruqee, eds., *Adjustment in Africa: Lessons from Country Case Studies*. Washington, D.C.: The World Bank, 1994: 238–285.

Fashoyin, Toya. "The Contribution of Social Dialogue to Economic and Social Development in Zambia," Working Paper 6, InFocus Programme on Strengthening Social Dialogue, International Labour Office (January 2002).

Fearon, J. D. "Signaling Foreign Policy Interests: Tying Hands Versus Sinking Costs." *The Journal of Conflict Resolution*, 41, 1 (1997): 68–90.

Ferguson, James. *Global Shadows: Africa in the Neoliberal World Order*. Durham, N.C.: Duke University Press, 2006.

Fomunyoh, Christopher. "Francophone Africa in Flux: Democratization in Fits and Starts." *Journal of Democracy*, 12, 3 (2001): 37–50.

Fonseca Lopes, Ana Maria Antónia Rocha da. Os Empresários da Construção Civil e as Relações de Trabalho: Estratégias e Desafios (1991–2004). Maputo: Imprensa Universitária, 2006.

Francis, Suzanne. "The IFP Campaign: Indlovu Ayisindwa Kwasbaphambili!" in Roger Southall and John Daniel, eds., *Zunami: The 2009 South African Elections*. Johannesburg: Jacana Media and The Konrad Adenauer Foundation, 2009.

Fraser, Alastair. "Zambia: Back to the Future?" in Lindsay Whitfield, ed., *The Politics of Aid: African Strategies for Dealing with Donors*. Oxford: Oxford University Press, 2009: 329–360.

"Introduction: Boom and Bust on the Zambian Copperbelt", in Alastair Fraser and Miles Larmer, eds., *Zambia, Mining, and Neoliberalism: Boom and Bust on the Globalized Copperbelt*. New York: Palgrave Macmillan, 2010: 1–30.

Fraser, Alastair and Miles Larmer, eds. *Zambia, Mining, and Neoliberalism: Boom and Bust on the Globalized Copperbelt*. New York: Palgrave Macmillan, 2010.

Freedom House. "Country Report: Mozambique." 2008. Accessed 2/10/2010. http://www.freedomhouse.org.

"Country Report: Zambia." 2008. Accessed 4/23/2009. *http://www.freedomhouse.org*.

"Comparative and Historical Data." Accessed 3/12/2009. http://www.freedomhouse.org

"Freedom in the World Survey, 2005." Accessed 3/15/2009. http://www.freedomhouse.org.

Frye, Timothy. *Building States and Markets after Communism: The Perils of Polarized Democracy*. New York: Cambridge University Press, 2010.

"Credible Commitment and Property Rights: Evidence from Russia." *American Political Science Review*, 98, 3 (2004): 453–466.

Fundanga, Caleb and Andrew Mwaba. "Privatization of Public Enterprises in Zambia: An Evaluation of the Policies, Procedures and Experiences," African Development Bank. Economic Research Papers no. 35 (1997).

Gallagher, Michael. "Election Indices." ElectionIndices.pdf. Accessed 5/25/2011. http://www.tcd.ie/Political_Science/staff/michael_gallagher/ElSystems/.

Indices.xls. Accessed 5/25/2011. *http://www.tcd.ie/Political_Science/staff/michael_gallagher/ElSystems/Docts/IndicesCalc.pdf*.

Gallagher, Michael and Paul Mitchell, eds. *The Politics of Electoral Systems*. Oxford and New York: Oxford University Press, 2005.

Games, Dianna. "Mozambique: The Business View. Results of a Survey on the Business Environment and Investment Climate." Business Leadership South Africa. Occasional paper number 4. November 2007.

Gautrain. Accessed 6/10/2011. *www.gautrain.co.za.*

Gautrain Management Agency. "Socio-economic Development Progress." 2008. Accessed 6/10/2011. *http://www.gautrain.co.za/contents/brochures/sed_brochure_final_print.pdf.*

Geddes, B. *Paradigms and Sand Castles: Theory Building and Research Design in Comparative Politics*. Ann Arbor: University of Michigan Press, 2003.

Gibbon, Peter. "Structural Adjustment and Structural Change in Sub-Saharan Africa: Some Provisional Conclusions" in Peter Gibbon and Adebayo Olukoshi, *Structural Adjustment and Socio-Economic Change in Sub-Saharan Africa: Some Conceptual, Methodological and Research Issues*. Research Report 102. Stockholm: Nordiska Afrikainstitutet, 1996: 9–47.

Gibbon, Peter and Adebayo Olukoshi. *Structural Adjustment and Socio-Economic Change in Sub-Saharan Africa: Some Conceptual, Methodological and Research Issues*. Research Report 102. Stockholm: Nordiska Afrikainstitutet, 1996.

Goldsmith, Arthur. "Foreign Aid and State Administrative Capability in Africa" in Nicolas van de Walle, Nicole Ball, and Vijaya Ramachandran, eds., *Beyond Structural Adjustment: The Institutional Context of African Development*. New York: Palgrave Macmillan, 2001.

Goldstein, Andrea. *Regional Integration, FDI and Competitiveness in Southern Africa*. Paris: OECD, 2004.

Gouws, Rudolf. "The Costs of State Intervention" in Graham Howe and Pieter Le Roux, eds., *Transforming the Economy: Policy Options for South Africa*. Durban: Indicator Project, University of Natal and Institute for Social Development, University of Western Cape, 1992: 25–34.

Gyimah-Boadi, E., ed. *Democratic Reform in Africa: The Quality of Progress*. Boulder: Lynne Rienner, 2004.

Gyimah-Boadi, E. "The Challenges Ahead." *Journal of Democracy*, 8, 2 (1997): 78–91.

Haber, S. H., N. Maurer, and A. Razo. *The Politics of Property Rights: Political Instability, Credible Commitments, and Economic Growth in Mexico, 1876–1929*. Cambridge: Cambridge University Press, 2003.

Habib, Adam. "Politics and Human-Oriented Development" in Raymond Parsons, ed., *Zumanomics: Which Way to Shared Prosperity in South Africa? Challenges for a New Government*. Johannesburg: Jacana Media, 2009.

Habib, Adam, and Collette Schulz Herzenberg. "Democratisation and Parliamentary Opposition in Contemporary South Africa: The 2009 National and Provincial Elections in Perspective." Unpublished manuscript (February 2010).

Habib, Adam, and V. Padayachee. "Economic Policy and Power Relations in South Africa's Transition to Democracy." *World Development*, 28, 2 (2000): 245–263.

Haggard, Stephan, "Democratic Institutions, Economic Policy, and Development" in Christopher Clague, ed., *Institutions and Economic Development: Growth and Governance in Less-Developed and Post-Socialist Countries*. Baltimore: Johns Hopkins University Press, 1997: 121–149.

Haggard, Stephan and Robert R. Kaufman, eds., *The Politics of Economic Adjustment: International Constraints, Distributive Conflicts, and the State.* Princeton, N.J.: Princeton University Press, 1992.
   The Political Economy of Democratic Transitions. Princeton, N.J.: Princeton University Press, 1995.
Haglund, Dan. "From Boom to Bust: Diversity and Regulation in Zambia's Privatized Copper Sector" in Alastair Fraser and Miles Larmer, eds., *Zambia, Mining, and Neoliberalism: Boom and Bust on the Globalized Copperbelt.* New York: Palgrave Macmillan, 2010: 91–126.
Ham, Melinda. "Zambia: A New Page." *Africa Report,* 37, 1(January–February 1992): 18–20.
Handley, Antoinette. "Business, Government and Economic Policymaking in the New South Africa, 1990–2000." *The Journal of Modern African Studies,* 43, 2 (2005): 211–239.
   Business and the State in Africa: Economic Policy-Making in the Neo-Liberal Era. New York: Cambridge University Press, 2008.
Hanlon, Joe. "Is Poverty Decreasing in Mozambique." *Instituto de Estudos Sociais e Económicos (IESE),* Maputo (September 9, 2007).
   "Mozambique Banking Crisis." Moçambique On-line, English version of an article published in Metical 1073. September 17, 2001. Accessed 8/3/2002. http://www. mol.co.mz/noticias/metical/2001/en010917.html.
   "Frelimo Is Now the Party of the Bureaucracy," "Mozambique News Reports and Clippings." *Mozambique,* 102, November 17, 2006.
   "Power Without Responsibility: The World Bank and Mozambican Cashew Nuts." *Review of African Political Economy,* 83 (2000): 29–45.
   ed. "2009 Elections." *Mozambique Political Process Bulletin,* no. 33 (October [sic] [November] 6, 2009).
Hansungule, Michelo, Patricia Feeney, and Robin Palmer. "Report on Land Tenure Insecurity on the Zambian Copperbelt." Oxfam GB in Zambia. November *1998* – Electronic Version with maps created 2004.
Harbeson, John. "Promising Democratization Trajectories in Africa's Weak States" in John Harbeson and Donald Rothchild, eds., *Africa in World Politics: Reforming Political Order.* Boulder: Westview, 2009: 109–139.
Harbeson, John and Donald Rothchild, eds. *Africa in World Politics: Reforming Political Order.* Boulder: Westview, 2009.
Harris, Laurence. "Nationalisation and the Mixed Economy" in Graham Howe and Pieter Le Roux, eds., *Transforming the Economy: Policy Options for South Africa.* Durban: Indicator Project, University of Natal and Institute for Social Development, University of Western Cape, 1992: 35–48.
Haque, Nadeem Ul, Nelson Mark, and Donald J. Mathieson. "Rating Africa: The Economic and Political Content of Risk Indicators" in Paul Collier and Catherine Pattillo, eds., *Investment and Risk in Africa.* New York: St. Martin's Press, 2000.
Hassen, Ebrahim-Khalil and Mawethu Vilana, "Accelerated Delivery and Worker Security." *Indicator,* 7, 4 (December 2000), 12–17.
Hellman, Joel. "Winners Take All: The Politics of Partial Reform in Postcommunist Transitions." *World Politics,* 50, 2 (1998): 203–234.
Hentz, J. J. "The Two Faces of Privatisation: Political and Economic Logics in Transitional South Africa." *The Journal of Modern African Studies,* 38, 2 (2000): 203–223.

Heritage Foundation, Index of Economic Freedom. Selected countries. Selected Years. Accessed 8/1/2010. http://www.heritage.org.

Heritage Foundation. "Seychelles." 2010 Index of Economic Freedom (2010), accessed 8/1/2010, http://www.heritage.org/index/pdf/2010/countries/seychelles.pdf.

Hibou, Beatrice. "The Political Economy of the World Bank's Discourse: From Economic Catechism to Missionary Deeds (and Misdeeds)." Les Etudes du Centre d'études et de recherches internationales, 39 (March 1998), English translation (January 2000).

ed. *Privatizing the State*. Translated from the French by Jonathan Derrick. New York: Columbia University Press, 2004.

Hicken, Allen. *Building Party Systems in Developing Democracies*. Cambridge: Cambridge University Press, 2009.

Hlahla, Monhla. "The Municipal Infrastructure Investment Unit: The Government's PPP-Enabling Strategy." *Development Southern Africa*, 16, 4 (Summer 1999): 565–583.

Hope, Kempe and Bornwell Chikulo, eds. *Corruption and Development in Africa: Lessons from Country-Case Studies*. New York: Palgrave, 2000.

Horwitz, Robert and Willie Currie. "Another Instance Where Privatization Trumped Liberalization: The Politics of Telecommunications Reform in South Africa – A Ten-Year Retrospective." *Telecommunications Policy*, 31 (2007): 446–462.

Houston, Gregory, ed. *Public Participation in Democratic Governance in South Africa*. Pretoria: HSRC, 2001.

Houston, Gregory, Ian Liebenberg, and William Dichaba. "Interest Group Participation in the National Economic Development and Labour Council" in Gregory Houston, ed., *Public Participation in Democratic Governance in South Africa*. Pretoria: HSRC, 2001: 17–82.

Howe, Graham and Pieter Le Roux. *Transforming the Economy: Policy Options for South Africa*. Durban: Indicator Project, University of Natal and Institute for Social Development, University of Western Cape, 1992.

Huber, John and Charles Shipan. *Deliberate Discretion: The Institutional Foundations of Bureaucratic Autonomy*. Cambridge: Cambridge University Press, 2002.

Hughes, Tim. "The South African Parliament's Failed Moment" in M. A. Mohammed Salih, *African Parliaments: Between Governance and Government*. New York: Palgrave Macmillan, 2005: 225–246.

Human Sciences Research Council (HSRC) with Rutgers University. "Mid-Term Review of the Expanded Public Works Programme: Synthesis Report." October 2007.

Humphreys, Macartan and Robert Bates. "Political Institutions and Economic Policies: Lessons from Africa." *British Journal of Political Science*, 35 (2005): 403–428.

Husain, Ishrat and Rashid Faruqee, eds. *Adjustment in Africa: Lessons from Country Case Studies*. Washington, D.C.: The World Bank, 1994.

Hutchful, Eboe. "The Fall and Rise of the State in Ghana" In Abdi Samatar and Ahmed Samatar, eds., *The African State: Reconsiderations*. Portsmouth: Heinemann, 2002: 101–129.

Iheduru, Okechukwu. "Organised Labour, Globalisation and Economic Reform: Union Investment Companies in South Africa." *Transformation: Critical Perspectives on Southern Africa*, 46 (2001): 1–30.

Institute for Democracy in South Africa (IDASA), Political Information and Monitoring Service (PIMS), compiled by Jonathan Faull with assistance from Pamela Masiko-Kambala, "Reading the ANC's National Membership Audit." *ePoliticsSA*, 4 (2007): n.p. Accessed 1/11/2008. http://www.idasa.org.

Inter-Parliamentary Union. "Cape Verde: Assembleia Nacional." Parline database. Accessed 8/1/2010. http://www.ipu.org/parline/reports/2057_E.htm.

International Federation for Human Rights. *Women's Rights in Mozambique: Duty to End Illegal Practices*, May 2007. n° 474/2. UNHCR Refworld, Accessed 5/5/2009.http://www.unhcr.org/refworld/docid/ 46f146890.html.

International Financial Law Review. "Mozambique: Legal Market Overview." IFLR 1000. 2006. Accessed 2/7/2010. http://www.iflr.1000.com/jurisdiction/86/ Mozambique.html.

Jerome, Afeikhena. "Privatisation and Regulation in South Africa. An Evaluation." Prepared for 3rd International Conference on Pro-Poor Regulation and Competition: Issues, Policies, and Practices. Cape Town, South Africa. Mimeo. September 7–9, 2004.

J and J Group. 2011. Accessed 6/10/2011. http://www.jandjgroup.com/about.aspx,.

Jolobe, Zwelethu. "The Democratic Alliance: Consolidating the Official Opposition" in Roger Southall and John Daniel, eds., *Zunami: The 2009 South African Elections*. Johannesburg: Jacana Media and The Konrad Adenauer Foundation, 2009: 131–146.

Jorgenson, Steen and Zlatina Loudjeva, "A Poverty and Social Impact Analysis of Three Reforms in Zambia: Land, Fertilizer, and Infrastructure." The World Bank, Social Analysis, Social Development Papers, no. 49. (January 2005).

Kagiso Trust Investments. Annual Report 2009. 2009.

Kahler, Miles. "External Influence, Conditionality, and the Politics of Adjustment" in Stephan Haggard and Robert R. Kaufman, eds., *The Politics of Economic Adjustment: International Constraints, Distributive Conflicts, and the State*. Princeton, N.J.: Princeton University Press, 1992: 89–136.

"International Financial Institutions and the Politics of Adjustment" in Joan Nelson and Contributors, *Fragile Coalitions: The Politics of Economic Adjustment*. Washington, D.C.: Overseas Development Council, 1989.

Kane Consult, University of Zambia Research Staff, Ness Associates and Participatory Assessment Group. "Post Privatization Impact Assessment Study." Zambia Privatisation Agency, May 31, 2005.

Kasanga, John, Robert Sichinga, and Chiwana Musonda. *Private Sector Development Reform Programme Review. Main Report*, vol. 1. Zambia Business Forum, 2007.

Kayizzi-Mugerwa, Steve. "Privatization in Sub-Saharan Africa: On Factors Affecting Implementation" in Steve Kayizzi-Mugerwa, ed., *Reforming Africa's Institutions: Ownership, Incentives, and Capabilities*. New York: United Nations University Press, 2003: 227–253.

Kayizzi-Mugerwa, Steve, ed. *Reforming Africa's Institutions: Ownership, Incentives, and Capabilities*. New York: United Nations University Press, 2003.

Keen, David. "Liberalization and Conflict." *International Political Science Review*, 26, 1 (2005): 73–89.

Key, V. O. *Politics, Parties, and Pressure Groups*, 4th ed. New York: Thomas Crowell, 1958.

Killick, Tony. "Principals and Agents and the Failings of Conditionality." *Journal of International Development*, 9, 4 (1997): 483–495.

Kitschelt, Herbert, Zdenka Mansfeldova, Radoslaw Markowski, and Gábor Tóka. *Post-Communist Party Systems: Competition, Representation, and Inter-Party Cooperation*. Cambridge: Cambridge University Press, 1999.

Kitschelt, Herbert and Steven Wilkinson, "Citizen-Politician Linkages: An Introduction" in Herbert Kitschelt and Steven Wilkinson, eds., *Patrons, Clients, and Policies: Patterns of Democratic Accountability and Political Competition.* New York: Cambridge University Press, 2007: 1–49.

   eds. *Patrons, Clients, and Policies: Patterns of Democratic Accountability and Political Competition.* New York: Cambridge University Press, 2007.

Knight, Jack. "Explaining the Rise of Neoliberalism: The Mechanisms of Institutional Change" in John Campbell and Ove Pedersen, eds., *The Rise of Neoliberalism and Institutional Analysis.* Princeton, N.J.: Princeton University Press, 2001: 27–50.

   Institutions and Social Conflict. Cambridge: Cambridge University Press, 1992.

Knight, Jack, and Itai Sened, eds. *Explaining Social Institutions.* Ann Arbor: University of Michigan Press, 1995.

Kogut, Bruce and J. Muir Macpherson. "The Decision to Privatize: Economists and the Construction of Ideas and Policies" in Beth Simmons, Frank Dobbin, and Geoffrey Garrett, eds., *The Global Diffusion of Markets and Democracy.* Cambridge: Cambridge University Press, 2008: 104–140.

Kołodko, Grzegorz W. *From Shock to Therapy: The Political Economy of Postsocialist Transformation.* New York: Oxford University Press, 2000.

KPMG. *100 Maiores Empresas de Moçambique.* XI Edição, Ranking das Maiores Empresas 2008. Maputo: Boom, 2009.

Kraus, Jon. ed. *Trade Unions and the Coming of Democracy in Africa.* New York: Palgrave Macmillan, 2007.

Kydland, Finn E. and Edward C. Prescott. "Rules Rather Than Discretion: The Inconsistency of Optimal Plans." *Journal of Political Economy,* 85, 3 (June 1977): 473–491.

Kuenzi, Michelle and Gina Lambright. "Party System Institutionalization in 30 African Countries." *Party Politics,* 7, 4 (2001): 437–468.

   "Party Systems and Democratic Consolidation in Africa's Electoral Regimes." *Party Politics,* 11, 4 (2005): 423–446.

Lanegran, K. "South Africa's 1999 Election: Consolidating a Dominant Party System." *Africa Today,* 48, 2 (2001): 81–102.

Larmer, Miles. "Reaction and Resistance to Neo-Liberalism in Zambia." *Review of African Political Economy,* 32, 103 (2005): 29–45.

   "Historical Perspectives on Zambia's Mining Booms and Busts." in Alastair Fraser and Miles Larmer, eds., *Zambia, Mining, and Neoliberalism: Boom and Bust on the Globalized Copperbelt.* New York: Palgrave Macmillan, 2010: 31–58.

Larmer, Miles, and Alastair Fraser. "Of Cabbages and King Cobra: Populist Politics and Zambia's 2006 Election." *African Affairs,* 106, 425 (2007): 611–637.

Leape, Jonathan and Lynne Thomas with Reg Rumney and Michel Hanouch. "Foreign Direct Investment in Africa," Regional Trade Facilitation Program (RTFP). Occasional Research Paper 1 (October 2005).

LeBas, Adrienne. *From Protest to Parties: Party-Building and Democratization in Africa.* Oxford: Oxford University Press, 2011.

Leftwich, Adrian, ed. *Democracy and Development: Theory and Practice.* Cambridge: Polity Press and Blackwell Publishers, 1996.

Levine, Daniel and José Molina, eds. *The Quality of Democracy in Latin America.* Boulder: Lynne Rienner, 2011.

"Evaluating the Quality of Democracy" in Daniel Levine and José Molina, eds., *The Quality of Democracy in Latin America*. Boulder: Lynne Rienner, 2011: 1–19.

"Measuring the Quality of Democracy" in Daniel Levine and José Molina, eds., *The Quality of Democracy in Latin America*. Boulder: Lynne Rienner, 2011: 21–37.

Lewis, Peter. "Economic Reform and Political Transition in Africa: The Quest for a Politics of Development." *World Politics*, 49, 1 (1996): 92–129.

"Economic Reform and the Discourse of Democracy in Africa: Resolving the Contradictions" in Mark R. Beissinger and Crawford Young, eds., *Beyond State Crisis? Postcolonial Africa and Post-Soviet Eurasia in Comparative Perspective*. Washington, D.C.: Woodrow Wilson Centre Press, 2002: 290–320.

Growing Apart: Oil, Politics, and Economic Change in Indonesia and Nigeria. Ann Arbor: University of Michigan Press, 2007.

Lindberg, Staffan. "Institutionalization of Party Systems? Stability and Fluidity among Legislative Parties in Africa's Democracies." *Government and Opposition*, 42, 2 (2007): 215–241.

Democracy and Elections in Africa. Baltimore: Johns Hopkins University Press, 2006.

Lindberg, Staffan, ed. *Democratization by Elections: A New Mode of Transition*. Baltimore: Johns Hopkins University Press, 2009.

Lindberg, Staffan and Minion Morrison, "Are African Voters Really Ethnic or Clientelistic? Survey Evidence from Ghana," *Political Science Quarterly*, 123, 1 (2008): 95–122.

Lodge, Tom. "The Future of South Africa's Party System." *Journal of Democracy*, 17, 3 (2006): 152–166.

"The ANC and the Development of Party Politics in Modern South Africa." *Journal of Modern African Studies*, 42, 2 (2004): 189–219.

Lund, Christian. *Local Politics and the Dynamics of Property in Africa*. Cambridge: Cambridge University Press, 2008.

MacLeod, Dag. *Downsizing the State: Privatization and the Limits of Neoliberal Reform in Mexico*. University Park: Pennsylvania State University Press, 2004.

Madrid, Raul. "Labouring against Neoliberalism: Unions and Patterns of Reform in Latin America." *Journal of Latin American Studies*, 35, 1 (2003): 53–88.

Mahoney, James and Kathleen Thelen, eds. *Explaining Institutional Change: Ambiguity, Agency and Power*. New York: Cambridge University Press, 2010.

"A Theory of Gradual Institutional Change" in James Mahoney and Kathleen Thelen, eds., *Explaining Institutional Change: Ambiguity, Agency, and Power*. New York: Cambridge University Press, 2010: 1–37.

Mainwaring, Scott. "Presidentialism, Multipartism, and Democracy: The Difficult Combination." *Comparative Political Studies*, 26, 2 (July 1993): 198–228.

"Multipartism, Robust Federalism, and Presidentialism in Brazil" in Scott Mainwaring and Matthew Shugart, eds., *Presidentialism and Democracy in Latin America*. Cambridge: Cambridge University Press, 1997: 55–109.

Mainwaring, Scott and Matthew Shugart, eds. *Presidentialism and Democracy in Latin America*. Cambridge: Cambridge University Press, 1997.

Mainwaring, Scott and Timothy R. Scully, eds. *Building Democratic Institutions: Party Systems in Latin America*. Stanford, Calif.: Stanford University Press, 1995.

"Introduction: Party Systems in Latin America" in Scott Mainwaring and Timothy Scully, eds. *Building Democratic Institutions: Party Systems in Latin America*. Stanford, Calif.: Stanford University Press, 1995: 1–35.

Manning, Carrie. "Assessing Adaptation to Democratic Politics in Mozambique: The Case of Frelimo" in Leonardo Villalón and Peter VonDoepp, eds., *The Fate of Africa's Democratic Experiments: Elites and Institutions*. Bloomington: Indiana University Press, 2005: 221–245.

"Assessing African Party Systems after the Third Wave." *Party Politics*, 11, 6(2005): 707–727.

"Conflict Management and Elite Habituation in Post-war Democracy: The Case of Mozambique." *Comparative Politics*, 35, 1 (2002): 63–84.

"Elite Habituation to Democracy in Mozambique: The View from Parliament, 1994–2000." *The Journal of Commonwealth and Comparative Politics*, 40, 1 (2002): 61–80.

"Mozambique's Slide into One Party Rule." *Journal of Democracy*, 21, 2 (April 2010): 151–165.

Marais, Hein. *South Africa: Limits to Change: The Political Economy of Transition*. New York: Zed Books, and Cape Town: University of Cape Town Press, 1998.

Maravall, José María and Adam Przeworski. "Political Reactions to the Economy: The Spanish Experience" in Susan Stokes, ed., *Public Support for Market Reforms in New Democracies*. Cambridge: Cambridge University Press, 2001: 35–76.

Market Tree Consultancy. "Facts and Statistics." Accessed 8/9/2009. http://www.markettree.co.za/fact_desc.html.

Maseko, Sipho. "From Pavement Entrepreneurs to Stock Exchange Capitalists: The Case of the South African Black Business Class." Thesis, D.Phil., School of Government, University of the Western Cape, Bellville, 2000.

Mattes, Robert. "Democracy without People: Political Institutions and Citizenship in the New South Africa." Afrobarometer Working Paper, no. 82 (2007).

McCarthy, Colin. "The SADC/SACU Interplay in EPA Negotiations – A Variation on the Old Theme of Integrating Unequal Economies" in Helmut Asche and Ulf Engel, eds., *Negotiating Regions: The EU, Africa and the Economic Partnership Agreements*. Leipzig: Leipziger Universitätsverlag, 2008: 109–130.

McDonald, David and John Pape, eds. *Cost Recovery and the Crisis of Service Delivery in South Africa*. London: Zed Press and Pretoria: HSRC Publishers, 2002.

McLennan, Anne and Barry Munslow, eds., *The Politics of Service Delivery*. Johannesburg: Wits University Press, 2009.

Metcalf, Simon and Thembela Kepe. "Dealing Land in the Midst of Poverty: Commercial Access to Communal Land in Zambia." *African and Asian Studies*, 7 (2008): 235–257.

Milaco, Armindo. "Intervenção Antes da Ordem do Dia." Speech by Renamo Member of Parliament (Cabo Delgado) to the Assembly of the Republic. Date unknown. Accessed 5/9/2009. http://www.renamo.org.mz.

Milimo, John. "Social Impacts of Privatisation: Findings from a Qualitative Participatory Research Exercise." Undertaken for the ZPA, field research by Mwiya Mwanavande and Nalishebo Katukula, Lusaka (May 2005).

Millenium Labour Council. "The Launch." Accessed 10/22/2010. http://www.mlc.org.za.

Miller, Darlene. "Transition in the Post-apartheid Regional Workplace" in Edward Webster and Karl Von Holdt, eds., *Beyond the Apartheid Workplace: Studies in Transition*. Scottsville, South Africa: University of Kwazulu-Natal, 2005: 243–265.

Miraftab, Faranak. "Governing Post Apartheid Spatiality: Implementing City Improvement Districts in Cape Town." *Antipode*, 39, 4 (2007): 602–626.

Mistry, Percy. "Commentary: Mauritius-Quo Vadis?" *African Affairs*, 98 (1999): 551–569.

Mkandawire, Thandika, and Charles Soludo. *Our Continent, Our Future: African Perspectives on Structural Adjustment*. Trenton, N.J.: Africa World Press, 1999.

Morrison, Minion. "Political Parties in Ghana through Four Republics: A Path to Democratic Consolidation." *Comparative Politics*, 36, 4 (2004): 421–442.

Mosley, Paul, Jane Harrigan, and J. F. J. Toye. *Aid and Power: The World Bank and Policy-Based Lending*. London: Routledge, 1995.

Mostert, C. *Reflections on South Africa's Restructuring of State-Owned Enterprises*. Friedrich Ebert Stiftung, South Africa Office, 2002.

Mozaffar, Shaheen and James Scarritt. "The Puzzle of African Party Systems." *Party Politics*, 11, 4 (2005): 399–421.

Mozaffar, Shaheen, James Scarritt, and Glen Galaich. "Electoral Institutions, Ethnopolitical Cleavages and Party Systems in Africa's Emerging Democracies." *American Political Science Review*, 97 (2003): 379–390.

Muneku, Austin. "Trade Union Membership and Profile in Zambia." ZCTU Economics and Research Department (2002).

Murillo, Victoria. "From Populism to Neoliberalism: Labor Unions and Market Reforms in Latin America." *World Politics*, 52 (2000): 135–174.

"Political Bias in Policy Convergence: Privatization Choices in Latin America." *World Politics*, 54, 4 (2002): 462–493.

Murphy, Kevin M., Andrei Shleifer, and Robert W. Vishny. "The Transition to a Market Economy: Pitfalls of Partial Reform." *The Quarterly Journal of Economics*, 107, 3 (1992): 889–906.

Murray, Martin. *City of Extremes: The Spatial Politics of Johannesburg*. Durham, N.C.: Duke University Press, 2011.

Mustapha, Abdul Raufu and Lindsay Whitfield, eds., *Turning Points in African Democracy*. Rochester: James Currey, 2009.

Mthimkhulu, Vula. "New Deal in the Offing for SMMEs." *Enterprise* (2008): 10–18.

National Democratic Institute. "Statement by NDI President Kenneth Womack on Suspension of Program Activities in Zambia." June 17, 1996. Accessed 10/06/2010, http://www.accessdemocracy.org/files/869_zm_statement_061796.pdf

National Democratic Institute (NDI) and the Foundation for Democratic Process (FODEP). "The State of Political Parties in Zambia–2003: Final Report." Lusaka, Zambia (July 2003).

Nattrass, Nicoli and Jeremy Seekings. "State, Business and Growth in Post-Apartheid South Africa." Research Programme Consortium for Improving Institutions for Pro-Poor Growth," Discussion Paper Series 34 (January 2010).

Ndulu, Benno, Stephen O'Connell, Robert Bates, and Paul Soludo, eds. *The Political Economy of Economic Growth in Africa, 1960–2000*, Vol. 1. New York: Cambridge University Press, 2008.

Nellis, John. "Privatization in Africa: What Has Happened? What Is To Be Done?" in Gérard Roland, ed., *Privatization: Successes and Failures*. New York: Columbia University Press, 2008: 109–135.

"Public Enterprises in Sub-Saharan Africa." World Bank Discussion Paper no. 1. Washington, D.C. (1986).

Nellis, John and Nancy Birdsall. "Winners and Losers: Assessing the Distributional Impact of Privatization." *World Development*, 31, 10 (2003): 1617–1633.

Nelson, Joan, and Contributors. *Fragile Coalitions: The Politics of Economic Adjustment.* Washington, D.C.: Overseas Development Council, 1989.

North, Douglass C. "Institutions and Credible Commitment." *Journal of Institutional and Theoretical Economics,* 149, 1 (1993): 11–23.

"Five Propositions about Institutional Change" in Jack Knight and Itai Sened, eds., *Explaining Social Institutions.* Ann Arbor: University of Michigan Press, 1995.

North, Douglass C. and Barry R. Weingast. "Constitutions and Commitment: The Evolution of Institutions Governing Public Choice in Seventeenth-Century England." *The Journal of Economic History,* 49, 4 (1989): 803–832.

Odendaal, Willem. "The SADC Land and Agrarian Reform Initiative: The Case of Namibia," NEPRU Working Paper No.111 (December 2006): 9, 20–47.

O'Donnell, Guillermo, Jorge Cullell, and Osvaldo Iazzetta. *The Quality of Democracy: Theory and Applications.* Notre Dame, Ind.: University of Notre Dame Press, 2004.

O'Dwyer, Conor. *Runaway State-Building: Patronage Politics and Democratic Development.* Baltimore: Johns Hopkins University Press, 2006.

Olson, Mancur. "Dictatorship, Democracy and Development." *American Political Science Review,* 87, 3 (1993): 567–576.

"The New Institutional Economics: The Collective Choice Approach to Economic Development" in Christopher Clague, ed., *Institutions and Economic Development: Growth and Governance in Less-Developed and Post-Socialist Countries.* Baltimore: Johns Hopkins University Press, 1997: 37–65.

Opoku, Darko. "Political Dilemmas of Indigenous Capitalist Development in Ghana under the Provisional National Defence Council." *Africa Today,* 55, 2 (2008): 25–51.

The Politics of Government-Business Relations in Ghana, 1982–2008. New York: Palgrave Macmillan, 2010.

Organisation of Economic Cooperation and Development. "South Africa Economic Assessment." *Economic Surveys,* 2008/15 (July 2008).

Parsons, Raymond, ed. *Zumanomics: Which Way to Shared Prosperity in South Africa? Challenges for a New Government.* Johannesburg: Jacana Media, 2009.

Pastor, Manuel and Carol Wise. "The Politics of Second-Generation Reform." *Journal of Democracy,* 10, 3 (1999): 34–48.

Pedersen, Mogens. "On Measuring Party System Change: A Methodological Critique and a Suggestion." *Comparative Political Studies,* 12, 4 (January 1980): 387–403.

Peerun, Reshma, Sumil Bundoo, and Kheswar Jankee. "Mauritius" in Pradeep Mehta, ed., *Competition Regimes in the World – A Civil Society Report.* Jaipur: Consumer Unity and Trust Society in Association with International Network of Civil Society Organisations on Competition, 2006: 254–259.

Pereira, João C. G. "'Antes o "diabo" Conhecido do Que Um "anjo" Desconhecido': As Limitações do Voto Económico Na Reeleição do Partido Frelimo." *Análise Social,* XLIII, 2 (2008): 419–442.

Picard, Louis. *The State of the State: Institutional Transformation, Capacity and Political Change in South Africa.* Johannesburg: Wits University Press, 2005.

Pienaar, Gary. "Procurement Corruption." *New Agenda,* 31 (August 2008): n,p. Reprinted by Idasa online, accessed 1/5/2012, http://idasa.krazyboyz.co.za/countries/output/procurement_corruption/.

Piesse, Jennifer and Bruce Hearn. "Barriers to the Development of Small Stock Markets: A Case Study of Swaziland and Mozambique." *Journal of International Development*, 22, 7 (2009): 1018–1037.

Pillay, Devan. "COSATU, Alliances and Working Class Politics" in Sakhela Buhlungu, ed., *Trade Unions and Democracy: COSATU Workers' Political Attitudes in South Africa*. Cape Town: HSRC, 2006: 167–198.

"COSATU, the SACP and the ANC Post-Polokwane: Looking Left but Does It Feel Right?" *Labour, Capital and Society*, 41, 2 (2008): 4–37.

Piombo, Jessica and Lia Nijzink, eds. *Electoral Politics in South Africa: Assessing the First Democratic Decade*. New York: Palgrave, 2005.

Pitcher, M. Anne. "Conditions, Commitments, and the Politics of Restructuring in Africa." *Comparative Politics*, 36, 4 (2004): 379–398.

"Forgetting from Above and Memory from Below: Strategies of Legitimation and Struggle in Postsocialist Mozambique." *Africa*, 76, 1 (2006): 88–112.

"Les élections générales de 2004 au Mozambique: Choix, conséquences et perspectives." *Politique Africaine*, 98 (2005): 149–165.

"Sobreviver a Transição: O Legado das Antigas Empresas Coloniais em Moçambique." *Análise Social*, xxxviii, 168 (2003): 793–820.

Transforming Mozambique: The Politics of Privatization, 1975–2000. Cambridge: Cambridge University Press, 2002.

"What Has Happened to Organized Labor in Southern Africa?," *International Labor and Working Class History*, 72 (2007): 134–160.

Pitcher, M. Anne and Manuel Teodoro. "The Impact of 'Technocratic Change Teams' on the Outcome of Political and Economic Reforms: Some Findings from Africa," paper prepared for the Annual Meeting of the Midwest Political Science Association, Chicago, April 22–25, 2010.

Pitcher, M. Anne, Mary Moran, and Michael Johnston. "Re-thinking Patrimonialism and Neopatrimonialism in Africa." *African Studies Review*, 52, 1 (2009): 125–156.

Ponte, Stefano. "The Politics of Ownership: Tanzanian Coffee Policy in the Age of Liberal Reformism." *African Affairs*, 103, 413 (2004): 615–633.

Posner, Daniel. *Institutions and Ethnic Politics in Africa*. New York: Cambridge University Press, 2005.

Posner, Daniel and Daniel Young, "The Institutionalization of Political Power in Africa." *Journal of Democracy*, 18, 3(2007): 126–140.

Posner, Daniel and David Simon. "Economic Conditions and Incumbent Support in Africa's New Democracies." *Comparative Political Studies*, 35, 3 (2002): 313–336.

Poteete, Amy R. "Ideas, Interests, and Institutions: Challenging the Property Rights Paradigm in Botswana." *Governance*, 16, 4 (2003): 527–557.

"When Professionalism Clashes with Local Particularities: Ecology, Elections, and Procedural Arrangements in Botswana." *Journal of Southern African Studies*, 29, 2 (June 2003): 461–485.

Prah, K. K. and Abdel Ghaffar Muhammad Ahmad. *Africa in Transformation: Political and Economic Transformations and Socio-Economic Development Responses in Africa*. Addis Ababa: OSSREA, 2000.

Przeworski, Adam. *Democracy and the Market: Political and Economic Reforms in Eastern Europe and Latin America*. New York: Cambridge University Press, 1991.

Przeworski, Adam and Fernando Limongi. "Political Regimes and Economic Growth." *Journal of Economic Perspectives*, 7, 3 (1993): 51–69.

Przeworski, Adam and James Vreeland, "The Effect of IMF Programs on Economic Growth." *Journal of Development Economics*, 62 (2000): 385–421.

Public Investment Corporation. "Annual Report 08." 2008.

Quist, Ronald, Corina Certan, and Jerome Dendura. "Republic of South Africa: Public Expenditure and Financial Accountability," Public Financial Management Performance Assessment Report, Final Report (September 2008).

Rakner, Lise. *Political and Economic Liberalisation in Zambia 1991–2001*. Nordiska Afrikainstitutet, 2003.

"The Pluralist Paradox: The Decline of Economic Interest Groups in Zambia in the 1990s." *Development and Change*, 32 (2001): 507–529.

Rakner, Lise and Lars Svåsand. "Stuck in Transition: Electoral Processes in Zambia, 1991–2001." *Democratization*, 12, 1 (February 2005): 85–105.

"From Dominant to Competitive Party System: The Zambian Experience 1991–2001." *Party Politics*, 10, 1(2004): 49–68.

Rakner, Lise and Nicolas van de Walle. "Democratization by Elections? Opposition Weakness in Africa." *Journal of Democracy*, 20, 3 (July 2009): 108–121.

Rakner, Lise, Lars Svåsand, and Nixon Khembo. "Fissions and Fusions, Foes and Friends: Party System Restructuring in Malawi in the 2004 General Elections." *Comparative Political Studies*, 40, 9 (2007): 1112–1137.

Randall, Vicky and Lars Svåsand. "Political Parties and Democratic Consolidation in Africa." *Democratization*, 9, 3 (Autumn 2002), 30–46.

Remmer, Karen. "The Political Economy of Patronage: Expenditure Patterns in the Argentine Provinces, 1983–2003." *The Journal of Politics*, 69, 2 (May 2007): 363–377.

Reno, Will. "The Privatisation of Sovereignty and the Survival of Weak States" in Béatrice Hibou, ed., *Privatizing the State*. New York: Columbia University Press, 2004: 95–119.

Riedl, Rachel. "Institutions in New Democracies: Variations in African Political Party Systems," Ph.D. diss., Princeton University, November 2008.

Ripley, Randall and Grace Franklin. *Congress, the Bureaucracy, and Public Policy*, 5th ed. Pacific Grove: Brooks/Cole Publishing Company, 1991.

Rodrik, Dani. "Promises, Promises: Credible Policy Reform Via Signaling." *The Economic Journal*, 99, 397 (1989): 756–772.

Roland, Gérard, ed., *Privatization: Successes and Failures*. New York: Columbia University Press, 2008.

Rolfe, Robert and Douglas Woodward. "Attracting Foreign Investment Through Privatization: The Zambian Experience." *Journal of African Business*, 5, 1 (2004): 5–27.

Rueschemeyer, Dietrich, Evelyne Stephens, and John Stephens. *Capitalist Development and Democracy*. Chicago: University of Chicago, 1992.

Rumney, Reg. "Overview of Progress to Date" in *BusinessMap Foundation, Restructuring 2004: A Change of Pace*. Johannesburg: BusinessMap Foundation, 2004: 1–6. Accessed 1/6/2006. http://www.businessmap.org.za.

"Calculating the Worth of SOEs" in *BusinessMap Foundation, Restructuring 2004: A Change of Pace*. Johannesburg: BusinessMap Foundation, 2004: 17–19. Accessed 1/6/2006. http://www.businessmap.org.za.

Salih, M. A. Mohammed. *African Parliaments: Between Governance and Government.* New York: Palgrave Macmillan, 2005.

Samatar, Abdi Ismail and Ahmed I. Samatar. *The African State: Reconsiderations.* Portsmouth, N.H.: Heinemann, 2002.

Sarakinsky, Ivor. "Political Party Finance in South Africa: Disclosure Versus Secrecy." *Democratization,* 14, 1 (2007): 111–128.

Sartori, Giovanni. *Parties and Party Systems: A Framework for Analysis.* Cambridge: Cambridge University Press, 1976; republished Colchester: European Consortium for Political Research, 2005.

Schamis, Hector. "Distributional Coalitions and the Politics of Economic Reform in Latin America." *World Politics,* 51, 2 (1999): 236–268.
  Re-forming the State: The Politics of Privatization in Latin America and Europe. Ann Arbor: University of Michigan Press, 2002.

Schedler, A., L. J. Diamond, and M. F. Plattner. *The Self-Restraining State: Power and Accountability in New Democracies.* Boulder: Lynne Rienner Publisher, 1999.

Schneider, Ben Ross. *Business Politics and the State in Twentieth-Century Latin America.* Cambridge: Cambridge University Press, 2004.

Seekings, Jeremy and Nicoli Nattrass. *Class, Race, and Inequality in South Africa.* New Haven, Conn.: Yale University Press, 2005.

Sen, Kunal and Dirk Willem te Velde, "State-Business Relations and Economic Growth in Sub-Saharan Africa." *Journal of Development Studies,* 45, 8 (2009): 1267–1283.

Shapiro, Ian and Kahreen Tebeau, eds. *After Apartheid: Reinventing South Africa.* Charlottesville: University of Virginia Press, 2011.

Shenga, Carlos and Amilcar Pereira. "Summary of Results." Round Four Afrobarometer Surveys in Mozambique. 2008. Accessed 11/2/2010. http://www.afrobarometer.org.

Shepsle, Kenneth. "Discretion, Institutions, and the Problem of Government Commitment" in Pierre Bourdieu and James S. Coleman, eds., *Social Theory for Changing Societies.* Boulder: Westview Press and New York: Russell Sage Foundation, 1991: 245–263.

Simmons, Beth, Frank Dobbin, and Geoffrey Garrett, eds. *The Global Diffusion of Markets and Democracy.* Cambridge: Cambridge University Press, 2008.

Simon, David. "Democracy Unrealized: Zambia's Third Republic under Frederick Chiluba" in Leonardo Villalón and Peter Von Doepp, eds., *The Fate of Africa's Democratic Experiments.* Bloomington: Indiana University Press, 2005: 199–220.

Simutanyi, Neo. "Copper Mining in Zambia: The Developmental Legacy of Privatization," South Africa Institute for Security Studies, Paper 165 (July 2008).
  "The Politics of Structural Adjustment in Zambia." *Third World Quarterly,* 17, 4 (1996): 825–839.
  "Political Parties and Party System in Zambia," Background paper prepared for Friedrich Ebert Stiftung, Lusaka, Zambia, October 2005. Mimeo.
  Presentation to the Political Parties Development Workshop, Lusaka, June 12, 2008.

Sklar, Richard. "Towards a Theory of Developmental Democracy" in Adrian Leftwich, ed., *Democracy and Development: Theory and Practice.* Cambridge: Polity Press and Blackwell Publishers, 1996: 25–44.

Soludo, Charles Chukwuma, Osita Ogbu, and Ha-Joon Chang, eds. *The Politics of Trade and Industrial Policy in Africa Forced Consensus.* Trenton and Ottawa: Africa World Press and International Development Research Centre, 2004.

Somerville, Keith. "Limits of Patience?" *African Business* (March 1995): 20.

Southall, Roger. "The ANC and Black Capitalism in South Africa." *Review of African Political Economy*, 31, 100 (2004): 313–328.

"The ANC for Sale? Money, Morality and Business in South Africa." *Review of African Political Economy*, 35, 116 (2008): 281–299.

"Zunami! The Context of the 2009 Election" in Roger Southall and John Daniel, eds., *Zunami: The 2009 South African Elections*. Johannesburg: Jacana Media and The Konrad Adenauer Foundation, 2009: 1–22.

Southall, Roger and John Daniel, eds. *Zunami: The 2009 South African Elections*. Johannesburg: Jacana Media and The Konrad Adenauer Foundation, 2009.

Southall, Roger and Roger Tangri. "Cosatu and Black Economic Empowerment" in Sakhela Buhlungu, ed., *Trade Unions and Democracy: Cosatu Workers' Political Attitudes in South Africa*. Cape Town: HSRC Press, 2006: 115–142.

Speck, Bruno. "Political Finance in Mozambique." Sao Paolo, Brazil, December 2004. Mimeo.

Spiller, Pablo. "Institutions and Commitment." *Industrial and Corporate Change*, 5, 2 (1996): 421–452.

Staffan Lindberg. "Institutionalization of Party Systems? Stability and Fluidity among Legislative Parties in Africa's Democracies." *Government and Opposition*, 42, 2 (2007): 215–241.

Stasavage, David. "Credible Commitment in Early Modern Europe: North and Weingast Revisited." *Journal of Law, Economics and Organization*, 18, 1 (2002): 155–186.

Public Debt and the Birth of the Democratic State. New York: Cambridge University Press, 2003.

Steinmo, Sven, Kathleen Thelen, and Frank Longstreth, eds. *Structuring Politics: Historical Institutionalism in Comparative Analysis*. New York: Cambridge University Press, 1992, reprinted 1998.

Stiglitz, Joseph E. "The World Bank at the Millennium." *The Economic Journal*, 109, 459, Features (1999): F577–597.

Stokes, Susan, ed. *Public Support for Market Reforms in New Democracies*. Cambridge: Cambridge University Press, 2001.

Storpor, Michael. "Lived Effects of the Contemporary Economy: Globalization, Inequality and Consumer Society" in Jean Comaroff and John Comaroff, eds., *Milleninial Capitalism and the Culture of Neoliberalism*. Durham, N.C.: Duke University Press, 2001: 88–124.

Strategic Partners Group PTY Ltd., "Company Profile." n.d. Accessed 6/4/2011. http://www.gautrain.co.za/contents/background/spg_profile.pdf.

Streeck, Wolfgang and Kathleen Thelen, eds. *Beyond Continuity: Institutional Change in Advanced Industrial Economies*. Oxford: Oxford University Press, 2005.

"Introduction: Institutional Change in Advanced Industrial Economies" in Wolfgang Streeck and Kathleen Thelen, eds., *Beyond Continuity: Institutional Change in Advanced Industrial Economies*. Oxford: Oxford University Press, 2005: 1–39.

Suttner, Raymond. "Transformation of Political Parties in Africa Today." *Transformation: Critical Perspectives on Southern Africa*, 55 (2005): 1–27.

Swamy, Gurushri. "Kenya: Patchy, Intermittent Commitment" in Ishrat Husain and Rashid Faruqee, eds., *Adjustment in Africa: Lessons from Country Case Studies*. Washington, D.C.: The World Bank, 1994: 193–237.

Swilling, Mark, John Van Breda, Albert Van Zyl, and Firoz Khan. "Economic Policymaking in a Developmental State: Review of the South African Government's Poverty and Development Approaches, 1994–2004." *Economic Policy & Poverty Alleviation Report Series Research Reports* 4 & 5(2004).

Sylvester, Justin. "Considering the framework for policy and delivery in SA – The NPC and more." IDASA. September 21, 2009. Accessed 10/19/ 2009. http://www.idasa.org.za.

Tangri, Roger. *The Politics of Patronage in Africa: Parastals, Privatization and Private Enterprise.* Trenton, N.J.: Africa World Press, 1999.

Tangri, Roger and Roger Southall. "The Politics of Black Economic Empowerment in South Africa," *Journal of Southern African Studies*, 34, 3 (2008): 699–716.

Taylor, Scott. *Business and the State in Southern Africa.* Boulder: Lynne Rienner, 2007.

te Velde, Dirk Willem. "Measuring State-Business Relations in Sub-Saharan Africa." Discussion Paper Series no. 4, Research Programme Consortium for Improving Institutions for Pro-Poor Growth, University of Manchester. November 2006. Accessed 1/25/2010. http://www.ippg.org.uk.

Tembe, Daniel. Director de IGEPE, Presentation to the Ministério de Planejamento, Brasil, 11 December 2008; Brazil, Ministério de Planejamento, "Moçambique procura o dest [sic] para melhorar gestão de suas estatais." December 12, 2008. Accessed 3/30/2009. http://www.planejamento.gov.br.

Transnet. "Transnet Annual Report, 2009." Accessed 12/13/2009. http://www.transnet.co.za.

Transparency International. "National Integrity System (NIS) Country Study Report Mozambique 2006/7." Written and Researched by Marcelo Mosse, Nelson Manjate, and Edson Cortez. 2007.

Trefon, Theodore, ed. *Reinventing Order in the Congo: How People in Kinshasa Respond to State Failure.* London: Zed Books, 2004.

Tsai, Kellee S. *Capitalism without Democracy: The Private Sector in Contemporary China.* Ithaca, N.Y.: Cornell University Press, 2007.

Tsebelis, George. *Veto Players: How Political Institutions Work.* New York: Russell Sage Foundation and Princeton, N.J.: Princeton University Press, 2002.

Unicef–Mozambique and Government of Mozambique. *Childhood Poverty in Mozambique: A Situation and Trends Analysis.* Maputo: UNICEF, 2006.

Union Alliance Holdings, (Pty) Ltd. Johannesburg, Gauteng, South Africa. Accessed 12/30/2009. http://www.mbendi.com/orgs/cp6l.htm.

Valodia, Imraan, Likani Lebani, Caroline Skinner, and Richard Devey. "Low-Waged and Informal Employment in South Africa," *Transformation*, 60 (2006), 90–126.

van Buren, Linda. "Malawi: Economy." Europe World Plus. Europe on-line. Accessed 3/5/2008. http://www.europaworld.com/entry/mw.ec.

van de Walle, Nicolas. *African Economies and the Politics of Permanent Crisis, 1979– 1999.* New York: Cambridge University Press, 2001.

  "Economic Reform: Patterns and Constraints" in E. Gyimah-Boadi, ed., *Democratic Reform in Africa: The Quality of Progress.* Boulder: Lynne Rienner, 2004: 29–64.

  "Meet the New Boss, Same as the Old Boss? The Evolution of Political Clientelism in Africa" in Herbert Kitschelt and Steven Wilkinson, eds., *Patrons, Clients, and Policies: Patterns of Democratic Accountability and Political Competition.* New York: Cambridge University Press, 2007: 50–67.

"Presidentialism and Clientelism in Africa's Emerging Party Systems." *Journal of Modern African Studies*, 41, 2 (2003): 297–321.

van de Walle, Nicolas and Kimberly Smiddy Butler. "Political Parties and Party Systems in Africa's Illiberal Democracies." *Cambridge Review of International Affairs*, 13, 1 (1999): 14–28.

van de Walle, Nicolas, Nicole Ball, and Vijaya Ramachandran. *Beyond Structural Adjustment: The Institutional Context of African Development*. New York: Palgrave Macmillan, 2003.

van der Heijden, Hendrik. "Zambian Policy Making" in Steve Kayizzi-Mugerwa, ed., *Reforming Africa's Institutions: Ownership, Incentives, and Capabilities*. New York: United Nations University Press, 2003: 77–104.

van der Westhuizen, Janis. "Glitz, Glamour and the Gautrain: Mega-Projects as Political Symbols." *Politikon*, 34, 3 (December 2007): 333–351.

van Donge, Jan Kees. "The Plundering of Zambian Resources by Frederick Chiluba and His Friends: A Case Study of the Interaction Between National Politics and the International Drive towards Good Governance." *African Affairs*, 108. 430 (2008): 69–90.

Vaux, Tony, Amandio Mavela, João Pereira, and Jennifer Stuttle. "Strategic Conflict Assessment: Mozambique." Prepared for the U.K. donor team in Mozambique. April 2006.

Villalón, Leonardo and Peter VonDoepp, eds. *The Fate of Africa's Democratic Experiments: Elites and Institutions*. Bloomington: Indiana University Press, 2005.

VonDoepp, Peter. "Institutions, Resources, and Elite Strategies: Making Sense of Malawi's Democratic Trajectory" in Leonardo Villalón and Peter VonDoepp, eds., *The Fate of Africa's Democratic Experiments: Elites and Institutions*. Bloomington: Indiana University Press, 2005: 175–198.

Von Holdt, Karl and Edward Webster. "Work Restructuring and the Crisis of Social Reproduction: A Southern Perspective" In Edward Webster and Karl Von Holdt, eds., *Beyond the Apartheid Workplace: Studies in Transition*. Scottsville, South Africa: University of KwaZulu-Natal, 2005: 3–40.

Von Soest, Christian. "How Does Neopatrimonialism Affect the African State? The Case of Tax Collection in Zambia." German Institute of Global and Area Studies. Working Papers no. 32. November 2006. Accessed 5/1/2007. http://www.giga-hamburg.de.

Walker, M. and L. Farisani. "SOEs Back Up 'Developmental State'." *South African Labour Bulletin*, 29, 5 (October 2005): 17–19.

Waterbury, J. "The Heart of the Matter? Public Enterprise and the Adjustment Process" in Stephan Haggard and Robert Kaufman, eds., *The Politics of Economic Adjustment: International Constraints, Distributive Conflicts, and the State*. Princeton, N.J.: Princeton University Press: 1992: 182–217.

Webb, Paul and Stephen White. *Party Politics in New Democracies*. Oxford: Oxford University Press, 2007.

Webster, Edward and Karl Von Holdt, eds. *Beyond the Apartheid Workplace: Studies in Transition*. Scottsville, South Africa: University of KwaZulu-Natal, 2005.

Webster, Edward, Geoffrey Wood, Beata Mtyingizana, and Michael Brookes. "Residual Unionism and Renewal: Organized Labour in Mozambique." *Journal of Industrial Relations* 48 (2006): 257–278.

Weimer, David, ed., *The Political Economy of Property Rights: Institutional Change and Credibility in the Reform of Centrally Planned Economies*. Cambridge: Cambridge University Press, 1997.

Weingast, Barry. "The Political Commitment to Markets and Marketization" in David Weimer, ed., *The Political Economy of Property Rights: Institutional Change and Credibility in the Reform of Centrally Planned Economies*. Cambridge: Cambridge University Press, 1997: 43–49.

Welz, Adam. "Ethanol's African Land Grab." Mother Jones. March/April 2009. Accessed 2/7/2010. http://motherjones.com/print/21671.

White, Oliver Campbell and Anita Bhatia. *Privatization in Africa*. Washington, D.C.: The World Bank, 1998.

White, Stephen. "Russia's Client Party System" in Paul Webb and Stephen White, eds., *Party Politics in New Democracies*. Oxford: Oxford University Press, 2007.

Whitfield, Lindsay. "Change for a Better Ghana: Party Competition, Institutionalization and Alternation in Ghana's 2008 Elections." *African Affairs*, 108, 433 (2009): 621–641.

"Ghana since 1993: A Successful Democratic Experiment?" in Abdul Raufu Mustapha and Lindsay Whitfield, eds., *Turning Points in African Democracy*. Rochester: James Currey, 2009: 50–70.

"The Politics of Production: Challenges to Economic Transformation in Ghana." Unpublished manuscript. May 2011.

Whitfield, Lindsay, ed. *The Politics of Aid: African Strategies for Dealing with Donors*. Oxford: Oxford University Press, 2009.

Williamson, John. "In Search of a Manuel for Technopols" in John Williamson, ed., *The Political Economy of Policy Reform*. Washington, D.C.: Institute for International Economics, 1993: 9–28.

Williamson, John, ed. *Latin American Adjustment: How Much Has Happened?* Washington, D.C.: Institute for International Economics, 1990.

ed. *The Political Economy of Policy Reform*. Washington, D.C.: Institute for International Economics, 1993.

"What Washington Means by Policy Reform" in John Williamson, ed., *Latin American Adjustment: How Much Has Happened?* Washington, D.C.: Institute for International Economics, 1990: 5–38.

Wood, Elisabeth. "An Insurgent Path to Democracy: Popular Mobilization, Economic Interests, and Regime Transition in South Africa and El Salvador." *Comparative Political Studies*, 34, 8 (October 2001): 862–888.

World Bank. *Beating the Odds: Sustaining Inclusion in Mozambique's Growing Economy*. Washington, D.C.: World Bank, 2008.

Bureaucrats in Business: The Economics and Politics of Government Ownership. Oxford: Oxford University Press, 1995.

Young, Daniel. "Is Clientelism at Work in African Elections? A Study of Voting Behavior in Kenya and Zambia," Afrobarometer Working Paper no. 106 (April 2009).

Zambia Congress of Trade Unions. "Zambia: Socio-Economic Issues and Unionization." Global Policy Network: Zambia Congress of Trade Unions, 2001. Accessed 1/3/2006. www.globalpolicynetwork.org.

Zambia Land Alliance (ZLA). "Land Policy Options for Development and Poverty Reduction." January 2008.

Zuern, Elke. "Continuity in Contradiction?: The Prospects for a National Civic Movement in a Democratic State: SANCO and the ANC in Post-Apartheid South Africa," study commissioned for project entitled Globalisation, Marginalisation & New Social Movements in post-Apartheid South Africa, a joint project between the Centre for Civil Society and the School of Development Studies, University of KwaZulu-Natal, 2004.

Index

Abdula, Salimo, 182
ABSA bank, 195–196
Accelerated and Shared Growth Initiative for
    South Africa (ASGISA), 226–230
Administrative Tribunal, Mozambique, 182–184
Africa, Sub-Saharan
    economic reform debates, 6–11
    foreign direct investment, 6–7
    judiciary, 32–33, 58
    Latin America, comparisons to, 19–21, 88,
        89, 94, 216, 219, 225
    partial reform syndrome, 7–8, 133–143
    presidency, office of, 93–96
    presidentialism and authoritarianism in,
        132–133
    structural adjustment policies, 9, 32–35, 248
    summary conclusions, 236–250
        credible commitments, 236–240
        cross-national comparisons, 242–247
        future trends, 248–250
        political dynamics of, 240–242
    see also specific countries, leaders and
        parties
African National Congress (ANC), South
    Africa
    adoption of neoliberalism and, 190–191
    benefits from privatization, 195–196
    business interests and, 221–234
    institutional reform and, 201–202
    opposition parties and, 90–92
    party organization, 205–211
    party splits, 81
    privatization and strategic compromise
        overview, 100–101
        discretionary authority, contingent use
           of, 215–216
        summary conclusions, 245–247
    as ruling party, 90–92

vote share, 211–215
Women's League, 206
Youth League, 195–196, 206, 208–209,
    215–216
see also South Africa
African Party for the Independence of Cape
    Verde. *see* PAICV (African Party for the
    Independence of Cape Verde)
Afrikaanse Handleinstituut (AHI), 222–224
Afrobarometer surveys, 79–87, 123, 166, 205
Akwetey, Emmanuel, 120
Alexandra Chamber of Commerce, 231–233
Alexkor, 226–230
Alliance. *see* tripartite alliance, South Africa
Anglo American, 193–195, 222–223
Anglo-Gold, 222–223
Anglo-Vaal Mining, 222–223
Angola, 9, 26–28, 39
Anti-Privatization Forum (APF),
    South Africa, 221
Archer, Ronald, 94
AT&T, 193–195
Australia
    corporate investment in Mozambique,
        148–149
    corporate investment in Zambia, 106–108
authoritarianism and privatization, 75
    cronyism, use of, 133–143
    populist agendas, use of, 133–143
    presidentialism and, 132–133
    ruling parties and, 19–21, 91, 110–116,
        170–178
    see also specific countries and parties
autocracy, Olson on, 3–4

Banda, Rupiah, 95–96, 121–122, 141
Bankers Association of Zambia (BAZ),
    125–133

Mali (*cont.*)
    ad hoc private sector development, 93–96
    ENPP scores, 83–87
    patronage and, 88–90
    policy dilemmas, 22–24
    reform delays, 88
    seat volatility, 83–87
    voter closeness, 83–87
  high-very high motivational commitment, 49
  imperative commitment scores, 54–63
  as limited democracy, 93–96
  political parties, 22
  poverty levels, 2
  presidency, office of, 93–96
  SOEs
    reform of, 44–45
    sales of, 1, 53
  summary conclusions, 242–243
Manning, Carrie, 166–169
Maqueval, Arlindo, 162
Masincazelane, 231–233
Matale, James, 111–112
Mattes, Robert, 245
Mauritius
  corporate investment in Mozambique,
    148–149
  design of privatization agencies
    after 2000, 46–48
  imperative commitment scores, 54–63, 240
  as liberal democracy, 74–75, 100–101
  privatization and strategic compromise,
    245–247
  discretionary authority, contingent use of,
    26–28, 68–71, 100–101, 235
  SOEs
    restructuring of, 13, 44
    sales of, 53
  stable party system
    economic reform and, 90–92
    ENPP scores, 83–87
    seat volatility, 83–87
    strategic compromise in privatization,
      100–101
    voter closeness, 205
Mauritius Telecom, 44
Mazanga, Fernando, 162
Mazoka, Anderson, 118, 120–121
Mbeki, Thabo, 207, 208–209, 211, 214–215,
  216–218, 219–220, 246
MCEL (Mozambique Cellular), 150–151
media, in liberal democracies, 74–75
Metal Fabricators, 112
Mexico, comparisons to, 19–21,
  216, 225
middle class
  in Mozambique, 153
  in South Africa, 197–200
  see also black middle class, South Africa

Millennium Labor Council (MLC), South
  Africa, 220, 222
Ministry of Commerce, Trade and Industry,
  Zambia, 125–133
moderate pluralism in party systems, use of
  term, 77–79
Molina, José, 72–73
Momade, Ossufo, 162
Morais, Herminio, 162
motivational commitment, overview, 12–15,
  16–18, 21–28, 31
  see also imperative commitment, overview;
    specific countries
motivational to imperative committment, in
  private sector institutions, 30–64
  from conditionality to commitment, 32–35
  dilemmas of conditionality, 35–38
  index of motivationally credible
    commitments (1988–2000), 38–43
    tables and figures, 43
  motivational commitment
    imperative commitment and, 50–63
    institutional variation and convergence,
      44–50
    sales of SOEs and, 50–63, 236–240
    summary conclusions, 236–240
    tables and figures, 52, 56, 59
  Shepsle on, 3, 11–13, 55
Movement for Democracy (MPD), Cape
  Verde, 83–87, 247
Movement for Multi-party Democracy
  (MMD), Zambia, 5–6, 22–24,
  105–144, 242–243
Mozambique
  agency autonomy, 48–49
  attitudes toward democracy, 1
  campaign finance, 161
  design of privatization agencies
    after 2000, 46–48
  economy, 187–188
  employment and unemployment, 115–116,
    153–154, 155, 174, 178–182
  foreign direct investment in, 6–7
  Freedom House indicators, 176–178
  IFIs and, 182–184
  imperative commitment scores, 54–63
  judiciary, 74–75, 155, 176–178
  land and investment laws, 45–46
  as limited democracy, 74–75, 96–100
    opposition parties, 90–92
    ruling party authoritarian practices,
      19–21, 91, 170–178
  organized labor, 154, 161, 170–182
  partisan private sector development,
    145–186
    democratic quality and, 170–185
    discretionary authority and, 26–28,
      68–71, 96–100, 178–185

Books in This Series